POST-CRITICAL MUSEOLOGY

Post-critical Museology considers what the role of the public and the experience of audiences means to the everyday work of the art museum. It does this from the perspectives of the art museum itself as well as from the visitors it seeks. Through the analysis of material gathered from a major collaborative research project carried out at Tate Britain in London, the book develops a conceptual reconfiguration of the relationship between art, culture and society in which questions about the art museum's relationship to global migration and the new media ecologies are examined. It suggests that, while European museums have previously been studied as institutions of collection, heritage and tradition, however 'modern' their focus, it is now better to consider them as distributive networks in which value travels along transmedial and transcultural lines.

Post-critical Museology is intended as a contribution to progressive museological thinking and practice and calls for a new alignment of academics and professionals in what it announces as Post-critical Museology. An alignment that is committed to rethinking what an art museum in the twenty-first century could be, as well as what knowledge and understanding its future practitioners might draw upon in a rapidly changing social and cultural context. The book aims to be essential reading in the growing field of museum studies. It will also be of professional interest to all those working in the cultural sphere, including museum professionals, policy-makers and art managers.

Andrew Dewdney is Professor of Educational Development at London South Bank University and has been the Principal Investigator and Director of the Tate Encounters project, Head of the School of Film and Photography at Newport College of Art, and Director of Exhibition and Photography at the Watershed Media Centre in Bristol. His teaching focuses upon new media and visual culture, and he is co-author (with Peter Ride) of *The New Media Handbook* (Routledge 2006).

David Dibosa is Course Director for MA Art Theory at Chelsea College of Art and Design in the University of the Arts London. His published work focuses on visual art and cultural difference and includes 'Cultural Diversity: Politics, Policy and Practices. The Case of Tate Encounters', with Andrew Dewdney and Victoria Walsh, in the edited collection, *Museums, Equality and Social Justice* (Routledge 2012).

Victoria Walsh has worked in various senior research, curatorial and project management roles at Tate since 1994 and was Head of Adult Programmes at Tate Britain from 2005–11. Trained as an art historian and curator, she holds various research and teaching positions within the UK and abroad and has published a number of titles on post-war British art.

POST-CRITICAL MUSEOLOGY

Theory and Practice in the Art Museum

*Andrew Dewdney, David Dibosa and
Victoria Walsh*

Routledge
Taylor & Francis Group

LONDON AND NEW YORK

First published 2013
by Routledge
2 Park Square, Milton Park, Abingdon, Oxon OX14 4RN

Simultaneously published in the USA and Canada
by Routledge
711 Third Avenue, New York, NY 10017

Routledge is an imprint of the Taylor & Francis Group, an informa business

British Library Cataloguing in Publication Data
A catalogue record for this book is available from the British Library

Library of Congress Cataloging in Publication Data
Dewdney, Andrew.
Post-critical Museology : Theory and Practice in the Art Museum / Andrew
Dewdney, David Dibosa and Victoria Walsh. – First [edition].
pages cm
Includes bibliographical references and index.
1. Art museums. I. Dibosa, David. II. Walsh, Victoria. III. Title.
N430.D49 2012
708.0068–dc23
2012016303

ISBN: 978-0-415-60600-4 (hbk)
ISBN: 978-0-415-60601-1 (pbk)
ISBN: 978-0-203-08459-5 (ebk)

Typeset in Bembo
by Taylor and Francis Books

CONTENTS

PART III
Hypermodernity and the art museum
165

FIGURES

ACKNOWLEDGEMENTS

This book is the culmination of a major research project, 'Tate Encounters: Britishness and Visual Culture', which was initiated by Tate Britain in 2005 and led by London South Bank University in collaboration with Tate Britain and the University of Arts. The project was enabled by a research grant from the UK Arts and Humanities Research Council. The research was immensely ambitious and has continued to be so, given the sustained level of support and valuable critique it has received from those who directly participated in it and those who followed its progress. At its heart, Tate Encounters embraced the value of the everyday as a form of 'radical empiricism' and sought to provide a more textured account of how lived experience, professional knowledge, and daily working practices connected and disconnected those that work in the museum and those that visit it.

In 2005 'tracing the everyday' seemed like a relatively gentle proposition. In reality it was considerably more demanding on all the project's participants than conventional forms of research practice. Invariably the project called up and called upon a great deal of goodwill, trust, flexibility, patience and a generous sense of humour of a wide range of people. We remain wholly indebted to all those that kept faith with the project through their contribution, endorsement and consistently high levels of open critical scrutiny.

Undoubtedly, the greatest scrutiny and counter-questioning came from the undergraduate students from London South Bank University whose lively encounters with Tate Britain over a three-year period formed the basis of the project's qualitative data. In particular, the project owes an enormous debt of gratitude to the group of students, and some of their families, who remained actively committed over a two-year period becoming Co-researchers in the process. We extend our thanks once more to Mary Ampomah, Aminah Borg-Luck, Adekunle Detokunbo-Bello, Tracey Jordan, Laura Kunz, Dana Mendonca, Cinta Esmel Pamies, Robbie Sweeny, Patrick Tubridy, Deep Rajput, Nicola Johnson Oyejobi and Jacqueline Ryan.

To describe the project as 'embedded' in Tate Britain says little of what ease of access was granted to the project and particularly the co-researchers to move through

Tate Britain, in and out of hours and equally how open Tate staff were in their interaction with the project, despite the pressures of work schedules and portfolios. Mike Phillips was instrumental in formulating the original AHRC grant application as Tate Britain's first Curator: Cross Cultural Programmes and in helping to bring the collaborating institutions to the table. Stephen Deuchar and Nigel Llewellyn were strategic supporters of the project and championed the value of audience research in the Art Museum. We also acknowledge the invaluable encouragement and perspectives offered through conversations with many Tate staff including the specific input of Felicity Allen, Jennifer Batchelor, Kirstie Beaven, Sarah Briggs, Indie Choudhury, James Davis, Kelli Dipple, Claire Eva, Paul Goodwin, Will Gompertz, Madeleine Keep, Mark Miller, Martin Myrone, Judith Nesbitt, Doris Pearce, Christine Riding, Rebecca Sinker, John Stack, and Chris Stephens.

Posing questions to the museum, as much as the academy, to policy makers as much as artists and critics, we also extend our thanks to all the contributors who gave their time to the month long public research programme 'Research in Process' which took place at Tate Britain in March 2009: Faisal Abdu'Allah, Andrew Brighton, Helen Charman, Anna Colin, Richard Colson, Michael Compton, Anna Cutler, Marc Garret, Raimi Gbadamosi, Charlie Gere, Will Gompertz, Honour Harger, Janet Holland, Toby Jackson, Roshini Kempadoo, Sylvia Lahav, Hew Locke, Matt Locke, Tim Marlow, Munira Mirza, Richard Morphet, Sandy Nairne, Ross Parry, Keith Piper, Malcolm Quinn, Peter Ride, Irit Rogoff, Paula Roush, Veronica Sekules, Marquard Smith, Gary Stewart, Damien Whitmore, Paul Willis, Simon Wilson and Lola Young. Their generosity, professionally and intellectually, and their critical interest in the project not only provided important data, but directed us towards many new lines of analysis. The collection of recorded discussion was notably enhanced by extended interviews with other key individuals connected to our research themes and questions, which we recorded for publication as audio files. We owe special thanks to them for allowing us to drill them for as long and as hard as we did without graciously complaining: Les Back, Tony Bennett, Donald Preziosi, Yudhishthir Raj Isar and Leon Wainwright.

The project was fortunate in being able to draw upon such a large and well qualified number of applicants for the research assistant posts. In drawing from over 700 applications the investigators were able to select three exceptional candidates whose enthusiastic and committed participation in the research stamped its own indelible character upon the fieldwork. The organisational study would not have been possible without the sensitivity Dr Isabel Shaw brought to the task. Sarah Thomas brought the skills of immersion to the family ethnography, which is amply reflected in her films. Morten Norbye Halvorsen provided an incisive perspective on the project's engagement with new media as well as providing crucial technical support to the project's digital documentation and website design. We would also like to acknowledge the independent contribution of Sophie Orlando, who joined the project as a seconded graduate researcher from the Sorbonne and whose own study of Tate Encounters formed a chapter of her doctoral thesis. In addition we would like to thank artist and teacher Paul Richards for acting as a producer for some of the co-researchers films and also to Nisha Matthews for co-ordinating the Research in Process Programme and to Sejul Malde for his keen participation as an invigilator during the Research-in-Process event.

In the early stages of the design of the research Jeffrey Weeks and Janet Holland were more than helpful in discussions of the project's methodology and remained interested offering sound advice on its progress. Our thanks are also extended to Tracey Reynolds, who joined the research team for a period, working with some of the co-researchers. Tahera Aziz and Katrina Sluis were project supporters who participated with their third year Digital Media Arts Students in creating an online digital encounter as part of the fieldwork. The University of Arts London also demonstrated their continued support to the project through the contributions of David Garcia, Malcolm Quinn and Oriana Baddeley. Our final thanks go to Kim Knott, the director of the AHRC strategic funded programme through which the project was, in the first and last instance, made possible.

INTRODUCTION

This book presents an argument to museology, but is not of itself museological. It draws upon sociological theory and method, but is not a sociology. It discusses art and aesthetics, but is not framed by art history or philosophy. It is an account of a research project but is also a theoretical speculation. In its use of theory it is eclectic, drawing upon sociology, art history, visual cultures, social geography, and science and technology studies. In its empirical research, it uses a mixture of ethnographic qualitative methods for gathering and recording people's experiences and ideas. As a result this book has strayed across many discipline boundaries and, in line with its characterization of the hybridity of the museum, is itself a hybrid. The book aims at transdisciplinarity and is written out of the uncomfortable position of 'general theory',[1] which the 'baggy monster'[2] of cultural and media studies is the familiar academic default. The book addresses the operations of the art museum, but cannot easily be operationalized. The book wants to argue constructively with those who practically make and manage the art museum, and those who make knowledge and teach about museums. In this sense the book, like many books, is an argument with itself since the authors are those very same people who, among other things, practice and teach in and about the art museum.

This book is a very contrary thing as it now appears to its authors who have spent most of their professional lives immersed in one or other aspect of the production, management, or, interpretation of the visual arts and in their personal lives could be euphemistically described as 'art lovers'. The authors are therefore avid supporters of museums in general and Tate in particular, upon whose hospitality and trust they depended and yet for all that have produced a 'critical' analysis of Tate's practices of audiences. Further, not content to rest upon the academic credentials of 'critical analysis', which, in the museological case, the book sees as the theoretical side of the 'same coin', on which practice misrecognizes audience in the museum, it also attempts to develop a position of the Post-critical Museology of its title. The production of the book and the research it was based upon relied upon the support of academia and government funding in equal measure to the generosity of Tate Britain, which offered itself as a site of practice-based research. In mitigating the circumstances of appearing to bite the hand that supported the view elaborated by the book, arriving at a position of post-criticality entailed a larger criticism of the instrumentalized culture of audit, which has held British cultural and educational institutions in such a tight grip over the period under discussion. The position of the post-critical is intended not to find the museum wanting from the remote position of analytical critique, but on the contrary, to develop a position which brings together academics, museum professionals and others in productive ways in order to open up new avenues of meaning and purpose through the agency of audiences.

Having located a certain contrariness as a response to the institutional organization and separation of the practices of the museum and academia, another source of discontent may well spring from more embodied and ingrained responses, which, differentially for the authors, are those of occupying institutional positions uneasily, of being acceptable insiders but intellectual outsiders, of being cultural migrants and internal exiles, or from occupying, as Stuart Hall once defined it, the tricky territory of ambivalent mainstreaming.[3]

Museums in Britain, and Tate is the exemplar here, have undergone enormous changes in their organization and position in culture over the past two decades, as a response to political, economic and social changes on a global scale, which have brought the value of heritage and contemporary art into wider public view. Tate in particular has transformed itself into a corporate world brand consisting of four galleries, Tate Britain, Tate Modern, Tate Liverpool and Tate St Ives. Tate's funding and organization is both public and private and this makes it a complex object of attention and the book has had to develop an analysis of the research data produced at Tate Britain equal to that complexity with respect to the framing of audience. As a public-private institution,[4] Tate can self-identify what audiences it seeks, but is also aware that it needs to understand that audiences are part of society and it is in the space between these two needs that the research identified and began to unravel a series of problems in how the terms 'audience' and 'public' were being used and how, within competing definitions, visitors were being misrecognized as social representatives.

The analysis of the book is based upon the research project, Tate Encounters: Britishness and Visual Cultures, which was a three-year collaborative research project, funded by the Arts and Humanities Council between 2007 and 2010 involving Tate Britain, London South Bank University and the University of the Arts London.[5] The research was directed by Andrew Dewdney, Professor of Educational Development at London South Bank University, working with co-investigators, Dr David Dibosa, a specialist in visual culture at the University of the Arts, London and Dr Victoria Walsh, an art historian and Head of Adult Programmes at Tate Britain at the time of the research.[6] Over a two-year fieldwork period, three research assistants, Dr Isabel Shaw, an anthropologist specializing in organizational studies, Sarah Thomas, a visual anthropologist film-maker and Morten Norbye Halvorsen, a

FIGURE 0.1 Compilation. Tate Britain 1897 (top left), Tate Modern 2000 (bottom left) (photo: Marcus Leith), Tate Liverpool 1988 (top right) (photo: David Lambert Rod Tidnam), and Tate St Ives 1993 (bottom right) (photo: Marcus Leith). © Tate, London 2011

new media artist, supported more than 600 arts and humanities undergraduate students from London South Bank University who visited Tate Modern and Tate Britain. Twelve students volunteered with their families to sustain and document their encounter with Tate Britain over an extended period of two years, and in the research process were constituted as co-researchers. The criteria for participation in the project stipulated that students should be the first in their immediate family to attend higher education and that either they, their parents or grandparents had migrated. The student visits produced 200 completed questionnaires, 300 essays, 143 hours of video interviews, 14 recorded workshops, 12 in-depth student research projects, and five edited ethnographic films on family participation. In an organizational study, Dr Isabel Shaw attended all internal meetings during the course of the production of The Lure of the East: British Orientalist Painting exhibition, Tate Britain (2008), and over a nine-month period interviewed 38 members of Tate staff. During the public engagement programme of Tate Encounters, Research-in-Process,

72 participants both external and internal to Tate gave recorded evidence. The research project was organized in relation to three major strands and three themes of investigation into Britishness, the National Collection of British Art and contemporary viewing experiences. The team of six researchers met weekly for two years (totalling 320 hours), in which all aspects of the research were monitored as well as the development of a reflexive methodological practice which led to 60 hours of further recordings within the research team. Beyond the fieldwork period the three investigators met over the following year to develop the resulting analytical framework from which the findings emerged.[7] In addition, the project was joined by five external researchers over three years who made structured contributions to the research outputs.[8]

For all of those working in and committed to what has come to be understood in Britain as the cultural industries, the broadening out of the aesthetic field has been nothing short of phenomenal and begs the question of why there should be a problem of audience at all. The research upon which this book is based was a response, at a particular historical policy juncture, to a practical problem of the lack of attendance of 'minority' audiences identified by Tate Britain. The investigation of the problem of 'missing audiences'/'non-attenders' involved understanding not only how people who would be classified as 'missing' or 'minority' might encounter the art museum, but also and crucially how this problem was framed and understood across the organizational networks of policy and practice.

Using the Tate Encounters[9] research, the book develops an explanation for why Tate Britain is currently caught up in a crisis of the very system of representation upon which it has depended since Tate opened to the public in 1897. The argument of a 'crisis of representation', which has been grounded within this account embraces a complex assemblage of the production of knowledge, institutions, modes of communication and the conduct of politics. Such an assemblage, what might be termed the pre-eminent system of representation, containing multiple sets of associations and practices, gathered its momentum as a formation of people, objects and ideas through the period of the European Enlightenment, and was continuously developed and widely disseminated through the periods of European colonialism and achieved its most 'universal' expression in the period of American cultural global dominance. What unites the many and variable elements in this system of representation is a subject/object dualism in which one thing – idea, sign or person – can stand-in for or represent another. Upon this most simple of distinctions, complex systems of ideas about the politics and interpretations of human reality have been constructed. Politicians represent their constituents, parliament represents the people, broadcasters represent public views and opinions, images represent the visible, literature represents the mind, art museums represent the continuity of visual culture and all of these uses of representational means ensure the stability of the existing order and relationship between people and things. So when this representational system is called into question, or, said to be experiencing a crisis, something is being pointed to that is creating change and undermining the stability of the existing organization of things. In this account, as in others already referred to, the two most compelling forces identified that are bringing about global change are those associated with technological advance and the convergence in digital form of a unitary code of information, and the ever greater accumulation and movement of capital and labour in urban centres across the world. Both processes produce cultural relativism and a general separation of people and ideas from historical forms of tradition.

The argument advanced over the following pages suggests that at Tate Britain, the general crisis of representation takes the specific form of a complex confusion of curatorial practices in relationship to the National Collection of British Art and the aesthetic logic of the modernist display of works that mitigates against the development of new audiences and inhibits a fuller exploration of the new informational networks. The organizational culture of Tate as a corporate institution demands quantitative measures of its audiences for sound operational reasons and the basis of the misrecognition of its audience arises in part from commonsense uses of the sociological encoding of demographics, a practice shared by most museums and perpetuated by government forms of monitoring. The book examines how racial and minority ethnic categories fail to match contemporary identities and, when used as a means of targeting specific groups to improve diversity statistics in museum attendance, fail to change core museum attendance demographics. In questioning British multicultural identity politics, the book pursues a new direction through an investigation of fluid subjectivities produced by transcultural experience. Through the Tate Encounters research, the book investigates the relationship between transcultural spectatorship, with what the book termed 'transvisuality', and Tate Britain's conceptions of audience. In doing this, the book has been led to understand how transculturality is a product of the movement of global labour. In a further extension, the book examines how global capital accumulation, coupled with the online circulation of images of collected objects has created both an image and display proxy for the actual collection, whose remaining function is to act as the reserve for the exchange value of the work of art in the global art market. The book works through understandings of the movement and dynamic of global capital and labour in order to develop its analysis of how multiple confusions entailed in the museum's practices of audience is restricting the exploration of the contemporary use value of art at a moment of expansion and change in global cultural communication.

One of the consequences of what is being termed here as the art museum's misrecognition of audience, in its commonsense use of sociological demographics, is that a redundant model of the social is also being perpetuated. The book examines how a cultural politics based upon a social deficit model of race and class no longer has explanatory reach in accounting for the contemporary cultural practice of emergent networks and collectivities and turns instead to a more problematized and shifting model of the social, contained in Latour's idea that the 'social is not a place, a thing, a domain or a kind of stuff but a provisional movement of new associations'.[10]

The mismatch between Tate's various historical and operationally fixed conceptions of its audiences and the social, understood as a provisional movement of new subjectivities and associations, brings the art museum's continuing claim to be a representative cultural authority of and in the public realm into question. There is a real problem for Tate Britain, that a potentially progressive cultural mission of custodianship of the National Collection of British Art and the display of historic, modern and contemporary art, will continue to be defined by the art market, canonical art history and bounded by a culture of hyper-consumption in which the idiom of heritage remains the only possible role allocated to a national art museum.

Yet, at the moment of this charge that Tate Britain is falling behind events in the world and that critical theory has reached a definitive point in time, a further contrariness of the book is revealed, as the very idea of a 'post' moment of critique, or, of a museum 'lagging behind' or being 'in front', appears to rely upon modernism's central conceit of time's unified historical progress. A key argument in the book is that time, linear historical time at least, has been eviscerated by the final loss of tradition and that time is better understood as having multiple dimensions. This is something argued by those associated with the analysis of the condition of post-modernity, including Harvey's account of time-space compression as a result of globally distributed forms of production (Harvey 2000: 211), which has subsequently been explored in studies of new geographies by, for example, Warf:

> Time-space compressions, therefore invites us to avoid thinking of space as a passive surface and time as a linear arrow; rather time and space loop around one another, fold in upon themselves and twist and turn in complex, contingent ways that can best be likened to origami.
>
> *(Warf 2008: 9)*

The Eurocentric and scientized account of linear historical time propelling the world in the modernist vision of progress was also challenged in post-colonial studies in which literary chronotropes representing colonial space and its subjects as non-contemporary and hence not modern were contested. In the case of museology, the same recognition of the exclusive dominance of a Eurocentric conception of linear time led Clifford to call for 'different chronotropes for art and culture collecting' (Clifford 1993: 71). The specific relevance of the post-colonial debate and its contemporary extensions in relationship to contemporary transmigration is extensively discussed in Section II of the book. The rejection of modernism's unified conception of time and space is also taken up in Section III, where the contemporary impact of global communications upon the art museum is discussed. Here the argument is developed from the starting point of post-modernist thinking, most notably expressed by Jean Baudrillard, when he argued:

> Something has changed, and the Faustian, Promethean (perhaps Oedipal) period of production and consumption gives way to the 'proteinic' era of networks, to the narcissistic and protean era of connections, contact, contiguity, feedback and generalized interface that goes with the universe of communication.
>
> *(Baudrillard 1985: 127)*

Insightful as this remains about changed conditions, it became associated with post-modernism's pessimism in calling a halt to the intellectual project of modernity, even while it was evident that the conditions of modernity were still at work. More recently, Baudrillard and Lyotard's perspectives have been extended to the idea of hypermodernity in which it is argued that historical time, which once located and inscribed memory and the subject in time and space, has been replaced by 'a paradoxical present, a present that ceaselessly exhumes and "rediscovers" the past' (Lipovetsky 2005: 57). In this ultra-modernity, the present is made up of different kinds of social time, by way of the development of heterogeneous temporalities, which compete for attention and give rise to new forms of the management of time.

As the book explores in its discussion of new media, Castells notes the increased tendency towards greater individualism, which is set against society and makes an argument for regarding museums, and Tate Modern in particular, as serving as a connector across a contradiction, which,

> ... consists of the current alternative between, on the one hand technological creativity and global cultural communication and, on the other hand, a strong tendency towards the individualization of messages, the fragmentation of societies and a lack of shared codes of communication between particular identities.
>
> *(Castells 2010: 427)*

The book explores a number of responses to a situation in which the separation of Tate Modern and Tate Britain left the latter in a temporal narrative defined by tradition, but in which both were entailed in the collective enterprise and project of modernism. In this view, tradition and modernity are examined using Giddens' notion of the post-traditional society (in Beck et al. 1994: 57), Beck's notion of reflexive modernization (Beck et al. 1994: 14) and Lipovetsky's paradoxical individualism (Lipovetsky 2005: 66). The idea that the modernist art museum is no longer at the 'leading edge' of time's forward march might be rephrased in the light of these understandings in the form of a question about how the art museum manages time. From where and to where is the art museum's journey and how is the history of Western European art henceforth to be arranged to make sense of the past to the global present? As Preziosi has observed:

> At this juncture it is often difficult to distinguish museum practices from the entertainment, tourist, and heritage industries; department stores and shopping malls; the art market; and even artistic practices. In such a world, the question of 'representation' (adequate or otherwise) is, to say the least, very complex indeed. The 'distinctiveness' of the museum as an institution and of museology as a practice, has come to be conceived as a mode of representation that deploys and disseminates knowledge. And many museums, aside from their ideological usefulness, are successful because they are good business

investments, in every sense of that term. ... It may be more useful today, to ask not 'What is a museum?', but rather 'When is a museum?'

(Preziosi and Farago 2004: 2–3)

The book's argument, if not plea, is for the art museum to recognize and work with a greater and more open sense of the paradoxical present. Such an 'opening out' of the art museum would require a renegotiation of its traditional form of authority and a new embrace of the informational networks, with its multitude of human as well as media migrations. The book makes the case as forcibly as it can, on the evidence used, that the most obvious way for the art museum to relinquish the constraint of the historical system of representation is to relocate the development of audiences at the centre of its practices and to work with it on a grand scale. This, it is argued, would be the start of reversing the terms of the selective and privileged routes of cultural value and authority which continues to rest solely upon the networks of private investment and acquisition around the art object, the artist, collectors, patrons and donors.

It is on the basis of the call to put audiences at the centre of the art museum's practices that the book is dedicated to the sublime of the ordinary, or the ante-conscious, or the profound unknowableness of the everyday and to what Walter Lippmann in 1925 titled 'the phantom public' (see Lippmann 2009). In this the book is indebted to a number of authors whose works have helped in developing the analytical framing of the Tate Encounters research. The work of Michel de Certeau, who also dedicated his book, *The Practice of Everyday Life* (1988), to the 'ordinary man' has been import-ant in the continuity of thinking about the relationship between subjectivity and practice. The more recent book by Nigel Thrift, *Non-Representational Theory* (2008), has helped populate the discussion of the general crisis of representational systems with an alternative sense of how to approach the idea of the distributed museum. Equally, Bruno Latour's work in general has been immensely useful in attempting to understand the problems of the sociological analysis of the social and to the disen-tanglement of a science of society from a politics of society. The question of what is the contemporary British public and how does it become visible to the art museum is perhaps the most crucial overriding question to arise from this book. In detail, the agency of visitor, audience and public are disentangled in order to reveal the prob-lematic surrounding the representational role of audience, acting as a stand-in term, a 'place holder', for the elusive 'public', which can no longer be understood simply as an aggregate of visitors acting as consumers. The hypermodern public have gone elsewhere and one of the aims of this book is precisely to trace the presence of the different lives that lie behind the term 'public' in the networks of the distributed art museum.

This is a book based upon a project, which set out to solve a problem about 'missing audiences' in the art museum. The way it finally 'solved' the problem with which it began was through a combination of radical empiricism, reflexivity and transdisciplinary synthesis. In addition to the arguments developed from the research findings, the book also proposes a radical reconsideration of how to study and bring together the practices and theories of the museum. It locates its account in a constructive relationship to international progressive museological thinking and practice and calls for a new alignment in what it announces as post-critical museology, one that is committed to rethinking what an art museum in the twenty-first century could be as well as what knowledge and understanding future museum practitioners might mobilize in a rapidly changing social and cultural context. The book argues that Western art museums, by embracing the market, while at the same time retaining the discourse of aesthetic modernism, have ignored the challenge of social and cultural difference. As a consequence, they have limited the potential for providing a democratically engaged basis upon which to develop the contemporary cultural role of the art museum.

The book equally asks why recently developed bodies of critical knowledge, which have so successfully revealed the museum's historic role in maintaining colonial and imperial worldviews, as well as their function of producing audiences based upon social distinction, have not had a wider impact upon the ways in which major art museums think about curatorial practice and audience development. Tate provides the book with a number of practical case studies whose key dimensions are those of the National Collection of British Art, the production of exhibitions and displays, modes of spectatorship and the use of digital media in and by art museums. But far more than examples, Tate Britain is the reason the book exists, for it was Tate Britain that saw the opportunity to apply for the resources for a sustained study of its audiences and it is Tate Britain that is the central complex and paradoxical object with which the book grapples.

FIGURE 0.2 Compilation. Duveen Galleries at Tate Britain and Turbine Hall of Tate Modern (photo Marcus Leith). © Tate, London 2011

A tale of two Tates

Tate Britain sits in the heart of historic London, less than a mile from the Houses of Parliament, along a stretch of the embankment of the river Thames between Lambeth Bridge and Vauxhall Bridge. It is located within the London borough of the City of Westminster and lies physically along a kind of liminal border between the political culture of the 'Westminster village' and the eastern edge of Pimlico, a mixed residential area of the city. Despite its central location, Tate Britain does not benefit from its location in terms of global visitor flows around central London, nor does it belong to a bustling retail or recreational district for Londoners. There is something odd and isolated about its position, although the move of Chelsea College of Art and Design to the buildings of the former Royal Army Medical College adjacent to Tate Britain in 2005 has created something of a nascent campus feel in the surrounding area. In short, Tate Britain is not somewhere Londoners or tourists happen upon, but is nearly always a deliberate destination. Tate professionals are often made aware of this by the sharp contrast with the new pivotal location of Tate Modern and its 6 million annual visitor footfall along the South Bank of the River, from the Hayward Gallery and South Bank Centre at Waterloo to Shakespeare's Globe along its east/west axis and the new north/south axis created by the opening of the Millennium Bridge in 2000, linking Tate Modern with the City and St Paul's Cathedral. For the foot-sore tourists of the South Bank, the walk west, beyond Westminster Bridge and across to Tate Britain, is for most, on audience figures alone, a bridge too far.

For its core visitors, Tate Britain is a comfortable and traditional art museum expressed through its neo-classical architecture of which modern extensions and alterations are mindfully respectful. Approached from the front elevation, the Corinthian columns, the decorated portico, topped by a statue of Britannia, and the imposing flight of steps are composed to humble and impress the most ardent sup-plicant. Once through the doors and across a lobby, the space opens out into a light filled Rotunda – the upper balconies of which more than nod to the High Renais-sance. The central Duveen Galleries stand before the visitor, so demonstrably a clas-sical temple. For over more than half of the twentieth century, the National Collection of British Art has been hung so that the historical collection was displayed according to periods along the walls to the west of the Duveen Galleries, while the modern British collection has, until the time of writing, been displayed to the east. The National Collection of British Art runs from the Tudor period of the 1500s to recent acquisitions and, until 2009, the annual exhibition of the contemporary work of the Turner Prize nominees was held at Tate Britain. As an institution, Tate holds more than 66,000 works of art, half are by Turner (the majority of which are on paper) and the other half includes more than 3,000 artists. Tate is able at anyone time to display 2,100 works over its four sites, which is 7 per cent of the collection across its four galleries. For those completely unfamiliar with art museums, Tate Britain is a less comfortable assemblage of spaces, objects and people. Social reserve, silence and restrained body movement is still largely the tacit mode of observance at Tate Britain as the book examines in the encounter of more than 220 undergraduates at Tate

Britain, and it is only when the visitor descends to the lower floor, or enters through the modern, Manton entrance along the western elevation, that the bustle and chatter of cloakrooms, coffee and lunches so familiar in the city reassert themselves.

Tate Modern stands in marked contrast to the traditional architecture, styles and modes of Tate Britain. As has been remarked upon in a number of accounts, Tate Modern's entry spaces are continuous with the street and the urban fabric of the city (Dean et al. 2010). Tate Modern was designed to be exactly what its title announces, modern. Sir Giles Gilbert Scott's 1947 towering brick power station lay derelict from 1981 until its opening in 2000 following its conversion by the Swiss architectural partnership, Herzog and de Meuron. The space of the power station's original Turbine Hall was retained and refurbished and with its stark, vaunted gantries still in place it retains its identity as a secular industrial cathedral, equal to the stark classicism of the Duveen Galleries at Tate Britain. Tate Modern was the first new contemporary art museum in Britain in the twenty-first century, housed in a building that is a memorial to an industrial age, a modern temple and an urban city space on a scale beyond any of the city's shopping malls. Tate Modern has giant spaces of circulation with lifts and elevators to department store gallery levels with corridors like streets in the sky, with information, coffee and retail stations along the way. The visitor ascends to a restaurant with panoramic views of St Paul's Cathedral and the City of London, looking down on the ant-like tourists crossing and re-crossing the Millennium Bridge. The visitor is transported by elevators to different levels leading to entrances of thematically displayed works from the collection or special ticketed exhibitions. The galleries of Tate Modern are relatively small in comparison to the overall space of the building and, once in the galleries, the urban streetscape recedes and an older reverence to the work of art reasserts itself against the sheer number of its visitors whose city exuberance not even the aura of the object can suppress.

While Tate Britain is the primary focus of this account, the uneasy relationship between the two museums forms an essential backdrop to the central narrative of this book. The division between the two London Tates revolves around the principle distinction between the display and exhibition of British art and the display and exhibition of modern and contemporary international art, reflected by their titles. Since its opening the success of Tate Modern has significantly eclipsed the status and profile of Tate Britain, often known as 'classic Tate' or 'old Tate', but the role of Tate Britain was of significant organizational value in assuming (courtesy of its representational remit) the primary responsibility to meet New Labour's cultural diversity policy objectives, and to continue to demonstrate Tate's contribution to the nation which validated the government's commitment to free access for all.

Policy, practices and problems

The other significant context for the initiation of the Tate Encounters research at Tate Britain can be found in British politics and government policy running in parallel to the period of modernization at Tate during the late 1990s. In Britain, Tony Blair's New Labour government came to power in 1997, after 17 years of Thatcherite

Conservative rule, with a popular manifesto promising greater equality and fairness, and policies aimed at the social improvement of the poorest, most marginal and excluded sections of society. Social inclusion and cohesion ran across many of New Labour's programmes for reform and improvement specifically in the state provision of education and health. In addition to increased funding for schools and hospitals, New Labour also had public culture within its sights and, through the Department for Culture, Media and Sport and the Arts Council of England, it set about implementing a systematic set of policy directives under the rubric of cultural diversity. In outline, New Labour's cultural policies for participation in culture were based upon the embrace of Britain as a multicultural society in which all individuals and communities should have equal access to arts and cultural activity. One of the direct outcomes of cultural diversity policy was that publicly funded arts organizations were required to monitor participation by race and ethnicity and performance indicators were generated against which funding was considered. These two framing contexts of New Labour cultural diversity policy and Tate corporate organization provided the starting point for the Tate Encounters research.

Taking the problematic of audience development focused around cultural diversity and its framing by British cultural diversity policies set by the New Labour government, the research argued that the failure of the art museum to sustain an engagement with difference is not the product of a political rejection or cynical manipulation, but the outcome of a complex set of organizational 'misrecognitions' of audience within a nexus of institutional knowledge practices evident in the spaces between the practices of education, curating and marketing. The book examines how, in detail, the maintenance and reproduction of the established art world knowledge economy resists, contains and limits the conditions as well as experience of the social reception of art.

The academic analysis of the discourse of the museum within the public realm has centred upon the museum as part of a social knowledge/power nexus. Previous critical analytical accounts of the role museums played were driven by the explanatory power of either Britain's colonial system of capital accumulation or industrial capitalism's social system of class division. In the former case, the development of the post-colonial critique within cultural and literary studies, notably in the works of Edward Said (1978), Gayatri Chakravorty Spivak (1987), Franz Fanon (1994) and Homi Bhabha (1994) were over time extended, particularly through anthropological interest in collections, to studies of museums (Barringer and Flynn 1998). In the latter case, the work of Pierre Bourdieu on social distinction also provided a historical bedrock for critical perspectives upon class-cultural reproduction, giving rise to a range of studies based upon his ideas of social and cultural capital. Equally, Michel Foucault's work in uncovering disciplinary discourses that organize knowledge and practices, notably in his study of punishment and prisons, was applied to the exhibitionary practices of museums and given forceful expression in the work of Tony Bennett (1995) and Eilean Hooper-Greenhill (1992). Approaches influenced by Bourdieu, Foucault and the post-colonial critique more generally have dominated academic literature in the formation of museum studies as an academic subject. One of the central arguments of the book is that important and seminal as these studies have been, under the new conditions of hypermodernity their explanatory power over the museum has now reached its limit. Newer forms of critical knowledge now need to build upon that legacy.

From the 1960s across Western Europe, the focus of critical attention was upon why it was that the working classes did not participate in the liberal culture of the public realm as prescribed by the arts in general. Four decades later, the intellectual as well as practical context of the Tate Encounters research of Tate Britain's audiences can be seen as a marked shift of attention from class practices to what has elsewhere in the book been called racialized practices focusing upon cultural difference. As the account develops across the book, the shift from class to race is reconceptualized as a bigger shift from the terms of race and class to those of new transcultural subjectivities produced by cultural difference emerging out of pronounced international migration. In the explanation offered for why social class has ceased to be the pre-eminent critical prism through which a singular and systematic logic of cultural value operates, the book advances the view that different cultural formulations have begun to dominate British, European and North American cultures; cultures emerging on the back of a transnational cultural space established under the aegis of international capital, which is bringing about a radical convergence in the systems of representation and a destablization of established forms of cultural value.

The Tate Encounters research reached a limit of the usefulness of a conception of cultural practices based upon a politics of representation, which underpinned state multiculturalism and the cultural diversity policies that emerged from it. In this highly established model of multiculturalism, culture is seen to be made up of identifiable, settled communities, formed along class and ethnic lines, of different sizes, shapes, interests and outlooks. Cultural diversity policy was a means of promoting proportionality and representativeness within state-funded cultural institutions. In marking out the limits of existing critical approaches to the reproduction of cultural inequalities in museums, the book explores the reasons why there remains a reluctance on the part of museum and policy practitioners to abandon the politics of identity and representation as the historic basis for progressive cultural engagement (see Dewdney et al. 2010). The book argues that the retention of identity politics is a residual and defensive 'left/liberal' response to the crisis of the representational system as a whole. As a defence against the potential accusation that the book abandons a cultural politics of cultural justice, it argues that progressive cultural thinking needs to recognize that globalization is producing ever greater, temporary and permanent kinds of mixing and mingling in global cities. In cultural terms, the recognition of increasing transnationalism led the Tate Encounters research to investigate whether and how moving across cultures brought with it new ways of experiencing and encountering the art museum and as a result the book develops one of its central ideas of transvisuality, or 'seeing on the move'.

The book continues to locate the discussion of the future of the art museum in a new account of the agency of different networks of users, using theoretical approaches associated with science and technology studies. In the book's terms, the art museum is continually made and remade through related networks and, instead of an approach that starts with traditional hierarchies of cultural knowledge and value, it develops an analysis of the art museum in terms of an extended set of objects and performances and examines the points of relationship between them. In this way, the book shows how the art museum in the first decade of the twenty-first century is no longer governed by the civic and civilizing mission of the nineteenth century nor ruled by the logic of modernist rationalism, while these remain as part of an institutional set of assumptions. For there is a very strong direction to the flow of cultural traffic in museum business that travels, in the standard metaphor, from the core to the margins with the source of the cultural flow originating in the triumvirate of artist, collector and patron. The production of art and the destination of the flow is understood to be the dispersal of cultural value through the museum in widespread appreciation. However, while the immediate source of cultural value is rendered as the consecrated material art object, a more complex grasp of the reality shows that the source of value is firstly in the nexus of relations involved in the production of the object. There is also a need to account for the subsequent processes by and through which the object is acquired by and remains an object of attention in the museum. In understanding and elaborating upon this, the book recognizes the importance of Stuart Hall's work on cultural reproduction and signifying systems in his cycle of representation (Hall 1999: 1).

While the book rejects any view of culture as 'reflecting' existing social structures and is highly critical of arguments based upon the representational role of museums, it retains the analytical importance of capital and labour as central organizing forces in the production of culture. This, of course, is the traditional ground of materialist analysis, only now without the narrative of historical determination applied in a continuing attempt to grasp the globalizing nature and effects of the movement of capital and labour upon patterns of production and consumption. A central observation of the book, which arises from every point of the Tate Encounters research, is that in the everyday flow of cultural traffic in the museum, the capital supply side of acquisition and collection, understood as the exchange value of the work of art, is organizationally separated from the labour demand side of exhibition and display, understood as the potential use value of the work of art in its reception by audiences. It is argued throughout the book that the naturalized specialist organizational divisions between acquisition, collection, display, learning and marketing, each serve as differential mediators in the networks of the capital-labour relations of cultural value and that the art museum thus participates in a larger field of market values, which is not presently visible to visitors in the practices of the art museum. Historically and conventionally, the visible link between capital and labour in the production of art is made through the biography of the artist, rather than the biography of the art object. However, it is suggested in this account that this form of narration belonging to a representational history is no longer a satisfactory substitute for an account of the object's agency in capital-labour networks and brings to a crisis point the practices of the museum across departmental communications.

The driving narrative of the book and its arguments is that a double set of global conditions, on the one hand the movement of capital and labour and on the other, the global informational network, is bringing about a radical reconfiguration of the production of cultural value and precipitating a crisis of the pre-eminent system of representation. Such a reconfiguration is evident in the convergence and remediation of previous analogue media in digital form as well as in the challenge to singular forms of cultural authority. The convergence examined in the book concerns the relationship between the art museum and what has been termed the expanded field of visual culture,[11] which it is argued is present for audiences as a feature of everyday life, but not as yet developed in the practices of the art museum. The substantiation of this argument takes the form of examining the media productions of the Tate Encounters co-researchers. The co-researchers' videos, images/texts, photographic essays and audio files were made as considered responses to their encounter with Tate Britain and are used across the book as supporting material for introducing two key linked concepts of the transvisual and transmedial used in concluding analysis. The transvisual is used to assign meaning to emergent forms of multiple and relative seeing which arise in transcultural experience. Transmediation is employed to define the process whereby meaning is recoded from one medium to another. Transmediation indicates how both digital remediation and convergence intercedes between the art museum and the expanded visual field. The book gives considerable space to thinking through the impact and significance of new media practices to the current ways in which Tate is using and organizing media.

Post-critical Museology

The book concludes by rehearsing the argument for the position of post-criticality and its importance in relationship to the art museum. Is it, as some might think, intellectual posturing, or, might post-criticality have practical utility? Does the concept and position of post-critical museology have a traceable agency, which might mark out a potential network of association, thinking and practice? In the introductory chapter of *A Companion to Museum Studies* (2011), Sharon Macdonald briefly and usefully traces three periods of academic investment in museum studies. She characterizes these as an 'old museology' focused upon practical improvement and a 'new museology', which was more theoretical, and developed a critique of the representational function of museums and the recent period reflected in the contributions to her book as:

> What we see in museum studies as represented here is a broader range of methods brought to bear and the development of approaches specifically honed to trying to understand the museum. Also characteristic is a renewed commitment to trying to bring together insights from academic studies with the practical work of museums – to return to some of the 'how to' concerns of the 'old museology' from a new, more theoretically and empirically informed basis.
>
> *(Macdonald 2011: 6)*

This book fits well with Macdonald's sketch of present interests and the title 'post-critical museology' is intended to signal a break with the theoretical critique of the representational museum and a call for a return to empirical and pragmatic research. The argument for a position of post-criticality emerges across the book from the analysis of the Tate Encounters: Britishness and Visual Cultures research project. The method of the project and its findings lays the ground for a wider and more open approach to both thinking and practicing in the art museum and by extension other museums. The work of the book and its analytical groundwork can be seen as a methodological struggle to remain in the space between the production of knowledge about the museum produced by the academy and the reproduction of know-how in the practices of the museum. In this sense, the book can be understood as a methodological rehearsal for the possible practice and position of post-critical museology and it labours to show how the methodology of the research and its analysis involves a reflexivity in both its theoretical and practice enterprise.[12] This foundational methodological position acted as a strong support to what was at times no more than a hunch that it was crucial to occupy as many interstices within and between the academy and the art museum as it was possible to see and to begin to populate and expand these spaces with new insights. This was the method and means of beginning to dismantle real and fictive established divisions in the production and reproduction of museological knowledge.

There is a recognition throughout the book that the academy produces and reproduces what is taken as knowledge through processes of institutional promulgation, i.e. its own reproduction, it also does so as a form of commodity exchange, in research assessments and in the Grub Street[13] of academic publishing. In the humanities and more particularly in cultural and media studies, the historical link, which was evident in the early formation of its knowledge domain, between political analysis and social change, has been decoupled in the process of its academic legitimation and at worst appropriated as a part of a largely self-serving technocracy.[14] The current epistemological turn, as it might be put, amounts to a revised political challenge to the passivity of institutionally reproduced knowledge and to its fragmentation and annexation to profession and career, rather than to progressive democratic change.

The book is offered as a further contribution to a body of scholarship that has been concerned to understand the ways in which the total assemblage of the museum, its buildings, collections, classificatory taxonomies and the penumbra of marketing, press and educational practices are constituent of and interact with the social organization of power, privilege and position. The undertaking here, based upon the Tate Encounters research, has been to review the critical tradition of post-colonial studies and museology in the light of further cultural change in order not only to add to our understanding of the museum's current relationship to its publics, but also to understand what the social and practical impact of the critical tradition amounts to at this point in time. As the Tate Encounters research has shown, however, although the academy is the traditional ground of expertise in research, museum professionals are rightfully wary of academic researchers who often know little of the practical pressures and exigencies of making an art museum 'work' successfully. The collaborative

Structure of the Book				
Structure	1. Policy and Practice	2. Displaying the Nation	3. Hypermodernity	4. Post-critical Museology
Contexts	CHAPTER ONE The Post-traditional Art Museum in the Public Realm	CHAPTER FOUR Canon-formation and the Politics of Representation	CHAPTER SEVEN New Media Practices and the Museum	CHAPTER TEN The Problem of Theory and Practice
Method and Data	CHAPTER TWO The Politics of Representation and the Emergence of Audience	CHAPTER FIVE Tate Encounters and the Transcultural Audience	CHAPTER EIGHT The Distributed Museum	Reflexivity and the Limits of Museum Studies
Analysis	CHAPTER THREE Tracing the Practices of Audience and the Claims of Expertise	CHAPTER SIX Reconceptualizing the Subject after Post-colonialism and Post-structuralism	CHAPTER NINE Museums of the Future	Transvisuality and the Transmedial Form

FIGURE 0.3 Plan of the book

and embedded nature of the Tate Encounters research provided an opportunity for the museum to test a new model of research practice that provided a means by which a more grounded research practice could be established, enabling it to claim new and revitalized forms of academic authority through the development of verifiable research methods that reflect the interests of its own practices, rather than the concerns of the academy.

The organization of the book

It goes without saying that there are countless ways to read this book, but it may be helpful to the reader to understand something of its organizational structure. The book is organized in three parts, based upon the research strands, with a final chapter, which provides a more abstract synthesis. It is quite possible to read any of the three parts independently as they each deal coherently with a specific dimension of the research at Tate: policy, spectatorship and new media. It is also possible to read the book chronologically as providing a past, present and future to the subject of the museum and its audience, such that the first section outlines a history of government policy and Tate practice in respect of audience, while the middle section discusses the contemporary practices of encountering Tate Britain and Tate Online, while the final section discusses issues of the future of the art museum.

The first part of the book, based upon the Tate Encounters research strand of cultural policy entitled, 'Policy, paractice and theory in the art museum', gives an account of the historical and contemporary cultural, economic and social conditions and contexts that led to the emergence of the public, visitor, consumer, viewer and finally audience through an analysis of the changing role of gallery education as the museum's pragmatic and strategic response to public engagement.

In tracing this organizational history, a history of the changing social and cultural role of the museum is examined and highlighted through the study of the museum's relation to the policies of cultural diversity enmeshed in the politics of post-colonialism. It concludes by demonstrating that the limits of audience development are realized in the limits of the museum's modernist aesthetic, the academy's theorization of the museum and its relation to post-colonialism, as well as the lines of tension between practices of audience and concepts of 'core and margin' audiences that operate between learning, curatorial, marketing and online.

Part II of the book draws upon the Tate Encounters research strand of Britishness and spectatorship, entitled, 'Displaying the nation'. It introduces the idea of a critical audience and demonstrates the opportunity and value of collaborative, grounded research through the presentation of insights gained from a critically engaged audience – the project's co-researchers. In providing an account and analysis of their encounter with Tate Britain the section identifies the misrecognitions and conceptual limits of 'difference' in the museum focusing around the lines of tension between the narratives and display of nation presented in the practices and galleries of Tate Britain and the grounded, lived encounters with the museum by the co-researchers, who collectively represent those constituted by policy and practice as 'museum non-attenders'. From the evidence of the project, the limits of academic post-colonialism and government policy to influence change towards a more inclusive and diversified culture within the museum and its activities is demonstrated. In mapping the existing premises on which academic theories, government policy, and museum practice bases its notions of difference and diversity, the section discusses how the museum continues to reproduce ways of viewing rooted in modernism that exclude difference and argues that new models and concepts for the understanding of contemporary practices of viewing are required that acknowledge the impact of transnational and transcultural experiences which the book proposes as 'transvisuality'.

Part III is based upon the visual culture and new media strand of the Tate Encounters research and transposes the terms of the arguments of the first two sections into a discussion of the art museum's relationship with new media. In doing this, it proposes the idea of the distributed museum and looks at the range of existing new media practices at Tate and discusses them in relationship to the impact of the internet, particularly the recent emergence of the term 'social media', ideas about the prosumer and how Tate and museums in general are responding to the potential of new media as either a virtual or distributed form of the museum collection and spaces. In doing this, the book focuses upon understandings of the interactivity of users and the ways in which Tate is considering developing its online resources. The book seeks to problematize existing notions of the motives and interests of online visitors in favour of a research-led, collaborative and investigative approach to visitor interest and response, which it argues, that the Tate Encounters co-researchers' media productions offered a potential model of audience engagement. The final chapter of the book, entitled, 'Post-critical Museology', revisits the relationship between the academy and the art museum, outlining the main historical ways in which the art museum has managed the co-production of scholarly and expert knowledge of works in relationship to the production of its own professional knowledge of display, exhibition, marketing, interpretation and education. It goes on to discuss how the academy and the art museum have not managed to establish ongoing and productive working practices in the field of the social reception of art and art museum audiences. It does this by focusing upon the relationship between professional museological practices and research methodologies. It gives an account of the collaborative and transdisciplinary basis of the research programme as a way of defining a new field of enquiry. It brings the critique of the art museum, based upon the suppression of difference, the occlusion of audience and the separation of curatorial and intellectual knowledge practices, to the threshold of defining a position of study, which would open up new relationships of knowledge between audience and the art museum. In doing this it discusses, in detail, a range of methodological problems associated with the empirical studies of Tate Encounters, in particular: anthropological film-making; organizational theory in science and technology studies; and critical reflexivity as method. From this basis, it moves to discuss the place of research in the museum and the framing of a transdisciplinary perspective and finally to a consideration of the position of post-criticality.

PART I
Policy, practice and theory in the art museum

1

THE POST-TRADITIONAL ART MUSEUM IN THE PUBLIC REALM

The year 1981 marked a historical watershed in British culture and society. In January of that year, a devastating fire took hold of a private party in New Cross, South London, claiming the lives of 14 black teenagers. As angry protests followed the tragedy, frustrated by the lack of police interest in claims of arson, the Conservative politician Enoch Powell, declared on 28 March that England was on the verge of 'racial civil war'. In April, the two-year-old Conservative government, led by Margaret Thatcher, announced major cuts and reforms to the public sector and official figures recorded the highest unemployment in 50 years at 2.5 million. On 10 and 12 April, major riots broke out in Brixton, South London, home to a predominantly African-Caribbean community, and an area defined by poor housing, high unemployment and high levels of street crime which police were tackling through an undercover street campaign named Operation Swamp 81.

As newspaper and TV coverage broadcast scenes of burning buildings, upturned cars and raging street battles between police and rioters, it became clear that the scale of protest and violence could not be dismissed or contained by political rhetoric and by 14 April the Home Secretary had commissioned Lord Scarman to undertake an inquiry into the causes of this major outbreak of civil unrest. As the summer months unfolded and much of the country began to settle back into national preparations for the Royal Wedding of Prince Charles and Lady Diana and media excitement replaced discussions of a broken England, a more disconcerting mood was reflected in the bleak lyrics of the song 'Ghost Town' by the British ska band The Specials, which topped the UK music chart and remained in the top 40 for more than ten weeks. On 4 and 5 July, three weeks before the Royal Wedding and as Lord Scarman was preparing his report, a second, significantly more intense and widespread wave of race riots erupted across England, starting in Toxteth, Liverpool, another city suburb of industrial decline, high unemployment and low life expectancy, which, like Brixton, had experienced large scale immigration from Africa and the Caribbean since the 1950s.

With the first ever use of CS gas against protesters in the UK and an increasingly nervous British public, the government recognized the imperative to actively engage with the protests of inner-city black communities. As Secretary of State for the Environment, Michael Heseltine, went to Liverpool for a week and consulted local communities, businesses and politicians, and rapidly recognized the need for substantial investment in the regeneration of such inner-city and post-industrial areas neglected or abandoned since the end of the Second World War. As the Scarman Report into the Brixton riots was published on 25 November – noting that 'complex political, social and economic factors' had created a 'disposition towards violent protest', concluding that 'urgent action' was needed to prevent an 'endemic, ineradicable disease threatening the very survival of our society' (Scarman 1982) – Heseltine was already in the throes of securing a major shift in government thinking and on 9 December he announced a £95 million package of funding initiatives to turn the tide of urban decay and inner-city unemployment.

It was in this heady mix of politics, economics and social unrest that the idea of a 'Tate in the North' began to take shape as a reality. The disused Albert Dock in Liverpool had already been identified in 1980 by the then Tate director, Alan Bowness, as a desirable location for a new national outpost to the Tate Gallery in London, but the impetus created by Heseltine's campaign to restore Liverpool's position and reputation as an economically dynamic and culturally proud city substantially bolstered this aspiration. After various stages of negotiation and essential building work was carried out on the allocated set of buildings in the Dock, crucial funding was confirmed from the Merseyside Development Corporation (the Liverpool regeneration body) and in March 1985 the government formally announced their approval of the Tate Gallery's plans (Spalding 1998: 222–7). As the Tate's biennial report of 1984–6 describes in detail, the ambition for this new gallery to introduce and share the Tate Gallery collections to new and larger national audiences was to be supported by innovative thinking made possible by allocating this first regional outpost 'a degree of autonomy from the Tate Gallery in London'. The report went on to say: 'In this way the new Gallery will, we hope, serve sensitively and flexibly the needs of the Northern community within reach of Merseyside. It will seek all means of integrating itself into the artistic and cultural life of that community' (Tate Gallery 1984–6: 23–4). In May 1988, the Tate Gallery Liverpool opened to the public.

In a series of interviews with past and present staff about the history and practice of education at Tate since its inception in 1970[1] including Toby Jackson, the first head of education at Tate Liverpool (and subsequently the first head of education at Tate Modern), it was revealed to what extent the creation and opening of Tate Liverpool had marked one of the most significant entries into cultural politics for Tate as an institution. Separated off from the neo-classical architectural language of heritage and power that defined the Tate Gallery in London, Tate Gallery Liverpool's contemporary conversion of its spaces in the Dock, designed by the architect James Stirling, firmly located it in the present, and with it the politics of the present. It was also the first time since its inauguration in 1897 that the Tate Gallery had to consider how to create and build a new and sustained audience. As Jackson recounted, despite being part of the government-led programme of urban regeneration, the gallery found itself under attack from all sides. On the one hand, the local authority was aggressively antagonistic towards the creation of a cultural centre of activity instead of housing developments ('Tate was not considered to be of any significance'), despite the promise of employment; and on the other, the scheduled displays of 'modern art' were deemed not to represent 'the right sort of art'. Equally, as Jackson went out into the local community he was met with strong and volatile levels of resistance which came 'as a surprise to Tate' and created intense levels of anxiety as the gallery found itself in 'the middle of all the debates around racism and institutional racism'. These debates were inextricably tied up with Liverpool's unacknowledged and unresolved history of slave trading, which the Tate Gallery's own history was perceived to be linked to through the founding philanthropic donations of Sir Henry Tate, whose financial success and art patronage was derived from his sugar business company, Tate & Lyle.

Having gained experience in local authority organizations working in the community, Jackson readily identified the need to develop a strategic way forward to overcome this resistance that would directly take on the questions of power, politics and representation that he was regularly confronted with when he met with local groups of potential audiences. Most importantly, this critically engaged view was shared and supported by the first director of Tate Liverpool, Richard Francis, and working in close collaboration the two developed a series of strategies to reconceptualize traditional modes of curatorial and educational practice in order to establish the Tate Gallery Liverpool as both a legitimate and culturally dynamic place in the life of the city. The form and impact of these strategies still resonate within Tate more than 20 years on, securing Tate Liverpool's reputation as the test-bed for much of the thinking that went into the planning and success of Tate Modern in 2000.

Invested with the authority of the Tate trustees and director in London to develop new forms of museum practice the two oversaw a key organizational shift to reorientate the gallery's culture from one of the custodial display of objects in an overtly controlled and supervised space to a more public-orientated environment in which the visitor was both directly acknowledged *and* encouraged to speak back to the gallery. This translated firstly into the redesignation of the role of security staff to the hybrid role of 'information assistants' (recruited locally) who were trained not only by Jackson in the master narrative of the museum framed by art history, but also in the arguments of cultural studies in order to develop a critical understanding of the role of the museum in society that could be confidently engaged with in conversation with the public. As Jackson noted in his interview, 'antagonism is a good point to start a conversation' and staff needed to develop a critically reflexive relation to the objects on display as much as to the institution of the museum if they were to forge open and meaningful dialogues with sceptical audiences. Such a move invariably demanded a shift in the knowledge-base of the museum and to realize this Jackson sought out new academic partnerships that introduced the social sciences disciplines of anthropology and ethnography, informed by an awareness of the need to develop levels of expertise and knowledge around public interaction with the work of art, as much as with the museum as an organizational structure with its own hierarchies of meaning and value.

In addition to brokering such external partnerships, the organizational separation between educational and curatorial knowledge and practice was addressed through the creation of a 'programme group' in which staff from both departments came together to plan and 'co-curate' changing displays of the collection that were reconceived thematically in order to break with the paradigms of art historical canons and the connoisseurial model of the museum that the Tate Gallery had historically assumed. To secure a productive level of collaboration with curatorial staff, Jackson recognized that the perceived role of educational staff as primarily 'servicing the curriculum' to schoolchildren had to be redefined and that equal professional value needed to be awarded to their work and own body of expertise. This recognition was achieved as the educational staff's work progressively moved from a dominant focus on responding to the demands of the school curriculum to a more proactive engagement with an adult audience through the establishment of 'public programmes', designed to encourage debate and dialogue, and to give validity and place to a politics of difference that, at the institutional level, the Tate Gallery had traditionally elided in its relation to the public. As Jackson won the argument that educational staff should be equally professionally recognized in their posts as 'curators', his own title changed from 'head of education' to 'head of education and public programmes'. This reflected his conviction that the role of education was 'not simply to amplify the role of collections and exhibitions' as an extension of marketing, but to critique it and 'engage people with larger issues around culture'. The need for this approach was still evident in the early 1990s as the city of Liverpool continued to experience poor levels of employment and social conditions and the relevance of the space and place of the gallery had to be constantly reconfirmed. Physically separated from the language of heritage and tradition invested in the Tate Gallery and its collection in London and dislocated from the authoritative status of both, the Tate Gallery Liverpool had to generate its own paradigms of value and meaning, not least given the vehement levels of antipathy that surrounded modern and contemporary art in the UK at this time.

Indeed, the category of art itself was highly problematic, perceived as it was as either the 'luxury commodity' of an elite patronage or as a form of cultural conceit (if not deceit), the understanding of which socially demarcated the educated from the working classes. Such perceptions of art were considerably bolstered by the media presentation of the visual arts, ranging from TV documentary series such as Kenneth Clark's 1969 epic series *Civilisation* (the first documentary series to be produced in colour by the BBC), and Robert Hughes' *The Shock of the New: Art and the Century of Change* (1980), to satirical cartoons of modern abstract and conceptual art in tabloid newspapers. The proliferation of the latter had particularly gathered momentum in direct association with the Tate Gallery following the debacle that is still referred to in British public life as the 'Bricks Affair'. As the collections curator Richard Morphet discussed in detail in his interview,[2] the 'Bricks Affair' played out on a rather distorted timetable given that the original purchase of Carl Andre's sculpture *Equivalent VIII* had taken place in 1972, the work had been on public display in 1974 and 1975, but it was only when a *Sunday Times* reporter reviewing the Tate Gallery's acquisitions in 1976 that a public furore broke out.[3]

In many respects, the 'Bricks Affair' was a very English affair, following in the footsteps of the Whistler *v.* Ruskin trial of 1878, at the heart of which was the public mistrust of modern abstract art and the prevalent belief that the value of a work of art rested on the material evidence of its labour, translated through technical skill and craft. In this light, clearly Andre's assemblage of 120 industrially manufactured firebricks arranged in a rectangular form on the gallery floor flouted the public's perceptions of what constituted a genuine and valuable art object. Furthermore, unlike other national museums whose collections were readily understood to hold established educational value – historical, scientific, technological – the history of the public art museum in England was considerably more stunted due to the lack of national belief in and support for the development of the visual arts. While it is beyond the scope or need of the current text to chart, suffice to say that the history and patronage of twentieth-century British and international art did not quite match the interest at the level of state or private individual as in America or other European countries; a fact made most explicit if one considers that the Museum of Modern Art (MoMA) in New York was founded from private monies in 1929 and the state-initiated and funded Centre Georges Pompidou opened in Paris in 1977.

Within such a context of cynicism and hostility, it was clear to Jackson from the outset that the restricted, conventional and albeit cursory nod to a public viewer in the form of an artwork's label was a hopelessly ineffectual form of communication. Based on the prerequisite template of information that defined the standard collection catalogue entry (artist's name, title, date of work, size and medium) and reflecting the practices of art historical scholarship and connoisseurial knowledge (provenance, authentication, scholastic citations and archival references), the conventional label was a technical tool of reference primarily of interest to a specialist audience and certainly of little value or currency to a non-specialist one. In response, Jackson oversaw the introduction of new 'extended labels' to the works and contrary to the Tate Gallery's tendency at the time towards presenting a unifying, 'consistent' voice to the collection, he actively encouraged 'inconsistency' by opening up the work of art to multiple textual accounts of meaning through inviting a dissonant range of 'voices' from different disciplines to be included in interpretative materials. In allowing the work of art to be understood as a site of dynamic meaning and contested knowledge, and situating it firmly within a contemporary cultural politics of viewing, Jackson sought to present the idea of a 'museum in motion'; a place of perpetual changing values and meanings which would question the prevailing Tate Gallery paradigm of the autonomy and universalism of art. As Simon Wilson, a contemporary colleague at the Tate Gallery in London noted in surprise at the end of Jackson's interview, however, there was little or no awareness among staff in London at the time that the Tate Gallery Liverpool had found itself operating in such a hostile environment and indeed official accounts of Tate's history do not quite capture the conditions of this moment either.

As Jackson reflected, 'you didn't speak of these things, but it was a story that had to be told and had to be heard'.

In resurrecting the history of the emergence and practice of education at the Tate Gallery since 1970, what became apparent throughout the interviews was the consistently uneasy relationship between collection and exhibition curators, and the educational department ('the poor cousin' in the gallery, as Jackson described it); the former invariably looking upon the latter as a necessary corollary to the public service of the museum, but not one significantly invested in the aesthetic or intellectual project of the art museum. This view was particularly reinforced as successive governments looked first and foremost to the educational work of the museum as the primary form of engagement with a museum's public, leaving the curatorial work of acquisition and display essentially uninterrupted by policies aimed at rendering the museum a more democratic space of cultural value. The circumstances in which the Tate Gallery Liverpool opened, however, combined with the need to create a new audience, clearly demanded a new model of collaboration between collection curators and education staff, but at the very same time that Jackson was developing critically reflexive practices of gallery and outreach programming to overcome the disjunctures between the public sphere of the art museum and the public sphere in which its potential audiences were located, the Tate Gallery in London was pursuing a diametrically opposed approach.

The subsequent institutionally pervasive silence in London surrounding the challenges that the Tate Gallery Liverpool had been forced to engage with was a functional response to preserve and protect the narrative of tradition and national heritage that the Tate Gallery in London drew its authority and public status from and, given the challenges it was also facing to demonstrate its public value, was in the process itself of reconstructing in order to build new audiences of a very different kind. For, while the Liverpool outpost was to assume more importance a decade later, its roots and critically reflexive practices were invariably underpinned by cultural and social conditions that explicitly questioned the value formation of tradition and heritage that the Tate Gallery drew its institutional legitimacy from. Seen within the arguments of 'reflexive modernization' posed by Beck, Lash and Giddens (Beck et al. 1994), the Liverpool gallery's negotiation of itself in a new spatio-temporal relation with art through the conditions of contemporary culture signalled its requisite place within a post-industrial, detraditionalized culture (Beck et al. 1994), or what Giddens terms the 'post-traditional'. Indeed, as Giddens notes:

> Modernity destroys tradition. However (and this is very important) a *collaboration between modernity and tradition* was crucial to the phase of modern social development – the period during which risk was calculable in relation to external influences. That phase ended with the emergence of high modernity or what Beck calls reflexive modernization. Henceforth tradition assumes a different character.
>
> *(Beck et al. 1994: 91)*

But as Beck stresses, 'to speak of detraditionalization is not to talk of a society without traditions', but 'rather the concept refers to a social order in which tradition changes its status' (Beck et al. 1994: vi). Fundamental to this argument is the demise of post-industrial certitude and the teleological certainty of the Enlightenment project on which the principles of modernity evolved, which, as the decay of the shipping industry and dock life in Liverpool demonstrated, along with the new patterns of post-war migration, the project of modernity could no longer lay claim. With the collapse of such anchoring narratives, 'reflexive modernization' emerges from the risk society that is generated out of the need to counteract the loss of certainty and social regulation that the organization of industrial society produced. In this light, the silencing of the Tate Gallery Liverpool's early history can be seen within the nascent risk management culture within the Tate Gallery in London at this time, which had readily identified the tactical value of promoting its values of tradition and heritage to safeguard its own strategic priority of building the case for the creation of the future Tate Modern.

In a historically illuminating Biennial Report of 1984–6, the then director Alan Bowness noted: 'The 1980s are bringing many changes in national museums. Political decisions have been taken to give the museum greater independence, and much is being done to stimulate an increase in private giving, in order to reduce the financial dependence on Government-provided funds' (Tate Gallery 1984–6: 17). In evidencing the significance of this new terrain facing the gallery, and in acknowledgement that 'the financial well-being of the museum' had shifted to the role of the Tate trustees, Bowness quoted extracts from a major draft policy review, initiated by the trustees, 'to redefine Tate's position in order to fulfill the role it must assume in a fast changing environment'. Most notably, in line with evolving government emphasis on increased public access, the extracts opened with the declaration, 'The public today look to museums not just as repositories of art, but as a source of inspiration, a place of enjoyment and education' and concluded with a section titled 'Public Affairs and Services':

> A key element in creating a distinct and dynamic image lies in the field of public relations. The role of the Tate Gallery is to provide the maximum service to the general public, key figures in the art world, the younger generation and the media. The aim of the Tate is to create an open institution which both draws people in and which also reaches out to new horizons by linking together with other institutions.
>
> *(Tate Gallery 1984–6: 8)*

As the report also documented, plans were afoot to establish 'new museums' in new buildings on the Tate Gallery London site to further display the collections of modern art, the process of which had begun with the building of the Clore extension (also designed by the architect James Stirling) that celebrated the Turner bequest and would provide extensive new education facilities to be opened in 1987. This conjunction of the need to develop new funding sources from the private sector (such as the Clore Foundation) while reconfiguring the public role of the gallery coalesced around a fundamental tenet of government policy that successful modernization inherently rested on an expanded market appeal. Following the logic of market-based ideology, the 'general public' was to be progressively configured as shareholders in the public ownership of the nation's assets and inherently invested with consumer rights not only to be granted access to their assets, but to be granted that access through the conditions of service that the marketplace awarded the 'consumer' of goods. The first move to reconstruct the public as shareholders and consumers, with return investment value, was to attract their attention and potential investment through the strategies of marketing and publicity that characterized the commercial construction of value of the commodity object. Given the contentious status of modern and contemporary art, combined with the elitist perception of the art museum, this presented the gallery with a considerable challenge and demanded an approach that would secure increased visibility without damage to reputation.

One of the first and most successful initiatives to generate publicity for the Tate Gallery was the creation of the Turner Prize in 1984. Funded through a network of private individuals established in 1982 called the Tate Gallery 'Patrons of New Art', the aim of the prize was 'to draw greater public attention to the high quality of the work being done by our artists today' (Tate Gallery 1984–6: 47), although the specificities of the selection criteria remained vague. In the Biennial Report of 1986, however, Bowness could confidently state: 'In two years the Turner Prize has become the highlight of the Tate Gallery's and country's artistic programmes. Brilliantly organized on a small budget, it has shown what can be done to capture the interests of both the public and the artist through the maximum use of media' (Tate Gallery 1984–6: 11), further commenting on the annual award: 'Both decisions were to some extent controversial, but there was very considerable publicity and extensive BBC Television coverage on both occasions for which we were most grateful' (Tate Gallery 1984–6: 47). While the controversial history of the Turner Prize in these opening years has been documented (Button and Searle 1998), suffice to say here that what rapidly surfaced was the problematic relation created by the private investment of individuals in public national institutions whose own assets, currency and legitimacy within the art world networks benefited by association; what, in time, would come to be formally scrutinized and monitored through 'conflict of interest' registers.

In such a climate of public animosity, framed by a government policy emphasis on 'value for public money', the role and investment of private patrons to financially support modern and contemporary art presented itself as an increasingly attractive option providing both a counterbalance to accusations of misuse of taxpayer's money and the freedom to invest in the acquisitions of such art without fear of public redress or critical rebuke. Under government pressure to generate publicity and attract new investors and increase awareness and access to the gallery, the Turner Prize was a bold and strategic move not only to positively exploit the value of controversy for media exposure but also to signal new alignments and networks that the Tate Gallery was both actively seeking and operating within. The unique capacity of public controversy to generate mass publicity was, of course, very well understood by the Tate Gallery following the 'Bricks Affair', as the archival history of the incident notes on the Tate website, according to one member of staff at the time, ' ... these bricks have really brought the public in. They can't make head or tail of them. Nothing has attracted as much attention as they have'.[4] Ascertaining the risk and balance between ways to generate press stories and publicity without bringing the institution into disrepute and compromising its institutional authority would subsequently become engrained in the organizational culture of the museum.

While the inaugural years of the annual Turner Prize met the demand to raise the public profile of the Tate Gallery, the equal if not greater imperative to simulta-neously lever funding from the private sector, while also making the case to gov-ernment for sustained public revenue, gained significant momentum as government cultural policy refined its thinking about the role and funding criteria for national museums. By the time the current Tate director, Nicholas Serota, took up his post in 1988, the year Tate Liverpool opened, the pressure to secure a radical new funding basis for the gallery based on the government's mixed-income model of income – often cited as the '30/30/30' model – (public subsidy, private sector income, and self-generated income) was gathering pace. An enthusiastic modernist, Serota's analysis of the challenges and opportunities facing the Tate Gallery were laid out in his two-page job submission statement, 'Grasping the nettle'. The Tate Gallery he inherited is well documented (Spalding 1998), the primary straplines being a critical lack of col-lection display space, a second-rate modern art collection with limited acquisition capacity, financial instability, buildings in need of repair and modernization, and an organizational structure that was no longer equipped to respond to the ever increas-ing demands placed upon it in the contemporary setting. And all of this within a strained context on the one hand, of public trust in the heritage and tradition of historical art but, on the other, a deep and engrained scepticism in the sincerity and value of modern and contemporary art.

Within the new market framework of Thatcherism, the baseline from which to argue and demonstrate the value of art to both the public and private sector essen-tially rested on the value assigned to the Tate Gallery's unique asset base, its collec-tion, against which it drew its authority and exchange value within networks of cultural and economic capital. Since the 1960s, however, the collection had been divided into two distinct categories: Historic British and Modern and Contemporary, with curatorial staff departmentally aligned according to knowledge and expertise. This division, which was organizationally split at the curatorial level and was physi-cally translated into the public display of the collection, invariably reflected and pro-duced two different value systems that coalesced around the disconnected networks of specialist interest (artists, curators, academics, critics), general public, and patronage (gallerists, dealers, patrons, auction houses). By default of this separation, the asset value of the collection was also bifurcated, undermining and diminishing its value as a collective entity. The asset value of the collection needed to be reconstructed and enhanced in order to attract greater financial investment and secure more leverage with which to negotiate and forge new relations and partnerships in both the public and private sector. The disconnected networks of connoisseurship and curatorship also needed to be reintegrated with the circulation of economic capital to bring new networks of patronage in sight and as Serota understood, the collection as a total entity was greater than the sum of its parts. The narrative of the collection equally needed reconnecting.

In 1990, after two years in post, the new director launched a radical rehang of the Tate Gallery collections, as the accompanying catalogue's foreword explained:

> The distinctive character of the Tate Gallery derives from the unusual range of its Collections. Most major museums across the world are devoted to either 'classic' or 'modern' art or to a 'national' or 'international' view. The Tate manages to combine all these forms in one small building and in so doing spreads confusion, but also the seeds of great potential ... In the sixties the Tate ... made a separation between the two collections 'Historic British' and 'Modern' absorbing twentieth-century British art into the story of the development of international modern art ... Now at a time when many different strands of contemporary British art are highly regarded abroad ... it is perhaps right to break the rigid divisions between British and Foreign, Historic and Modern.
>
> *(Tate Gallery 1990: 7)*

In a complex set of tactical moves the rehang realized a number of objectives that lifted the collections, and by implication the gallery itself, out of association with its recent past, reissuing it in a new format. Firstly, in reintegrating the collections into a general chronological hang titled *Past, Present and Future*, a temporal continuum was created, as Serota wrote in the catalogue:

> A museum is conventionally regarded as an assembly of objects recording the achievements of the past but as Eliot has pointed out it also exists as 'the present moment of the past', throwing a light both backwards and forwards from history into history from our own time. A museum which continues to add works by living artists to its collection is in a specially privileged position.
>
> *(Tate Gallery 1990: 8)*

Such a temporal continuum enabled the inferred values of the Historic British collection – tradition, heritage and cultural authority – to extend and run through to the Modern and Contemporary collection of art, legitimizing its place not only within the gallery context but within the public's perception and understanding of the category of art. This point was reiterated on the back cover of the second edition of the catalogue, which emphasized the display's treatment of 'the present as continuous with the past' which gives 'equal attention to the work of historic old masters', 'established masters of the modern era', and 'the more controversial achievements of the most recent generation of artists' (Tate Gallery 1991).

Secondly, in introducing 'in depth' and 'cross-current' displays to show 'the richness of the collections' rather than 'an even handed representation of everything at all times', the major gaps in the Modern collection (the outcome of the gallery's historically fragmented acquisition policy and troubled relation with modernism) could be effectively concealed. Thirdly, the introduction of a rotational hang in order to display more works from the collection than a static, permanent one, introduced the dynamic of programming which, while demonstrating the Tate Gallery's critical lack of space to show its full collections (crucial to making the public case for a new museum of modern art), also afforded multiple opportunities to generate press and publicity on each rehang. A key aspect to this reintegration of the collection was not only the revalidation of modern and contemporary art, but also the merging of the national narrative of the British collection with the international narrative of modernism that underpinned the modern and contemporary collection, creating an interchange of cultural values. Furthermore, while posing a more substantial challenge to the historical and canonical ownership of modernism that MoMA in New York and the Pompidou Centre in Paris monopolized at this time, the historical realignment of the collection also brought into sight many new international networks of private and corporate interest, and particularly north America, seduced by the prospect of the cultural capital to be gained through association with British heritage while simultaneously being firmly anchored in culture of the twentieth century.

Last but not least, the curatorial approach to rehanging the collection was framed by the Kantian logic and aesthetics of Greenbergian modernism with its emphasis on the critical self-referentiality of the art object and its aesthetic self-realization through the progressive specificity of its medium-based experience. As Greenberg wrote in his seminal essay 'Modernist Painting' (1965): 'That visual art should confine itself exclusively to what is given in visual experience, and make no reference to anything given in other orders of experience, is a notion whose only justification lies, notionally in scientific consistency' (Greenberg 1965: 6). Strategically, the logic of Greenberg's modernism also crucially supported the homogenizing narrative of the newly conjoined collections in *Past, Present and Future*, for, as Greenberg had also postulated:

> And I cannot insist enough that Modernism has never meant anything like a break with the past. It may mean a devolution, an unraveling of anterior tradition, but it also means a continuation. Modernist art develops out of the past without gap or break, and wherever it ends up it will never stop being intelligible in terms of the continuity of art.
>
> *(Greenberg 1965: 9)*

Sparsely hung, in what the press rapidly termed a 'minimalist' aesthetic, the history of art was now constructed in the new Tate Gallery hang as a teleological development underpinned by an essentialist and Romantic paradigm of the artist as creative individual and the art object as a hermetically sealed entity latent with meaning. To secure the optimum aesthetic conditions for the art object to be appreciated the Tate

Gallery spaces were decluttered and stripped back to reveal the splendour of their original neo-classical architecture setting up a further dialogue between history and the present. The modernist reification of both the art object and the space itself, within an atemporal construction of tradition, is perhaps nowhere better displayed than on the front cover of the catalogue to the rehang which reproduces a photograph of the French artist Auguste Rodin's sculpture 'The Kiss' (1901–4), located in complete isolation in the octagon space of the central spine galleries, the Duveens. One of the most popular works in the Tate Gallery collection at the time, and a work produced on the cusp of modernism, the image confidently announced the professional art of curatorship and a new encounter with a modernist aesthetic of beauty that had eluded the visual arts in Britain while the art centres of Paris and New York had established their pre-eminence. As a sculpture representing the forces of desire and seduction, so the image extended out from the catalogue calling forth a new relation with the visitor based on the market principles of generating desire and consumption; as the back cover of the second edition noted, 'this enlarged edition … is at once a flexible companion to the Tate Gallery Collections, a resource book for students and a splendid gift book and souvenir' (Tate Gallery 1991). From this point on, the idea of the aesthetic would define the operational default position from which all other practices were registered and negotiated, not only in and of itself in terms of the visual, but also as a key organizational tactic by which to reanimate and manage the asset value of the collection through the reification of the art object.

While the opening of the rehang *Past, Present and Future* was greeted with much praise and debate in the newspapers and art press in 1990, the UK was in a period of political turmoil as Margaret Thatcher was ousted and replaced by John Major as Conservative Prime Minister and a major economic recession started to take hold of the country. As government policies to 'roll back the state' continued in favour of privatization, deregulation and free market economies, public sector bodies also continued to be encouraged and progressively compelled to scrutinize and modernize their operations under new public management systems to make them more efficient and cost effective, again demonstrating and justifying their value for money from the 'public purse'. Following the general election in 1992, the re-elected Conservative government established the Department of National Heritage (DNH), which marked a watershed in the relation between government and cultural bodies as the DNH was, for the first time, awarded the status of a Department of State with representation at the Cabinet level of government. This transformed the relationship between publicly funded national cultural institutions, such as the Tate Gallery, and government in both encouraging and problematic ways. On the one hand, it indicated a positive shift in the status of the arts and culture in public life and presented a more direct link to the Treasury and funding negotiations, while on the other hand, the closer proximity also presented the means for more potential government intervention in the management and policies of the arts and culture. What it certainly produced was a greater emphasis on the Arts Minister to account for public investment and expenditure in order to maintain and secure funding from the Treasury, which in turn was dependent on gathering evidence to indicate how successful funded arts institutions were in meeting government objectives of access, income and financial management (Selwood 2002). The role of the National Audit Office, established in 1983, subsequently took on a considerably more active intermediary role between government and pubic cultural institutions collating and analysing data.

A second, equally momentous change in Britain's national museum culture was brought about through the introduction of major new legislation under the Museums and Galleries Act 1992. Under this Act, the Tate Gallery's status as part of the Civil Service was terminated and the gallery was reconstituted as an independent organization with its own corporate status, responsible for its own financial management, buildings and staff employment, while continuing to receive core revenue government funding through 'grant in aid' agreements. Invested with this new corporate status, the Tate Gallery, in line with government advocacy of commercial business practice, energetically set about modernizing itself to meet the new financial pressures and demands to construct and deliver corporate and strategic business plans. In a series of radical organizational changes, major new departments such as Development were established and the previous Civil Service-style Press Office was transformed from being a reactive information distribution point to a proactive publicity team located within the newly established Communications Department that also incorporated Marketing and Publications. As Tim Marlow who worked in the Education Department recalled in his interview,[5] the gallery swiftly became more 'business orientated towards the art object'. With the appointment of Damien Whitmore as the Head of Communications in 1992, a new strategically integrated approach to press, marketing and publicity began to emerge with the clear objective to transform the public image and reputation of the Tate Gallery as a national collection of works to that of a dynamic, contemporary, innovative and homogeneous institution with a clear corporate vision. This emphasis on not just building the asset value of the collection through the new collection displays but also the asset value of Tate itself, was underpinned by commercial product marketing principles aimed at expanding the market share and building product loyalty. The professionalization of these practices also evolved as, in keeping with Thatcherite policies of good business practice in the public sector, outside specialists and consultants from the private sector were brought in to support or lead on key projects or exhibitions and partnerships were forged through strategically aligned sponsorship often in the form of in-kind contributions. The rapid rise in the use of external consultants was also importantly facilitated by the new corporate status of the museum that freed it from the employment regulations of the Civil Service under which it had historically operated, transforming the inherent idea of 'public service' into one of professional expertise based on competitively proven 'best practice'.

Like other museums at this time, the Tate Gallery also accelerated its level of programming to generate more public interest and increase attendance and revenue through exhibition ticket-sales underpinned by a progressive ethos of providing high quality service to the new 'visitor-consumer'. As the title of the first major National Audit Office report of 1993, 'Department of National Heritage, National Museums and Galleries: Quality of Service to the Public' (Department of National Heritage

1993), indicates the concept of service was paramount in terms of monitoring institutional performance that was carried out through highly detailed qualitative and quantitative auditing and analysis of work undertaken that was contributing to the provision and delivery of 'customer' experience. Throughout the document, the emphasis on marketing and publicity as the drivers towards change is clear, as is the call for increased use of external expertise in relation to visitor/market research. (Department of National Heritage 1993: 5/13/23). What is perhaps more striking in retrospect is not only the level of detail under operational and financial management headings, and other primary headings such as 'Education' and 'Access', but also under very individual and localized aspects of museum production such as the interpretation on offer through exhibition leaflets, guides, catalogues, object labels, etc. As the forms and methods of data-gathering and auditing rapidly developed under such monitoring processes, significantly enabled by new computerized database technology, many new organizational practices were rendered visible through their representation as statistical, quantitative data that also inevitably gave rise to the proliferation of descriptive and evaluative categories that assumed a scientific legitimacy in their numerical and systematic form; categories that in time would assume the status of established practice concealing their instrumental origins of conceptualization.

While the Tate Gallery entered the arena of cultural and social politics through its urban extension in Liverpool, Sylvia Lahav, who worked in the Education Department, highlighted in her interview[6] the shifts in education practice in London during the early 1990s as the gallery's income streams began to diversify through the rise in levels of corporate sponsorship that demanded not only a range of 'outreach projects' as forms of civic engagement and 'corporate social responsibility' towards urban renewal, but also high quality 'entertainment' events with prestigious names that carried the promise of social and cultural mixing that could not be found elsewhere. The rapid rise of interest in creating 'privileged' opportunities for the public that corporate sponsors enjoyed offered new ways to acquire social and cultural capital that, due to their success, became the driving force of much of the Adult Education work in the Thatcher years, turning income generation into one of the key objectives for this area of work. And it was easy work, according to Lahav, as the institution's profile swiftly changed from being a static museum with a permanent collection to a gallery with a constantly changing exhibition and displays programme, and a new high profile spotlight on the contemporary represented by the annual – and reliably controversial and headline-hugging – Turner Prize. This income-generation friendly and aspirant public, who recognized the new asset value of Tate as a total entity, began to define what would increasingly be strategically identified as the 'core' audience of the institution. In extending the ethos of privilege and exclusivity that private sponsors enjoyed to a ticket-revenue public through an increase in programmed 'events' and private views through membership schemes, the reconceptualization of the art gallery not only as a place of knowledge but also as a space of aesthetic pleasure, socialization and affective experience fed into and off the new forms of self-fashioning individualization – promoted by the advertising industry and media through lifestyle magazines in the UK – and the increasingly present 'arts review' sections. In this context, the marketplace for a modernist aesthetic in the UK was assured, given its symbolic break with the class confines of tradition and heritage that had dominated national taste and culture and its accessibility through the belated arrival of modernism in the UK through the opening and success of IKEA in 1987.

The progressive income-generation value of 'Public Programmes' within the Education Department invariably began to shift the historical and primary focus of educational activity away from the predominance of serving the school curriculum of the 1980s (based on the idea as Simon Wilson described it of 'inoculating' children so that they would come back in later life) and paralleled the impetus that had gathered under Toby Jackson in Liverpool towards establishing adult education as an independent and legitimate concern of the gallery to forge new publics. As Andrew Brighton, curator of public programmes in London in the mid-1990s noted in his interview,[7] the objective of his programming was to make public 'the discussion about what constituted artistic value'; a programme that would invariably reflect the ethos of his previous practice as an academic lecturer and cultural theorist. Moreover, Brighton, like Jackson, was adamant that this critically-based programme would not act as an extension of marketing for the collection and exhibition programme and to that end he consistently tried to protect it from 'incursions by curators' by ensuring he met, and regularly exceeded, income generation targets, although there were, 'periodically, various assaults to work more closely with curators'. Like Jackson, Brighton's aim was to engender critique and 'spread uncertainty' while 'making artist's discourse public and intelligible', although unlike Jackson, whose public was defined by the local community of Liverpool, Brighton's self-identified 'paradigmatic audience' was the artist community of London. While at the institutional level Brighton negotiated and secured much of his programming autonomy through sustained levels of income generation, both his appointment and his programming, which was overtly based on a material culture model of both the art object and the museum itself, was often seen by other staff as diametrically opposed to the aesthetic project of the new modernist Tate Gallery. Indeed, Brighton had a reputation at the Tate Gallery having provoked quite a considerable debate in the art world of the 1970s, along with his polemical friend and early collaborator, the art critic Peter Fuller, when they aggressively attacked what they deemed the orthodoxy of modernism in the Tate Gallery's acquisitions of this period. However, Brighton's appointment (personally ratified by Nicholas Serota) and his programme were organizationally valuable in terms of stakeholder development, indicating as it did to an important (and highly invested) body of artists, students and academics not only a level of institutional confidence regarding its modernist paradigm, but also its liberal-minded approach to acknowledging and embracing alternative critical positions and perspectives.

In particular, there was a growing awareness of the vulnerability of the Tate Gallery to the evolving debates and increasingly vociferous attacks from academics aligned to the New Art History that had brought the art museum into its sights as a key object of enquiry and one that stood accused of the silencing and writing out of the history of class, race and gender conflict in order to maintain and perpetuate the values of a dominant ideology. At its heart lay the politics of identity and representation that had particularly come to the fore in relation to the rise of modernism. Indeed, at the very point at which Serota was constructing a modernist aesthetic for the public con- sumption of art and building the asset value of the collection, a major moment of conflict emerged between the museum and the academy within the walls of the Tate Gallery itself. The occasion was the 1993 international conference of the Association of Art Historians, which had been developed by Tate Education staff in collaboration with the University of London to take place at the Tate. As the conference pro- gramme made clear, the opportunity and relevance of the location was central to the theme of the conference 'Identity and Display', which 'is concerned with the nature of personal, sexual and national identities and the many different ways in which they are represented. A number of the academic sessions will examine these questions in relation to museums and galleries in general and to the Tate's current displays in particular. Guest speakers include Helene Cixous, Stephen Lukes, Richard Sennett, Michelle Roberts, Carol Duncan and John Brewer'. As Nicholas Serota acknowl- edged in 2008,[8] the conference marked a significant stand-off between the academy and the gallery following three days of relentless attack on the composition of its collections, the knowledge-base of curatorial staff and the modernist mode of display. By bringing 'the enemy within', as Brighton's appointment was described to him by another member of Tate staff, accusations of cultural elitism could be effectively negotiated and offset through the public demonstration of open debate and the expansion of the public programmes remit.

Which knowledge-bases and which audiences the Tate Gallery should be addres- sing equally came to the fore in relation to the core educational practice of inter- pretation. As the National Audit Office report of 1993 had discussed at length, a fundamental concern of all national museums should be the creation of better public understanding and enjoyment of national collections. The primary tool for this was through the various mediums of interpretation, not least the labelling and texts to accompany objects on display. Not surprisingly perhaps, the practice of 'interpreta- tion' as a mode of public engagement presented itself quite early on as one of the most contentious and indicative practices of the gallery's changing role in relation to the public. Toby Jackson's assessment that interpretation represented a challenge to institutional notions of expertise and scholarship among collection curators was strongly endorsed by Simon Wilson's account[9] of his proposals to Nicholas Serota on the latter's appointment, which he presented in his 'Epistle to Nick' (Lahav 2012). These proposals argued for the introduction of a caption for every work of art on the gallery walls and texts that were based on indisputable 'facts' combined with infor- mation that created a visual point of entry for the reception of the work of art to the visitor, rather than a canonical account of artistic merit or value. Like Jackson, Wilson shared the view that collection curators were ill-disposed to communicating effec- tively with a wide public, although his points of contention rested primarily on their incapacity to translate their knowledge into a public discourse, rather than the type of knowledge they would utilize, which concerned Jackson.[10] As Wilson noted of the collection displays: 'No-one other than a professional art historian could understand it so it was like a private reference collection,' or more esoterically, the displays appeared to reflect the individual taste of curators who hung works 'like flower arranging'. Ever alert to the need to facilitate support and appreciation of the collection by the public, in whose name the gallery sought funding and from which it made its claim as the nation's guardian of its national art heritage, Serota agreed to the introduction of extended texts, but in keeping with the need to equally build a coherent and consistent authoritative 'Tate' voice, the agreement was based on the principle that all curatorial captions would go to Wilson who would 'convert a technical language [art history] into common parlance'; a practice that led Wilson to produce a style handbook for all Tate Gallery public communication materials.

As a site of the most regular and exposed form of public engagement, the need to align the practices of interpretation with wider corporate strategies of public communications was clearly understood within the organizational operations of the gallery and marked what can be seen as either the morphing or hybridization of education and communications practices in the mid- to late 1990s. As the National Audit Office report had noted in 1993, the role of interpretation was even more important in the production of exhibitions as income generation sources if the public were to be provided with sufficient means to enjoy and understand what was on offer. This need for explanation had in fact historically informed the establishment of the Education Department at the Tate Gallery in 1970, which was set up on the occasion of the departure of the gallery's exhibition programme that had been led and organized by the Arts Council of Great Britain, but which came to an end with the opening of their own independent space in the form of the Hayward Gallery at the South Bank Centre in London.[11] As exhibitions were primarily focused on modern and contemporary art, explanation had been seen as fundamental to introducing the public to new and difficult art forms.

It is not surprising that, as exhibitions of contemporary art increased in frequency at the Tate Gallery in the mid-1990s, the role of interpretation took on greater significance. This change took place in the new more pressurized context of attracting visitors as well as building their interest alongside their trust in modern and contemporary art. The need to shape and manage this interaction took on a new dimension. As a key strategic tool for generating publicity and visitor numbers, the Turner Prize presented a unique challenge to balance the art of controversy with publicity, while strategically managing the risk of damage to the Tate Gallery's reputation as a national and culturally responsible institution. In a move that reflected the new corporate management approach to risk, Wilson moved from his role as Head of Education to Curator of Interpretation in the Communications Department, where he became responsible for the Turner Prize while also taking on the role as official spokesperson for other high-profile moments of potential public controversy that needed to be managed. A prime example was provided by the display of the installation 'Twentieth Century' by the contemporary artist Maurizio Cattelan, which showed at the gallery in 1999. The work was comprised of a dead horse's body suspended from the roof of the Rotunda space of the Tate Gallery as part of the contemporary art exhibition *Abracadabra*. This coalescence of education and publicity management protected the curatorial project of modernism from exposure to the politics of contemporary reception while simultaneously diminishing the exclusive authority of curatorial knowledge to articulate the public value of the art object. That is to say, curatorial expertise was no longer sufficient to independently guarantee the organizational need to secure public validation. This was particularly true in relation to the exhibition form of production, which was both a crucial form of income generation and a strategic currency through which to build both the changing identity of the Tate Gallery as a dynamic and contemporary institution while extending national and international networks of patronage as well as sponsorship alongside high quality museum loans. As temporary forms of aesthetic production, exhibitions offered expedient means to demonstrate innovative and progressive programming while generating publicity and revenue. They carried, in equal measure, a higher risk of courting controversy, given their implicit role of either proposing new interpretations of canonical art or arguing the aesthetic value of new art. While the role of interpretation would become a prerequisite to negotiating the public reception of exhibitions, they crucially, however, also drew their legitimacy, by proxy, from the permanent status and authority of the Tate Gallery as well as from the monolithic status of the collection, which acted as the guarantor/reserve to their temporary claims of attention.

In what can be seen as a pincer-like movement, the reconstruction of the Tate Gallery as a distinct and dynamic entity, defined by its unique asset base in the collection, consolidated with its own individual but fluid identity expressed through exhibitions and projects, enabled it to assume a notably commanding position on the national and international stage of art museums, investing it with invaluable new currency to negotiate and secure unprecedented levels of leverage of public and private investment and support. As Damien Whitmore observed, every organizational activity throughout the 1990s was focused on creating the optimum conditions for the planning and building of the future Tate Modern, the first British museum of modern art, and not least in respect of raising the necessary funds to build it. The final move in this strategic journey was to establish the first museum brand in the UK that was conceived and designed by the award-winning brand consultancy Wolff Olins, whose practice, defined by the motto 'making strategy visible', had won them many high-profile British commercial contracts. Commissioned to be launched with the opening of Tate Modern and the redesignation of the Tate Gallery site as Tate Britain in 2000, the Wolff Olins website records the creation of the brand:

> With help from Wolff Olins, Tate reinvented the idea of a gallery from a single, institutional view, to a branded collection of experiences, sharing an attitude by offering many different ways of seeing. The new Tate would become a part of everyday national life, democratizing without dumbing down. Wolff Olins created the Tate brand under the idea 'look again, think again': both an invitation and a challenge to visitors. Instead of the confusing 'Millbank' and 'Bankside' we named the London sites Tate Britain and Tate

Modern to signal what kind of art people would find inside. We designed a range of logos that move in and out of focus, suggesting the dynamic nature of Tate – always changing but always recognizable. And we shaped Tate's visual style, influencing its posters, website, publications and shops.[12]

The conversion of the Tate Gallery into a 'branded collection of experiences' in preparation of the opening of Tate Modern in the new Millennium was clearly in-keeping with the circulating ideas of the 'experience economy' (Pine and Gilmore 1998), which was perceived to be replacing the 'Service Economy', bringing forward a new emphasis on 'customer experience management' as well as the need to create memorable and individualized experiences that would emotionally bind the con-sumer to the product, nurturing a sustainable relationship. In practice, this informed an overhaul of how the Tate Gallery's invigilators, 'wardens' and other 'front of house' staff would interface with the public, and, as piloted in Tate Liverpool in 1988, the role of security management shifted to a more public-orientated mode, most clearly witnessed in the abandonment of civil service style uniforms for a more informal and contemporary uniform created by the leading British fashion designer Paul Smith. The language and conceptualization of the 'experience economy' was clearly an exceptionally good fit with the discourse and practice of art and the prin-ciples of aesthetic display. Moreover, the associated conceptualization of the 'experi-ential society', with its emphasis on informality, socialization and pleasure presented a new framework in which to reconsider the tenor and formats of curatorial and edu-cational programming for public engagement such as artists' commissions, late event openings and all-day festivals. The potential to mesh the art of consumption with the consumption of art through the expedient language of experience was undoubtedly not lost on Nicholas Serota when he presented and published the Walter Neurath lecture in 1996 *Experience or Interpretation: The Dilemma of Museums of Modern Art*, concluding with the final statement: 'Our aim must be to generate a condition in which visitors can experience a sense of discovery in looking at particular paintings, sculptures or installations in a particular room at a particular moment, rather than find themselves standing on the conveyor belt of history' (Serota 1996: 55).

One key aspect of the success of the Tate brand was its effectiveness in creating a homogenous identity, which by 2000 had grown to what the gallery often describes as a 'family of four Tates', encompassing the newly created Tate Britain and Tate Modern as well as Tate Liverpool and Tate St Ives, which had become increasingly important regional outposts in meeting the political demands to create greater national access to the national collections of British historic, modern and con-temporary art. The discourse of nationalism had begun to emerge at government policy levels in the late 1980s, but by the mid-1990s there was a greatly enhanced urgency to respond to this emerging agenda as the prospect of accessing historically unprecedented levels of public funding began to unfold which the Tate Gallery clearly wanted to pursue for the creation of both Tate Modern and Tate Britain. In 1994, the Heritage Lottery Fund was set up from the newly established National Lottery. Within it, the Millennium Commission was also founded with the aim 'to encourage projects throughout the nation which enjoyed public support and would be lasting monuments to the achievements and aspirations of the people of the United Kingdom'. Tate was clearly in a potentially strong position to secure such funding as the number of visitors to the Tate Gallery at Millbank increased year on year, and its high quality of public service and access was publicly acknowledged. The role of Communications became ever more important in drawing attention to the 'national' status of the gallery, and the discourse of public ownership was brought into play more frequently through high-profile public campaigns that surrounded collection acquisitions – often described as purchases 'on behalf of the nation' – and the ongoing debate about free access to national museums.

This discourse of vested national interest inherently played off the historical construction of national museums in the nineteenth century as institutions of 'public good' disseminating the values of knowledge and civilization through education as well as cultural exposure. The extent to which these narratives of national importance and public value were successfully constructed and mediated by the Tate Gallery is clearly revealed in the levels of public and private sector funding that it succeeded in attracting in order to realize the creation of Tate Modern, and its byproduct Tate Britain. In the case of Tate Modern, various sources of public sector funding were secured: £50 million from the Millennium Commission, £12 million from English Partnerships, £6.2 million from the Arts Council of England, and £5 million from the government's Department of Culture, Media and Sport. The success of the gallery to also generate equally significant sums from the private sector is evidenced in the final funding model that approximated to 60 per cent public funding and 40 per cent private. From the private sector, the Clore Duffield Foundation donated £2.5 million for educational spaces, and the industrial company Unilever agreed to £1.25 million sponsorship deal for a programme of contemporary commissions in the Turbine Hall. Of particular significance, was the success that the gallery had had in achieving unprecedented levels of international funding, most notably from North America through the American Fund for the Tate Gallery which had been established in New York in 1988 with a $6.5 million endowment (Donnellan 2011).

From the perspective of the New Labour government, only two years in office, the Tate Gallery's unrivalled success in meeting the cultural policy rubric of modernization and accessibility through the development of a mixed ecology of funding and particularly private sector investment, marked out both the Tate Modern building project and the Tate as an institutional organization as exemplary forms of 'best practice'; a fact acknowledged in the government's externally commissioned report *Efficiency and Effectiveness of Government-sponsored Museums and Galleries-Measurement and Improvement, Private Initiative Incentive (PFI)*, which sought to encourage the cultural sector to exploit the potential of the private sector more vigorously. As the Tate Gallery's own biennial report of 1998–2000 also noted, however, the need to continue to develop the asset base and value of the Tate brand also demanded significant organizational change to support this and to increase the level of production and revenue opportunities (Tate Gallery 1998–2000). The hybrid and paradoxical narrative of nation, heritage and modernism, which had been so effectively constructed under the banner of an aesthetic modernist tradition and had framed the arguments of the original amalgamation of the Historic British and Modern and International Collections, left, however, a highly problematic legacy for the logic of collection and exhibition display at Tate Britain in its resumed original status as the National Collection of British Art. Where narratives of a teleological history had originally bound the two disparate collections together in one building, the Tate brand now had to take on this unifying role to account for the distinction between the temporal narrative of Tate Modern as a universal representation of modernism and Tate Britain's representational identity defined by the geopolitical construct of nation and narratives of Britishness circulating at the time of its opening. The Tate brand identity, 'always changing, always recognizable', became a strategic glue to hold these two galleries together in one corporate entity defined by one Tate collection.

As Kevin Robins has argued, 'tradition and heritage are also things that entrepreneurs can exploit: they are products', but 'they also have human meaning and significance that cannot easily be erased. At the heart of contemporary British culture is the problem of articulating national past and global future' (Robins 1999: 27). Key to Robins' argument is the proposition that a 'relational logic' exists between the emergence of enterprise culture and the practices of tradition and heritage that are produced by the impact of global market forces: 'Enterprise culture is about responding to the new global conditions of accumulation. British capital must adapt to the new terms of global competition and learn to function in world markets.' As an institution, Tate's identity as a sector leader in cultural enterprise was secured by the turn of the new millennium. As a symbol of modernity and change (albeit belatedly in the UK), Tate Modern's capacity to register with the new geographies of the global market was potentially left open by the designation of 'modern'. For Tate Britain, however, as the original historic site of the Tate Gallery and housing the National Collection of British Art from 1600, its location within a nation-state history inevitably enmeshed it in the more localized, representational politics of nation, however hard it tried to suspend these through the continuity of modern and contemporary displays of British art, reflecting what Robins has described as the 'neurotic ambivalence' that lies at the heart of 'cultural transformation'. The idea of 'neurotic ambivalence' presents a useful frame in which to view Tate Britain's negotiation of its own national identity and its relation to cultural diversity policy under New Labour, which, courtesy of the nature of its collection and representational claims, it inherently assumed an explicit role and responsibility to represent ideas of nation not only in its collection displays, but also in its programming and public engagement practices.

Tate Britain's negotiation with cultural diversity policy clearly called up the gallery's historical relation with the politics of post-colonialism, which it first encountered through the confrontational positions produced by academics aligned with the New Art History of the late 1980s and 1990s, and manifested at the Art Historians conference of 1993, at which one of the leading proponents of this new disciplinary approach was Carol Duncan, whose *Civilizing Rituals: Inside Public Art Museums*

(1995) had particularly brought the museum into critical debate, as had Tony Bennett's *The Birth of the Museum: History, Theory, Politics*, published in the same year. On the one hand, the historical construction and analysis of the museum in these important early days of museum studies, which primarily understood the museum as a monolithic hangover of the imperial days of cultural authority clearly established a relationship of mistrust. On the other hand, for the museum such studies contributed towards a progressive scepticism and perceived naivety within the museum of the work of the academy, which seemingly remained either disinterested or relatively unaware of the ever-increasingly complex economic and political environment in which museums were negotiating and navigating their way towards increased financial independence. The need for this financial independence was prompted not only by Thatcherite policies of corporate self-sufficiency, but necessitated by the fragility and short-termism of public sector funding, and the subsequent decline in the principles of arm's-length funding, all of which coincided with a fiercely competitive commercial environment of the leisure industries with which the Tate Gallery had to compete. The perpetuation of post-Marxist and post-structuralist critiques of the museum, announcing the art work either as a material expression of class and difference or as a text to be read and decoded in the absence of the artist or artistic intention, further contributed to an academic positioning of museum studies that was crucially at odds both with the account and curatorial enactment of aesthetic modernism that the Tate Gallery deployed in the 1990s. It also proved contrary to the account presented more latterly at Tate Britain, which fed off the Romantic narrative trope of a national story of art held together by a canon of individual 'geniuses'; in the case of Tate Britain, through such figures as Turner, Constable, Gainsborough and Reynolds.

This specific context of economic change, cultural policy and museum practice in which the Tate Gallery had to simultaneously develop its relationship with both the public and with the private sector has for the most part remained elusive in museum studies accounts of this period, thereby concealing the largely forgotten and singular history of the extraordinarily poor reputation and low status that both modern and contemporary art experienced in the British public domain in the 1980s. This 'missing history' primarily arose out of museum studies of the 1980s, which framed museums as a collective object of study to reveal the larger narratives of their agency as organization of public culture. However, relatively little attention was paid to the specificity of museums' collections, rendering them of equivalent ontological value, despite their distinct historical formations, epistemological histories and cultural trajectories in contemporary life. This is particularly noticeable in terms of the number of anthologized publications that entered the market as academic course 'readers' for museum studies courses. Last but not least, as a consequence of this ontological reduction, the specificity of the modes of presentations and the modalities of spectatorship were also flattened out across different object-based collections. This rendered the idea of the audience either as a passive byproduct or as an effect of the engagement with objects, rather than an active agent or co-constituent of their making, meaning and experience within the specific paradigms of the art museum (Trodd 2003).

Awareness of the lack of impact and connection between academic accounts of the museum and the academy has, however, become increasingly evident, calling forth a new, more critically reflexive negotiation of the location of the museum in the public sphere. As Irit Rogoff has observed:

> 'Criticality' as I perceive it is precisely in the operations of recognizing the limitations of one's thought for one does not learn something new until one unlearns something old, otherwise one is simply adding information rather than rethinking a structure ... the ever increasing emphasis on allocating blames and pointing out elisions and injustices has created alliances between critique and such political projects as 'identity politics' and diminished the complex potentiality of occupying culture through a set of productive dualities and ambiguities.
>
> *(Rogoff 2006)*

For Tony Bennett, building on the work of Stuart Cunningham, this also translated into an awareness of the need to move beyond a confrontational mode of critique with the museum, and towards the:

> ... contention that the incorporation of an adequate and thorough-going policy orientation into cultural studies would see a shift in its 'command' metaphors away from rhetorics of resistance, progressiveness, and anti-commercialism on the one hand, and populism on the other, toward those of access, equity, empowerment and the divination of opportunities to exercise appropriate cultural leadership.
>
> *(Bennett 1999: 381)*

In considering the relation between policy and practice, and carrying forward the arguments of how aesthetic modernism became a strategic tactic to build both the asset value of the collection and a new paradigm of the public experience of art, the upcoming discussion reveals to what extent, as a museum caught up within the post-traditional moment of reflexive modernization, Tate Britain created a new precarious framework of sociopolitical reference points and a new set of challenges for the management of the Tate brand. Indeed, 'the rewriting of Tate's history through the brand', as Tim Marlow described it in his interview, found itself in a potential direct line of conflict with the politics of multiculturalism, which prompted a significant increase in risk-management strategies to protect the new Tate history. Twelve years on from the opening of Tate Gallery Liverpool, the practices of education would once again come into focus to mediate the relation between art and the public, but in the newly politicized forms of cultural diversity policy, the value of education would not only be seen within its service role to offset policy demands of audience development and inclusion, but also as an integral agent to manage the increasing range and levels of risk presented by the closer relation now forged between the museum and society, the collection and the market.

2

THE POLITICS OF REPRESENTATION AND THE EMERGENCE OF AUDIENCE

On 1 July 1997, Nicholas Serota greeted Princess Diana at the steps to the Tate Gallery, welcoming her as guest of honour at a lavish gala dinner, sponsored by the fashion house Chanel, to mark the Tate Gallery's centenary. As much a symbol of tradition and monarchy as of contemporary culture and social equality through her charity work, Diana undoubtedly represented some of the challenges and paradoxes that narratives of nation were facing Britain in the late twentieth century. That same year, the Tate Gallery announced the creation of a major Centenary Development to its neo-classical building at Millbank, which would add a new contemporary architectural component to support its conversion into Tate Britain in 2000, occasioned by the concurrently scheduled opening of Tate Modern, and the relocation of the gallery's collection of international art. This announcement coincided with a year of tumultuous change in the political and social landscape of Britain. In May 1997, New Labour came to power in a landslide victory bringing to a close 18 years of Conservative government. But as the British press and public were preparing for a new era of political governance, the narrative of nation was to take on a new rhetoric as the death of Princess Diana was announced on 31 August 1997 and Tony Blair declared, 'We are today a nation in a state of shock', concluding, 'She was the people's princess, and that's how she will stay, how she will remain.'[1]

As spokesperson for the 'people', Tony Blair had already made clear in the party manifesto that the idea of nation was no less important to New Labour than it had been to the Conservatives, but the new focus was to be on a nation marked by an ambition to realize equality and social justice for all, to create 'a fairer society'; as Blair declared: 'I want a Britain that is one nation, with shared values and purpose, where merit comes before privilege, run for the many not the few, strong and sure of itself at home and abroad … I want a Britain that does not shuffle into the new millennium afraid of the future, but strides into it with confidence.' This translation from the idea of nation comprised of an abstract body of citizens to the more social and embodied concept of 'the people' marked a significant shift in the construction of the public realm. For New Labour 'the people' of the public realm was understood to be constituted by diverse communities defined by categories of difference – class, gender, race and disability – and by their status of inclusion and exclusion in national life, through access to education, employment, housing, welfare – and culture. As change was dependent on the recognition of difference, the status of representation within the nation body became increasingly important. As the New Labour manifesto also made clear, the arts had a very specific role to play in this reconfiguration of nation:

> The arts, culture and sport are central to the task of recreating the sense of community, identity and civic pride that should define our country. Yet we consistently undervalue the role of the arts and culture in helping to create a civic society – from amateur theatre to our art galleries. Art, sport and leisure are vital to our quality of life and the renewal of our economy. They are significant earners for Britain. They employ hundreds of thousands of people. They bring millions of tourists to Britain every year …

In many respects, both Tate Britain's conception and its opening displays in 2000 were symptomatic and reflective of this political and social climate of the late 1990s. During this period, there had been a concerted move to rebrand Britain as a dynamic, innovative and creative new player on the global stage, most clearly symbolized by the celebration and export of contemporary popular culture in the forms of Britpop, Brit-art, Cool Britannia and the creation of the Millennium Dome in London. Much of this emphasis on the 'new' of Britain was generated by the political language and strategies of New Labour after its election to government to rebrand Britain and create distance between the heritage-orientated era of Thatcherism and the dawn of a new political era moving into a new millennium; a fact effectively signalled by the renaming of the Department of National Heritage to the Department for Culture, Media and Sport (DCMS).

As the DCMS's first report signalled in 1998, its aims reflected the manifesto policies of the government as a whole with a focus on 'the promotion of access, for the many not just the few; the pursuit of excellence and innovation; the nurturing of educational opportunity and the fostering of creative industries' (Selwood 2002: 7). It also responded assertively to the agendas and policies presented by the Social Exclusion Unit, set up by the government in 1997 to consider ways in which joined-up government departments could address and overcome issues of social exclusion: 'art and sport can not only make a valuable contribution to delivering key outcomes of lower long-term unemployment, less crime, better health and better qualifications, but can also help to develop the individual pride, community spirit and capacity for responsibility that enable communities to run regeneration programmes themselves.'[2] Furthermore, in 1999, the Secretary of State for Culture, Media and Sport, Chris Smith, identified 'cultural diversity' as one of eight reasons to fund the arts, declaring:

... we must recognise and celebrate the cultural diversity of our country. It is no longer true to conceive British culture as being a monolithic entity: we need rather to speak of British cultures. And a healthy, thriving, publicly funded arts system needs to develop organically as society develops, reflecting and sustaining the full diversity and richness of our national identity and our cultural traditions.[3]

While the politics of representation had vigorously unfolded in artists' practice in the preceding two decades (see Part II), it had found little purchase in the national museum sector, and had only very cursorily been taken up in Tate's acquisition policy. This position was, however, to come under intense scrutiny when once again events took place that shook British society and put the issue of race back at the top of the political agenda. Like the riots of 1981, the murder of Stephen Lawrence in April 1993 acted as a major catalyst in reconfiguring the relation between culture and society. The political need and conviction to address the issues of racial inequality and discrimination was highlighted on 31 July 1997 when, in one of the first high-profile moves of the three-month-old government, Lord Macpherson was commissioned to undertake an enquiry into the high-profile murder of Stephen Lawrence and the management of the criminal and justice processes that had failed to deliver any convictions. The impact of the Macpherson Report, published in February 1999, was significantly greater than many had anticipated as its findings resonated well beyond the institution of the police and the criminal justice system, carrying as it did more refined and extended definitions of racism in public life:

'Racism' in general terms consists of conduct or words or practices which advantage or disadvantage people because of their colour, culture or ethnic origin. In its more subtle form it is as damaging as in its overt form.

(Macpherson 1999: 46.25)

'Institutional Racism' consists of the collective failure of an organisation to provide an appropriate and professional service to people because of their colour, culture or ethnic origin. It can be seen or detected in processes, attitudes and behaviour which amount to discrimination through unwitting prejudice, ignorance, thoughtlessness, and racist stereotyping which disadvantage minority ethnic people.

(Macpherson 1999: 46.25)

The full import of the Macpherson Report, however, came to the fore in 2000 with the passing of the Race Relations (Amendment) Act 2000, which not only extended what constituted racial discrimination and the types of institutions subject to the law, but also placed specific responsibility on public authorities 'to promote race equality'. As the new millennium began and Tate Britain opened its doors for the first time on

24 March 2000 (and Tate Modern on 12 May the same year), the emphasis on not just engaging with cultural diversity as a public institution, but actively promoting it and supporting positive action programmes was beginning to take shape at Tate Britain. Both through its new representational name and national status, Tate Britain found itself inextricably tied to the politics of representation and subsequently invested with a more overt responsibility to demonstrate its inclusivity and active engagement with local and national communities defined by the government's cultural policy category of 'black and minority ethnic' (BME).

Whereas the primary focus of cultural policy under the previous Conservative government had been on maximizing the quantity of visitors and the quality of visitor experience within a framework of service and value for taxpayers' money and income generation, with the added remit of contributing to civic renewal through urban regeneration (such as Tate Liverpool), New Labour's emphasis on cultural provision for all, within a framework of cultural access and entitlement, placed a new emphasis on the category of 'audiences'. While in many respects, since the passing of the Museums and Galleries Act in 1992, the national museums had realized a greater distance from the direct impact of government cultural policy through their enhanced institutional autonomy and increasing financial independence, underpinned by 'the arm's-length' principle relation to government, New Labour's cultural policy particularly identified national museums and galleries as key agents of social and cultural change in the public domain. Under more detailed contractual terms outlined in the new Public Service Agreements introduced in 1998, the Department of Culture, Media and Sport's focus on public engagement was reformulated under the terms of 'New Audiences' and 'Audience Development', which carried the explicit responsibility to secure and demonstrate increased attendance and participation by BME audiences. The imperative to respond to this new cultural access and 'widening participation' agenda was not only informed by government monitoring processes of auditing audience numbers against the policy category of BME, but also by the new legal terrain laid out both by the Macpherson Report's definition of institutional racism and the legal requirements of public bodies to promote equality under the Race Relations (Amendment) Act 2000.

As the principles of cultural diversity policy were rolled out across cultural organizations and agencies in the first half of the first decade of the new millennium, highly contested debates emerged around what was subsequently deemed the political racialization of culture by both second and third generation black artists, critics and curators such as Sonya Dyer (2007a; 2007b), Richard Hylton (2007) and Munira Mirza (2006). Opening up discussions around the positive action funding programmes being directed at BME groups, they had begun to question whether targeted initiatives inadvertently helped to support the status quo, by contributing to the further marginalization of artists, writers and curators through the emphasis on difference. Further opposition from these constituencies also took on the wider debate of the political instrumentalization of cultural policy as can be seen in the publication of collected writings *Culture Vultures: Is UK Arts Policy Damaging the Arts?* (Mirza 2006) and *Art For All? Their Policies and Our Culture* (Wallinger and

Warnock 2000). As Richard Hylton has comprehensively charted in *The Nature of the Beast: Cultural Diversity and the Visual Arts Sector: A Study of Policies, Initiatives and Attitudes 1976–2006* (Hylton 2007), minority arts funding emerged in Britain in the 1970s out of certain political discourses of the time, most notably race relations, and to a large extent retained this association and remit. Looking back, Hylton identifies Naseem Khan's report *The Arts Britain Ignores: The Arts of Ethnic Minorities in Britain*, published in 1976, as a key moment in the political racialization of cultural policy. In her report, Khan focused on the benefits that ethnic arts could bring to a multicultural Britain and emphasized the ethnicity of different forms of cultural practice, such as festivals, that could be conceived under the umbrella of 'ethnic minorities' community arts'. Later the same year, Rasheed Araeen, the artist, critic and later founder of the journal *Third Text*, published a clear counter-challenge to these views with his publication *The Art Britain Really Ignores* (Araeen 1984). For Araeen, *The Arts Britain Ignores* represented a 'recipe for cultural separatism' and offered no analysis or ways forward for black artists to be recognized and valued in the mainstream narrative of modernism. On the contrary, for Araeen, the report reasserted the view that 'somehow the sensibility in the art activity of black people is inherently related to their "ethnicity" and is necessarily different from and alien to the mainstream'. This distinction between focusing on the essentialized politics of identity that underpinned New Labour's policies of cultural diversity (what came to be labelled as 'State Multiculturalism' by the end of the decade) and a new politics of integration, rather than assimilation, which would produce a reconfiguration of the mainstream as opposed to a form of cultural extension, emerged as a central debate for Tate Britain through its reactive practices of display and audience development.

As a gallery, Tate had a complicated history with its British aspect. When it first opened to the public in 1897, its official name was the 'National Gallery of British Art' and it had been specifically built and designed to house the collection of nineteenth-century British painting and sculpture given to the nation by the industrialist Sir Henry Tate. Together with British paintings transferred from the National Gallery in London, the gallery's responsibilities were specifically for modern British art, defined then as artists born after 1790. In 1917, however, the gallery assumed the additional responsibility for the national collection of international modern art and for British art dating from the sixteenth century and was subsequently renamed the 'Tate Gallery'. The emphasis on 'British' however, was always retained to some extent in the displays of the permanent collection up until 1990 with the introduction of the first rehang *Past, Present and Future*. The embodied value of the collection, as the representation of British art, culture and identity, was nonetheless evident and clearly open to critique in the late 1980s and 1990s, during which time revisionist art history focused on collections as the manifestations of historic formations of society, race and gender organized by the dominant, elitist classes.

Following the controversial hosting of the Association of Art Historians conference at the gallery in 1993, which had taken its theme as 'Identity and Display', the Tate Gallery understood the need to acknowledge these new politics of representation and recognition and indeed to try and engage with the Academy on its own terms of debate, and particularly those of post-colonialism. As an academic discourse, post-colonialism featured strongly within British cultural studies in the 1980s through the seminal writings of Stuart Hall and Paul Gilroy, but its permeation into the visual arts within national institutions was slow and fragmented. In 1996, however, the gallery invited Paul Gilroy to select and curate works from the collection in the exhibition *Picturing Blackness in British Art*. The display brought together works from across three centuries and included the artists Benjamin Robert Haydon, Dante Gabriel Rossetti, William Powell Frith, Sir Joshua Reynolds, Sonia Boyce and Lubaina Himid. As Gilroy argued in the exhibition's text, 'Any discussion of the representation of blackness in British art demands political as well as aesthetic sensitivities':

> ... when so ignored by official history, black British citizens, and indeed citizens of any minority group, can become vulnerable to exclusion from the nation's sense of itself. Since 1945, Britain has frequently been perceived as a society disrupted by the arrival of colonial immigrants who have supposedly brought disharmony, division and a brash, assertive multiculturalism. This idea of intrusion has triggered appeals to a mythic past, an imaginary, culturally simple, racially homogeneous and monochrome Britain in which there were no blacks. Such misinterpretation has served to soothe continuing uncertainty surrounding Britain's post-war, post-imperial identity, culture and national character. This display addresses some of the myths of Britishness ... The changing perception of blackness and Britishness presented in this display is not a minority issue. It is not something of significance primarily only to those who have previously been excluded and ignored. It is an essential ingredient in the development of a sense of nationality free of 'racial' division. This is an urgent goal for us all.
>
> *(Gilroy 1996)*

While seeking to appease academic debate and to demonstrate its openness to new revisionist art history, the gallery found itself inadvertently provoking and alienating one of its key constituencies and strategic objects of attention, the national press – who responded with headlines such as, 'A Black Mark for the Tate' and lambasted the gallery for betraying its duty, while another called it 'a wretched little exhibition'.[4] As one commentator noted, however, the critics were as much 'irritated with the polemic that was forced upon them' as they were with the alternative historical reading of the works that lifted them out of the national story and canon of British art and relocated them in the imperial and subsumed past of Britain's history abroad. That the polemic had been imported by an external and radical academic rather than a Tate Gallery curator also offended the established idea of connoisseurship that was particularly associated with the British collection on which the narrative of nation had been constructed through the genius status of the single artist canon of artists such as

Hogarth, Reynolds, Gainsborough and Turner; a canon of taste on which the cultural authority of the Tate Gallery was rooted and deemed to represent. For a core audience and significant body of experts and patrons invested in this legacy of British art history, the direct challenge was both aesthetic and political, and further questioned and potentially compromised the emphasis on aesthetic modernism that the gallery had so carefully set up in the rotational rehang initiated by the *Past, Present and Future* installation. Furthermore, it brought into focus the political and economic conditions from which Britain had secured its relation with modernity through the project of imperialism and colonial trade, on which it had secured its status as a world trading nation. While not entirely comparable to the public controversy of the 'Bricks Affair' of 1976, the negative publicity and exhibition profile that *Picturing Blackness* generated nonetheless resonated throughout the Tate Gallery and entered the organizational memory as a curatorial experiment from which important lessons needed to be taken on board.

By 2000, with renewed debates of multiculturalism circulating around the policies of cultural diversity and social inclusion being introduced by the New Labour government, Tate Britain resumed its engagement with the discourses of post-colonialism in its opening hang of collection displays. As with Tate Modern, Tate Britain adopted a seemingly more radical and contemporary curatorial approach by thematically hanging the collection that replaced the art historical approach of a linear, chronological sequence of displays telling one 'story' of British art. While wishing to signal both a new account of the history of British art, as with Tate Modern again, the format also offered the strategic means by which to conceal the 'gaps' in the collection that would be ever more visible through the removal of key canonical works in the collection to the new displays of the Tate Modern. Through this thematic approach, however, the work of artists of different historical periods was juxtaposed creating new and multiple readings of the collection and challenging the orthodoxies of traditional art historical discourse based on genre, medium or artist. While some displays were more successful than others, one that drew attention from academics was titled 'Artists Abroad', which brought together the Zanzibar-born British contemporary painter Lubaina Himid with nineteenth-century British-born painters such as Lawrence Alma-Tadema, Richard Dadd and Philip Wilson Steer, among others. As Andy Morris analysed in his essay, 'Redrawing the Boundaries: Questioning the Geographies of Britishness at Tate Britain' (Morris 2003), this display signalled the gallery's desire to present a notion of a Britain that was rooted firmly in the world beyond the geographical confines of Britain and acknowledged the changing world within Britain.

Within this context, the 'Artists Abroad' display clearly acknowledged the new rhetoric and identity of an inclusive Britain as the display text noted: ' ... what home and abroad mean have become more complex with the growth and recognition of a culturally diverse Britain'. But as Andy Morris argued: 'There is a need to talk of multiple identities and differences within Britishness and this is what brought Himid and Turner together ... but it is this "bringing them together" which causes problems ... ' (Morris 2003: 178). For Morris, the display opened up discussion, but a discussion framed principally by the act of juxtaposition that suggested simple journeys of departure and arrival for the 'migrant' as well as shared meaning with real or imaginary trips for the artist traveller; the act of travel being the binding principle of display. This approach to presenting diverse stories within the collection was recognized by Morris as a positive move, albeit a partially realized one, 'if it is to remain a coherent reappraisal, reflexivity demands that the quest for a more nuanced, complex understanding goes to the very centre. The criticisms of Tate's approach ... seems to endorse the notion that, at present, the Tate is caught "between camps"' (Morris 2003: 180). To a large degree, Tate Britain had identified for itself, the paradox of its condition as both being a manifestation of tradition and cultural heritage while also assertively committing itself to the practices and discourse of the contemporary and contemporary art, as Stephen Deuchar, the Director wrote in the foreword to the first collection catalogue of the new Tate Britain:

> Though the concept of a national gallery of British art may not seem automatically modern, with its roots in a nationalistic, centralist Victorian ethic scarcely in harmony with twenty-first century society, Tate Britain's agenda is determinedly contemporary. As its, and the name of this book [*Representing Britain*] tend to imply, its concern with art's place in the political and cultural entity that is Britain – and questions about art's contribution to varying kinds of national identity – will certainly form an undercurrent to our programme of displays, exhibitions and publications.
>
> *(Myrone 2000: 8)*

For, in an attempt to present inclusive representations of 'diverse artists' work the display inherently re-enacted the story of British migration as one of a journey of the departure from an essential origin to the arrival in the monoculture of Britain, emphasizing the notion of essentialized difference rather than a manifestation of two-way travel that the colonial project of Britain as a trading nation had established over centuries, creating settled communities of migration now integrated into British culture. In so doing, the geopolitical construction of Britain as simply the end point of the migrant's journey constructed the artist as 'visitor', or as in Georg Simmel's definition of the 'stranger', someone 'who comes today and stays tomorrow' (Beck et al. 1994: 81). As Mike Phillips notes:

> ... the conventional way of talking about migration in Britain almost always focuses on the 'moment of arrival' because there is always a demand that ethnic minorities should be framed within this 'moment of arrival' – a moment which appears to value and privilege the arrival but which also, much more powerfully, is an argument that defines cultures as separate and alien to each other and extends that definition into the past. But this moment of arrival is an imaginary moment ...
>
> *(Phillips 2007: 11)*

While, as Morris identified, for Tate Britain to pursue its well-intentioned revisionist form of display demanded greater reflexivity and re-engagement with how notions of difference and identity were imbibed into the idea of travel that was essentially conceived from a geopolitical positioning of Britain at the centre and the 'visitor' travelling from the periphery towards it. But such a renegotiation of Britain's historical past in relation to the contemporary experience of a multicultural Britain would inevitably also demand a renegotiation of Tate Britain's own institutional identity that was simultaneously highly invested in maintaining its status as a place of distinct nationalist heritage (despite its aspirations towards the contemporary), in the competitive market of international tourism in which its tradition of 'Britishness' was its unique selling point.

While at the curatorial level such internal contradictions between policy aspirations and objectives of increasing cultural diversity representation (and through the representational assumption an increased diversity in audience engagement) were problematic, the opportunity to widen the knowledge-base of post-colonialism through recourse to the discipline of art history offered little aid towards a position of reflexivity. As Donald Preziosi has argued, the relation between art history and the museum is not co-existent nor co-dependent, but rather 'their relations are anamorphic – each transforming the other – rather than direct or transitive' (Preziosi 2011: 50–1). But as Leon Wainwright has also argued, the limits of British art history to extend its account to the actual production of diasporic British artists beyond the linear and representational narratives of post-colonialism has also proved reductive, exclusionary and problematic and supported the malaise with which the museum has taken up an enquiry into a more complex and inclusive account of British art in the twenty-first century. In an interview documenting his own trajectory to develop a more integrated history of British art,[5] Wainwright reflected on the issues of the relationship between the post-colonial and the global from the perspective of his own academic career in relation to the evolution of art history as a discipline, which, when he encountered it as a young lecturer in the 1990s was 'failing its subjects and students'. Actively interested in the history and contemporary practice of black British art, Wainwright identified that while there was a network of critics, curators and gallerists engaged in promoting this, there was a notable vacuum of interest within his own discipline. This led him to contribute to the establishment of the 'Globalising Art, Architecture and Design History' (GLAADH) in 2001 which brought together 47 institutions in a project funded by the Higher Education Funding Council for England that would foster and promote teaching through revised curriculums within the context of the global and encourage reflection on the relation between multicultural Britain and a globalising world. This 'radical approach to teach art history … was intended to disabuse the discipline of its racism. … [and] ethnicisation of knowledge'. Despite the emergence of World Art History, and, indeed the Academy's own engagement with New Labour's agenda of 'widening participation' in education, the continued emphasis on 'positioning artists and artworks so as to appeal to a notion of difference that leads to an ethnicizing caricature' has perpetuated throughout the discipline (Wainwright 2009: 100).

That Tate Britain understood its task to demonstrate inclusiveness through representational practices is not surprising: between the politics and racialized policies of government cultural diversity and the critical hostility engendered in New Art History, post-colonial theory and in particular, post-colonial studies centred on the museum (Duncan 1995), the first strategic response could only be in terms of acquisition (Preziosi 2004: 2) of works by 'diverse' artists. As Nicholas Serota reported in his speech at the closing of the Commission for Racial Equality in December 2006, Tate had recently acquired work by artists including Mona Hatoum, Isaac Julien, Yinka Shonibare, Zarina Bhimji, Chris Ofili, Steve McQueen and Rosalind Nashashibi, who, 'all draw productively upon past events and narratives of international conflict, exchange and migration'.[6] This was subsequently followed by the announcement in the Tate Biennial Report of 2004–6, under the section heading 'Audiences, Diversity and Learning', that 'an audit of the British art collection to highlight gaps' was underway to identify further artists and works for collection (Tate Gallery 2004–6). But in understanding inclusion and diversity on the exclusive terms of representation also implicitly led to the conceptual alignment with fixed notions of identity based on an essentialized understanding of subjecthood, as Stephen Deuchar's introduction to Tate Britain's catalogue *Representing Britain* stated:

> In today's immediate climate of progressive regional devolution on one hand and European integration on the other and with increasing awareness of a population representing many ethnic and social positions, interrogating the roles of art in defining and challenging ideas of national identity may be a responsibility of Tate Britain, but it is also an exciting opportunity. For as well as providing a rich diversity of meaning and aesthetic pleasure, art can offer a key to opening up some of the pressing questions and debates about the nation, its history and future. Tate Britain's programme is not intended to be an extended investigation into the Britishness of British art.
>
> *(Myrone 2000: 8)*

The translation of national identity into the amorphous idea and discourse of Britishness that was circulating at this time, and the need to name it, albeit contestedly, reflected the momentum it had gained in political debates around the need to assert a more coherent and inclusive national identity that would engender and facilitate greater social cohesion. From the government's historical perspective, the museum presented itself as a ready-made site and agent to promote identity through its representational mode, but as the government consultation report *Understanding the Future: Museums and 21st Century Life: The Value of Museums* (DCMS 2005) revealed, within this conceptualization of the museum rested a series of conflations and misrecognitions of the nature of collections as both universal and representational in that they present:

> … a way for us all to see our place in the world. This is all the more important as society changes and new values of nationality and community emerge …

They are a means of helping citizens understand their place in the world and its heritage … museums are spaces where people can explore personal beliefs in amongst universal truths. In short, they can show how events and beliefs from the past shape people's experience of the present, and help create a sense of identity. Because cultural identity in the 21st century is not necessarily defined by national borders.

(DCMS 2005: 10)

The paradoxes that this government strategic framing of the museum created, paralleled an equal set of paradoxes established by Tate Britain through its embrace of aesthetic modernism (predicated on a universal subjective experience of the art object) and the increased emphasis on the representational role the museum was offering itself up to in terms of cultural diversity policy. This was clearly brought into sharp focus through the flirtation with post-colonial thought that determinedly called into question the atemporal claims of aesthetic modernism and the historical condition of the post-colonial subject, provoking further representational questions of 'whose heritage?' and 'whose history?' In resisting calls to purposefully pursue 'an investigation into the Britishness of British art', Tate Britain was not necessarily constructing a position of resistance, however, but rather a more strategically flexible and advantageous one that would allow a greater historical fluidity to the designation of British in relation to artists and the formation of the Tate collection. Indeed, Tate had consistently avoided defining what constituted British in terms of both artist and collection and had consistently avoided cataloguing works of art on the basis of national origin, neither designating works as belonging to the British or the international collection, but rather one whole Tate collection. This is particularly evident in the way the definition of British had shifted many times in relation to the short-listing criteria of the Turner Prize. This level of operational ambiguity was clearly also understood as a preferable stance by New Labour, which noted in the 2007 Green Paper *The Governance of Britain*, that, 'our relative stability as a nation is reflected in a relative lack of precision about what we mean to be British.'[7] If 'British' was an elusive and problematic concept in relation to the politics and policies of the present, it was, however, a far less complicated concept to invoke in relation to arguments to government for the preservation of free access for and in the name of the British public, and indeed the public was invariably summoned up as key beneficiaries of major acquisition funding bids to the Heritage Lottery Fund.

As one curator observed, while concerns with Britishness circulated at Tate Britain, at the level of actual curatorial practice it held very little interest or significance and was primarily understood as a strategic discourse for national funding or, more visibly through the practices of the marketing department. A good example of this was the marketing creation of Tate Britain's 'British Art Week' in 2004, which was conceived to highlight new hangs of the collection galleries, sponsored by the British oil company BP. In one of the more high-profile projects, the black artist Hew Locke was invited to work with the grand neo-classical façade of Tate Britain for which he produced the monumental installation 'King Creole', which straddled the full scale of the classical pediment. The work featured the Portcullis coat of arms of the British seat of elected government, the House of Commons, emblazoned with a skull and cross bones and festooned with artificial flowers, which the artist described: 'The design is based on an original Pugin design for the House of Commons coat-of-arms, also shown on the back of every penny. My piece refers to the buccaneering, piratical attitude that has existed in British history as well as the often vicious cut and thrust of debate in the House, and of the real wars that can result.'[8] But as Hew Locke observed in interview, while such an opportunity of exhibition was both important and appreciated, it did raise questions as to why he should be seen particularly as 'British' at Tate Britain while other British artists were understood simply within the category of 'artist' at Tate Modern, or 'international artist'. This was particularly resonant following the high levels of publicity and debate around the international market-setting exhibition *Documenta XI* in 2002, curated for the first time by a black curator, Okwui Enwezor, and focused on the work of artists both inside and outside the geographies of established Western modernism. For as, Locke pointed out, the impact of this *Documenta* had encouraged British curators, including Tate Modern curators, to start 'chasing all over the world looking for the latest thing from Mexico, India ... ', travelling to non-Western metropolises to secure this new 'global art' (the representational term and place holder for non-white art) now legitimized as

FIGURE 2.1 Hew Locke, 'King Creole' (2004). Reproduced by kind permission of the artist. Photo Mark Heathcote © Tate 2005

'international', leaving him to offer the flippant but incisive jibe at Tate Modern curators, 'Come on folks, what's going on? I'm here … in Brixton.'[9]

Struggling to overcome the negative perception that Tate Britain's creation was necessitated by its byproduct status of the creation of Tate Modern, and wishing to pursue 'a determinedly contemporary' programme as well as being seen as the home of the historical collection of British art, Tate Britain commissioned the advertising company Fallon to review its marketing strategy in 2005 and to create a high-impact campaign that would transform the public profile of the gallery from 'old-fashioned' and 'establishment' forged through its distinction from Tate Modern. Fallon subsequently observed: 'Gallery marketing [at Tate] was dominated by the artist being elevated beyond the art – like a modern day celebrity, or cult of the artist.' In their analysis of what was needed to refresh the image of Tate Britain and lift it out of its historical associations and render it more 'contemporary', Fallon arrived at the conclusion that the most contemporary aspect of Tate Britain was the viewer/visitor and their engagement with the work of art. Since works of art, 'masterpieces', were created by artists 'to display their feelings, emotions and mood; connect to other people; and stimulate an emotional response' they surmised that it was the work of art, not the artist, that dealt 'with feelings we all have in common'. Completing this analysis, the conclusion arrived at was that 'mood, feelings and emotions are timeless. When based on an emotional response Tate Britain and its permanent collection are as contemporary as Tate Modern. This was our epiphany'. The resulting campaign, 'Create your own collection' envisaged visitors in relation to 'everyday' life scenarios and moods and created a variety of self-selecting tours through the collection displays such as 'I have a big meeting', 'I'm hungover', 'I've just split up', and slightly out of sync 'The Britannia Collection'.[10]

The success of the campaign as a marketing strategy was reported as a 20 per cent increase in visitor numbers. This reorientation of the marketing strategy towards the interests of the art visitor/consumer of art clearly reflected the continued currency of the 'experience economy' on which marketing practices were based in the 1990s and equally coincided with the reorientation of cultural policy to the use value of museums for the public initiated by the Conservative government's agenda for museums to demonstrate their public value. As the institutional primary owners of visitors/audiences since the Conservative government emphasis in the 1980s on commercial revenue, the role of the marketing department had significantly increased following the introduction of the Museums and Galleries Act in 1992 that, as previously discussed, passed corporate financial independence and responsibility to the Tate Gallery. The rapid rise of visitor studies emerging out of market research models established in the 1980s and 1990s, encouraged by the National Audit Office's commercial model of product development and customer care, had clearly informed the Tate Gallery's overhauling of its management approach to front of house staff (converting them from security wardens to gallery assistants in informal uniforms) and repositioning Visitor Services as an extension of marketing. The need to actively maintain and build a knowledge-base of visitors, given the pace of market change, was simultaneously consistently pursued. Following the creation of Tate Britain and

Tate Modern in 2000 and the rebranding of Tate, the need to refine this knowledge-bank to support marketing activities and protect the coherence and market value of the new brand, while simultaneously engaging with the site-specific requirements of both London sites, led to both commissioned visitor research from commercial specialists and internally from departments directly involved with audience engagement (namely interpretation) as the section 'Audiences, Learning and Diversity' recorded in the Tate Biennial Report of 2004–6:

> Over the last two years, Tate continued to track the demographic profiles of its visitors, helping to spot visitor trends and informing future communications campaigns. At Tate Modern and Tate Britain this was done three times a year around the exhibition programme and has been undertaken for the last five years by the research agency BDRC. After wide consultation on the shape this research should take in future, MORI were appointed to continue this research.
>
> *(Tate Gallery 2004–6)*

As the report also noted, a major qualitative visitor audit had also been undertaken by the strategic research consultancy Morris Hargreaves McIntyre (MHM) who produced a report titled 'Anatomy of a Visit'. The impact of this report was immense, introducing as it did a new segmentation model of visitors to Tate that, rather than interviewing and recording visitors' responses in quantitative terms against socio-logical demographic categories of gender, age, race, employment and so forth, analysed them in terms of the motivation for visiting and the kind of experience the visit elicited. As the company's website quotes from Tate Marketing, 'the segmentation model revolutionized the way we understand our audiences at Tate'.[11] Incorporating this segmentation model, a substantial piece of internal research was undertaken at Tate Modern to understand the interaction and engagement of visitors with interpretation resources included in an exhibition of the American artist Mark Rothko. As the research observed:

> MHM considers motivation and behaviour the two most defining factors to influence the visitor experience. Their research has resulted in a segmentation that recognizes four types of motivation for a museum visit: social, intellectual, emotional and spiritual. These four groups can be further divided into eight segments by looking at who the visitor arrives at the museum with (mainly if there are children under fifteen in the party), if the visitor has visited Tate before, and the level of knowledge/whether or not a visitor is a professional.
>
> *(Meijer and Scott 2009)*

The eight segments that the MHM produced from their research fell under the categories of 'Aficionados, Actualisers, Sensualists, Researchers, Self-improvers, Social Spacers, Site-seers, and Families'. The success of MHM's motivational analysis of audiences was reflected in the currency the modelling assumed across the museum sector and notably informed the arguments put forward by New Labour's Department of Culture, Media and Sport (DCMS) in a major piece of research commissioned in 2007, *Culture on Demand: Ways to engage a broader audience* (DCMS 2007). The DCMS report was, however, not concerned with the analysis of existing visitors, or rather 'visits' that MHM had sought to interrogate, but was focused on the cultural policy agenda of diversity, social inclusion and widening participation, that is to say 'audience development'. Policy research into understanding the 'barriers to access', had by 2007, gained significant momentum, and the Arts Council of England had equally published a major research survey *Taking Part* (ACE 2007) which the DCMS report asserted, 'confirmed the challenge for providers of these services in terms of three priority groups: disabled people, Black and Minority Ethnic (BME) communities and lower socio-economic groups' (DCMS 2007: 7) and went on to argue: 'Driving or stimulating demand ... needs to go beyond the removal of barriers and the identification of contextual factors to take in the arguably more important effects of motivations, group behaviour and experience in determining perceptions of the relevance of culture and therefore individuals' propensity to engage.'

As the primary owners of visitors and audiences, the escalation of audience development as a strategic objective at Tate naturally fell within Marketing's remit, not least as it progressively assumed greater importance within public sector funding applications such as the Heritage Lottery Fund, which Tate necessarily and consistently sought support from in terms of collection acquisitions, capital projects, regional and educational initiatives and digitization projects. While the work of the Learning Department also accrued greater responsibility to conceive and deliver national projects aligned with audience development objectives within such funding applications, for Marketing the emphasis lay directly on increasing access to collection displays and exhibitions. In seeking to combine MHM's segmentation model, which had proven more than successful in increasing attendance at the Tate galleries in terms of what constituted the 'core' audience, with the new socio-demographic categories of government cultural policy such as BME, a second highly popular marketing model derived from the seminal work of the American psychologist Abraham Maslow was drawn upon. Maslow's model, developed in 1943, proposed a motivational theory for individual behaviour based on what he identified as a 'hierarchy of needs' derived from the individual's attainment of the hierarchical levels of 'self-actualization, esteem, belongingness, safety, and physiological' at the bottom of this pyramidal analysis. In synthesizing MHM's segmentation model of existing visitors with Maslow's model of motivational needs, Marketing produced a hybrid model known as the 'wheel of appeal' in which the core, existing audience of Tate was located at the centre and the missing categories of audience development at the margin, occupying a position of cultural need as opposed to one of cultural attainment.

To comply with DCMS requirements of performance indicators under the heading 'percentage of UK visitors from an ethnic minority' and to meet funding agreement targets of audience development, the need for Tate to gather both quantitative and qualitative data about 'missing audiences' encouraged the development of marketing strategies that would attract both core (identified as 'journalists, artists and the public') and marginal audiences, primarily defined by the category of BME. To realize both sets of audience objectives, the market research principle of targeting was refined, underpinned by a conflation of national marketing demographic categories (A, B, C1, C2, D and E) and segmentation modelling. A key tool in this process of targeting was provided by the commercial marketing sector's database 'Target Group Index' that maps target groups next to media consumption (TV, radio, and print) and provides 'a snapshot of the population' and 'guidance as to the sorts of magazines and newspapers ... [to be used in marketing] in relation to targeted groups'.[12] This was particularly utilized in relation to the marketing of exhibitions that were also understood as 'personality expressions of the brand' and against which the brand equity was developed. Whereas the early days of the Tate brand had been conceived in order to change the public profile and appeal of Tate by encouraging the public to re-engage on the basis of 'look, look again', Tate Britain's dual remit to display both historical and contemporary art led to the new adage 'always changing, always Tate', continuing the ethos of a temporal continuity of past, present and future created in the late 1990s before the Tate collection was split between modern and British.

That diversity was understood at the organizational level to be the work of departments associated with audiences was indicated by the section heading of the Tate Biennial Report – 'Audiences, Learning and Diversity', although contained with this was a wider statement of intent:

> Two major pieces of work were undertaken on diversity. A cross-Tate Diversity Group was formed to review Tate's performance to date across the range of its activities. In response to this, a strategy and plan, Tate for All, was drawn up and discussed widely across the organisation. This described Tate's achievements to date, and set out what needed to be done if Tate is to fulfill its vision. A central theme was that diversity is not an additional programme of activity but a set of principles that will be carried out by all, over time.
>
> *(Tate 2004–6)*

As the section also highlighted, the period covered by the report marked 'the beginning of a far-reaching, cross-cultural programme stemming from Tate Britain's 'Interpretation and Education Department' (I&E) and a more direct reference to the work of the I&E department in delivering against these objectives appeared in Tate's Funding Agreement for the same period which reported under section four, 'Tate's Contribution to the delivery of Government Objectives: Audience Development – Diversity' that 'Tate has become experienced and successful at engaging a wide range of audiences through its education programme'.

Charting the history of the educational function of the museum from its inception in the nineteenth century to the contemporary moment of 2005, Helen Charman, then Curator of Teacher Programmes at Tate Modern, noted in her article, 'Uncovering Professionalism in the Art Museum' (Charman 2005: 2), that 'the history of education in the museum sector is to a large extent a shared history from a policy perspective'. Under New Labour, this was perhaps ever more evident, particularly following Tony Blair's high profile speech in 2007 that opened with the now famous rhetorical statement: 'Ask me my three main priorities for government and I tell you: education, education and education.' That education was seen to be the means to create a fairer, more socially inclusive society invested it with a whole new import for museums, which now looked to their education departments to deliver these policy objectives through targeted audience development programmes. As already discussed, this was not just a policy obligation in relation to funding, but also the means by which to lever funding from other public sector funding agencies as evidence of social inclusion and public value. The dramatic increase in project funding for education projects, while investing education staff with considerable more agency within the museum than previously, also paradoxically instrumentalized it further as a service department to offset policy agendas evidenced through the quantitative audit culture of audience attendance based on the socioeconomic target categories of marketing.

That this emphasis on education was seen as a partial infringement on the core purposes of collection for national museums was reflected in the final report of a major research enquiry that the National Museums Directors' Conference (NMDC) commissioned from the London School of Economics in 2004. This was launched as part of a museum and gallery sector-wide 'Manifesto for Museums: Building Outstanding Museums for the 21st Century' as a pitch to government in advance of the Treasury's Spending Review. The research comprised both a qualitative report *Museums and Galleries: Creative Engagement* and a quantitative report *Valuing Museums: Impact and Innovation* (NMDC 2004) and highlighted the increase in demands on the museum as it had to progressively play out a more complex role in public life than ever before; demands that 'even private companies committed to the highest standards of corporate social responsibility would not be expected to pursue' (NMDC 2004: 13). As the *Valuing Museums* document described:

First, they must continue to hold and display the collections that they were originally created to preserve. This, for many people, is the pre-eminent role of such institutions. Second, they must now use the collections to educate, at all levels from university to school. Third, they undertake research of the kind found in private companies and university departments. Fourth, they must now act as mass visitor attractions, on a par with theme parks and other modern leisure facilities. Fifthly, they provide public space for organisations and individuals to meet and communicate. Sixth, they often have to preserve their built heritage on historic sites. To all of these objectives, the Government now requires a greater involvement in making good failures within society, including efforts to reduce crime and regenerate areas of social decline.

(NMDC 2004: 42–3)

As both reports evidenced through detailed case studies, despite limited funding capacity, the museum sector had developed a range of innovative practice (described as 'creative' in the policy language of the moment) to respond to this growing and changing list of 'requirements', which was predominantly realized through its capacity to 'make links', i.e. to develop partnerships with external bodies well-positioned to support new forms of activity, generate new knowledge and, potentially, new audiences. As the list of case studies revealed, these 'links' were as much with the private sector as the public sector. Notably, however, was the accepted framing by the National Museum Directors of the 'socially-orientated' demands on the museum as 'additional' activity to the core work of the museum, reconfirming the established view that gallery-education, as the prime agent of socially-engaged practice, was consistently conceived and received within the museum as 'added value'.

As the documented interviews on the history of education practice at Tate since 1970 also charted, this relatively marginal position to Tate's activities was (and is to a large extent still is) characterized by comparatively low levels of core funding and dependency on external project funding, secured either through government-funded initiatives, charitable foundations or corporate funding with criteria generally aligned to government policy directives (i.e. Corporate Social Responsibility). Putting aside the precarious position that project-funding produces (short-term contracts, lack of opportunity to develop expertise and authority, short-term partnerships, discontinuity of expertise through the employment of freelancers), what the interviews also revealed was that in being aligned with external policies and directives set outside of the traditional curatorial and scholastic interests of the museum, education practice had inevitably been the conduit and agent that dramatically altered the proximity of the museum to the wider social and cultural context in which it was located, bringing with it networks and interests remote, if not in direct opposition, to the networks of private interest invested in the rarefied art object and the project of aesthetic modernism. The public was no longer an abstract idea or an income-generation figure on paper, but rather an increasingly individualized set of relations, not set out in the community (as outreach), but progressively more present in the spaces of the museum – and not just the demarcated educational spaces at a distance from the collection galleries. Much of this had, quite clearly, already been understood and experienced in the development and early years of Tate Liverpool as Toby Jackson had highlighted in his interview.

One important difference between the period in which Toby Jackson had developed the role of education at Tate Liverpool and this first decade of the twenty-first century was, however, the overt modelling of gallery education on constructivist pedagogical principles employed not, nor primarily, in relation to discursive knowledge-exchange, but rather through increased emphasis on creative participation. The practice of partnership and collaboration as part of 'outreach' gallery education had a long established history in relation to community development (Dewdney 2008; Allen 2008), but under New Labour cultural policy the ethos of such work had assumed a new set of values in relation to working with 'young people' who were identified as one of the most disenfranchized and excluded categories of British

society. The role that the arts could play in this particular policy area was proposed by
Francois Mattarasso, a cultural researcher, in his report *Use or Ornament? The Social
Impact of Participation in the Arts* (Mattarasso 1997), published in 1997 and 'targeted at
policy makers in the arts and social fields', which argued that:

> The election of a Government committed to tackling problems like youth un-
> employment, fear of crime and social exclusion is the right moment to start
> talking about what the arts can do for society, rather than what society can do
> for the arts. Un-fettered by ideology, the new pragmatism can extend its
> principle of inclusiveness to the arts by embracing their creative approaches to
> problem-solving.
>
> *(Mattarasso 1997: Foreword)*

But as the artist and critic Dave Beech argued in his assessment of the prolific take-up
of participative art practice (Beech: 2008), or 'socially engaged art' as it became
termed in the art sphere, the potential folly of participation to construct unequal
relations of power between participant and the conditions of participation,
thereby undercutting its social value as a form of democratic inclusion in meaning-
making and reinscribing the very conditions of unequal power relation it sought to
address, needed to be critically confronted. For Beech, the answer lay in the practice
of 'collaboration' rather than participation, which, invested collaborators with the
agency to 'share authorial rights over the artwork that permit[s] them ... to make
fundamental decisions about the key structural features of the work'.

This distinction between participation and collaboration was well understood
within the practice of Tate Britain's curators in the Young People's Programme and
was consistently and rigorously built in to the programming of youth projects. In so
doing, the areas of interest often generated by young people's interaction with
Tate Britain's exhibitions and displays raised questions of the social and political in
relation to both displayed art works and art practice itself; questions that often ran
across and into the discourse of aesthetic modernism framing curatorial practice.
One such project, 'Tate Shift' (2008), which targeted 14–16-year-olds 'who are
on the borders of losing interest in the formal school curriculum' invited them to
'explore exhibitions and displays at Tate Britain while developing their own critical,
contextual and practical responses to the works'. As the information laid out, the
project would:

> ... explore the narrative of space, culture and mobility. Related to the 'Trien-
> nial – Altermodern', 'Turner Prize' and 'Drawn from the collection' displays
> and exhibitions. Exploring time (anthropology, real-time), space (architecture,
> geography) and mobility (movement of culture in relation to the physical,
> media, and technology) as a catalyst to define culture. Within these themes
> some of the focal points will be borders, economic, geography, history, class,
> exile, mobility and access. Economics and reactions against standardisation and

commercialism through the theories of a new mobility. Using space to construct or deconstruct cultural, social and political issues. Time and space as a process to construct a non verbal experiential narrative.

('Tate Shift' project information leaflet, 2008)

But as one of the artists working in collaboration with young people on the project, Raimi Gbadamosi, discussed in an interview with Paul Goodwin, Tate Britain curator, 'the pedagogical turn' in contemporary art marked a significant shift from the conventional practices and expectations of the 'art education project' to that of the independent 'art project' and presented considerably more tangled issues for the museum, producing as it did art works of ambiguous status within the exhibition and collection-based practices of the museum.[13] As Gbadamosi also identified, a further problem for the museum in relation to 'the pedagogical turn' was the extent to which the knowledge-base of an artist's practice lies not in the museum, but rather within culture and social history, which is inextricably underpinned by diversity. Culture and social history, invariably embodied and animated in young people's creative engagement, always precedes the practice of art history that the museum holds as its paradigm of interpretation. It is at this juncture in the museum, where culture meets heritage, that the greatest potential tension arises within learning-based projects, where the fluid meanings of culture meet the institutional, national narratives of heritage.

FIGURE 2.2 'Tate Shift' (2009). Reproduced courtesy of the artist. Photo © Raimi Gbadamosi/Britt Hatzius

This culture of critical reflexivity that pervaded Tate Britain's Interpretation and Education Department also informed the creation of the post of 'Curator: Cross-cultural Programmes' in 2005, which, while clearly responding to organizational needs of audience development in terms of diversity, also sought to expand internal debate in relation to the operational understanding of cultural diversity. As Mike Phillips, the first holder of the post, noted in an interview in 2007,[14] the explicit objective of 'realigning relationships with potential new audiences' was not one based on trying to increase the low level of attendance by BME audiences at Tate Britain through more targeted programmes, but rather to reframe the terms of reference in which cultural diversity was understood and to shift the knowledge-base in relation to both cultural production and reception rather than reception alone, as he put it, 'it's not the people who need to be inclusive, it's the ideas'. Acutely aware of the history and formation of cultural diversity policy within British politics and society, having been professionally active within these circuits at a senior level and being on the receiving end of them as a black writer, Phillips understood the interpretation and limits of representational practice in the museum, the construction of minorities as groups marked by a cultural deficit and, by extension, the framing and marginalization of educational work at the institutional level as a form of added value or cultural welfarism.

The politics of representation and racial discrimination in terms of government cultural policy took on a very particular momentum, however, in the run up to 2007 which marked the bicentenary of the Abolition of the Slave Trade Act in Britain in 1807. In the preface to a publication produced by the Department of Communities and Local Government (DCLG) and under the 1807/2007 logo 'Reflecting on the Past, Looking to the Future', the Prime Minister, Tony Blair, noted:

> The bicentenary of that event offers us a chance not just to say how profoundly shameful the slave trade was – how we condemn its existence utterly and praise those who fought for its abolition – but also to express our deep sorrow that it ever happened and to rejoice at the different and better times we live in today. The bicentenary is also an opportunity for us to recognise the enormous contribution of Black African and Caribbean communities to our nation.
>
> *(DCLG 2007: 1)*

Significant amounts of funding were ring-fenced across government departments and funding made available through such national funding bodies such as the Heritage Lottery Fund to support public projects and initiatives that promoted the government's agendas set next to this historical anniversary. As the publication noted under the section 'Today's Issues – Legacy of the Bicentenary/Increasing Race Equality':

> Many Black and Minority Ethnic communities are already thriving in Britain today. But some communities still suffer poorer outcomes in education, health, housing and employment ... The Government is seeking to address these

inequalities by ensuring that every individual, whatever their racial or ethnic origin is able to fulfill their potential through the enjoyment of equal opportunities, rights and responsibilities ... 'Improving Opportunity, Strengthening Society' is the Government's strategy to increase race equality and community cohesion. It brings together practical measures across Government to improve opportunities for all in Britain – helping to ensure that a person's ethnicity or race is not a barrier to their success. It signals the Government's intention to give greater emphasis to the importance of helping people from different backgrounds come together, supporting people who contribute to society and taking a stand against racists and extremists.

(DCLG 2007: 26)

At Tate Britain the response to engage with the bicentenary manifested itself in the form of an exhibition *1807: Blake, Slavery and the Radical Mind* (30 April–21 October 2007), curated by Mike Phillips and two collection curators which, as the press release stated, 'focuses on William Blake (1757–1827) and the circle of radical writers and artists associated with the publisher Joseph Johnson (1738–1809) in the 1790s and 1800s. In Blake's poetry, prints and actions we can clearly see his protests against the enslavement of Man's mind and body which have continued to inspire generations of artists, writers and political dissenters'. As Mike Phillips discussed in interview, the overriding ethos of the exhibition was not to place exclusive focus on the narrative of slavery through visual representations of race and persecution, but rather to engage with the wider historical and cultural context in which ideas of freedom, democracy and artistic expression emerged and circulated and informed the cultural, social and political context in which the Abolition Act came to fruition. Behind this curatorial approach was a decisive attempt not only to retrieve a British cultural history of radical artistic production that engaged, but was not defined by slavery, but also to create a disjuncture between the historical narrative of slavery and victimhood generated by government rhetoric around the 1807/2007 anniversary with the contemporary debates and experiences of racial inequality and cultural diversity. For, however well-intentioned government attempts to link the events of 1807 with questions of racial inequality in 2007 were, the linkage between the two timeframes defined by a narrative of transatlantic slavery and individual subjugation inflected the same narrative of victimhood on a contemporary diverse population simply on the basis of racial difference, exacerbated by the targeting of BME audiences, and thereby invariably enhancing the idea of racial difference and marginalization. For Paul Gilroy, this meshing of the politics of post-colonial guilt with the contemporary politics of social reconstruction and renewal, in a wider public context of racial fear and blame for Britain's national decline and loss of cultural identity, lay at the heart of Britain's 'melancholia' as he termed it which was characterized by the 'signature combination of manic elation and misery, self-loathing and ambivalence' (Gilroy 2006).

The paradoxical reproduction of racial marginalization through narratives of slavery and disempowerment was confronted head-on in a major youth project 'Stolen

Sanity', which was a collaboration of young people with the artist Faisal Abdu'allah. As with 'Tate Shift' the project evolved out of meetings with collection and education curators involved in the 1807/2007 displays from which the young people 'explored, formulated and communicated their opinions, questioning and debating aspects of the art-making process and its relevance to liberty, revolution and slavery'. The resulting large-scale photographic portrait works, produced to high production levels of professional practice, were, in an unprecedented move, subsequently displayed in the central gallery spaces of Tate Britain where they assumed both visually and spatially the equivalent status of collection exhibits. In an interview with the project curator, Mark Miller, Abdu'allah outlined the complex nature and implications of the project for the museum in relation to its collaborative nature and the final output of art works that matched the aesthetic qualities and production level of other contemporary art works on display in the gallery.[15] Through both the collaborative process of production and the final installation location (as opposed to the marginal educational spaces of the Clore Foyer), the project raised provocative questions for the artist and student collaborators about how aesthetic, cultural and market value is bestowed on the art object and legitimized in the museum setting. As Abdu'allah stated, such questions remain silent and unanswered at the curatorial and acquisition level of the museum, which continues to accumulate such collaborative art works that 'must be worth millions' but cannot formulate a position on how to accommodate them within the museum's collections, leaving Abdu'allah to conclude, 'it's a minefield' and 'a question of ethics'.

FIGURE 2.3 'Stolen Sanity' (2007). Tate Britain. Photo © Ellie Laycock

The creation and process of Tate Britain's 1807 programme, generated directly by the imperatives of government cultural policy, marked a significant moment in the gallery's engagement with practices of programming beyond its own strategic objectives of collection and display. Moreover, although both the 1807 Blake exhibition and the 'Stolen Sanity' project had essentially generated from within the Education Department, the presence of their outputs in the curatorial domain of Tate Britain's main galleries also represented a new spatial location (if not incursion) of education practice, previously only realized through the Clore Foyer or the dedicated educational display gallery known as the Goodison Room (or colloquially known among front of house staff as the 'Black Gallery' due to the earlier annual displays associated with Black History Month).

While New Labour's commitment to racial equality initially unfolded in the development of cultural diversity policy focused on the African-Caribbean community of post-war colonial migration, an expanded international context forced open a wider model of diversity after 9/11 in 2001 and the sense of national unrest around the politics of the Iraq War in 2003. But the London bombings of 7 July 2005 dramatically reoriented the terms of reference of cultural diversity policy towards British Muslims, first as part of an educational strategy to support counter-terrorism and social inclusion, and subsequently as part of a more strategic programme of international cultural diplomacy and business development. Yet again, Tate Britain found itself navigating a new complex terrain well beyond the aesthetic category of art, and with all the potential risk to damage its reputation as the 'Bricks Affair' had done in 1976.

The occasion was the long-term planned exhibition of the work of the artist John Latham, which was to include the work 'God is Great No. 2' (1991). This work, acquired by the gallery earlier in the year, existed as a freestanding sculpture of a sheet of glass cutting through books that included copies of the Koran, Talmud and Bible. Scheduled to open on 5 September 2005, two months after the London bombings, the work was removed from the list of exhibits before the show opened. The removal of the work, however, did not go unnoticed as Latham decided to speak out against the decision in various interviews with press and TV media and in an interview with the *Observer* newspaper he exclaimed: 'Tate Britain have shown cowardice over this. I think it's a daft thing to do because if they want to help the militants, this is the way to do it … It's not even a gesture as strong as censorship: it's just a loss of nerve on the part of the administration' (Smith 2005). Extending the realm of debate, the article also sounded out Shami Chakrabarti, director of Liberty, an independent civil rights organization, who supported the artist's position:

> 'We share his concern,' she said. 'I don't know what precise thought processes were going on at the Tate but I am concerned about the signal this sends at a time when we see free speech quite significantly under threat. I think that after 7 July we need this kind of artistic expression and political expression and discourse and disagreement more than ever, which is why this is worrying. Is three holy books in a piece of glass going to incite controversy? Frankly,

whether it does or doesn't, controversy is what we have in a flourishing democracy.' She added: 'I ultimately level my criticisms against legislators and certain lobby groups who've allowed free speech to be put in such peril and are making the climate that leads the Tate to have this kind of nervousness.'

(Smith 2005)

As the article further continued, Stephen Deuchar, Director of Tate Britain, defended the gallery's decision to hold back the piece:

The artist and curator discussed the exhibition and wanted to include it. We had every intention of doing so but in the light of events in London in July we felt we should exercise a little caution, so we altered our plans towards the end of August. It was a very difficult decision but we made it due to the exceptional circumstances of this summer and in the light of opinions that we value regarding religious sensitivities. We didn't want John Latham's work to be misrepresented and given a political dimension he didn't intend. We didn't want our motives to be wilfully misrepresented because of a particular social and political resonance.

(Smith 2005)

The next morning, Monday 26 September, the gallery issued a press release with the following statement:

God is Great, 1991, a work by John Latham featuring copies of the Bible, a Koran and a Talmud, which have been physically manipulated, is not included in the display of the work of John Latham, which opened at Tate Britain last week. Having sought wide-ranging advice, Tate feels that to exhibit the work in London in the current sensitive climate, post 7 July, would not be appropriate.

What the incident revealed was the extent to which the political and cultural climate in England had become enmeshed with the display and reception of art within the gallery context and had catapulted Tate Britain into a nexus of contemporary debates and arguments beyond its control over meaning and interpretation. As an institution that had invested heavily in establishing a homogenous brand of aesthetic modernity, the politics of internationalism and religion raised an even more problematic challenge to the practice of curating and audience development than the post-colonial politics of representations or national concerns with Britishness posed by the early formation of cultural diversity policy. As Stephen Deuchar had noted, the gallery was as much concerned with protecting a misinterpretation of the artist's work in a heightened social and political context as much as protecting Tate Britain from being misrepresented in its motives for display. In a move of partial appeasement to the artist, as much as an attempt to counteract the impression of 'nervousness' that Shami Chakrabarti had perceived in the decision, a public panel discussion 'Sacred,

Sacrosanct or Just Art? The Politics and Place of Art in the Public Arena' was organized by the Education Department to openly engage with the issues surrounding the public debate of the artist's work and its ramifications in the contemporary moment.

The decision to remove John Latham's 'God is Great No. 2' (1991) from exhibition was clearly a pre-emptive attempt to reduce the risk of damage, whether to people, property, or reputation, and whether successful or not, the legacy of the Latham controversy undoubtedly added a new impetus to the role of the Interpretation and Education Department (I&E), which found itself increasingly called upon to actively mediate between the complex policy conditions of developing new audiences and the curatorial selection, display and interpretation of art works. Although, as the Latham controversy demonstrated, there was no evident interest or protest from Muslim communities per se, the anxiety produced by anticipating unknown risks from audiences, increasingly defined through concepts of racial and ethnic difference, placed a new value on the knowledge and experience of audiences held within the I&E Department; both of which were being significantly developed through the ever-increasing range of project-based programmes supported by both public and private sector funding defined by cultural diversity and social inclusion policy agendas.

This was particularly apparent the year after the Latham exhibition when Tate Britain organized a series of collection display interventions under the title *East–West: Objects Between Cultures* (1 September 2006–14 February 2007). As the exhibition information described:

> East–West: Objects Between Cultures explores Christian–Muslim encounters and exchanges over the past five hundred years by introducing a selection of related objects into the Collection displays. Rather than impose a rigid version of this complex history, fresh connections are suggested between traditions, objects and historical contexts. The variety of objects on display provides an insight into the relationship between societies sometimes considered distinct. This is revealed in the hybrid nature of many of these artefacts, which have been formed and transformed between cultures. Some represent mercantile goods, some document the establishment of Muslim communities in Britain, while others reflect contemporary politics. It is hoped that this project will challenge static ideas of national history, art and identity.

In recognition of the lack of knowledge and expertise pertaining to objects outside of the Western European and American canon of art held within Tate Britain, knowledge and advice was sought from three external academics (Lisa Jardine, Matthew Dimmock and Matthew Birchwood) to select appropriate objects and curate a series of interventions that would establish a dialogue with Tate Britain's own collection on display. While such a curatorial collaboration was far from unprecedented, what was considerably more experimental was the introduction of objects that not only fell outside of the Western fine art tradition, but also that of traditional art history. The need therefore to supply both a greater amount of explication and new types of interpretation more aligned with visual culture and contemporary cultural politics fell to the responsibility of the I&E Department and, as with the 1807/2007 exhibition, to the work of the department of Tate Media under which the production of video film interviews for online access was undertaken.[16] As the filmed interviews with cultural critics, journalists, and young people discuss, one particular problem with the exhibition was the disparity in scale between the fine art paintings on the gallery walls of Tate Britain and the discreet scale of the selected artefacts, such as a copy of the Koran, which however aesthetically impressive, were visually overwhelmed by their environment.

Within the practices of Tate and the general management of press and publicity, and the Tate brand, the public dissemination of such critical commentary on the exhibition remains noteworthy in the online interviews and highlighted a new approach to audience at a more open and discursive level with targeted audiences. The need to understand a more individual idea of the visitor was also unfolding as the museum recognized the need to create a less mono-institutional role of information transfer to a more 'editorial' position that recognized additional perspectives to its own, as Nicholas Serota had anticipated in 2006 in an article written for the Commission of Racial Equality:

> Our vision for the future of Tate demands a shift towards what could be described as editorial operation: we will develop as a creative 'publisher' of many ideas drawn from inside and beyond the organisation, whereas, in the past, we tended only to act as the author of our own. While sustaining and continuing to share our traditional expertise, we need to open ourselves up to new expertise through partnership and collaboration, in a process of exchange. In this way, we will be able to serve more people, in more ways. We need to make space for new ways of working that may create a more diverse workforce, programme and collections and a different institutional model, in keeping with highly mobile and diverse communities in a digital and global age.
>
> *(Serota 2006)*

The production of this film of interviews also marked out what can either be seen as a new merging of the work of marketing (Tate Online existing within Tate Media as an extension of marketing) and education through the practice of interpretation, or as an extension of the role of interpretation that began in the 1990s when interpretation moved into the Communications Department. Whatever the status of the online interviews, the overall strategic value was understood under the umbrella of 'audience development' and, as Will Gompertz, then Head of Tate Media, discussed in interview,[17] the direct recruitment of staff from I&E to Tate Media was an obvious one given both had a central interest and understanding of audiences, rather than purely a knowledge of objects. One critical distinction, however, between the motivations of producing interviews with a variety of individuals and perspectives: for the I&E Department, the interest was to represent alternative socially and culturally inclusive interpretations that represented diverse audiences, whereas for Tate Media, whose role was to protect the Tate brand from controversy while promoting its inclusivity, the multiplicity of external voices simultaneously displaced the risk of controversy away from the institution and redistributed and dispersed it to a far wider constituency. In doing so, however, the embrace of a wider constituency also brought it in greater proximity to the gallery, raising the potential scenario that Beck identifies: 'Risks are infinitely reproducible, for they reproduce themselves along with the decisions and the viewpoints with which one can and must see decisions in pluralistic society'(Beck et al. 1994: 9).

As Charman has noted, 'the Education curator's professionalism is janus-faced, both looking inwards to the institution and collection, while at the same time being inherently outward looking, towards the particularities of audiences' (Charman 2005). Whereas in the 1980s, cultural policy focus on the 'public' value of the museum had produced a concept of the public as the marketing category of visitor, and in the 1990s the project of aesthetic modernism and institutional branding had produced the experientially defined viewer, cultural diversity policy, through the practices of learning had brought a substantially more embodied and socially-engaged concept of audience directly into the curatorial space and narratives of the museum. Engaged to enhance museum attendance from culturally diverse audiences, however, educational practice was highly limited in its capacity to impact on the core audience of Tate Britain through inherent contradictions of both its own practice, as primarily a transformative one through creativity, and the museum's interpretation and take up of cultural diversity policy through marketing and targeting techniques. While many accounts of individual change have been documented qualitatively, collectively this has brought little change to the core practices of collection and display. Furthermore, while cultural diversity policy was conceived to increase cultural participation, the conceptually reductive account of difference, focused on an essentialized racial representation, produced the unintended consequence of reinforcing a model of British culture based on the marginalized category of black and minority ethnic. In targeting this category and further combining it with agendas of social inclusion and social marginalization, a model of minority audiences emerged as one defined by cultural deficit, the institutional response to which was to produce a needs-based programme of activity as form of cultural compensation.

Within the project of cultural change and transformation that underpinned the critically reflexive practice of the Education Department's work at Tate Britain, also lay the means by which it presented itself organizationally as an expedient agent to meet statutory legal and funding commitments, but equally, through its localized and particularized knowledge of audiences, to manage the risk presented by such audiences to the core museum project of aesthetic modernism. The rise in organizational status and increased professionalization brought about through the expansion of externally funded education projects invariably interrupted the cultural authority of curators by un-anchoring their exclusive hold over the interpretation of the art object and shifting the institutional knowledge-base and paradigm of both the art object and the museum's audience. It equally questioned, through lived direct experience of audiences as individual members of the public rather than racialized categories of targeting, the technical practices and knowledge-base of Marketing.

While these internal organizational shifts in cultural and organizational authority might initially be seen simply as the political dynamics of any large public or corporate institution, they suggest, however, a far more potent form of cultural change and imminent institutional crisis if understood as part of the new processual shift in cultural experience, which Thrift has described as producing 'a new epistemic ecology of encounter' (Thrift 2008: 34). As Beck has also discussed at length, the modernist project of 'staging the people' has been undone by the processes of reflexive modernization, which has produced 'a chaotic world of conflicts, power games, instruments and arenas which belong to two different epochs, that of the "unambiguous" and that of "ambivalent modernity". On the one hand a political vacuity of the institution is evolving and, on the other hand, a non-institutional renaissance of the political. The individual subject returns to the institutions of society' (Beck et al. 1994: 17). Caught between tradition and heritage of an imperial national past, and the contemporary cultural condition of society converted into organizational practice through policy imperatives, Tate Britain's capacity to hold authorship over its curatorial project of modernism becomes inextricably compromised. As Beck concludes:

> The decisive point, however, is that the horizon dims as risks grow. For risks tell us what should not be done but not what should be done. With risks, avoidance imperatives dominate. Someone who depicts the world as risk will ultimately become incapable of action. The salient point is that the expansion and heightening of the intention of control ultimately ends up producing the opposite.
>
> *(Beck et al. 1994: 9)*

The specific limits of both cultural diversity policy, based on post-colonial 'melancholia' at both the level of British government politics and Tate Britain's response, and its conversion into the politics of representation was specifically located by Gilroy in social and economic conditions beyond the nation-state:

> This country outgrew the 1960s model that associated integration and immigration in government policy. Two generations beyond their coupling, the anxieties which fuel contemporary concern about the integrity of national culture and national identity have very different sources. Their origins lie, not as we're routinely told, in immigration, but in broader effects of globalization, de-industrialisation and de-colonisation …
>
> *(Gilroy 2006)*

3

TRACING THE PRACTICES OF AUDIENCE AND THE CLAIMS OF EXPERTISE

At an operational level, the knowledge-base and expertise from which organizational change has been generated within Tate over the last 20 years has primarily been developed through the purchase of commissioned research from external consultancies, and indeed this knowledge-base has dramatically diversified and extended during the last 20 years in response to the changing cultural, social and economic conditions to include economics, business and finance; architecture, urbanism and engineering; design, media and communications; retail, publishing and catering; and information technology. More often than not though, such consultancy research was invisible at the level of the delivery workforce having been mediated through organizational change or project initiatives at director level of strategy and implementation. But despite Tate's entry centre-stage into the cultural and social politics of the public domain, comparatively little independent research has been commissioned towards the creation of change within the practices of the museum in relation to the cultural or social, despite the epistemological shifts in the gallery's activities towards these domains. Tate Encounters: Britishness and Visual Culture was the first sustained piece of internally authorized research in this area.

In many respects, the key research questions of Tate Encounters centred on audiences in terms of non-attendance, essentially echoing a substantial body of academic enquiry into making visible the relationship between museums and their publics, and the conditions out of which cultural value and exclusion is produced and reproduced by the museum; a field of enquiry most notably forged by the work of Eilean Hooper-Greenhill (1994b) and Richard Sandell (2003; 2007) at the School of Museum Studies at University of Leicester and, Tony Bennett (2005; 2007), including the extensive research carried out at the Centre for Research for Economic and Social Change based at Manchester University. Furthermore, during the last decade, the academic scrutiny of the museum has particularly gained momentum, not only in the field of museum studies and cultural management – in which discussions of public culture have been increasingly located within an understanding of the commodified system of exchange values (Sandell and Janes, 2007) – but also within curatorial and cultural studies that have been concerned with moving beyond institutional critique and questions of representation to those around the strategies and practices of display, interpretation and audience participation (Greenberg et al. 1996; Pollock and Zemans 2007; O'Neil and Wilson 2010). While this body of work continues to generate new accounts of museum practice and arguments for change towards a more democratic and transparent cultural arena, there has been a notable lack of take-up by the museum of the key debates posed by this body of work, characterized by a sustained discursive disengagement and by the limited recognition of value in terms of employment from within these disciplines. A further key factor that played into this dissonant relationship with the academy was also the extent to which, in framing museums as a collective object of study to reveal the larger narratives of the agents and organization of public culture, relatively little attention was paid in museum studies to the specificity of museum collections, rendering them of equivalent onto-logical value, despite their distinct historical formations, epistemological histories and cultural trajectories in contemporary life.

A final point for consideration is the issue of the relationship between the acad-emy's own theoretical ruminations on the museum and the perceived lack of con-nection with the 'real work' of the museum, the everyday practices, practicalities and realities in which decisions are made and unmade, along with the circulation of meaning, through a complex interrelation of socioeconomic factors as much as intellectual and aesthetic ones, logistical and programmatic: or what de Certeau, quoting Lukacs' eloquent phrase, cites as 'the anarchy of the chiarascruo of the everyday' (de Certeau 1988: 199). It is perhaps most notably at this juncture of theory and practice that the conditions of non-engagement between the academy and the museum have been and continue to be most defined, ensuring that the common-sense, sedimented language of the museum and the theoretical language of the academy rarely meet outside of an educational context, if fleetingly there. But as Sharon Macdonald has noted, as editor of the recent and academically progressive anthology *A Companion to Museum Studies* (2011), this situation has not only come about through the restrictive nature of disciplinary practice, but also through the lack of access for academics to the daily workings of the museum, paralleled by the lack of time museum employees are allocated to pursue research and critically reflect on their practice. Beyond this, understandable organizational sensitivities need to be acknowledged and respected, not least in terms of protecting financial and corporate strategy information in a competitive market environment.

The opportunity presented to undertake a major, three-year, research project within the museum was, however, occasioned by two particular facts. Firstly, Tate was in the process itself of securing its own independent research status from the British Arts and Humanities Research Council (AHRC), granting it equal status to universities in accessing national public funding for research. Secondly, the launch of the AHRC's first strategic programme, 'Diasporas, Migration and Identities' in 2005 invited collaborative research bids that allowed Tate Britain to directly interrogate the stubborn lack of movement in audience figures from culturally diverse groups in society under which it was both legally obliged to develop and organizationally seeking to attract. The central problematic that was identified was the disconnections and tensions between the practice and policies, the rhetoric and effect, of cultural diversity in creating sustained relationships with what this policy identified as the missing audiences; an audience categorized by the designation of 'black and minority ethnic' (BME). This set of perceived tensions seemed to be supported by the fact that despite substantial levels of funding invested in project-based activity dedicated to developing culturally diverse audiences, the level of participation deno-ted by the BME group remained well below the national demographic. A further problematic was the paucity of research in the sector conceived independently of the processes of advocacy or auditing, which summarily rested on quantitative and qualitative data gathered in response to the predetermined socioeconomic categories of race, gender, age and class. The currency of this research and data-gathering had also increased substantially as New Labour embraced the concept of 'evidence-based policy' leading to the commissioning of research both by government agencies (DCMS 2007; ACE 2007) and by the cultural sector keen to demonstrate the social impact of museums and galleries, and hence their value for public money (NMDC 2004).

At the same time of developing the AHRC proposal, there was also vigorous debate in the arts unfolding around the racialization and instrumentalization of cul-tural diversity policy (Mirza 2006; Furedi 2004; Hylton 2007), which built upon the recognition that the audit practice of measuring culture and impact was deeply prob-lematic, if not flawed (Selwood 2002; Belfiore 2002). Although Tate was not constituted by the AHRC as an independent research organization until 2006, after the project began, the prerequisite need to create a collaborative research project with the aca-demic sector was understood and welcomed by the initiating Tate Britain department of Interpretation and Education (I&E). The initiation of a research project was seen as an important opportunity to create an interdisciplinary project that would test the fundamental paradigms and models of quantitative and qualitative research, under-pinning cultural diversity policy. As curatorial staff in the I&E Department were also acutely aware, there were also internal lines of tension that needed unravelling. The tension centred on ideas of culturally diverse audiences and in particular on how they figured in and in-between the departmental work of Education, Curatorial and Marketing. These lines of tension often emerged at points during which the work of education teams felt at odds with the marketing practices of audience engagement as well as the curatorial practices of exhibitions and displays, despite a shared set of objectives around strategies of audience development. From this, the need to study the organizational practices of the museum in relation to audience development was recognized. The problem needed to be addressed in a way that did not position the missing audience as if they were not exclusively located in their own social fact. Implicit within the project was also a quest to create a more intellectually sound account of cultural diversity at the level of lived experience. The account would need to lift cultural diversity out of an institutional misalignment with cultural welfarism. The policy positioning cultural diversity within education defined the latter as a service programme providing 'added value' to the core work of the museum, or otherwise as cultural therapy carried out through the practice of creativity.

It was with an understanding of these disconnected lines of research enquiry between the museum, the academy and government, acknowledged again in part by Hooper-Greenhill (1994a: 255–68) and McClellan (2007), that the opportunity to collaboratively create a research funding application to the AHRC's 'Diasporas, Migration and Identities' funding programme was pursued.

In formulating a research project it was clear that, in order to capture a more subjective account of the individual encounter with the museum, an action research project should be configured to capture how Tate Britain figured in the life worlds of diasporic individuals rather than at a conceptual level of policy categories. The commitment to establishing a sustained longitudinal enquiry and analysis was funda-mental to this endeavour. It would test the working assumptions of cultural diversity policy in action, while ensuring that a sufficient timescale was realized in which to generate significant quantities of practice-based and participant data. More com-plex readings would be drawn from such data than could be realized through the exigency of commercially commissioned research. The team aimed at creating a research project that benefited from the insights of the 'bottom-up' approach of grounded theory (Charmaz 2006) and principles of critical reflexivity were also applied (Alvesson and Sköldberg 2009) with the ambition that new knowledge could be gained of as much value and interest to Tate Britain as to academic debate and government policy-making. To realize this end, the need to fully embed the research project within the art museum was seen as a prerequisite so that highly situated and multitextured accounts of an action research project and an organizational study of Tate staff could be secured.

The project specifically embraced reflexivity as a critical method of guarding against the dangers of data-orientated methods of grounded theory, ethnomethodol-ogy and inductive ethnology as, 'missing the main part of the interpretative prob-lematic, so that the data appear as more or less unmediated, pure, and the research process is endowed with a naïve character of gathering and threshing empirical material' (Alvesson and Sköldberg 2009: 88). Bringing together the disciplines of sociology, anthropology, visual cultures, museum studies and art history, critical self-reflexivity was also the means by which the epistemological assumptions of each dis-cipline were cross-examined and interrogated in relation to the research questions and data-gathering methods. Critical distance was also sought from both the academy and Tate Britain. Through such distance new forms of knowledge-exchange and practice would emerge. This emergent form of method coincided equally with Tony Bennett's observation that:

> Critical thought, no matter who its agent might be, is most productive when conducted in a manner which recognises the need to take account of the contributions of different forms of expertise without any a priori prejudicial ranking of the relations between them and equally, when it takes account of

the forces – social, economic, political and moral – which circumscribe the field of the practicable.

(Bennett 2007: 149)

In addition to the bottom-up approach of grounded theory and critical reflexivity, actor-network-theory (ANT) was also adopted. The aim was to move beyond a determinist model of positivist social science research that generates data for interpretation through existing paradigms and theories. Such models were seen as supporting the epistemological work of emancipatory knowledge as well as the project of social engineering. In this respect, ANT also offered a path beyond the archaeological project of Foucault's reading of the institutional relations of power and knowledge, a reading that typifies much museum studies research. The problem with such museum studies research is that it constructs institutions as stable and coherent formations acting as conduits of the policies of governance and state, thereby obfuscating the complexity of the relation between policy and practice on the ground; that is to say, the field of the practicable. At this juncture, de Certeau's reclamation of the 'everyday' (de Certeau 1988) in making visible the tacit knowledge of individual practice rather than the institutional discourse of organization and planning also provided a lens through which to approach both the proposed action research project and ethnographic organizational study. Equally, Thrift's understanding of the need to move beyond representational perceptions of practice, but rather to work with the everyday 'as found' (Thrift 2008: 7) and to document it through a 'radical empiricism' (Thrift 2008: 5), resonated well with the project's objective to avoid reproducing the critical deconstructive model of the museum, which had stunted earlier accounts from being of interest or value to the museum itself. In this respect, Latour's account of the work of art held significant import and appeal. For rather than emptying it out of all aesthetic value, as a coded form of materialist production, his more reconstructive, or in his terms 're-assemblage', of the work of art, acknowledged its multifaceted role. The accumulation of the artwork's relations and connections in the course of its various forms of animation called into play by disparate, even opposing practices:

> ... in the old paradigm you had to have a zero-sum game – everything lost by the work of art was gained by the social, everything lost by the social had to be gained by the 'inner quality' of the work of art – in the new paradigm you are allowed a win-win situation: the more attachments the better ... the more 'affluence' the better. It is counter-intuitive to try and distinguish 'what comes from the viewers' and 'what comes from the object' when the obvious response is 'to go with the flow'. Object and subject might exist, but everything interesting happens upstream and downstream. Just follow the flow. Yes, follow the actors themselves or rather that which makes them act, namely the circulating entities.
>
> *(Latour 2005: 237–40)*

The organizational study at Tate Britain subsequently took the form of an ethnographic case study of the planning and delivery of the exhibition, *The Lure of the East:*

British Orientalist Painting (2008) and included 39 interviews with both staff and external individuals connected to the exhibition. (The selected exhibition was not chosen for any reason related to its subject matter but rather was the only exhibition in the early development stage that coincided with the fieldwork period of the research; that said, its subject matter did invariably put a more intense spotlight on the issues of cultural diversity.) At the outset of the research team discussions around the methodology of the organizational study, the initial criteria proposed for interviewing members of staff was determined by their place within the formal organization of departments and levels of seniority. However, as a more useful understanding of science and technology studies and ANT unfolded, alongside embedded contact with Tate Britain staff, it became apparent that many of the processes and acts of everyday decision-making did not take place within the formal, organizational structures of Tate Britain. Rather such decision-making took place between networks of individuals that came together and separated out according to the agency they assumed, claimed or were awarded at different points of individual pragmatic, rather than strategic need. In this regard, the organizational study interviews also revealed the extent to which tacit knowledge, what might internally be described as 'the Tate way', was mobilized, claimed and made visible at different moments where the practice of daily work often coincided with practices of risk management.

First mooted as a curatorial proposal nearly a decade earlier, Tate Britain opened the major exhibition *The Lure of the East: British Orientalist Painting* in 2008. It explored the 'responses of British artists to the cultures and landscapes of the Near and Middle East between 1780 and 1930, offering vital historical and cultural perspectives on the challenging questions of the "Orient" and its representation in British art'. As plans for the exhibition began to take detailed form, two years before its opening, the dramatic changes in the cultural, political and social context of the Middle East and Britain's relation with this geopolitical region created a much more charged environment than when the exhibition was first considered. As such, the organization of *Lure of the East* substantially magnified the institutional challenges that Tate Britain had faced in the earlier exhibitions of John Latham and East–West. It also, as will become clear, revealed the extent to which significantly different conceptions of audience and practices of audience development, as well as audience engagement were circulating within Tate Britain across the departments of Curatorial, Learning (renamed from Interpretation and Education) and Marketing.

While a primary understanding of an exhibition audience as the source of income generation through ticket sales with an emphasis on the quality of visitor experience existed across departments, other considerations propelled the idea of audience up the *Lure of the East* exhibition planning agenda in response to levels of anxiety about how targeted British audiences would perceive and receive the exhibition in relation to the strategic policy objectives of audience development and cultural diversity, which the exhibition was deemed it should serve well. While the prolific 'meeting culture' of Tate is well-established, the scale and scope of the planning meetings that brought together more than 30 individuals from 14 teams within eight departments demonstrated the seriousness with which careful planning and management of the exhibition's realization was taken. A further smaller cross-departmental group of 14 was also identified to help strategically manage and direct sensitive areas of content development and audience engagement. There was also a further proposal of a third additional body of external advisors 'to double check'. The general awareness and acceptance from the outset was that insufficient knowledge and expertise resided within Tate Britain to plan and deliver the exhibition to the usual Tate standards, and there was insufficient confidence to be able to effectively anticipate any risk of causing offence, misrepresentation or misinterpretation; a heightened sense of public responsibility; brand management awareness; as well as issues of professional ethics and integrity consistently pervaded these concerns to differing levels across departments.

The long gestation and development period and shifting staff portfolios invariably led to various changes in the curatorial leadership and management of the project, but as interviews with both internal and external contributors revealed, however, the belief in the curatorial value and timeliness of the project remained constant. As one curator noted:

> … the exhibition [covers] an episode in British art that has not been covered by an exhibition at Tate Britain before. We have worked with 19th century works a lot … and the political and social background is very interesting … this is the first reason for doing the show – it is an important aspect of 19th century British art. We also wanted to engage with 150 years of continued culture and post-colonial critique, in addition to bringing the pleasure of the work before the audiences.

As interviews with curators across the development period of the exhibition reasserted, the 'pleasure' principle was the primary curatorial consideration:

> You need to establish a focus and pace for the visitor. It is an act of choreography. It is also about staging the exhibition, its pace, rhythm and drive which you understand through experience. First of all it has to be a visual experience – it has to be animated and have a visual pull … The aim is to create some chemistry between the works and the space … The art should not be constrained or hijacked by the design idea. We need to be careful to strike a balance between the animation of the works and not falling into a cliché or work by trying to open up the work from fixed cultural associations. We try and tune into the spirit that is already there in the work and try and transfer what the artist wanted.

As all the curatorial interviews testified, this concern with choreography balanced with a conscious objective not to overstage the paintings was translated into an aesthetic of display that, while aiming to avoid mimicking or re-presenting the colours, textures, and designs associated with 'exotic orientalist' settings, would equally offset the works to 'their best effect':

With the design of the exhibition we have gone for a neutral colour system. This has been influenced by [an] understanding of the aesthetic aspects of the works as they need a neutral palette and this happens to work with the sensitivities of the exhibition. We didn't want the exhibition to go down the historicizing route, we didn't want any gimmicks, we wanted a fresh and uncluttered appearance because the works themselves are intensely coloured. We wanted to create a nurturing environment. For instance, we didn't want to use heavy Victorian colours. The role of the designers was to translate these ideas visually and problem shoot.

Inherent within this aesthetic discourse and decorum of display was also the operative understanding that a contemporary visual experience – 'judging how the images look together in terms of factors such as scenes, frames and colours' – supersedes all other considerations such as 'theoretical arguments.' First and foremost exhibitions are 'about play within the gallery'. As one curator described, this 'curatorial orthodoxy' is hard to question given that the curator is 'a prisoner of traditional expectations':

You have to understand that most paintings are rectangles and therefore there are limited ways in which to arrange them without them looking wrong. There is a tradition in Europe where you have the same line, symmetry, balance, ratio and proportion. The room hangs itself. There are certain key decisions such as the vistas and the immediate effect of a room as you enter it; it has to look powerful, elegant and authoritative ... these are professional standards. They are really unspoken, no one says what they are, you are not taught them and they are the hardest to change.

The 'political situation' of the Lure of the East exhibition was potentially inescapable due to the complex and complicated range of stakeholders invested in the exhibition. There was a fundamental awareness, however, that any political implications of the exhibition needed to be carefully managed, or ideally managed out, to ensure that the public value and credibility of the exhibition, as well as the associated value of the works of art themselves was not corrupted by negative publicity or controversial criticisms. Building on the legacy of East–West and its direct knowledge and experience of audiences, the Learning Department identified, from the outset, the need to explicitly acknowledge and incorporate an understanding of the seminal work of the cultural theorist Edward Said and his theoretical analysis in *Orientalism* (1978). Said discussed the ways in which ideas and representations of the East were historically constructed by the West within imperial systems of power; constructions that it was argued continued to pervade contemporary Western culture and thought. As the exhibition introduction explained: 'The argument for and against Said's Orientalism has continued for thirty years. Its resonance for an exhibition such as this one, however, is as strong as ever given that, by the 1920s (the end of the period covered by the exhibition), Britain was in direct control of much of the newly abolished

Ottoman Empire, including Egypt, Palestine and Iraq. As Said's followers argued, these images cannot be viewed in isolation from their wider political and cultural context.'[1]

Whether indeed the full text of Said's extensive analysis in *Orientalism* was ever directly or fully engaged with is uncertain. What is clear though is the degree to which it readily assumed high levels of currency as a conceptual and managerial trope around which the production and consumption of the exhibition should be configured in order to alleviate and displace concerns of the exhibition reproducing, or being perceived to reproduce, colonial representations of the 'other'. Indeed this was increasingly significant as the 'other' had become positioned as potential exhibition audiences and visitors aligned with the interests and/or identities of the Middle East and Islam. Throughout the various project development meetings that took place, what became apparent to all involved was the unprecedented level of interaction between curatorial and education staff that the anxieties around the exhibition had brought about. This led to a noticeable change in institutional practice, leading to the fact that 'rather than the usual conveyor belt where the exhibition is passed on to be interpreted', education staff were actively involved in the curatorial meaning-making and decision-making processes of the exhibition. As with *East–West* this was particularly notable in terms of how the practice of interpretation was called upon to act as a crucial mediator between the curator and art object and the visitor. The decision was taken to create a large scale resource of audio interpretations and responses from a diverse range of external contributors (more than 40 individuals were approached) from the world of journalism, cultural politics and the arts, in order to simultaneously capture a diverse range of perspectives, 'redistribute the institutional voice', and 'like carbon foot-printing, hopefully offset any potential toxic damage'. As another collection curator described it, 'the audio guide is the non-political aspect of the exhibition; it's like Wikipedia – without value judgement'.

Following extensive early discussions as to how to define the 'Orient' in terms of faith, politics or geographies, and taking into primary consideration the issue of how constructions of 'a timeless Orient' had underpinned stereotypical representations of the 'other' of Said's argument, a decision was made to create a space within the exhibition under the working title of the 'Documentary Room', finally named 'Mapping the Orient', which would act as a key information point to document the changes in the geopolitical landscape captured within the timeline and subject-matter of the paintings in the exhibition. As the wall text explained:

> While British Orientalist painters may have chosen to present a timeless 'Orient', this was a period in which the Middle East changed and developed as the Ottoman Empire itself waxed and waned. The map, photographs and city plans featured here explore some of the complexities of the region at a time when so many British artists chose to travel there. The map projection shows some of the political fluctuations of the Middle East between the late seventeenth and early twentieth centuries, which affected those who travelled to, and within, the region.

As discussions unfolded with designers about the technical format and presentation of the digital map, which ultimately manifested in the form of a digital video wall projection, other concerns arose around the use of photographs within the space. Discussion centred on whether these photographs might be confused as works of art with object status within the exhibition, as opposed to purely 'documentary' sources of information. The concern was resolved through the technical mediation of the photographs as images on plasma screens, reducing any ambivalence that might be created by their object status if presented as artefacts. Within the curatorial paradigm of 'staging the exhibition', the room also functioned as a 'breathing space' for visitors and a physical and visual pause before 'you turn around the corner and you experience a moment of visual drama when you see the screen in the Harem room. This is the experience that people are paying for … '. By all accounts across various departments, the high level of interpretation for *Lure of the East* was deemed exceptional and despite the extended level of internal debate and meetings that it generated, and the level of resource it took, it was understood by staff to have brought into greater cross-departmental focus the rationale and working assumptions of different departments' practice, which were usually 'siloed' off in the more established linear process of exhibition-making at Tate Britain. For the Learning Department, which experienced itself often at the 'service' end of this process, the escalation of the role of interpretation also prompted reassessments from other departments with observations such as, 'I find it fascinating that interpretation is currently the custodian of Tate's voice' and 'it began to [make me] wonder why we weren't so sensitive with other exhibitions'.

In comparison to the levels of risk and anxiety that circulated around the curatorial and interpretation strategy of Lure of the East, the engagement with contemporary political implications of the exhibition presented a less fraught if not positively rich context for audience engagement, given that its remit was directly to engage with the contemporary politics of the Middle East. As with the majority of major exhibitions, an international conference was organized by the public programmes team of the Learning Department. Within a tradition of public programmes, initiated by Toby Jackson at Tate Liverpool (and later under his leadership at Tate Modern), the understanding of the role of public conferences to critically engage with the curatorial scope of exhibitions (rather than amplify them as an extended form of marketing) and to move beyond the curatorial paradigm of art history by bringing together academics and cultural commentators from other disciplines, was well-established. The Lure of the East conference[2] subsequently posed a series of questions: 'What is the current debate on Edward Said's radical book *Orientalism*? Is his argument too binary between East and West? What is the relevance of the Middle Eastern art market? And how did people of the Middle East view it?'[3] In proposing a discussion into how cultural value systems were circulating beyond the immediate concerns of the exhibition, the conference took its steer from the international dimension of the exhibition that was related to its touring programme to the Pera Museum, Istanbul (which the Tate had never toured to before), and the Sharjah Art Museum in the United Arab Emirates. The tour was crucially supported by the government-sponsored agency the British Council.

Although a major stakeholder in the exhibition, the British Council's involvement with *Lure of the East* was unusual given that its primary curatorial interests and experience rested in contemporary cultural practice rather than historic. However, the British Council's support of the Tate Britain show was financially integral given that Tate's indemnity agreement with its government sponsoring department, the Department of Culture, Media and Sport (DCMS), only covered national venues, whereas the British Council, sponsored by the Foreign and Commonwealth Office, provided the necessary international indemnity for works of art. With its interests in artistic development in relation to internationalism, the British Council worked in contrast to the DCMS's agenda of developing cultural diversity and audiences at a national level. Indeed the British Council's cultural agenda and strategic objectives were aligned with government agendas that focused on enhancing counter-terrorism through the development of new and improved cultural relations with the Islamic world, which invested the exhibition tour with strategic value and interest. In response to the British Council's desire to give more contemporary significance to Lure of the East, a public panel discussion was organized at Tate Britain. Whereas the British Council confidently advertised it as ' a frank discussion about our shared history – including areas of connection and conflict', the Tate Britain event publicity more conservatively announced:

> Based on the format of the famous BBC TV series Question Time, Cultural Questions will mark the occasion of the Lure of the East: British Orientalist Painters exhibition at Tate Britain with a contextual debate about the role of culture and the arts in the future development of peace and security in the Middle East. Questions to be discussed include: Is cultural diplomacy a new form of 'soft' imperialism? What role do artists and intellectuals have to play in socio-political change in the region?[4]

Tate Britain's programme involvement with the British Council, in relation to the Middle East, had already been established via an educational initiative with young people in a project named 'Nahnou-Together' (translated from Arabic as We-Together), which has been 'a two-year exchange programme involving artists, curators, teachers and young people from the UK, Syria and Jordan'. Between 2006–8 the project involved 'sixty young people aged from 13 to 21, from a range of different cultural, social, school and economic backgrounds, [who] have participated in the programme, the majority travelling to the countries involved, and taking part in workshops with artists and young people there'.[5] Programmed to coincide with *Lure of the East* at Tate Britain, a display exhibition was presented within the main galleries of the building that brought together the prints, drawings, films and other material created through the collaborative project, highlighting and documenting the developmental process of dialogue and interaction between participants and the international partner institutions. The visual manifestation of Nahnou-Together, however, posed its own set of problems and challenges at the organizational level of Tate Britain; rather than conforming to either a modernist object-based display or present an 'aesthetic' product or output, its aim to capture the more open-ended process of cultural exchange and its attempts to distribute ownership of representation across its diverse range of participants left it open to charges of 'messiness' and 'incoherence'. As Felicity Allen, then Head of Learning at Tate Britain, wrote a year later: 'This process opened up the possibility of individual critique of the institutions that represented, and were represented by, the participants. However most of us feared the consequences of becoming "unprofessional", and to a lesser or greater extent were conscious of different imagined or actual forms of professional reprobation. The borders being crossed included the concepts of amateur and professional, an integral part of the authority of institutions' (Allen 2009).

The concerns of the Learning Department were generated as much by a model of the cultural construction of value within *Lure of the East* as by direct, professional interaction with the individuals of their programme audiences such as Nahnou-Together. However, the concerns of Tate Media, the department under which marketing, press, publicity and Tate Online sat, were clearly first and foremost centred on a formulation of audience as the target number of visitors that the exhibition should attract, in terms of income generation through ticket sales. At a management level, the data and knowledge gathered by Marketing on audiences was clearly of strategic interest. As one curator noted:

> ... if the press and marketing don't understand the main goals of the show then we miss the audience ... Marketing tend to think about audiences and how we reach them. We are working with accepted scientific ideas from professional practice that informs the size of the font in the introductory text, the forms that the leaflet take, the aspect of the physical layout of the show. The information comes to us from visitors and focus groups.

At a level of curatorial delivery, however, a more remote relation to audiences circulated. As one curator admitted, the concept of audience was highly elusive and understood mainly as the 'core', which constituted press and artists, and 'presumably' one 'not alienated by what we do'. A more acute degree of scepticism was expressed by another who commented in interview that 'audiences are not quite the enemy but something to be dealt with', since 'audience is never curatorially located as the object is outward facing and the curatorial is towards the object'. This disconnection of interests in audience between Marketing and Curatorial was also characterized by some degree of professional scepticism by curators who questioned the evidence-base and audience modelling under which the Marketing Department operated. They also questioned the concomitant principle of targeting, which one curator claimed assumed 'authority by naming the public', denouncing them as 'total mythologies that just get passed on and accrue power without being challenged. What's the evidence for this mirroring?' This analysis of 'mirroring' and targeting was, however, contradicted by curators in relation to the Learning Department. There was 'a tendency in Curatorial to treat Learning as "suspect" ... the feeling that Learning is imposed on them', while holding some respect for their 'worthy enthusiasm'.

However, many curators identified an important role for Adult Programmes (responsible for conferences, seminars, events) on the basis that, at a professional level of 'intellectual curiosity and knowledge', it produced programmes that correlated with the adult work of artists intended for an adult audience of viewers.

Marketing's ability to realize its targets of both extending audience engagement and audience development was also further hindered by a lack of knowledge-sharing and an emphasis on project-based work rather than long-term programming. Marketing was also caught between Curatorial scepticism and the Learning Department's emphasis on promoting and protecting the interests of minority audiences, while carrying a prerequisite responsibility for generating income through audiences. As one member of the Marketing Department noted, 'targeting would work if we followed through' and 'if there was greater consistency to what was meant by audience development', rather than just the assumption that it was defined by low-income status. Within this context, *Lure of the East* invariably became a microcosm of how differential notions of audience were circulating, from the Curatorial construct of the 'viewer', the under- and mis-represented 'other' of Learning, to Marketing's data-driven 'visitor'. In many respects, early discussions around the selection of the title and poster image for the exhibition made the terms of cross-departmental debate unusually explicit. From a curatorial perspective, while complex to organize in terms of securing loans, group thematic shows were often easier to manage ('thematic can be used very well if you can't get certain works. ... [it] makes it less obvious that certain works are missing'). Whereas, from a marketing perspective, it is considerably harder to sell such a show compared to a monographic one, the prevalent tradition at Tate, as it necessarily denies the modernist biographical narrative of the unique, creative artist. Moreover, group exhibitions are, by their very nature, underpinned by a proposition or 'argument' that precedes the narrative of the artist and the works of art gathered under it. This takes place unless the exhibition remains within an established modernist 'ism'. Tate though had at one level dismantled such approaches through the introduction of thematic displays. Marketing an artist is much easier than marketing an idea or argument as group shows demand that the idea or argument is clear and simple for ease of communication and packaging. They place considerable more pressure on the exhibition title and the choice of poster to be self-explanatory, attract attention and position the exhibition succinctly in the marketplace.

However, as the preceding discussions have evidenced, while the concept of the *Lure of the East* show might have been construed as clear and simple, the 'institutionally fraught' discussions and anxieties around issues of representation, political sensitivities and audience reception and misperceptions, rendered it a highly complex exhibition to navigate as an idea. Consideration of the exhibition's title could also not be separated out from the choice of poster image, as the two were read in relation to each other when juxtaposed in the public domain. The final selection of the title, however, *The Lure of the East: British Orientalist Painting* did not necessarily work well for marketing purposes as initial focus groups indicated that both the word 'Orient' and 'East' suggested an exhibition of work about China. The choice of image, therefore, had much work to do to counteract this impression and, as one curator commented, 'we don't want a kitsch or exoticized approach ... we wouldn't want to give the impression of Arabian Nights'. Consideration was also given to Learning's concerns about reproducing the very stereotypical and imperial view that Said had made the subject of his work, and issues over the poster image led to the discarding of Marketing suggestions of one of the paintings of a harem. While Marketing were no less aware of the arguments and issues around representation, the onus on them to secure a major tabloid media partner for the show to attract a core audience, and for whom an image of the harem would potentially resonate, drove discussions forward. In the event, the proposed media partner was not sufficiently interested in the exhibition to associate itself and an alternative cropped image taken from Arthur Melville's painting 'An Arab Interior' (1881) was used. Further aspirations towards audience development were also problematic as the cultural policy category that national audiences of Middle East origin or alignment came to be understood by, 'the invisible audiences of Islamic sensitivities', were not usefully catered for within the more well-established category of BME. Furthermore, as the Target Group Index database used by Marketing revealed, the category of art did not feature in the target media outlets for this new 'Middle East' audience, being essentially a construct and product of Western modernism and the work of art history as a discipline.

Despite the acute levels of institutional anxiety that the organization and delivery of *Lure of the East* generated, the show passed by without much attention. Many staff, both directly and indirectly involved, were left bemused at the amount of time, resource and energy that had been invested in 'managing' the 'public aspect' of the show, which as one curator exclaimed, 'didn't even occur to the touring partners' in Turkey and the United Arab Emirates. While the study of *Lure of the East* demonstrated the variation between organizational notional concepts of audience and more localized, individualized and embodied ones – from the 'general public', to 'visitors', 'audience', 'participants', 'collaborators', 'viewers' – the lines of tension between the traditional cultural authority of the curator and the more recently acquired agency of Learning became explicit. It was in this line of tension that the need to maintain and protect not just the aura of the work of art, but the aura of the Tate brand through the strategic value of aesthetic modernism, became a tangible issue. Indeed, in the final instance, what seemed to be of more dynamic institutional value was the symbolic role and value. That the exhibition played not in the local national context, but elsewhere: the new networks of potential patrons of existing and proposed art museums in the emerging globally competitive markets of the Middle East. A fact that *The Art Newspaper* would ponder over two years later in an article titled 'The Lure of the East', as it reviewed a plethora of comparable exhibitions in Europe taking place at the same time and asked, 'Does all this translate as an overall re-evaluation of academic painting and Orientalism in particular, or is it more a reflection of commercial realities, as new money, particularly in the Middle East, drives the market forward?' (Adam 2011).

The prominence of Learning in relation to the production of *Lure of the East*, reasserted the historical emergence and role of the Education Department. In 1970 it had been brought into being to explain to the public the complexities and abstract ideas of modern and conceptual art as well as to help overcome their resistance to it. In 2008, Learning was brought in not just to offer interpretation of the content of *Lure of the East*, but to overcome perceived resistance and hostility from a targeted public in relation to the policies of cultural diversity and audience development. In the final analysis, however, it also acted as a risk management strategy to safeguard Tate Britain's reputation – and by extension the reputation of the Tate brand – in relation to the organizational prospects of new global markets and patrons, namely those of the Middle East. This particularly came to the fore when the Tate hosted a major two-day conference on art in the Middle East. The conference was held across both Tate Britain and Tate Modern the following year.[6] Whereas in the 1990s, the strategic need to build the asset value of the collection had underscored all organizational practice towards establishing Tate's reputation as a national and international cultural authority, by 2008 the 'exhibition' had acquired, if not replaced, the collection, as the lead currency of exchange. For, compared to the museum loan of an individual work of art from the collection, the exhibition form, given its technical and conceptual flexibility and mobility, was inherently a more effective vehicle through which to promote, market and enhance the value of the Tate brand globally. In this respect, in the 1990s the collection display had functioned as a 'proxy' to the collection operating as a 'gold standard reserve', drawing its status and authority from the collection as a historical entity of national heritage. By 2008, the exhibition had assumed this role of proxy drawing its authority from both the collection per se and the brand. In its first iteration of the 'proxy' the 'collection display' in the 1990s hang *Past, Present and Future* increased the asset value of the collection when the two collections of Historic British and International Modern and Contemporary were forged together. The re-hang reinvested the collection with symbolic value as one entity, coalescing the invisible but networked interests of connoisseurship, heritage and British patronage with the international networks of patronage and sponsorship. The exhibition as the second iteration of the proxy increased the asset value of Tate as an institution globally.

In this context, it is easier to understand how the exhibition format had become a site of great conflict in terms of claims to expertise and cultural authority as once again the audience of the exhibition became an imaginary construct, equivalent to the 'national public' of the 1980s and 1990s. However, by the first decade of the new millennium it has been brought into being through the anxious practices of risk aversion and management. Within the narrative of the post traditional condition of reflexive modernization set out by Beck, Giddens and Lash (Beck et al. 1994), this 'neurotic ambivalence' towards the public mediation practices of the art museum was fully accounted for, through the repetitive and reproducing process of anticipating and then managing risk. Such a process produces and multiplies the risk register (Giddens' 'array of "scenarios"', Beck et al. 1994: 59), which subsequently stimulates more risk aversion action and so forth until a pernicious cyclical action is set in motion in which cultural authority is so fully distributed across different expert domains that it fragments. This leads to reassertions of cultural authority through recourse to expertise based on epistemic forms of knowledge production that are the very sources from which the risk was first generated. This double negative effect does not lead to productive, rational action but rather the opposite. It produces greater appetite (if not need) for risk conditions to be manufactured, in order to revalidate the practices under pressure to stabilize the situation and to self-authenticate the value of the expertise brought to bear upon its resolution. Such a situation is typified by Giddens' references to the compulsive appetite for risk that the poker player embodies.

As Lash also notes (Beck et al. 1994: 145), in reflexive modernization, 'aesthetic reflexivity', the confrontation with the staging of the visual as the primary means through which to self-identify (the stylization of culture and commodities) equally creates a condition of anxiety, bringing into consciousness what Thrift has described as 'the art of artificiality and the artificiality of art'. It also brings to the fore an awareness that what at first presented themselves as the processes of aesthetic choice and experience are in fact highly mediated and externally constructed value systems that undermine the sense of personal freedom. Paradoxically, according to Giddens, in this moment of self-reflexive awareness and scepticism towards the political organization of contemporary culture, individuals turn for reassurance to public institutions as the embodiment of freedom and expression. The institution's cultural authority is assured by reference to both tradition and the expertise maintaining it in the present. Tradition offers a way to master the present through the past

> Tradition is an orientation to the past, such that the past has a heavy influence, or more accurately put, is made to have a heavy influence, over the present. Yet, clearly ... tradition is also about the future, since established practices are used as a way of organizing future time ... Repetition ... reaches out to return the future to the past, while drawing on the past to reconstruct the future.
>
> *(Beck et al. 1994: 62)*

Given that, 'The integrity or authenticity of a tradition ... is more important in defining it as a tradition than how long it lasts' (Beck et al. 1994: 63), the claims of expertise become ever more vital to shore up the trust and authority invested in the tradition. However, as the *Lure of the East* organizational study revealed, the location and status of expertise within Tate Britain has invariably become contested through the object of audience and the work of art. Curatorial expertise, through the project and strategy of aesthetic modernism, works hard to maintain the legitimacy of universal access and value. At the same time it serves the vested interests of the private networks of art around the art object (patrons, dealers, auction houses, and so forth). Learning's concern is to uphold its ethos of social and public responsibility focused on the audience. It sits not so much in opposition to curatorial imperatives, but rather at a tangent to them and nonetheless contestedly situated elsewhere. Caught up in practices of risk management, expertise is brought into crisis for as Beck observes: 'In risk issues no one is an expert or everyone is an expert because the experts presume what they are supposed to make possible and produce: cultural acceptance' (Beck et al. 1994: 9). For Giddens, the conflicting claims to expertise, brought about by reflexive modernization, also separates out 'experts' from 'guardians': 'Guardians are not experts, and the arcane qualities to which they have access for the most part are not communicable to the outsider ... status is the traditional order, rather than competence is the prime characteristic of the guardian' (Beck et al. 1994: 65).

Historically designated as 'keepers' until renamed as 'curators' in the early 1990s, curators are also now coming under scrutiny to articulate their expertise but within a practicing culture of aesthetic modernism in which their own identities are inextricably entwined and committed to perpetuating; as one curator put it, being a collections curator used to be the most desirable in terms of 'the gold dust effect' but had been eclipsed though by the more 'prestigious and international' role of exhibition curator. What Preziosi has termed 'stagecraft', and what internally many of the curators interviewed referred to as 'the Tate way', this tacit knowledge of hanging works of art at Tate, was institutionally underpinned by an explicit scepticism of the epistemology of both New Art History and art theory, which derived from a cultural studies perspective. Such perspectives were understood to 'taint' appreciation and enjoyment of the artist's intention by relocating it within a constructivist tradition of cultural production; a tradition that rendered the work of art as either illustrative or symptomatic of its historical moment rather than as evidence of the individual imagination and expression of the artist framed by a Romanticist paradigm of creative genius. As several curators also reflected, this resistance to academic knowledge based on culture rather than the aesthetic category of art also manifested itself in the approach to curatorial recruitment which sought staff primarily at an undergraduate or Master of Arts level and therefore more open to being trained up in the 'Tate way' through practice rather than theory. As one curator exclaimed, 'this is not a fantasy, this is felt and real', while another regularly referred to the Curatorial Department as the 'dark arts' in light of the lack of explicit rationale for their practice. Some variation to these accounts did emerge, however, indicating that 'historical British art within Tate Britain has always been expected not to drift into the area of theory but provide a historical narrative' whereas 'contemporary art is expected to deal with theory'. The impetus behind these distinctions invariably fell to an understanding that, 'as an employee you have a responsibility towards the object – that you have to preserve it as a beautiful object otherwise you'd be mistreating [it]. This tends to be the line drawn when there is a political situation'. Such a formulation reasserts Giddens' contention that, 'Tradition has the hold it does ... because its moral character offers a measure of ontological security to those who adhere to it' (Beck et al. 1994: 65) and moreover, 'Tradition is unthinkable without guardians, because the guardians have privileged access to truth; truth cannot be demonstrated save in so far as it is manifest in the interpretations and practices of guardians' (Beck et al. 1994: 80).

In questioning, if not challenging, curatorial expertise in the production of the *Lure of the East*, Learning's professional rise in status in the museum was more than evident. Equally, as it became increasingly clear what its risk-management role was, it prompted questions regarding how education practice at Tate Britain had found itself positioned in the role of 'servicing' the gallery in terms of a response to cultural diversity policies, despite its serious and sustained commitment to sympathetically translate such policies within the conventions of museum practice and production. That is to say, at a defining level, Learning curators mutually share with collection and exhibition curators a deep commitment to and curiosity about the value of art in society. They also share an understanding about the museum as an entity, which makes its positioning as complicit and embedded in the process of cultural administration and the political project of social management even more difficult.

The interviews with Toby Jackson about Tate Liverpool and the interview with Anna Cutler, the first to hold the new position of 'Director of Learning'[7] demonstrated, the extent to which they both agreed that the work of art marked out the clearest territory between the primacy of curatorial knowledge within the organization and the relative marginality awarded to education practice ('the poor cousin' as Jackson described it). As a shorthand to the debates around the conflicted views of the status of the individual viewer in relation to the work of art (rather than the more manageable and abstract notion of the 'audience'), discussions about the role of interpretation in Tate Britain today, and in particular in relation to the *Lure of the East* exhibition, resurrected many of the same, if not identical, arguments and models that Jackson had established in Liverpool 20 years before. What this comparison revealed, however, was that whereas in Liverpool Jackson's emphasis had been purely on building audiences, at Tate Britain it had assumed a dual strategic role. However, as Helen Charman discussed in her interview,[8] the legacy of innovative practice and open challenge to the hierarchy of knowledge that Jackson brought from Tate Liverpool to Tate Modern, with its emphasis on building a distinct body of professional knowledge for Learning, established the conditions within Tate by which to extend these debates of meaning-making and public engagement through the work of practice-based research within Tate.

Indeed, both Toby Jackson and Anna Cutler forcefully asserted that the fundamental prerequisite of all education activity in the museum was the role of research that alone could award the right for Learning 'to sit at the table' of both museum and government policy-making, on the basis that authority can only be claimed and argued for through expertise based on knowledge and understanding. Despite the apparent professionalization of education practitioners, without the foundations of critically examined models and contexts of practice assessed by a peer community, 'soft' evidence could only be provided through the project-based form of 'evaluation reports', which could not build knowledge capacity or new theorizations of practice. The opportunity to build such research capacity was, in part, recognized as limited in relation to short-term projects that were externally funded. The case made for research by Jackson and Cutler took Tate Encounters as such an example of the need to interrogate an area of policy concern and activity. However, it also brought to the fore the vulnerable ground on which Learning practice at Tate Britain operated, despite the very best of practice at the level of delivery. Without the ability to 'make the case' (or 'box smart' as Jackson described it), for the role and value of learning practice independent of either government policy or gallery directives, the shifting ground on which its practice rests renders it both mutable, unlocated and instrumentalized, both within and without. However, when presented well, the case can not only be made and won, it can also be explored more deeply both in the interests and to the benefit of the museum – a cited example being the original case that was made for the creation of Tate Online by Jackson.

For all the enthusiasm and discussion for research that emerged during the organizational study interviews, however, one key condition was consistently cited that mitigated against the potential of research within the museum to generate new useful knowledge: the paradoxical relation between the levels of productivity within the museum driven by an output orientated programme, which nonetheless was always encouraged and promoted as engendering innovation and new expertise. Moreover, as Bennett notes, such levels of activity (Furedi's 'dramatisation of change') often emerge out of 'structurally restless' organizations which 'owing to the incorporation within them of principles of reflexive self-monitoring' lead to a 'remorseless capacity for unending change' (Bennett 2007: xx). While the interviews with staff testified to the institutional appetite for risk, which was invariably linked to a sustained narrative of change as innovation, the critically reflexive practice of research was consistently subsumed with a meeting culture discussing the potential of research that curators described as 'displacement activities' or 'therapy sessions' although, as one curator reflected, 'If the aesthetic is the problem don't we need to understand why?' In this context, Beck's analogy with the traffic jam comes into focus: 'The instrument of power in sub-politics is "congestion" … as the modernized form of the involuntary strike. The phrase that Munich motorists can read in a typically congested location, "You are not in a jam, you are the jam", clarifies the parallel between strike and congestion' (Beck et al. 1994: 23).

While the predominant public narrative of Tate continues to posit the collection as its primary organizational imperative and *raison d'être*, its more recent embrace of the role of art history as a joint partner in an enterprise of change and recontextualization in a global world was noted in Tate's Financial Report for 2010–11:

> Changing trends in society and the impact of new research into art history means that there is a continuous rethinking of Tate's collecting priorities. Tate remains committed to contributing to a reshaping of art history by reflecting local histories across the world, as well as reflecting a broader range of national and artistic views in the Collection.

However, in light of the new strategic value of exhibitions, as part of the global project of expansion, Mark Rectanus' contestation in his article 'Globalization: Incorporating the Museum' also raises the importance of looking beyond the narratives and practices of acquisition:

> Exhibitions reveal an interplay and recontextualisation of the global within the local. The contents of the exhibition and the aesthetics of their presentation relate to the symbolic exchanges of culture which globalize … These tensions

in turn, relate to the broader disjunctures of global flow among ethnoscapes, technoscapes, finanancescapes, mediascapes and ideoscapes which characterize globalization [...] and are simultaneously played out through the museum's own implication in each of these 'scapes'.

(Rectanus 2011: 383)

The belief that the role, interpretation and experience of the collection can continue to still be understood within representational practices, framed by either epistemological knowledge or cultural policy, is undoubtedly beginning to make visible its limits within the new globalized context in which audiences both encounter and understand works of art. For, with the restructuring of capitalist economies, one also sees the restructuring of social and cultural relations, as Robins states, 'As territories are transformed so too are the spaces of identity' (Robins 1999: 17). The one-way direction of economic and cultural traffic determined by colonial and post-colonial forms of labour and capital flow are now giving way to new, non-centred circuits of exchange and dismantling the geographies of centre and periphery, core and margin. This is no less true for the museum, as it is for audiences of the museum. However, as Robins has asserted: 'Globalization, dissolves the barriers of distance, makes the encounter of colonial centre and colonized periphery immediate and intense' (Robins 1999: 18) leading to the conclusion that 'it is the experience of diaspora that we may begin to understand the way beyond empire' (Robins 1999: 28).

When Tate Britain first grasped the opportunity of research to help understand what the barriers to access for new 'diverse' audiences were, the missing audience of the 'margins', it did so with the inherent understanding that existing research disciplines and methodologies were also needed. Effected through both a trans-disciplinary approach and a Latourian 'tracing of the social', what emerged, however, was not merely an account of missing audiences but rather a larger account of how practices of audience played out in the everyday work of the museum across departments. To understand the emergence of audience, consideration of the connections and disconnections between practice, policy and theory, also had to be usefully addressed. In so doing, a more complex analysis of the museum emerges: one that acknowledges both the specific economic, cultural and social conditions under which Tate and indeed Tate Britain has come into being. It provides a recognition of the barriers it itself is now confronting as it renegotiates its role and position in the twenty-first century. The transition from the connoisseurial museum to the globally connected, and now accelerated, hypermodern museum was a journey created by Tate out of strategic necessity and professional desire to build the exchange value of the collection and the institution in order to sustain the validity of modern and contemporary art alongside the authority of the institution. This move through modernization towards the present extraordinary success of Tate has clearly generated immense numbers of visitors. However, the first stage of this process, what might be termed a belated modernism, in the 1990s took place on the cusp of globalization and under the conditions of reflexive modernization, which allowed it to build success in international market terms. It is, however, increasingly limiting its organizational capacity to negotiate audiences in the hypermodern moment. The strategies and tactics of heritage and tradition, when combined with the contemporary moment of globalization, begin to reveal their limits in the fragmentation of authority, trust and expertise creating the emergent spectacle of aesthetic modernism as the new heritage aesthetic. The new spatio-temporal relations between the museum and society, between Tate Britain and its audiences, while creating anxiety and ambivalence, can nonetheless be thought of more opportunistically; what is not in doubt, is that change is in process, as Thrift notes:

> ... space times are always accompanied by their phantoms, which rehearse the 'the active presence of absent things' ... space-times very often provide the 'stutter' in social relations the jolt which arises from new encounters, new connections, new ways of proceeding.
>
> *(Thrift 2008: 120–1)*

PART II
Displaying the nation

4

CANON-FORMATION AND THE POLITICS OF REPRESENTATION

Canon-formation, under the aegis of national art museum collecting practices, remains a highly defended zone. It is in the name of the canon that Tate curators have continually advocated the safeguarding of curatorial independence. From a curator's point of view, Tate Britain's implicit role as the guardian of British cultural values heightens the need to protect curatorial autonomy.[1] Critiques of such a position have emerged from those commenting on conventional museology, such as Preziosi (2003: 39), who suggest that canon-formation, particularly at the level of the national art museum, remains connected to statecraft. Canonized objects in national art collections form part of the body of the nation. Such a role assigned to art objects finds its corollary in the project of engaging populations in the observance of the canon. Such notion of 'observance' retains, as Jonathan Crary has pointed out, a disciplinary aspect (Crary 1999) through which observation – viewing artwork – and observing convention – (self-)regulation – operate in tandem. In similar terms, critical museology reached the position that modernity had rendered museums as instruments to not only exercise control over objects, but also, by so doing, to discipline urban populations into a well-functioning bourgeoisie and a quietly civilized working-class (Bennett 1995: 28).

The national art museum in the contemporary period has made a decisive break from its trajectory in modernity. The museum has ceased to be one organization with a coherent set of aims but rather has become susceptible to institutional dynamics that produce organizational dissociations. The affinities between professionals and practices do not rely on identification within one organization, but rather on affiliations across networks that move through different organizational frameworks. The analytical model, thereby, shifts from a central focus on one institution to an awareness of the dispersal of expertise across various networks. In a Bourdieu-influenced analysis, such as that expounded by Grenfell and Hardy (2007), such issues are discussed in terms of the notion of 'overlapping fields' rather than networks. However, the distinction is

made here because in the modality of the network, the museum organization is disaggregated: it is no longer a unitary entity situated in a broader field; it is a nexus of
disaggregated interests that only make sense in relation to interests articulated elsewhere. Such an approach allows each organization to be understood as a matrix
through which different networks interlace. Thus, educational networks, curatorial
networks, corporatist networks, family networks and political networks must be seen
as separate nexuses that cross the institutional space. Curators need not meet the
families that visit the museum every day. Equally, policy-makers who set the framework for institutional operations need not meet the educationalists who work within
the parameters that they set. Indeed, Tate provides an example of how elite political
networks operate across the organization independently of any other network. From
its inception, Tate Britain's geographical proximity to the historic political institutions
in Britain (Palace of Westminster, Downing Street, Whitehall, Buckingham Palace)
made it part of an elite political network. In fact, when the then Tate Gallery opened
on 21 July 1897, it did so in the presence of HRH The Prince of Wales, later King
Edward VII. More than a century later, rumours abounded and apocryphal stories
were often told, at Tate Britain, of the museum being opened at 'special hours' to
allow various eminent figures to view exhibitions of prominent artists to whom they
might have particular attachments. Such distinguished visitors, of course, were never
seen, and such rumours of the dim-lit corridors of 'special hours' with solo attendants
on special watch always went unsubstantiated. The fact that even the knowledge of
such activity belonged to the particular register of 'rumour' and 'apocrypha' supports
the argument that certain networks criss-crossed institutional space completely
unnoticed, undisturbed, disconnected from and, significantly, *unbeknown to* other
networks.[2] Indeed, the institutional dynamics intensified such dissociation.

At Tate, the handling of cultural politics as matters to be discussed within policy
networks alone must be addressed. Black and Afro-Asian artists' critiques of institutionalized 'canonical' exclusion of their work was not handled by curatorial networks,
but was instead pushed outside the domain of the curatorial and transformed into a
policy matter to be assigned solely to those operating within policy networks. The
handling of the National Ethnic Minority Arts policy, developed in the 1980s, provides an example of how such practices worked. Sandy Nairne, Director of Visual
Arts at the Arts Council during that period, spoke in 2009 about his earlier role. He
outlined how the thinking in his department had taken place within the wider
national cultural policy body. He reflected on a department that had aimed to construct a more systematic approach to issues concerning black and other ethnic minority cultural practitioners. Nairne explained that, at senior levels of the Arts Council
in the 1980s, thinking had begun to centre on the politics of representation, as it was
deemed that a proportion of the available arts funding should be allocated to every
national arts organization for specific activities aimed at attracting and reflecting the
proportions of ethnic minority people in the UK population as a whole.[3] Such
thinking would eventually lead to a culture of 'target-setting'. Policy development
from the 1980s, therefore, began to centre on 'representational' forms of target-setting
in relation to social demographics. Those people visiting museums who were

identified as 'black and minority ethnic' (BME) were seen as representing black and ethnic minority people in general. Such an approach was pursued later during the 1990s. It was via this route that critiques of institutionalized 'canonical' exclusion of black and Afro-Asian artists were sutured to concerns about the institutional marginalization of migrational peoples. As part of a policy rubric, such questions also extended to Tate's activities. It is, therefore, crucial to note how this policy entered into the practice and thinking of curatorial networks via arts policy formulation rather than through curatorial discussion of artwork.

Arts policy formulation became welded to the social inclusion policy agenda promoted by Tony Blair's New Labour Administration in the late 1990s. Policies were targeted at those who were regarded as socially marginalized. Black and ethnic minority people were counted among that group. Issues raised by black and Afro-Asian artists were drawn into the social inclusion debate. In response to New Labour's continued advancement of the social inclusion agenda, the National Museums Directors' Conference (NMDC) proposed practical steps to deliver objectives that were seen as addressing the concerns raised about the exclusion of black and Afro-Asian art practice from mainstream institutions. Social and institutional exclusion were, by those means, brought together under the New Labour Social Inclusion agenda. Set up in 2004, the NMDC's Cultural Diversity Working Group reported in 2006 with recommendations aimed at setting the terms of institutional implementation of cultural diversity policy. The recommendations separated the Working Group's work into three areas: emphasis on ensuring the diversity of workforce; focus on exhibitions and public programmes; prioritizing work with external bodies, such as the Greater London Authority – through the London Mayor's Commission on African and Asian Heritage. By tackling exhibitions and public programmes as a matter of policy, the cultural critique of black and Afro-Asian artists became reformulated and transformed, via Arts Council policy machinery. It was then later placed within the national government's policy networks. The ideas, thereby, reached the executive suites and directorial offices of national cultural institutions – the exact configuration from which curatorial networks insisted that they had to protect themselves. As Sandy Nairne, who had chaired the NMDC Working Group, explained: 'It was obvious that some of the structural issues that needed to be changed were to do with who had power and who had control. [it] centred on curatorship ... we had to create an environment in which things might be different.'[4] What Nairne's view did not reflect, however, were the institutional dynamics dissociating curatorial networks and their work of curatorial knowledge-formation from the pressures coming from museum directors, national policy-makers, arts bureaucrats and other people working in policy-networks, such as Nairne and his colleagues on the NMDC. It was clear, for instance, from the Tate Encounters organizational study, that a number of curatorial staff explicitly sought to resist the influence of such policy.[5] Indeed, it was suggested that moves to make changes that were clearly seen as being policy-driven became counterproductive. Resistance built up within museum departments to the issues concerned. Policy drives issuing either from the national cultural policy body or directly from government departments, such as the

Department of Culture, Media and Sport, were seen as being taken up at the strategic level. Museum directors were expected to respond to the relevant issues raised by policy-makers so that curators, in fact, would not have to.

A clear account of curatorial disengagement from policy must be given: the imposition of institutional limits, the setting up of strategic exclusions, the repeated misrecognitions – all need to be traced and understood. For, systematic disengagement with political structures has its corollary in the institution's distancing from societal conditions. By refusing the reality of the sociopolitical conditions in which the institutional body is situated, the museum produces an affirmation of a different set of conditions: the relations between objects and people over which the museum exercises control by setting the terms of reference and evaluation. Every exclusion of the determinations of the social, every 'no' to political conditions, can be counted as a 'yes' to another set of conditions – museological conventions. These now demand a specific, detailed and located account in order to understand the processes that make their functioning possible.

The domain of the political was set out as an explicit line of exclusion within the constitution of the museological discourse at Tate Britain. As a means of sustaining the precept that curatorial knowledge is produced primarily through relations to art objects, the notion of 'non-political' expertise was reified. As interviews with curators at Tate Britain, as part of the Tate Encounters' organizational study, revealed, an insistence that curators needed to remain 'independent' and free from outside influence was a point reiterated by practitioners at several levels of curatorial expertise. Curatorial knowledge, according to such practitioners, was constituted, in part, through a specific refusal of anything that came under the banner of the 'political'. Calls to be more 'political' or to engage with political issues were redirected to spaces of policy-making and organizational strategic direction. Politics, then, was seen rather more as the currency of those involved in organizational governance. Tate trustees, together with the officials of the national government's culture department, had the remit to deal in political matters. Any insistence that such issues ought to have influenced curatorial decision-making and museological practice was treated as undue political interference from above.

The independence of curatorial knowledge and museological discourse from political matters remains an epistemological claim representing a facet of certain 'classical' approaches to curatorial practice within the modernist museum: the autonomy of curatorial knowledge is seen as deriving from claims for the autonomy of the art practice to which it professes to defer. Critiques of such assertions to autonomy are not new: Peter Burger's work in the 1970s, which appeared in English translation in the 1980s, underlined the ways in which the modernist category of art-making, 'bourgeois art' in his terms, relied on a problematic 'separation of art from the praxis of life' (Burger 1992). The insistence on an autonomous category of art came under sustained scrutiny through the late 1970s and 1980s, as the claim to separation from everyday life became subjected to arguments influenced by the sociological thinking of figures such as Bourdieu (1977). Gretton, for instance, suggested that:

> ... aesthetic criteria have no existence outside a specific historical situation; aesthetic values are falsely taken to be timeless ... the category of 'art' cannot be taken to have an absolute existence. Rather it is the name of a social relationship.
>
> *(Gretton 1986: 64)*

The use of the category of the social to formulate critiques of art institutions was sustained in discussions that led from the sociological disciplines into museology, informing moves towards what can now be termed 'new museology' or, more precisely, 'critical museology'.

Critical museology did significant work in asserting the importance of a socio-political dimension in museums study. An emphasis on the category of the social can be seen in the work of Bennett (1995), Hooper-Greenhill (1994b) and Sandell (2002). Such work has addressed specific areas of museological practice, such as audiences, education and learning. Work in the area of education and learning provides a good example of the way that critical museology resorted as much to social sciences as to arts practice and cultural theory to develop its critiques. For instance, it brought together developments in learning theory, psychology, audience analysis and institutional critique to produce what has been termed a 'critical museum pedagogy' (Hooper-Greenhill 1994b: 4). Hooper-Greenhill's work is cited here as exemplary because of its direct engagement with policy formation.[6] Her analysis stood explicitly on the theoretical ground laid down by Foucault (Hooper-Greenhill 2000: x). As such, her input belongs to a swathe of thinking grounded in Foucault's work on disciplinary regimes and governmentality (Foucault 1977) – thinking that has remained influential in respect of policy and practice in the museums and galleries learning field over a significant period of time (Bragg 2007; Bennett 1995).

A late Foucauldian framework, emphasizing strategies of subjectivization undertaken within a range of institutional contexts – what Foucault himself termed 'practices of the self' (Foucault 1984) – became an important dimension of critical museology's approach. It facilitated an understanding of the museum as operating within a social context in such a way as to produce knowledge that helped inform practice. Indeed, such understanding has continued to influence the debates surrounding the social agency of the museum and its concomitant responsibility to act as an agent of transformation within the social world (Sandell 2002: 3–5). Foucauldian thinkers, such as Hooper-Greenhill, however, would be the first to recognize that such knowledge cannot stand outside the institutional relations that make it possible to be formed and disseminated. It becomes increasingly imperative, then, to expose the institutional relations within which such knowledge is embedded and upon which it relies.

The assertion of the independence of curatorial knowledge, despite the decades of critique emerging from critical museology has to be taken seriously as an institutional phenomenon. A detailed focus on the institutional responses to academic critiques advanced by critical museology has to be applied. Equally, an account must be given of the museum's misrecognition of critiques emanating from cultural practitioners aligned with migrational cultures. Reference to the institutional dynamics of museums, such as Tate Britain, accounts for the ways in which sustained theoretical critique was channelled away from the formation of curatorial knowledge. The institutional dynamics protected such areas of museum activity by exposing other parts of the organization to the force of critique. One such exposed area was the policy arena, alongside others such as education, interpretation and, later, learning.

An example of the propensity to protect the curatorial knowledge arena was uncovered during the Tate Encounters organizational study: leading curators at Tate Britain spoke, for instance, of the tendency not to appoint people who held doctorates to the Curatorial department. The entry level preferred was Masters level. This was seen as a means of protecting the formation of curatorial knowledge from the tendencies of those immersed in the latest museological research. Rather, it was preferred that research training should be undertaken within the museum so that curatorial knowledge-production could be formed according to the needs of the museum itself – rather than in concert with the latest prevailing academic trends. Such a stance, according to information received in the Tate Encounters study, was particularly true of the historical (i.e., pre-1900) part of the collection. In that section, a connoisseurial model of knowledge predominated. Emphasis was placed on the ability to generate an historical narrative. Where the latest developments in art historical or museological theory interfered with such purpose, these were set aside. The relation to the historical art object had to remain paramount.

A strong example of the privileging of the art object at the expense of developments in theoretical thinking was the handling of the *Lure of the East* exhibition in 2008. The organizational study demonstrated that the curators of the show were more than aware of debates on theories of Orientalism, particularly those surrounding the work of Edward Said (1978). However, a series of arguments were advanced as to why ongoing debates around the theory of Orientalism should not be allowed to overshadow the intrinsic worth of the artworks that had been brought together for the exhibition. First, there was the suggestion that theory had generated analytical categories that were not significant for addressing the paintings themselves. Theoretical preoccupations with 'feminism', 'gender' and 'identity' were seen as not central to an understanding of a group of Victorian painters responsible for generating the works on show.[7] Second, the thematic concerns that emerged out of theoretical debate – concerns around figurations of the 'harem' or 'gay relations' or 'female relations' – were also regarded as themes that were not central to the concerns of the painters themselves. Third, the thematic preoccupations evidenced in the artwork – the male figure, for instance – were seen as having been marginalized within postcolonial theory.[8] Finally, it was viewed that the theory was not specific to the art form. Said's work (1978), for instance, centred on literary criticism, dealing primarily with literary sources.[9]

The applicability of such theory, then, not only to visual sources but also to the pictorial specificities of the paintings in the exhibition, was seen as questionable.[10] Academic preoccupations with theory were, furthermore, viewed as having a trajectory of their own, with the movement between one theoretical position and another being rendered as 'faddish'. On several counts, then, the argument was made that theoretical knowledge was not useful in the necessary engagement with artwork. In respect of the *Lure of the East*, however, theoretical insights were not entirely discounted; they were, more accurately, reassigned a place within the institutional paraphernalia surrounding the exhibition. For instance, it was argued that reference to Said needed to appear somewhere in the exhibition, as a means of signalling to the show's academic audiences that Tate was *au fait* with current debates in academia.[11] The role of making such overtures to the museum's academic audiences was assigned not to the curatorial department but to the department of Interpretation and Education (I&E). This was because the national art museum worked through a set of institutional dynamics that assigned specific roles to different parts of the museum structure. In the case of the *Lure of the East*, the allocation of roles – policy to directors, theory to educationalists, art objects to curators – produced a form of organizational dissociation.

By stressing the term organizational dissociation, emphasis is placed on the ways in which different sections *within* the museum interfaced all too directly with different networks *outside* it. Indeed, the directness of the interface meant that certain organs within the museum had more in common with other bodies in external networks than they did with parts internal to their own organization. For instance, the education and learning departments interfaced so much within educational networks (schools and colleges, academia, education and learning departments in other art institutions) that their language, ideas and practices had more in common with people in such educational networks than they did with curatorial discourse in their own organization. The institutional dynamic worked to ensure that the appropriate discourse circulated within the allocated network. The handling of theoretical knowledge was not seen, then, as being proper to the curatorial network. Rather, the interpreters and educationalists were asked to deal with it and keep it circulating within an academic discursive context. In so doing, they allowed curatorial knowledge to reconstitute the *artwork without theory* as the proper object of curatorial discourse.

The insistence of a dissociation between art production, politics and theoretical thinking can be seen as one of the reasons why Tate curators took so long to recognize the artwork of black artists in the UK? The sense that the work was seen as emerging from an explicitly political discourse was reiterated. As a case in point, the reflections of the artist Rasheed Araeen should be addressed. He commented on the contrast between the warm popular welcome of his 1989 survey show of Afro-Asian art in Britain, *The Other Story*, as opposed to the poor critical reception of the exhibition:

> What was perhaps unusual about the works in *The Other Story*, in addition to their modernism and avant-gardism, was their representation of the social experiences specific to Afro Asian immigrants. That this [British] society had not previously confronted such experiences and their representations in art, perhaps accounts for their difficulty in being accepted ...
>
> *(Araeen 1991: 24)*

The move to render Afro-Asian art, as a practice engaging directly with the social experiences of migrational peoples, placed such artwork outside the autonomous space of the aesthetic. Although such an autonomous space, claimed within the protocols of the national art museum in its modernist guise, could not open itself up to what was seen as the sociopolitical agenda of the Black Arts Movement, educators could be assigned the task of dealing with it.

The continued isolation of the category of the 'aesthetic' from the categories of the 'political' and the 'theoretical' within national art museums parallels an insistence that the aesthetic should be insulated from the intellectual debates questioning the formation of the art historical canon. For instance, thinkers, such as the British scholar Leon Wainwright have pointed towards the problematic teleology of conventional Western art history with its failure to address its geopolitical biases: 'The opportunity,' he wrote, 'has not been taken for the merging of British and Caribbean horizons and art histories' (Wainwright 2010: 101). Wainwright's view is that the Western art canon generates a selective teleology, leaving out whole geographical areas, such as the Caribbean. The intimate relationship to the Caribbean, enjoyed by several of the artists recognized as part of the Western canon, such as Chris Ofili and Peter Doig, suggests that the exclusion of wider Caribbean art practices from the Western canon remains an unresolved contradiction. Wainwright has recognized the ways in which such ongoing issues in art history have become marginalized within the discipline itself and thereby have impacted negatively on the work of mainstream art institutions: 'phenomena such as the art history canon serve to structure the art mainstream and so inevitably assist in marginalization and exclusion' (Wainwright 2010: 102). The art historical canon and the critiques that surround it, such as that advanced by Wainwright, have been assigned a place within the intellectual spaces of debate within the museum. However, at the same time, there is a specificity within museum practice that means that the successive canons generated by museum collecting practices seem built to withstand any nuanced position that might emerge from art history. The passage between art history and collecting remains a carefully monitored one – one that turns aside any tricky questions that might derail the incessant reification of the existing canon.

Even when critiques of the canon come from neither intellectual debates nor from politicized discourse but from art practices themselves, careful strategies can be observed at work in defence of Western art's modernist canon. For example, the exhibition *From Two Worlds* (1986), which was curated at the Whitechapel Art Gallery by Nicholas Serota and Gavin Jantjes, took place shortly after Lubaina Himid's groundbreaking show, *The Thin Black Line* (1985). Himid's exhibition platformed a range of black women's art practices, displaying the work at London's Institute of Contemporary Arts (ICA). Jantjes and Serota's Whitechapel show presented artists who had been in Himid's exhibition, such as Sonia Boyce and Lubaina Himid herself. What was interesting to note about *From Two Worlds* was its emphasis on a notion of 'cultural synthesis', suggesting that one could delimit artists whose work was grounded in two cultural traditions – the eponymous 'Two Worlds' – from those artists whose practice was only located in one. Jantjes and Serota wrote:

Of principal importance to … [the] selection was the works' achievement as an innovative synthesis of a 'lived' cultural plurality. Artists whose work draws on other cultures primarily as a stimulus for their own artistic development, but without a deep understanding of that culture, were of lesser interest here; we were looking for artists whose work synthesized their non-Western cultural roots with those of Europe and Britain.

(Jantjes and Serota 1986: 8)

The curatorial framing of the exhibition demonstrated that there was an awareness of the problems of setting up artists who worked 'within' the traditions of Western European art and those who worked 'outside' of them. The curators admitted that ' … the "ethnic" label can be used to diminish or at least to question the standing of art which draws on such [ethnic] traditions, rather than on the traditions of Western European art' (Jantjes and Serota 1986: 6). What becomes clear here is that, whether inadvertently or not, art practices associated with Afro-Asian art and/or the Black Arts Movement, were being cited as not being fully located within the Western European canon. Their work was seen as not sharing and, therefore, not properly belonging to the modernist traditions of Western European art. It took the words of Adeola Solanke, another writer published in the exhibition catalogue, to clarify this point in the essay 'Juggling Worlds':

The debt owed to African sculpture by various non-African artists (Picasso, Braque, Brancusi, etc.) is generally acknowledged but their demonstrable dependence on African aesthetics is not deemed to diminish their 'Europeanness'.

(Solanke 1986: 9–10)

Solanke's arguments, albeit valid, were placed among a series of intellectual positions that critiqued conventional canon-formation. The exhibition of the artwork itself did more to provoke a change in curatorial perspective as it took only another year before Sonia Boyce's work *Missionary Position II* (1985) entered the Tate Collection. Other artists in *From Two Worlds*, soon followed suit after Nicholas Serota's appointment to the directorship of Tate in 1988, which led to much more of their artwork being deemed to merit preservation in perpetuity in the national collection of British art.

More than 20 years after Serota's appointment as Tate Director, a new display opened at Tate Britain, *Thin Black Line(s)*.[12] Opening on 22 August 2011, the show was curated by artist Lubaina Himid with Tate curator Paul Goodwin. It featured the work of a selection of black women artists who had been living and working in the UK during the period of the British Black Arts Movement of the 1980s. Indeed, the display acted as a reprise, a direct citation of the exhibition, *The Thin Black Line*, curated by Himid more than a quarter of a century earlier at London's Institute of

FIGURE 4.1 Sonia Boyce, 'Mr Close Friend of the Family Pays a Visit Whilst Everyone Else is Out' (1985), charcoal on paper. Arts Council Collection. Southbank Centre, London. © Sonia Boyce, all rights reserved. DACS 2012

Contemporary Arts (ICA). During a public debate of the 2011 rendition of *Thin Black Line(s)*,[13] Himid and Goodwin were joined by artist Claudette Johnson in a discussion of the cultural and political context surrounding the original mounting of the exhibition at the ICA. Such a context included calls for the greater accountability of cultural institutions to the publics whom they were meant to serve, as well as a consequent expectation that such institutions would reflect the wealth and diversity of the arts practices that were growing up around them. Both Himid and Johnson acknowledged the close proximity of debates around visual arts practices to discussions of broader feminist and black politics throughout the period surrounding the 1985 show. The wider politics of feminism and black struggle through the 1980s then later the 1990s and early 2000s provided a backdrop that marked a specifically British context alongside a broader international setting, particularly in the USA. The debates that arose around exhibitions, such as the 1993 Whitney Biennial as well as Catherine Lord's *Theatre of Refusal* exhibition, shown in California in the same year, for instance, demonstrated the links between concerns being raised in the United States, alongside those raised in the United Kingdom, in respect of the politics of race, sexuality and gender.

The trajectory of contestations around cultural practice reached as far back as the late 1970s/early 1980s, when matters relating to racial equality were discussed in terms of cultural politics and the work of visual artists, as well the arts institutions that engaged with them. Indeed, the period of the 1980s provided a rich range of interventions from literary practitioners (Dabydeen 1985; Okri 1988), cultural theorists (Gilroy 1987) alongside visual artists (Himid 1985; Araeen et al. 1987) whose artwork sat alongside their curatorial interventions, which acted in tandem with a number of significant exhibitions throughout the decade.[14] Such exhibitions brought forward a range of talent, including artists who were emerging in the 1980s period, such as Sonia Boyce and Keith Piper, together with artists with more established practices whose work had not been platformed by major collecting institutions. The painter Frank Bowling, for instance, entered the collection of the Arts Council of Great Britain, as early as 1962 with the acquisition of his oil on canvas work, 'Birthday' (1962). However, it took another 25 years before Bowling entered Tate's collection through an acquisition, during the significant 1980s period, of his artwork 'Spreadout Ron Kitaj' (1984–6), an acrylic and mixed media on canvas piece by the painter, bought in 1987. Such moves underlined the significance of the 1980s in the UK as a period in which major cultural institutions were forced to take note of the range and quality of the artistic and critical interventions with which they were surrounded.

Taken as a whole, the artistic and critical interventions of the 1980s not only generated critiques on existing institutional practice, they also advocated the formation of strategic resistance to the exclusionary practices of cultural as well as broader societal institutions. In the long run, such strategic resistance could not achieve its aims for two key reasons: first, there was not a detailed enough understanding of the institutions against which critiques were mounted – the work of curatorial

FIGURE 4.2 Frank Bowling, 'Spreadout Ron Kitaj' (1984–6), acrylic and mixed media on canvas. Tate Collection. © Frank Bowling, all rights reserved. DACS 2012

knowledge-formation could not be understood through theoretical or museological means, it needed to be understood through its functions; secondly, the strategic 'fronts' developed within the Black Arts Movement successively presented unified voices behind which there were varied and differential interests that remained under-explored. Much more work needed to be done to bring forward the different investments in practice, ideas and concerns. Such an approach would have linked the various practices developed by artists to the range of available networks rather than marshalling all resources either in the direction of the 'community' or in a full-scale assault on the ramparts of 'Fortress Tate'.

By the early 1990s, further thinking proposed the putting forward of more varied stances to add to the strategies of resistance that had been supported up to that point. For instance, Stuart Hall's notion of 'enunciation' (Hall 1994: 392) analysed the way in which writers and artists from migrational cultures engaged with the cultural imaginary to produce nuanced identity-positions. Such strategies were taken further in the mid-1990s with the emergence of an emphasis on the interrelatedness of place (Gilroy 1993; Bhabha 1994). The complication of ideas of geography and location led in turn to discussions of ideas of indeterminacy and self-narration (Enwezor 1999: 273). Such critiques, rich as they were, suffered from their location in academic discourse. The presumptions around national sovereignty and bourgeois individualism, around which museum practice at the then Tate Gallery were situated, could not be dismantled by academic reasoning because they had not been built by academic reasoning in the first place. Their reification was established through institutional activity that was *naturalized* through reiterated practice. It did not need to articulate itself through intellectual rationale. The museum was not susceptible, then, to the conceptual work done to rethink approaches to migrational subjectivity.

It was only by the early 2000s, when thinking around migrational subjectivity had undergone a recast into the international context, that Tate became prepared to engage with the issues expressed by black and Afro-Asian artists who had become part of a broad international agenda. The artist Mona Hatoum, for instance – who had shown alongside other artists associated with the Black Arts Movement, such as Simone Alexander, Zarina Bhimji and Veronica Ryan in an exhibition titled *Dislocations* (1987)[15] – was the first artist to show in the series of Sculpture Displays by British artists in the Duveen Galleries in the newly opened Tate Britain in 2000.[16] Hatoum, as a Palestinian artist who lived between London and Paris, encapsulated the subject-position with which Tate could deal, as regards the attention it could bring to the issue of cultural difference. Hatoum's work provided a politics of difference that could be firmly located elsewhere – Palestine – but artwork that could be located in proximity to Tate. Although intensely political, her artwork could be disengaged from immediate policy concerns and returned to the curatorial arena. The opening up of international platforms to British artists such as Hatoum, Bhimji and film-installation artist Isaac Julien, allowed debates around difference to continue circulating on an international visual arts stage – a stage with which Tate could connect. Such a stage came to fruition when artists, critics, curators and theorists came together to fully elaborate thinking around issues of migration and diaspora via the platform provided by the international art event, held in Kassel, Germany, *Documenta XI* (2002).

The construction of subjectivity within migrational culture became a theme reiterated by artists because it was seen as central to an appreciation of the post-colonial condition itself. The engagement of migrational peoples with the social conditions that framed their experience of late twentieth-century Britain remained intimately linked to an understanding of British culture still operating under the shadow of historical empire. Such themes were developed through a series of interrelated ideas, which emerged between the 1980s and 2000s across different fields of cultural practice, including literary scholarship, fiction and poetry as well as cultural theory and visual arts practices. The ways in which such practices were consolidated must be addressed alongside the means by which cultural institutions were engaged. In the light of such an approach, the sense of how a notion of cultural politics was constituted thereby becomes clarified more specifically in relation to the actual practices, gestures and institutional networks that were activated. This highlights the discursive formation within which critical and artistic interventions worked at the time. By looking at that formation, it becomes evident how the conditions of the political formation of the Black Arts Movement made it impossible for it to realize its stated aims.

When showing at the ICA, *The Thin Black Line* (1985) featured a number of emerging black women artists, such as Sonia Boyce, Ingrid Pollard and Sutapa Biswas. The show was one of several exhibitions in the mid- to late 1980s platforming black British art as a set of practices that had been ignored much to the cost of British culture in general: *Into the Open*, selected by Pogus Caesar and Lubaina Himid (Mappin Art Gallery, Sheffield, 1984); *The Image Employed*, curated by Keith Piper and Marlene Smith (Cornerhouse Gallery, Manchester, 1987), and *The Essential Black Art*, curated by Rasheed Araeen (Chisenhale Gallery, London, 1989) as well as *The Other Story*, also curated by Araeen (Hayward Gallery, 1989), were prominent examples. The aim of such activity, according to figures such as Himid, was to restore the appropriate level of visibility to black artists who had otherwise been marginalized. *The Thin Black Line* thus became emblematic of the strategy of resistance that can be seen to mark cultural activism of the 1980s. In her commentary for the exhibition catalogue, Himid gave voice to some of the concerns surrounding 'visibility' and 'representation' that had begun to characterize the cultural politics of the period:

> All eleven artists in this exhibition are concerned with the politics and realities of being Black Women. We will debate upon how and why we differ in our creative expression of these realities. Our methods vary individually from satire to story-telling, from timely vengeance to careful analysis, from calls to arms to the smashing of stereotypes. We are claiming what is ours and making ourselves visible. We are eleven of the hundreds of creative Black Women in Britain. We are here to stay.
>
> *(Himid 1985: i)*

The foregrounding of black women in the original *Thin Black Line* exhibition can be seen as a move to transform the figuration of black women in wider politics in Britain during the 1980s. Such transformation can be seen in Marlene Smith's artwork. She exhibited a mixed media-work in *The Thin Black Line* titled 'Good Housekeeping I'. Made principally of household materials (chipboard, chicken wire, jay cloths and plaster), the work consisted of the following: a framed family photograph; a three-dimensional mixed media rendition of a black woman, the artist's mother; lettering running in two lines across a wall as well as along a partition perpendicular to it, stating: *My Mother Opens the Door at 7 am. She is not Bulletproof.* The words made explicit reference to the brutal treatment of black women at the hands of police, particularly during an incident in 1980s London, involving the serious injury of a black woman, Dorothy 'Cherry' Groce.

The name Cherry Groce had become closely associated with the counter-repression struggles across urban centres in Britain in the 1980s as she became known as the black woman whose maltreatment at the hands of police led to riots in Brixton, South London, in the mid-1980s. It was contested that she had been shot and paralysed by the London Metropolitan Police on 28 September 1985 during an armed raid on her home in search of her son. Marlene Smith's work epitomized the kind of intervention made by artists, as a means of countering what was seen as the repressive and exclusionary practices of British state institutions. Smith recently commented on the work, stating:

> I had been on a march protesting police brutality around the time I decided to make this piece ... Having a show in that particular corridor [in the Institute of Contemporary Arts, London] across the road from the [Buckingham] Palace was really significant and I did want to make a big statement about humanity and justice and brutality and myself in relation to all that.[17]

Following the uproar that followed this incident, public institutions that represented the forces of oppression – the police, the criminal justice system, the education system and art institutions themselves were also open to question. Through their artwork, black women saw a means of liberating themselves from both the sacrificial economy of police brutality and from the logics of victimization. Neither victims nor sacrifices, black women would pose the difficult questions, make the troubling statements. Interrogating and intervening, one could say: *Black women ... are here to stay*.

Keeping the pressure up on art institutions to recognize the significance of the contribution of black artists to British culture was of particular importance to artists and curators like Marlene Smith and Lubaina Himid. During a television interview in 1986, Himid stated her viewpoint clearly: 'It's difficult for me to say that the white art world is racist ... I have to look at the white art world as something that can be changed'.[18] Such themes of resistance to the logics of objectification of dominant society also ran through the work of prominent men within the Black Arts Movement of the 1980s, such as Eddie Chambers and Rasheed Araeen. Cited in the opening of the catalogue to a retrospective held in the 1980s, Araeen discussed the theme of resistance to notions of white superiority:

> Who am I? Where do I come from? How do I, a non-European, relate to the European society I find myself living in but do not belong to? How do I react to its assumptions of white superiority? Are a few of the questions that confront me today and which I'm trying to deal with in my work.
>
> *(Araeen et al. 1987)*

Rasheed Araeen's celebrated mixed-media work from the late 1970s *How Could One Paint A Self-Portrait!* (1979), drew attention to the artist's critical strategy of subversion, as a means of resisting the paradigms of ethnicity erected by dominant white culture. Critic Desa Phillipi referred to the 'subversion of ethnic status through its radical adaptation' (Phillipi 1988). Araeen's work depicted an image of the artist over which racist graffiti such as 'blacks out' and 'paki go home' had been deliberately scrawled to obscure Araeen's self-image and thereby thwart his attempts to find a voice. The work remains one of the most poignant elaborations of the struggle to find artistic agency within the antagonistic context of racist Britain. Araeen's work rearticulated the problem of political agency within an arena other than the explicitly political, thereby legitimizing cultural practice as a site of resistance and a place where the struggle to generate another form of agency could take place. Eddie Chambers' work, 'The Destruction of the National Front' (1979–80), also posited artistic production as a site of resistance, suggesting that artistic action impacts directly on the political arena. Chambers stated: 'The work of the black artist should be seen as having specific positive functions: a tool to assist us in our struggle for liberation, both at home and abroad' (Chambers 1988/9: 45).

The artwork of Araeen and Chambers found resonance with theoretical and critical voices that, by the end of the 1980s and the beginning of the 1990s had placed the theme of resistance at the top of the critical agenda. Paul Gilroy, for instance, in an essay titled, 'It Ain't Where You're From, It's Where You're At … The Dialectics of Diasporic Identification' (1991), foregrounded the need to analyse resistance, asking 'how resistance itself is to be understood' (Gilroy 1991: 3). The political context of Britain during the 1980s, with the culmination of the Reagan–Bush–Thatcher era, informed such thinking, particularly as regards attempts by those forming part of migration cultures to find some means of articulating political agency. Such articulations, set against the ultra-nationalist rhetoric of Britain in the wake of the victory over Argentina in the Falklands War, had to be framed in terms of 'resistance'.

'Resistance', however, would not make it possible to advance the different rhetorical, artistic and economic practices in which artists working in that era were engaged. The needs of a sculptor such as Veronica Ryan (1985: 11), preoccupied with sculptural language and natural form differed demonstrably from that of photographer Ajamu,[19] concerned with portraiture and documentary. There were shared positions between practitioners: the insistence on the 'political' use of the term 'black', for instance, to embrace African, Afro-Caribbean, East Asian, South Asian, West Asian, and for a time, what would now be described as Latino/a subject-positions, emphasized a willingness to deploy an 'umbrella' term without disregarding the specificities of the interests of different racial and ethnic affiliations. The liveliness of the tension in such circumstances can be seen with the emergence of the term 'Afro-Asian', which came to be used alongside 'black' (Araeen 1991: 19). Questions of gender, nation and sexuality were also addressed in respect of the politics of resistance. Difference could be articulated in terms of subject-positions set out in those terms. However, it remains important to emphasize the ways in which, with the exception of lens-based media – photography and film – subject-positions as constituted through different art practices were never fully articulated. The 'black painter', 'black sculptor', and 'black print-maker' were not elaborated as subject-positions in the way that the 'black photographer' and 'black film-maker' were. The politics of resistance, working through a representational modality that emphasized the resolving image of 'the black artist', not only failed to do the work to draw out those other subject-positions; they actively stood in its way.

Albeit difficult to grasp from a twenty-first century standpoint, the 1990s context for cultural production among artists associated with migrational cultures in the UK and, to a certain extent, in the USA, was one in which a (white) dominant culture was seen as marginalizing everything judged to stand outside of it. National art

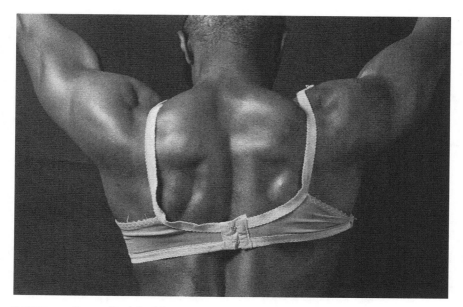

FIGURE 4.3 Ajamu, 'Bodybuilder in a Bra' (1990), silver gelatine print. Collection of the artist. © Ajamu, all rights reserved

institutions were implicated in the normative processes that marked out those with cultural affiliations beyond the dominant culture as other, different, peripheral. Corollary activity could be observed in the USA with cultural commentators observing that issues relating to identity politics were often positioned as matters that should remain outside of the networks forming critical judgements about art. Writing in relation to *The Theater of Refusal* (1993) exhibition, which featured artists such as Renée Green, David Hammons, Adrian Piper and Carrie Mae Weems, the critic Catherine Lord discussed the way in which shows willing to embrace matters relating to race, sexuality and gender often encountered a difficult critical reception in the United States. She referred in some detail to the response to the Whitney Biennial (1993):

> ... the press had more than a month to pronounce its verdict on the Whitney Biennial. It was worse than usual. The show had been assigned not to a committee but to a chief curator who chose to focus on the idea of 'sexual, ethnic and gendered subjects' and included fewer artists and noticeably fewer white men than the norm. The result caused what the critics ... agreed was a 'critical riot'.
>
> *(Lord 1993: 23)*

The positing of the Whitney Biennial as 'issue-heavy' and 'missing the pleasure principle' (Lord 1993) underlines the ways in which art practices that had been developed to counter the effects of dominant culture were systematically delegitimized: the domain of the political was consistently placed in opposition to the space of aesthetic pleasure. By imposing such a false dichotomy, the critical establishment was able to refuse the concerns of artists working around sexual, ethnic and gendered issues, suggesting that they were not engaging in the legitimate preoccupations of art practice.

The failure of national art museums in the UK, such as Tate, to legitimize the work of black artists, in general, and those associated with the Black Arts Movement, in particular, became the focus of constant critique among such artists as well as the theoretical practitioners working alongside them. The target of such critique was not only the question of collection but also, through the politics of representation, the issue of recognition more broadly. It was agreed that black and Asian artists formed part of British society and history. The history of British art would never be accurately and fairly represented without their inclusion. Such arguments were articulated as an insistence that the work of black artists should be placed in a wider context of mainstream art production in the UK. It was a call that, for some time, went unheeded. Practitioners, such as Rasheed Araeen, advocated the contextualisation of black artists' work in terms of interventions in the advancement of British modernism. His approach was to consistently question why this was not taking place, as well as to point out the costs of such omissions: 'why are black or Afro-Asian artists generally invisible or/and excluded from modern discourse of art history, even when the cultural plurality of our society is recognized?' (Araeen 1991: 19). Araeen's critique underlined the failure to locate black or Afro-Asian art practice at the heart of modernism.

Araeen saw such failures in terms of the inability to recognize the black or Afro-Asian artist as a modern subject whose predicament directly expressed the contradictions and impossibilities of modernity itself. He wrote that, 'black or Afro-Asian artists are removed from the authentic space or experience of the modern age. As a result, all signs of modernity in their work become *in*-authentic representations, making it almost impossible to understand the real significance of their work in their broad social and historical contexts' (Araeen 1991: 19). Such misrecognition of the complex modernity of the subjectivity of black and Afro-Asian artists continued as a wilful refusal to reconsider the constitution of modernity in respect of postcolonial experience. Time and again, national art institutions demonstrated their reluctance to accept that modernism could be expressed as a critical response to modernity in terms that were not already known and acknowledged by dominant culture.

The importance of Araeen's intervention was that it sat alongside a series of practices emphasizing the constitution of the subjectivity of the other as critical to an understanding of migrational cultures. Stuart Hall's notion of 'enunciation' also provided an example of the ways in which the migrational experience called upon the migrating subject to develop ever new and ever more elaborate means of constructing a subject-position or identity: retelling the past, refiguring and, to some extent, mythologizing as a means of survival (Hall 1994: 394). Such construction was not seen as direct or simple, 'who speaks, and the subject who is spoken of, are never identical' (Hall 1994: 392). Rather, the emphasis was on the complex process through which subject-positions had to be negotiated:

> Identity is not as transparent or unproblematic as we think. Perhaps instead of thinking of identity as an already accomplished fact, which the new cultural practices then represent, we should think instead of identity as a 'production' which is never complete, always in process, and always constituted within, not outside, representation.
>
> *(Hall 1994: 392)*

Such nuanced strategies as 'enunciation' were, however, also associated with a wider range of cultural production, such as music and literature, as well as the visual arts. While Stuart Hall associated his rendition of enunciation with lens-based media – such as new Caribbean cinema and the photo-work of Caribbean-British photographer Armet Francis – others, such as Paul Gilroy, focused on the potential of music (Gilroy 1991), while writers, such as Jacob Ross (1988) stressed the importance of literature.

In such terms, a resistance to dominant culture was advocated, alongside the call for attention to be placed on the complex and contradictory ways in which those engaged in migrational cultures developed practices to facilitate their inhabitation of difficult, sometimes oppressive, conditions. An advance was made, then, on the 1980s exhortations for resistance. Practice came to the fore. However, there was still a need to distinguish art practice as a self-subjectifying strategy from art-making as an institutional network practice. Category errors were made in not insisting on such a distinction and thereby not allowing distinct modalities of thought around the different sets of practices to develop.

Thinking beyond the mid-1990s brought to the fore an emphasis on movement between places as an important aspect of migration cultures. Britain's post-imperial complex was seen by Gilroy as informing its practices on a political, social and cultural level (Gilroy 2004). However, some of the national cultural institutions in post-imperial Britain, such as Tate, failed to recognize the need to engage with post-colonial migrational culture. Such a failure came from a wilful misrecognition of the significance of a set of cultures that contributed to the constitution of the conditions of modernity within which those cultural institutions operated. Continued misrecognition, undervaluing the production of cultural value and form within the arts practices associated with migrational peoples were contiguous with the failures to address the conditions of liberation struggles in Britain's colonies. Such issues cannot be discounted as marginal or political or tangential to the aims of museums. Disengagement with such matters meant that the conditions of decolonization in Britain itself were barely grasped and never clearly articulated through its national cultural institutions.

Misrecognition of the realities of Britain's post-colonial condition remained in marked contrast to the expression of Britain's imperial grandeur articulated through cultural institutions such as London's Great Exhibition of 1851 and, of course, Tate itself. Tate's turn to aesthetic modernism in the post-imperial period was a reaction to the historical conditions in which the institution saw the nation as being situated in the post-war, post-colonial era. Conventional art history, for example, cited the two World Wars as drivers for establishing the modernist paradigm, as Amy Dempsey wrote in her comments on the rise of abstract expressionism, 'the Depression and World War II had led to a loss of faith in prevailing ideologies and the artistic styles associated with them' (Dempsey 2002: 189).

The movement within modernism was towards, 'the artist's commitment to the act of creation in the face of continual choice, tying their work to the prevailing climate of the immediate post-war era, in which a painting was not merely an object but a record of the existential struggle with feeling, responsibility and self-definition' (Dempsey 2002: 189). The insularity of the modernist aesthetic, championed by national art institutions, such as Tate, in the decades following World War II, was not, however, complemented by an active engagement with the conditions that made modernism itself possible. Continued institutional disengagement from migrational cultural formations was not only as the result of the modernist tendency to disengage with immediate social context in order to connect with a deeper reality on a higher level. It also acted as an alibi for the institution's consistent misrecognitions of contemporaneous social and political conditions.

The practices of black and Afro-Asian artists could not align themselves with curatorial and museum networks, from which they were largely excluded. This was partly because of the intransigence of such networks, transfixed by a rigid understanding of the modernist paradigm. It was also partly because of the rhetoric that accompanied the artwork of black and Afro-Asian artists – a rhetoric that became too closely associated with 'political' agendas to enter the necessary curatorial and critical networks, even if such networks had been open, which they were not. Prevailing perspectives among black and Afro-Asian artists set a tone for the rhetoric. Artist Eddie Chambers, for instance, sought to emphasize the role of artists associated with the Black Arts Movement in the struggles against the racism of the established British institutions. The arguments he drew upon rested principally on representation through the assertion of racialized difference under the umbrella of singular terms, such as 'black community' and 'black experience':

> I would define Black art as produced by black people largely and specially for the black audience, and which, in terms of its content, addresses black experience ... The function of Black art ... was to confront the white establishment for its racism, as much as to address the black community in its struggle for human equality. I think Black art has still that role to play.
>
> *(Araeen and Chambers 1988/9: 52)*

A contrary perspective was offered by artist Rasheed Araeen in his insistence on the need to ensure that black artists ought to be granted equal access to national and other mainstream institutions: 'The institutions of this country must belong to all the people, and if they are dominated by whites only then it is the right of black artists to demand their share of the pie' (Araeen and Chambers 1988/9: 53). The assertion of the 'right of black artists' alongside the notion that one could meaningfully speak of 'their share of the pie' remained rooted in a different political position from that advocated by Chambers. However, Araeen's views still relied on the substitution of varied interests of different visual arts practitioners for the political category of 'black artist'. The rhetoric advanced by the Black Arts Movement showed that it, too, suffered from a set of misrecognitions – namely the misrecognition of the different needs and interests of the practitioners associated with it. Equally, the misrecognition of key issues on the part of institutions meant that the rich political and intellectual discourse populated by the artists of the British Black Arts Movement could not have brought about the changes that they insisted were necessary within national art institutions such as Tate. For, in terms of the way that Tate operated, the production of the significant cultural idioms of modernism was never solely a political or even intellectual process. Instead, it needed to be understood as part of a socioeconomic complex, involving networks of patrons, dealers, gallerists and collectors. Such complex networks remained inaccessible to the political lobbying of the Black Arts Movement and indifferent, at least for a time, to the intellectual rationale of post-colonial theorists.

It was only when black and Afro-Asian artists connected with international curatorial networks that national cultural institutions in the UK, such as Tate, began to take note. This happened mainly through the emergence of internationalist perspectives among cultural practitioners associated with migrational cultures. The development of nuanced takes on issues of identity, such as mutability, among visual arts practitioners, took place against a curatorial backdrop pointing towards a broader geographical perspective among those organizing exhibitions. The phrase, 'new internationalism', for instance, became a fiercely contested term during the mid-1990s. It signalled, however, a stronger articulation of a global perspective. Exhibitions such as Sunil Gupta's *Disrupted Borders* at the Ikon Gallery in Birmingham in 1994, with its emphasis on art practices drawn from across the globe, were cited as exposing the inability of modernism to encompass a broader constituency of art-makers and viewers of art (Hylton 2007: 109). With such new internationalist approaches, the aim seemed to be to focus on a transnational outlook, seeing cultural production as emerging from a series of interrelated discourses emanating from several sources across the world. The effectiveness of such an outlook did not go uncontested, however. Criticism, for instance, crystallized around the founding of the Institute of International Visual Arts (inIVA) in London in 1994. According to curator and historian, Richard Hylton, questions arose as to 'how applicable the term "new internationalism" could be … to a rapidly internationalizing artworld' (Hylton 2007: 113). The exponents of new internationalism were left open to the accusation that they were producing no more than a 'bureaucracy of cultural theory'.[20]

However, the global economic drivers, increasing the circulation of artworks through ever more numerous and ever more accessible international biennales, meant that new internationalism's agenda coincided with the growth of internationalized networks. Exhibitions, such as *Mirage: Enigmas of Race, Difference and Desire* (1995), curated jointly by Gilane Tawadros of inIVA and Emma Dexter of ICA, featured artists drawn from the US, the UK and Martinique. The insistence on working on an international platform, reconstituting an international discourse around migrational issues with visual arts practice at its heart contributed to the integration of black and Afro–Asian cultural practices in Britain into a global network of art practice. Such integration culminated in 2002, when artists, critics, curators and theorists working around issues of migration came together via the international art event *Documenta XI*. The event reshaped and reconsolidated thinking on migrational issues across a range of cultural practices at the turn of the new millennium, contributing to a refocusing of debates that had taken place in Britain, North America, the Caribbean, Africa, Asia and Europe in respect of issues of contemporary migrational culture. It is interesting to note that artists, such as Zarina Bhimji and Mona Hatoum, who had also participated in exhibitions associated with the Black Arts Movement of the 1980s, such as the *Dislocations* show held in 1987 (Kettle's Yard Gallery, Cambridge) appeared in the *Documenta* event.

One influential idea circulating within *Documenta XI* was the notion of 'creolization', elaborated by the event's artistic director, Okwui Enwezor (Enwezor 2002). His rendition of it emphasized a polycentric or multicentred model of contemporary experience in many parts of the world. Such polycentrism embraced the idea that those forming part of migration cultures carried with them a multicentred worldview.

According to 'creolization', individuals built such worldviews knowing that they could only inhabit particular places in full consciousness of other centres in the world. Creolization, then, put forward a model of migration in which migrational peoples carry with themselves an awareness of a multicentred, interdependent world. The idea of creolization was embedded in the structure of *Documenta XI* in the form of the themes of the event's five 'platforms' or main features. The platforms took place in different continents: Africa, the Caribbean and Europe.[21] Each continent provided a location to stage different debates. The programme, thereby, benefited not only from an actualization of the rhetorics of 'de-centring' associated with post-colonial thinking, it also provided a means of giving effect to broader international dissemination. Visual artists, such as the film-maker Isaac Julien, discussed the importance of creolization within works, such as his film *Paradise Omeros* (2002). Although 'creolization' was specifically formulated in respect of experiences of the Caribbean, it has been taken as a model for analysing the experience of those forming part of migrational cultures across the world. As Enwezor put it: 'In recent years, through waves of migration and displacements Creolization has emerged as a dominant modality of contemporary living practices, shaping patterns of dwelling that are crossed and differentiated by massive flows of images and cultural symbols expressed through material culture and language' (Enwezor 2002: 51)

The flows of images and cultural symbols across a multicentred world rendered creolization a significant theme for national art institutions and their relationships with their audiences. Models that underline an interrelatedness between the national territories with which migrational peoples engage became crucial. It is with notions of 'creolization' and the *Documenta XI* that issues relating to identity and difference within the British context resonated with critical issues surrounding migration in a global setting. Through such moves, a series of ideas and practices found another platform, inserting themselves into debates that *commented upon but did not activate* the politics of the post-imperial context of contemporary Britain. The cleaving of political commentary from political action was a critical step. It announced the end of one formulation of the cultural politics in Britain, in terms of the Black Arts Movement and those associated with it. At the same time, it heralded the recognition of a number of artists that the Black Art Movement had championed for some time.

The move to an internationalist approach allowed cultural practitioners to bypass national cultural institutions, such as Tate, on their way to taking up positions on international platforms like *Documenta XI*. However, it left the inner workings of the national museum intact. The wilful misrecognition of sociopolitical contexts on the part of cultural institutions could be surpassed by reference to such notions as creolization but they could not have been entirely undone. Nor could they be unravelled through the political and intellectual advocacy advanced by artists, writers and theorists associated with the Black Arts Movement; nor by thinkers aligned with post-colonial thought more broadly. There was a need to understand more clearly the mechanisms and workings of the cultural institutions that continued to generate the disengagement with migrational cultural formation. The critiques of such institutions as regards, for instance, the limited understanding of the conditions of modernity, were perceptive. The analyses were cogent. However, the advocacy of institutional change in national arts institutions could only be strengthened by more detailed and specific accounts of how such institutions actually functioned. Macrological approaches, discussing national art institutions in terms of their societal roles or their relation to varying cultural formations remained necessary but not sufficient. A detailed micrology was also necessary to facilitate a deeper understanding of the institutional environment in which decisions were made, strategies were formulated, policies were implemented and people were either promoted or sidelined. An understanding of museum practice, involving case studies looking at the ways in which people interacted with the institution, pushing at its limits and exploring new possibilities, needed to sit alongside the critical analysis of the museum's societal role. Such an approach takes this study beyond the critical framework that has emerged out of visual arts practice and cultural theory over the past 30 years. As the critical gaze sits in the body of the museum, inhabiting its corridors of power, as well as its cafés and car-parks, a different understanding of the interrelation between the national arts institution and the networks in which it is situated begins to emerge.

5

TATE ENCOUNTERS: BRITISHNESS AND VISUAL CULTURES, THE TRANSCULTURAL AUDIENCE

The targeting of groups considered to be representative of the composition of society as a whole, yet under-represented in the museum's core audience is essentially a problem with the ways in which social categorization is used and interpreted by the museum. For museums, the problem arises in the conflation of statistical methods of socioeconomic and ethnic classification, with the historical notion of the public and civic realm. A further problem arises in the conflation of statistical categories with individual identities. Measuring the composition of core audiences repeatedly shows that art museums are overwhelmingly populated by people classified as white and of the higher percentiles of education and income. As a result of this stubborn fact, cultural policy in Britain, as elsewhere, has focused upon encouraging museums to find ways of achieving a greater diversity of their audiences in order to bring them more into line with regional and national demographics and in doing so produce a more inclusive culture. The means of achieving greater diversity of audience has been to target black and minority ethnic (BME) groups in the belief that if the museum can break down the initial barriers to access over the long term, then their audiences will change. However, the experience, as Tate Britain has demonstrated, is that such targeting measures over a long period of time have done little to change their core audience demographic. The Tate Encounters research project set out to understand in more depth the barriers for BME access and on the basis of its fieldwork, in talking to museum professionals and student participants, came to the preliminary conclusion that the attempt to realize the aims of cultural policy by targeting policies not only instrumentalized groups of people, but also essentialized them on the basis of racialized and ethnicized categories. More importantly the research found that such targeting on the basis of BME categorization was resisted and ultimately rejected by student participants as a basis for defining identities.

Over the course of the Tate Encounters research project, the collaboration with London South Bank University facilitated visits to Tate Britain of more than

600 first-year students who participated in documenting their experience of the art museum either through completing surveys, writing essays or uploading images and text to an intranet site. For a group of 12 students, it also meant a sustained ethnographic encounter over the following two years in which they undertook a larger scale set of media projects, which were screened to a public audience and discussed in the Duveens Studio at Tate Britain at the end of the fieldwork period in March 2009. The data collected over the fieldwork period was considerable. The essays and surveys helped the research understand the broader social profile of the student group. The essays in particular gave a strong portrait of the 2008 cohort's initial reactions to the spaces and displays of Tate Britain. However, it was the group of 12 students who elected to stay with the project over the following two years who provided the research with invaluable in-depth understandings upon which the analysis of contemporary modes of transcultural spectatorship has subsequently been developed. On the basis of an evolving and reflexive relationship in the ethnographic encounter with the 12 students, the research team took the decision, nine months into the project, to define the student participation as that of co-researchers. Their questions and responses to the research and to Tate Britain as an integral part of the overall analytical response. To explain why extracts from the material produced by the co-researchers is reproduced here is to rehearse a number of understandings about the ways in which Tate's 'missing audience', specifically the BME category, was operating in cultural diversity discourse. Including extracts from the co-researchers' media production also provides an understanding of what it is possible to produce, given permission to take photographs and film in the galleries. Both the framing of missing audiences and the use of media in museums are part of the larger problematic with which the book deals. More specifically, both issues formed the initial problematic the Tate Encounters research project attempted to grasp.

During the very first stages of recruiting volunteer students, through presentations and workshops at Tate Britain, the project was met with considerable hostility and resistance, as it soon became apparent that in initially titling the project 'Tate Encounters: Britishness and Visual Culture: Black and Asian Identities', it had fallen prey to reproducing the same racialized categories of cultural diversity policy that it was interrogating. The project thereby, inherently repeated the same practice of 'targeting' that characterized the marketing techniques of the museum. All of the project's early engagements with voluntary student participants pointed to the fact that they resisted being addressed through, as well as constituted by, race and ethnicity categories. The deep resistance from the students to be hailed and interpellated through notions of a fixed identity constructed around categories of race and ethnicity continued to be demonstrated through the students own data generation. Such refusals were also evident in the ethnographic films focusing on the students' everyday life worlds, which insisted on a recognition of the fluidity of identity alongside the primacy of subjectivity in relation to forging meaning in and through the visual. As the students' auto-ethnographic research also revealed, this emphasis on the fluidity of identity arose out of patterns of transmigration from Africa and greater

FIGURE 5.1 The co-researchers, Tate Britain, March 2009. Back Row: Patrick Tubridy, Laura Kunz, Tracey Jordan, Robbie Sweeny, Adekunle Detokunbo-Bello, Mary Ampomah, Deep Rajput, Nicola Johnson Oyejobi, Aminah Borg-Luck; Front row: Cinta Esmel-Pamies, Jacqueline Ryan and Dana Mendonca

movement within the expanded European Union that were distinct from the patterns of migration that essentially underpinned the formation of UK cultural diversity policy – that of post-war migration from West Africa, the Caribbean and South Asia.

The one criteria of participation, that the student or their family must have migrated to Britain in the last three generations, produced a global set of migrational journeys with family ties and roots from Malaysia, Bangladesh, Latvia, Ukraine, Norway, Finland, Poland, Eire, Spain, Nigeria, Ghana and the Caribbean. All the engagement with participants on the project indicated that the social categories and discourses around race and ethnicity, which developed with the patterns of post–war migration to Britain from West Africa, the Caribbean and South Asia, no longer fitted with the reality of global migration for an aspirational group in education.

For the Tate Encounters research, the problem with demographic typologies was not only registered as a problem in cultural diversity policy, but was also connected to the ways in which British and European continental sociology had framed the study of immigration. As Mike Phillips records in his account of the early developmental stage of the AHRC proposal (Phillips 2007), a core set of working assumptions regarding the fixed identity of individuals were inherent within this body of research. Those assumptions failed to recognize the fluidity of cultural and social capital within contemporary culture, as well as, more specifically, the fluidity of identity created by the migrational experience. Furthermore, the scientizing gaze of sociology, which underpinned most of this research, not only freeze-framed and silenced the migrant as an object of study, but also as a static entity, defined by post-colonial narratives of departure and arrival, rather than the free-moving, transmigrational individual defined by an experience of subjectivity.

It became clear in the early discussion of possible academic research collaborators that in approaching questions of diasporic audiences, different but contemporary approaches were necessary: first, a knowledge base that could trace relations between the life worlds of participants and the museum was required; second, a field of study was needed to recognize the specificity of the visual, not as defined by the category of art, but as a practice of viewing that connected the visual of the everyday with the practice of viewing and spectatorship inside the art museum. One of the major ways in which sociological research had theorized identity, group belonging and social composition in the second half of the twentieth century was through the prism of the concepts of social and cultural capital.

Bourdieu's (1977) notion of cultural capital was important in demonstrating how culture was not a determined reflection of economic power but an active arena defined by 'habitus' and 'field', in which individuals negotiated their agency through the social structure. Bourdieu extended the concept of economic capital, derived from Marx, to include symbolic operations and practices within the family, civil society and, crucially, in education. He did so in order to explain the unequal distribution and possession of material and cultural resources alongside the positioning of identity and subjectivity that followed. Within the academic expansion of the study of sociology taking place in the 1960s and 1970s, Bourdieu's modelling of cultural capital provided a powerful explanation of the rooted educational and cultural privilege enjoyed by the French bourgeoisie and the British upper classes. His work was particularly convincing for the political cultures of Paris and London and more significantly, however, Bourdieu's work also offered European post-war democratic and meritocratic governments a model of social reform on the basis that cultural capital could be acquired and could, therefore, produce upward social mobility as well as social change in the rise of the meritocracy.

Bourdieu discusses three forms of cultural capital in terms of individual competence, objects and institutions. The mobilization of understandings of cultural capital led many educationalists in both the US and Britain to consider how alternative or radical pedagogies might extend the acquisition of dominant forms of cultural capital to working class and migrational groups as well as extending historical forms of know-how, or 'really useful knowledge' drawn from the experience of community and labour (Giroux 1983). The use of cultural capital had also been mobilized to account for the social class fractions that attended museums and those that didn't on the basis of Bourdieu's significant work, *Distinction* (1979) – a work that was subsequently applied by DiMaggio (Powell and DiMaggio 1991), to the experience of North America.

In the 2008 cohort of students who attended Tate Britain and Tate Modern as part of Tate Encounters, the utilization of all three of Bourdieu's notions of cultural capital can be seen in their encounter with the museum. The cultural capital of the students is demonstrated in their individual competences, while the cultural capital of Tate is constituted in the objects of collection and its institutional structure. However, while it is possible to explain some of the students' responses in terms of whether they possessed certain forms of cultural capital or not with respect to the museum, the wider utility and value placed upon such observations sociologically did not easily fit with the students' own assessments of Tate Britain. This was particularly the case in relationship to their sense of how cultural value now operated, i.e. participation was not about learning to like art nor acquiring the habit of attending museums.

The 2008 cohort of students who completed the questionnaire and essay comprise a qualified representative snapshot of one of three student cohorts who were enlisted on the periphery of the project over the fieldwork period and from whom the co-researchers were drawn. The analysis of the questionnaire is instructive in terms of its fit with contemporary social and cultural classification of British Higher Education students in post-1992 British universities (formerly polytechnics), and in terms of core and targeted audience groups for Tate Britain.

Of the respondents, 76 per cent had British nationality with the majority of non-British students coming from European countries (18 per cent) while other non-British students made up the remainder. When considering the wider framework of migration, 46 per cent of one or both parents were born outside of the UK. This was significant in relationship to one of the two criteria of long-term supported participation used in the project; the other being that the participant was the first in their immediate family to attend university.

Nearly half of the cohort had families with migrational experience or had migrated themselves for educational purposes. The questionnaire did not ask students to

British	Western Europe	Central Europe	British Caribbean	British African	British SE Asian	British Asian	Other	Other
	Sweden	Croatia	Jamaica	Zambia	India	Malaysia	Turkey	Australia
	Germany	Lithuania	Cuba	Sierra Leone	Bangladesh	Hong Kong	Israel	NZ
	Denmark	Slovakia	Barbados	Congo		Thailand	Iran	Ireland
	Finland	Estonia	St. Lucia	Zimbabwe		Vietnam		
	France	Poland	Grenada	South Africa				
	Greece	Romania		Ghana				
	Spain	Serbia		Algeria				
	Italy	Czech Republic						
	Portugal	Hungary						
		Ukraine						
		Russia						
107	19	19	13	9	9	5	3	5
54%	9%	9%	6%	4%	4%	2%	1%	2%

Parents born in UK	107	54%
Parents born outside UK	88	46%

FIGURE 5.2 Chart of migrational backgrounds of LSBU student participants.
Source: Tate Encounters Student Questionnaire, administered to 220 first-year students at Tate Britain, October 2008

designate a racial or ethnic classification, although interestingly of the 6 per cent of students with one or both parents of Caribbean descent, most self-designated as black British, while a small portion of students whose parents were born in Britain self-designated as white British. The snapshot that emerges is of a student group that reflects continual migration with two historically distinct patterns: first, migration from former British colonies that led to British urban settlement from the 1950s; second, recent economic migration associated with European Union and its enlargement in the post-Soviet period. This is a picture in which migrational family and cultural experience becomes of equal standing to that of 'indigenous' British family and cultural experience. Taken together with the parental occupation distribution, the profile of this cohort of students can be defined as both culturally mobile and socially aspirational. A situation in which education is negotiated as both gatekeeper and instrument of advancement.

In terms of the second form of cultural capital – cultural capital as personal competence – the cohort clearly expressed a range of differences in habits and tastes. What is more interesting and more obvious is the commonality of popular media and the marginality of the traditional high arts. They were a group comfortable with and confident in contemporary media environments while being uncomfortable in formal cultural institutional settings. Tate Modern was more popular for this group precisely because it is less like a traditional museum and more like many of the ambient spaces of shopping. The cultural competences of this group, as registered by the questionnaire, are perfectly in line with the ways in which they have chosen to invest in higher education. This was a cohort aspiring to be creative technical media practitioners and administrators. In this equation, art history and the art museum were on the periphery of their interests.

In his book *The Long Revolution*, Raymond Williams (1965: 42) makes the point that for art to exist at all it must be actively transmitted and actively received. His stress on the active reception necessary to complete what we ordinarily think of as the autonomous work of the artist, was a new emphasis, although he was not alone in wanting an account of art that was fundamentally social and material. More than 40 years later, the effort to fully understand and account for the social process of making, collecting, exhibiting and experiencing art remains a complex task, if not in theory then most certainly in the practices of the art museum. In Tate Encounters, the research strove to understand the participation of students and in particular the contributions of 12 student co-researchers within a framework in which viewing works of art was an active and extended 'social' process.

In understanding how Tate Encounters finally positioned the co-researchers and their contributions, Williams' perspective on the creative process is apposite. For Williams, while talented individuals compose and play music, write or make artefacts, to mention only the most established forms, they do so from within a general process of discovery and creative communication based upon human physiological, historical and social development. More than this, Williams wants to insist that even though the artist has come to be defined as an exceptional individual, the art s/he produces is the outcome and product of countless individuals and groups who form the whole process in which exceptional communication takes place. However, the intellectual project of Williams and Bourdieu were formed in the period of the end of Britain and France's empires caused in part by the struggles of former colonies for national independence. The local European cultures that both men were attempting to understand, in progressive and ultimately socialist terms, were still strongly bound by the nation-state. This led to the problematic perspective that progressive liberation struggles were first and foremost considered as arising from the homegrown seed of liberty, arising out of British and French historic forms. The independence struggles and colonial wars liberation became marginalized within those perspectives. Williams' argument for progressive social change, based only upon the recognition of a common British culture, was thus limited. This is the situation in which Appadurai (1990) developed his account of ethnoscapes, mediascapes, technoscapes, financescapes and ideoscapes in order to address what he defined as:

> The central problem of today's global interactions is the tension between cultural homogenization and cultural heterogenization. A vast array of empirical facts could be brought to bear on the side of the 'homogenization' argument, and much of it has come from the left end of the spectrum of media studies ... and some from other, less appealing, perspectives ... Most often, the homogenization argument subspeciates into either an argument about Americanization, or an argument about 'commoditization', and very often the two arguments are closely linked. What these arguments fail to consider is that at least as rapidly as forces from various metropolises are brought into new societies they tend to become indigenized in one or other way: this is true of music and housing styles as much as it is true of science and terrorism, spectacles and constitutions.
>
> *(Appadurai 1990: 295)*

Williams' emphasis upon a 'social' model of artistic production, can be retained but expressed in the newer terms of the entry of the individual into global mediascapes by virtue of interactive and personalized media. A 'social' or as it might now be put, interactive model can be applied to the practice-based work of the Tate Encounters research in which the media productions of the co-researcher were understood as the counterpart to how meaning is encoded in the National Collection of British Art and its display in the art museum. The framing of the co-researchers' practice and its outcomes in a globally 'social' account provides a basis for understanding how the processes of response and dialogue with Tate Britain took place. It also shows how the research came to understand them in terms of transvisuality.

The somewhat vexed question of the status of art or media practice as research within the academy can be usefully related to the work of the co-researchers. The initial paradigm for using media practice was as a means of recording participants' encounters with the museum. However, over an extended period of time, the research team came to understand the co-researchers' media productions as a more sophisticated process of response to both the art museum and the research questions.

Through a complex set of theoretical moves and practical negotiation with the co-researchers, their media projects gained the status of a parallel research process with definitive research outcomes. It could rightfully be said about the co-researchers' media practice that, while it began as a practice without a theory, it ended in a theory of practice.

The co-researchers' media practices, carried out over the fieldwork period, had been established as the form and language of participation on the basis of the pervasiveness of media encoding in everyday life. The familiarity that young people have with digital recording devices also played a part in the thinking. Media practice thus constituted the means of sustaining participation. It also, over the duration of the research, became a means of developing greater dialogue while creating a pool of shared knowledge.

This process of constitution as a co-researcher demanded of the students an equally rigorous process of self-reflexivity. They enacted this through the project's intranet, in which they documented two key elements: their engagement with Tate Encounters; and their connection of such engagement to their own life worlds outside the museum. From this process, they were also invited to submit proposals of auto-ethnographic accounts, from which they identified their own questions of practice and research in relation to Tate Britain. These proposals were subsequently shared and discussed in a series of 12 workshops. Further reflections and contributions were also captured on the intranet and published in various formats of film; photography; and writing – all of which appeared in a series on online 'editions' that also carried the working papers of the project (*Tate Encounters*, editions 1–6).[1] Within this selected group of twelve students, five students also enlisted the support of their families to extend their own enquiries into the value and place of Tate Britain in their families' life worlds. These were documented through film, photography and sound recordings with the directorial support of Sarah Thomas, the team's visual anthropologist. The project used digital media technologies as the default mode through which participants documented their experience. The final productions of their accounts were screened as part of the programme 'Research in Process', a month long project programme of public discussion at Tate Britain, during which each of the co-researchers further reflected upon their media productions and involvement in the Tate Encounters project.[2]

From the second period of fieldwork in 2008, all remaining student participants were offered the opportunity to become co-researchers on the basis of proposing a practice-led research project, which the research team would support. This was communicated in a proposal feedback form in October 2008.

> Thank you for your continued participation in the project and for submitting a project proposal for the research display. The display will be held at Tate Britain in Gallery 62 between February and April 2009. We have decided upon a format for the gallery, which will be combination of a TV studio, Video screening and Online research office. We have thought about how your proposals will fit into this format (see Tate Encounters Intranet for details). The

display will mark the end of the practical project and we are now trying to bring all of the different parts of the research together. To this end we are trying to connect your own investigations with that of the overall project and our response to your proposals is a first step in this direction. We would encourage you to look again at our research questions and see to what extent they match up with your own encounter or whether you have posed different questions. We aim to interview you again, during the research display so that we can discuss the journey we have all taken on the project.

A further attempt at defining the approach was made by the principal investigator in February 2009. This aimed at deepening the understanding of the ways in which the co-researchers' own investigations at Tate Britain fitted with the overall research programme. The strands of investigation and the variety of ethnographic methods employed were also further elaborated. The principal investigator wrote:

It is my view that the co-researchers' projects achieve the status of research when their projects are narrated and in dialogue with our questions. It is the 'co' preface to researcher that we need to concentrate upon now because it stresses that sense in which their practice is entailed in a research process, not that it stands independently as research. It is in the co-dependency of the relationship between participants and investigators that it is possible to define the outlines of a research process. This can be expressed as follows [see Figure 5.3]:

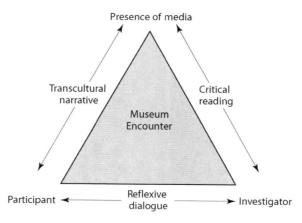

FIGURE 5.3 Diagram of reflexive methodology. Tate Encounters Research Team 2009

The above description of the process of student participation had crucially been extended to include the process of registering their reflections upon the research itself as part of the encounter with Tate Britain. This was a turning point in understanding that the participants were not the subjects of research but equal collaborators in defining the objects of attention. This understanding was expressed in a further response by a co-investigator in January 2009:

> The visual media interventions of the Tate Encounters' co-researchers can be seen as points of departure within the investigation. As such, they do not respond to questions outlined within the research literatures from which the project emerged. Indeed, one could argue that the co-researchers' works escape a responsive mode altogether. Rather, they can be seen as an opening up of parallel routes of investigation as well as a deepening of the lines of enquiry that became more evident as the research progressed.

In rehearsing how 'the museum might see itself reflected' in the co-researchers' productions, questions raised within the intellectual field of visual cultures were introduced. Most significantly the issue of 'transvisuality' as a mode of address was put forward. Transvisuality had been generated by the questioning of the relationship between Britishness and migration. Such thinking was reflected in the same internal working paper:

> The role of visuality in the constitution of subjectivity becomes rendered as the starting point for a series of questions that challenge our assumptions about subject-constitution. In such terms, visuality cannot, for the time being, at least, act as the basis for a series of programmed strategies of engagement. As regards the former, transvisuality offers an opportunity for questioning the framing of modes of address.

The final piece of the jigsaw of theorizing the media practices of the co-researchers and its role in the research process came in questioning how their productions could be staged within Tate Britain. The audience would be made up of art museum-goers as well as academic professionals, alongside an extended audience of the co-researchers' families and friends. Such a staging of the research results had been written into the research funding application and Tate Britain had agreed to hold a display in the Duveens Studio (Gallery 62) in the final year of the project. Questions emerged such as: *What form would this display take? Who was it for?* and *How would it be understood?* Those queries formed the basis of an extensive series of internal discussions, which revolved around wanting to avoid putting the co-researchers in a position of a learning group. It was also important to avoid their media productions being seen as artwork. The question became one of how to stage research about the art museum in the art museum without allowing it to become co-opted into the art museum's forms and categories of display. The solution found was the staging of the month-long series of recorded interviews and public discussions in the Research-in-Process programme. This took place in the Duveens Studio during March 2009. It consisted of a four-week public programme in which the major themes of the research were presented and discussed with Tate staff as well as invited external speakers.[3] Through the Research-in-Process event, the co-researchers' participation in the research was able to be understood as a progressive dialogic staging and

Co-researchers productions			
Name	Course	Project title	Output
Aminah Borg-Luck	BA (Hons) Media and Society	Tate Encounters and Finnish Roots Lie Back and Think of England A Little Bit of Hamalainen	Video (3.54) Edition 1 Video (23.04) Edition 4 Video (20.19) Archive
Adekunle Detoknbo-Bello	Research Degree	Nollywood Springs Up in London	Video (15.46) Archive
Dana Mendonca	BA (Hons) Digital Photography	What Does Britishness Mean To Me Please Tick the Appropriate Box Donate to Tate	Text. Edition 2 Image/Text. Edition 3 Video (8.41) Archive
Jacqueline Ryan	BA (Hons) Arts Management	Travel to Kerela Trading Cultures	Image/Text. Edition 1 Video (13.11)
Nicola Johnson Oyejobi	BA (Hons) Criminology	Tate and Me	Video (14.08)
Patrick Tubridy	BA (Hons) Digital Photography	Tate Encounter Men Learn to Fly Reignited Memories, Ellen Terry as Lady Macbeth The Process of Identity Homemade	Video slideshow. Edition 1 Video slideshow (3.40) E2 Image/Text. Edition 3 Image/Text. Edition 4 Video slideshow (6.13)
Robbie Sweeny	BA (Hons) Digital Photography	This is Tate, But This is Britain Art Imitates Life or Life Imitates Art?	Image/Text. Edition 2 Image/Text. Edition 3
Mary Ampomah	BA (Hons) Media and Society	Talking About Paintings	Video (11.21)
Tracey Jordan	BA (Hons) Arts Management	My Journey to London My Journey to Tate Britain	Text/Video. Edition 1 Video (9.34) Archive
Rebecca Cairns	BA (Hons) Arts Management	My Armenian Grandmother	Video (13.12)
Deep Rajput	BA (Hons) Sociology	On Busta Rhymes via Nigel Henderson Sikhism via Herbert Draper The Last Judgement. John Martin	Audio over still image Archive ditto
Cinta Esmel Pamies	BA (Hons) Arts Management	Avalanche in the Alps. Philip James de Loutherberg Where I Come From the Sky is Brightest Identity Remix at Late at Tate. March 2009	Video (3.50) Archive Image/Text. Edition 1 Photography/Video. Archive

FIGURE 5.4 Chart of co-researchers' productions. Tate Encounters 2009

documentation of their responses to Tate Britain. Artist and writer Raimi Gbadamosi responded directly to the co-researchers and Irit Rogoff, Veronica Sekules and Marquard Smith, academics who have an intellectual investment in thinking about visual culture and museum spectatorship, discussed questions raised by the co-researchers' productions.

In total, 28 media productions were made by the co-researchers and are available on the project's archival website.[4] In what follows, a selected narrative is presented using extracts of the media productions from five of the co-researchers. This is to give the reader a small indication, both of the material itself, as well as of the argument that has been made about the status of the material.

Case study 1

Deep Rajput joined the study in 2008, when he was in the second year of a sociology degree. During his school years, Deep visited Britain's national art institutions in London as part of a series of educational museum trips. Such trips also included visits to non-art institutions, such as London's Science Museum and the British historical institution, the Imperial War Museum. Of South Asian parentage, with a mixed Sikh and Hindu background, Deep described himself as a 'British-born Punjabi'. His family settled in West London, where he grew up. Deep's later occasional visits to museums formed part of his continued engagement with his Sikh heritage, in support of which he visited exhibitions such as *The Art of the Sikh Kingdoms*[5] held at the V&A Museum in London in 1999. Deep's Sikh heritage can be seen as providing a network of engagement with relations to music, such as that of mantra singer Snatam Kaur, as

well as visits to Sikh temples. Alongside such activity, Deep also maintained a relationship to his Hindu heritage. He spoke in terms of connection with images drawn
from Hindu iconography. It remained clear that Deep sought ways of maintaining his
relation to his aspects of both Sikh and Hindu traditions, as these were also embedded
in his family relationships and background. He became a co-researcher on the basis of
proposing to make a series of audio-guides for paintings in the collection. On a very
early first visit to Tate Britain, Deep made a series of comments upon his encounter
in the galleries and possible choices of works for further investigation, which were
noted by the project's new media research assistant, Morten Norbye Halvorsen.

Spaces
  Duveens – likes the feel of the 'oxygen circulating' and the lack of
congestion
  Manton staircase – likes the openness, and the bright colours of the paintings
there. They reminded him of the bright colours of the living room in
American TV series Dharma and Greg, which cheered him up while his leg
was in plaster.
  Room 26 – reminds him of Goldfrapp music videos, esp for 'Ride on White
Horse'.
  Artworks
  Room T6 – Michael Landy – Sweep to Victory – found that the sole of the
Converse shoe depicted related to his fashion tastes.
  Room T5 – Paul Noble – Paul's Palace – Skate boarding half-pipe reminded
him of a skate boarding accident he had, the pins in his legs he has as a result,
and how this affects him when he is trying to sit cross legged for long periods
of time in his Gurdwara (Sikh temple).
  Room T4 – Tacita Dean – The Roaring Forties: Seven Boards in Seven
Days – particularly the one of the choppy seas close up. The kind of thing he would
like to have in his dream house where the dining room would be large with a
long table and have black walls (Gothic-esque) like the one in Evanescence's
music video for the song 'Call Me When You're Sober'.
  (All these 3 are up until 15 Feb 09)
  Room 21 Graham Sutherland OM – Head III – reminds him of Alien the
movie. Henry Moore – King and Queen – reminds him of figures in a Lloyds
bank ad currently on TV. Reg Butler – Woman – The kind of thing he would
'expect to see in Marilyn Manson's house'.
  (This room changes after 22 March 09)
  Room 23 – Nigel Henderson – Stressed Photograph – reminds him of the
'fisheye lens' effect in some music videos he likes such as: Busta Rhymes,
Beastie Boys 'Check It Out' that he saw on The David Letterman show.
  (This room changes after 22 March 09)
  Room 24 – Richard Smith – Slot Machine – reminds him of a trip he made
to Las Vegas, playing on the slot machines and only winning $5 while his
cousin won $45.

(This room changes after 15 March 09)

Room 8 – Cecil Collins – The Poet – reminds him of Sikh belief in the Third Eye and the separation of 'mind' from 'soul'.

William Blake paintings in general. Knew he was also a poet, who had inspired Jim Morrison (of The Doors). Mentioned in particular the songs 'Break on through to the other side' and 'Riders of the Storm'. Mentioned also that Snoop Doggy Dog had done a remix of 'Riders of the Storm', that is used in the computer game 'Need for Speed II'.

Room 9 – James Ward – Gordale Scar – Loves the magnificence of it.

John Martin – The Last Judgement – finds it spiritually relevant, esp the pathways between Heaven and Hell opening up and the suggestion of becoming one with God.

Room 10 – Edward Burne-Jones – The Sleep of Arthur in Avalon – reminds him of the Eminem track 'Like Toy Soldiers' about the futility of rappers who disagree on things killing each other (see E3).

Room 15 – George Frederic Watts – Eve Tempted (triptych) – reminds him of the out of body experiences through meditation that his religion teaches him is possible (although he has never experienced one).

John Brett – The British Channel seen from the Dorsetshire cliffs – likes the serene light and could not guess where in the world it was.

Herbert Draper – The Lament for Icarus – Reminds Deep of a fallen angel, who has tried his best to be an angel but done something wrong, and so fallen to the material world He may have committed one of the Sikh '5 Deadly Passions': Lust, anger, greed, attachment, and pride. He is trying to pray but God is not listening. Instead mermaids are attempting to listen to his lament.

Over subsequent months, Deep made a number of video and audio works based upon a smaller number of works at Tate Britain. The following example is a narration Deep made over a video he recorded showing a painting entitled, 'An Avalanche in the Alps' (1803) by Philip James De Loutherbourg (1740–1812). It is an oil painting and measures 1099 × 1600mm, depicting a moment when an avalanche smashes the bridge crossing a mountain pass. The mountains loom large against the diminished figures of three travellers.

Ok in this small presentation I am going to be discussing the painting by Philip James De Loutherbourg 1740–1812, An Avalanche in the Alps 1803, Oil on canvas. I'm going to give you first of all an overview of the painting itself. It's an incredible work of art, which has been richly framed. Now in my perspective, well in my perception of the work itself, in the way I can relate to it, is basically when I first saw the painting the first thing to cross my mind was exam stress. Now, whenever I go through a time of intense study I just feel I have a mountain to climb and that is how I relate to this painting through that emotion I'm feeling. Now it looks as if there are characters, which appear at the bottom of the painting, which I am going to focus into and give a brief discussion about. For example here we have three characters who are over-whelmed by this accident that is happening in the Alps. For example if we look carefully at this particular character, the way I can relate to him is basically at times when I think to myself I can get through this exam no problem its easy well not easy, there's going to be a lot of hard work but I can get through it. Now as we move further along the painting and have a look at this particular character it clearly seems as if she is stressed out, as if she is snowed under with the stress of the mountains, which is how I would be snowed under with a lot of revision. Now with this character who appears to be in prayer with the heavens above him. The way I can relate is that I am praying to god the night before that I can easily get through it. Now moving further along the painting there appears to be some further catastrophe, as though people have just fallen down a collapsed bridge. And it seems as looking at this particular character he has fallen through a collapsed bridge and it reminds me of how I've felt after failing an exam. Now there's another character here further along who's got over the collapsed bridge. So putting that into my perception I can often get through an exam after going through a lot of hard work I've passed it just about got over the bridge could have done better result but I made it through to the next level. Well that's just about it and thank you very much for listening.

Deep's digital video narrative of De Loutherbourg's painting, in which the shock and awe wreaked by nature on the terrified human subjects became an allegory for overcoming the exam stress that Deep had clearly experienced, also animated the implied narrative of the still image through the use of a time-based visual medium. The video was shot in one take, with Deep holding the camera and providing the commentary. The piece opens with a shot of the accompanying wall text and widens to show the whole painting and frame. As he starts his narrative, the camera zooms into the lower left section of the painting where the first figure is looking up, out and across the scene of devastation with his arms held open in alarm. Staying closely focused, the camera then follows the path from left to right across the canvas, stopping at a middle group of two figures, a woman gesturing wildly back to the first figure, while the second figure is kneeling in a position of prayer. Moving on, the camera pauses on a partially visible figure trapped by the avalanche, before moving on again to a final figure who appears to have just managed to save himself from the abyss below the collapsed bridge. The camera follows, in close-up, the narrative device of the painting, 'reading' a series of figures from right to left, whose gestures and positions narrate the story of the disaster. Deep refers to the figures throughout as 'characters', which are diminished and gestural, in comparison to the expanse of canvas given over to the depiction of mountains and the dramatic storm painting which make the nineteenth-century idea of the sublime bearable to witness.

Deep's interest in this particular painting is contiguous with his extensive knowl-edge and deep appreciation of the *Star Wars* films and computer games as well as the collection of detailed scale models of the characters. As in De Loutherbourg's painting, the *Star Wars* characters undertake hazardous journeys, crossing immense spaces in landscapes where they might be confronted by an abyss, or have to cross deep chasms spanned by frail unprotected bridges. In *Star Wars* the characters are driven onwards in search of their destiny. Striving always, as Deep remarks about the figure in De Loutherbourg's painting, to make it to the next level.

Deep's engagement with the *Star Wars* saga was instigated in part through his involvement in West London local networks. His neighbourhood friends introduced him to a range of popular entertainment forms, including the hit TV series *The A-Team*, which, like *Star Wars*, had been developed in the US. In Sarah Thomas' film, Deep's study room contains *Star Wars* posters and models, but he also refers to a further source of visual imagery within his life world in which a cast of characters are used to tell a creation story in Hindu mythology.

> As I was growing up and as a kid, where I lived and especially when my Gran lived with us, we kept a shrine of photos of Hindu gods and goddesses, which is known as a 'Mundhir' and I would just be inquisitive, you know, like who's that and who's that and why that picture, that god, why is his skin blue, why has that goddess got eight arms, why is she sitting on a tiger, you know, why has that other one got an elephant's head. I was always inquisitive about that and then, like, we had teachings of Sikhism as well, so I would be going to Gurdwaras, Sikh temples, you know, quite often as a kid as well as Hindu temples as well, so I, and it never bothered me, and I never saw any difference, going to either of those places of worship because it's good to learn about what your parents believe in and where they come from.[6]

Case study 2

Aminah Borg-Luck's reflexive account of her participation in Tate Encounters, as one of the student co-researchers, embraces the value of contradiction, as she unravels her conflicted and conflicting journey through both Tate Britain and the Tate Encounters project, noting that: 'I had the feeling that Britishness was both irrelevant and integral to me, that I absolutely was and was not Finnish and that the awe that the Tate Britain building encouraged was both off-putting and dazzling. I believed the very contradiction of all the contradictory impulses I had was worth pausing on as it offered its own insight.' Reflecting on the initial perception and avid rejection of the project's 'call' on racialized identities, Borg-Luck worked through her own subtle and complex negotiation of her personal background alongside her relationship to the framing and politics of identity. Through the discussion of her two films *Lie Back and Think of England* and *A Bit of Hämäläinen*, she noted 'that as identities (national, personal, other) tend to be in a constant state of flux, attempting to locate any fixed or stable Britishness in Tate Britain's galleries was hugely problematic'.

A Bit of Hämäläinen, a 20-minute film, was written, produced and directed by Aminah Borg-Luck, as an undergraduate student in 2009. The video is a complex montage structured by an interview with the principal research investigator on the Tate Encounters project shot at Tate Britain. It is divided into a numbered, but non-sequentially arranged set of parts; 'On Dominant Narratives'; 'Of Histories and Texts'; 'On Questions'; 'On Answers'; and 'On Regulated Spaces'. The central interview is intercut with extracts from out of copyright film footage now in the public domain, including: the coronation of George VI (1937); the films *The Scarlet Pimpernel* (1934) and *Sword of Lancelot* (1963); and a brief newsreel shot entitled 'Churchill Homecoming' (1941), showing the eponymous historical figure walking in a public march. These were inserted as humorous, stereotypical representations of 'Britishness'. In addition the film contained a sequence of a musician friend of the director, playing a set of skin drums in the Duveen galleries, which reads as a very 'un-British' event. The interview with the researcher takes place in the Duveen galleries, early in the morning and out of hours, during an exhibition changeover with art handlers moving trolley boxes in the background. Indeed, at one point the noise being made overcomes the interview. This was not a planned sequence of events but its inclusion is a deliberate punctuation and disruption of the spoken delivery of the expert investigator attempting to summarize what the research had found out. Shots of installation work taking place in the background as well as behind closed doors, are used elsewhere in the video, as if to underline that the museum is a fluid work-in-process. It also underlines a 'behind the scenes' sense of the museum. In the opening of the video there is a black and white sequence of the exterior of Tate Britain, shot from a car panning along the north-west elevation and around to the front entrance on Millbank. A poem by a friend of the co-researcher is spoken over the scene:

An anomaly
An anomalous
homogenous
morass of nonsense
An historical construct
of indigenous in-constants
rendered ridiculous
inevitably redundant
broken between economy
and systemic dysfunction
Identity conundrum's complex text
rejects spoon fed knee jerk simplistic reduction
denies identity as set in space like 'where d'ya come from?'
denies identity as set in place like 'we from London!'
denies identity per-se as fixing someone
to something objectified categorised and static
written in blood cut hot on cold granite
written in blood lines split on stone tablets
I I-dentify my I-dentity by integrating signs
I relate to signify authenticity's defunct

commodified style artifacts
colon-ised while globalised mobile
iconoclastic art state-ment meant to represent
plastic content of nationality
spins in the default code of an anomaly

Martin Daws

In the section entitled 'On Regulated Spaces', the main video sequence is of the musician friend drumming in the Duveen Galleries at Tate Britain, while cleaners move in and out of the shot. There is also a set of captions written by the director as follows:

Who sets the rhythms of Tate
Who controls what is seen
The visitors with their various view
Modifying histories and backgrounds,
Or those who arrange the Tate's spaces?

Part two of the video, *Of Histories and Texts*, is introduced by a series of titles, again written by the director, making up the following text:

Eventually, I came to think on the stories I would weave through hidden layers of Tate. I'd probably be quite mischievous when fooling around with the sub-textual visuality of the space. I would most likely have a play with the traditional trappings of Britishness preserved by the Tate. That is, an essentially unlocatable bit of Tate. I may even attempt to turn the Tate's big hall into a forest.

The text is followed in the film by a slow fade from an image of the Duveen Galleries to a forest in which the classical columns of the gallery march the trunks of trees. The film cuts to a text saying:

If I were a curator, I might wonder about the voices I would hear from, for instance, the John Singleton Copley in Room 9.

This is followed by a still of the painting, 'The Death of Major Peirson', a large oil on canvas painted by John Singleton Copley (1781), illustrating a successful counter-attack by the British army after the fall of St Helier to the French. The Union Jack and the bright red tunics of the British are prominent in the foreground of the painting, as is a depiction of Major Peirson's black servant, shown avenging his master's death.

The caption text continues:

By the mighty spirit of the Finnish legendary hero, Vainamoinen, I could not celebrate grandeur, great battles or great noblemen. But would rather overlay the Tate's collection with lines from the Kalevala

FIGURE 5.5 Three video-frame grabs from the film *A Bit of Hämäläinen* (2008), Aminah Borg-Luck

This is followed by the soundtrack of a Finnish folk poem, the text of which is superimposed over a number of Tate collection historic paintings:

As Old Vainamoinen played
There was none in the forest
Running on four legs
Or hopping on foot
That did not come to listen
Marvel at the merriment
Vainamoinen, ancient minstrel,
Played one day and then a second,
There was no fellow
Nor any brave man
Neither ancient dame, nor maiden,
Not in Metsola a daughter,
Who did not fall to weeping:
Whose heart did not melt:
The young wept and the old wept
And the unmarried men wept
And the married fellows wept
And the half-grown boys wept
Wept the mothers, wept the daughter
Wept the warriors and heroes
At the music of his playing
At the songs of the magician.
Vainamoinen's tears came flowing,
Welling from the master's eyelids.

The film is complex and contains more than has been indicated here. The methodological point is not that the film is ethnographic data to be interpreted as a representation of subject position, but rather that the film is itself an interpretation or, better, a figuration of the research itself. The film is also an intervention into the space of Tate Britain. Screened in the Duveens Studio in March 2009, and viewable online, it invites others to think about and see Tate Britain differently.

Case study 3

Cinta Esmel-Pamies joined the project in 2007 as a first-year BA arts management student. She remained with Tate Encounters until the completion of the fieldwork period in March 2009. She made a series of contributions over that period, two of which are touched upon here: 'Identity Remix', a photographic event at Late at Tate Britain in 2009; and a paper to *Tate Encounters* online editions entitled, 'Into the Politics of Museum Audience Research' (Esmel-Pamies 2010) bringing together and tracing the emergence of the 'public' as audience in museum culture in the UK over the last 20 years. The paper resituates a history of visitor studies and market research practice at Tate from two points of view; museological and cultural policy analyses of the relation between the state, governance, accountability; in the light of and the rise of consumer-orientated modelling of audiences within corporate strategies. The following extracts appeared in the paper in the form of 'boxed inserts', intended to signal the subjectified and reflexive position of the author in an otherwise academic essay. The use of this device is used to create a personal counter-narrative of resistance and scepticism, which Esmel-Pamies describes:

> Explicitly and implicitly combining media theory, museum studies, sociology, visitor studies, philosophy and political philosophy, this extended paper is considered a piece of ritual resistance. Using and adapting the academic setting inevitably connected to the imposition of shared cultural norms, this piece aims to increase reflexive awareness of the fundamental sources which cause the previously stated feelings of exclusion and oppression upon entering an art museum.
>
> *(Esmel-Pamies 2010: 5)*

This is a position that emerged for Esmel-Pamies through her participation in the Tate Encounters project as a co-researcher and her subsequent detailed research (which formed her B.A. dissertation) into the practice, policy and theory of audience research and development within the UK museum sector, taking Tate Britain as a case study.

Example 1

Subjective Museum

The museum, understood as a medium, is a subjective piece of social engineering. While museums collect and conserve, classify and display, research and educate, they also engage in the production and delivery of messages and arguments. More importantly, they acquire, conserve, study, interpret and exhibit not only objects and collections, but also segments of population.

Subjective Oppression

The call for museums to meet specific targets could be understood as a means of social control that feeds the dynamics of inequality, and therefore oppression. Even if adopted in order to promote equal opportunities, this call structurally reproduces hierarchical beliefs and its results perpetuate not only social fragmentation, but also social subjugation of those initially targeted as implicitly less serviceable to the society, unable to understand by themselves the value of *high-civilising culture*.

Subjective Democracy

The means to understand, demonstrate or measure museums' 'public value' and 'social impact' should take into consideration not only the intrinsic contradictory dynamics of these institutions and their contexts, but also the essence of democracy. The monitoring and regulation of visitors' conduct and behaviour in relation to an agreed 'common norm' and ratified extra-ordinary is characteristic of autocratic practices; the analysis on how museal commodity, power/knowledge, is biasedly imparted to some and imposed onto others within the everyday of an unequal society would be symptomatic of genuinely visitor-centred museums.

Subjective Resistance
My 'uncivilized' self may not be able to communicate on equal terms with the museum, thereby genuinely resisting its potential 'disciplinary power'; however, I am occasionally able to subvert the 'belief system' that this seeks to impose upon the segment of population I belong to. As it was said in the introduction, this work should be read as a personal subversive act, articulated through an everyday practice, of someone who resists consuming what has been packaged as an act of democracy.

(Esmel-Pamies 2010: 31, 34, 35)

Example 2: 'Identity Remix', Late at Tate 2009

Is 'LATE AT TATE' an attempt to collapse object and subject? Or are they trying to amuse me in TATELAND★?

★TateLand: Theme park of real TATE available once a month. Tate's carnival, when it challenges and questions itself and its own Status Quo, allowing visitors to eat olives inside the museum (£2 a pot), listen to a DJ and see projections not suitable for epileptics.

–LANDS (Creative/Cultural and Leisure industries) are more and more a reflection of 'our' society. A society which is moving into a 'magic world Disney'; where there are two people to clean poo for every pony; where pony mess is offensive; where the natural and organic is obscene; where everything is painted in accordance with Disney pantone★, artificially coordinated; where the odd one out has no place; where nothing ages and everything keeps fresh and is carefully updated; where ideas feed themselves through mirror walls; where the selves perpetuate themselves to the infinite. Consumer-centred paradises without Gods but with princesses.

The Lord help us! To Tate Britain you are an aficionado, actualiser, sensualist, researcher, self-improver, socialite, tourist, student, child, family. But who are you really? For one night only register your own identity within Tate with a toolkit of labels and personal portrait photo.

Late at Tate visitors were invited to write and print up their own identity labels. At the same time, they were invited to be professionally photographed at the event and video of all the photographs taken was subsequently screened to the Late at Tate public and again during the Research-in-Process event.

FIGURE 5.6 Cinta Esmel-Pamies, 'Identity Remix', Late at Tate, March 2009. Photograph Pablo Goikoetxea

Case study 4

Adekunle Detokunbo–Bello, or Toksy as he preferred to be known in the university, joined the project in its second year in 2008. He was working at London South Bank University as a part-time security person, while studying on a part-time Masters programme in creative media arts. He had visited Britain's national art institutions in London as an adult, having grown up in Ibadan, Oyo State, in the Yoruba region of southern Nigeria. One of the key networks in which Toksy operated during his youth was a drama network, having trained as an actor and having acted in a number of dramas, including video features, among which were Yoruba-language video-works, such as *Arewa* by Bucky Amos. Toksy's acting network drew him into a parallel network of video-making through which he distributed video-features, such as those shown in cultural centres in London, among them the South London Gallery.[7] Another parallel network in which Toksy participated was the academic research network, which involved him in a research study of the contemporary Nigeria video-making industry, colloquially known as 'Nollywood', for which he generated a documentary examining the cultural milieu of contemporary Nigerian diasporas in London. Among his central concerns have been the workings of diasporic audiences centred on Nollywood viewing. Toksy has addressed themes such as 'nostalgia', researching it as a modality of viewing for diasporic audiences. He has also elaborated his interest in the questions of shifts in the development of aesthetic approaches within Nollywood. He has cited the Yoruba language film, *Abeni*, with its emphasis on production quality, as being of particular interest.

Toksy's main engagement with Tate Britain, during the Tate Encounters study was as an institutional backdrop through which to further his examination of the question of aesthetics in the production values of Nollywood output. As he explained during interview, aesthetic concerns had conventionally been relegated as an aspect of Nollywood productions. Production values per se had been downgraded in favour of placing more emphasis on a clear elaboration of themes and high emotive content. By focusing his engagement with Tate Encounters on his own Nollywood production, Toksy addressed the museum as a space that prioritized aesthetics and high production values. As such, the museum setting would enable Toksy to provide a contrast with the then existing Nollywood conventions. Similarly, the clear elaboration of themes demanded by Nollywood conventions would also bring a refreshing clarity to the workings of Tate Britain as an institution.

Toksy's concerns were fully elaborated through the making of his film, *Whirlwind at Millbank: Nollywood Springs Up in London* (2010), which was screened in the museum itself. The film tells the story of Taribo, a Nigerian student based in London who has taken a part-time job at Tate Britain 'to help him with his student upkeep'. Taribo's experience of the institution is one of 'racism and segregation', in which a clear racial hierarchy is in operation with racist humiliation and insults barely masked. Taribo's views of the intransigence of the institution are challenged after a couple of chance encounters with a white upper-middle-class curator, Leonie. Having heard Taribo's account of his negative experiences of the institution, Leonie invites him to consider the pleasures that the museum has to offer. In accepting her invitation, Taribo makes a date to meet with Leonie at Tate Britain. They spend time in the galleries looking at works by Lawrence Alma-Tadema and Dante Gabriel Rossetti. Leonie offers an exposition of the works, encouraging Taribo to experience the pleasure of looking at art. The development of a love theme is made evident through Leonie's excitement and their enjoyment of each other's company in the gallery. The film ends with the two of them hand-in-hand while a narrative voice-over tells of Taribo's reconsideration of art alongside a reappraisal of the museum's racist environment, as a result of his experience with Leonie.

The playing out of some of the Nollywood conventions remains explicit in *Whirlwind at Millbank: Nollywood Springs up in London*. The clear articulation of the central themes – institutional racism and the way in which love overcomes it – are notable features of Nollywood productions. Another convention is the inconsistent acting-style, embodied, in particular, in the performance of Leonie's role: demonstrable mistakes are consistently made with the actress tripping over lines and obviously missing cues. Her failure to maintain eye-lines with inappropriate glances at camera and crew during shooting adds to the amateur effect. The main contrast

FIGURE 5.7 Six video-frame grabs: from *Whirlwind at Millbank: Nollywood Springs Up in London*, Tate Britain (2009). Directed by Adekunle Detokunbo-Bello

with conventional Nollywood drama is provided by the luxurious backdrop of the museum, in particular, its historic nineteenth-century galleries, which provide luscious interiors and rich colours, offering a ready-made art direction for the production. Art direction was certainly an area that remained deliberately underdeveloped within Nollywood productions. Such a feature provided a clear contrast with African Third Cinema, especially the films that had emerged from Francophone directors such as Med Hondo and Ousman Sembene,[8] who paid increasing attention to art direction, landscape and architecture in their films. By being able to introduce such aesthetic preoccupations to a Nollywood format, courtesy of the interiors provided by Tate Britain, Taribo was able to advance his concerns.

The film was produced and directed by Toksy. It involved members of the research team with research assistant Isabel Shaw working in an associate producer role, co-researchers and research team members playing various parts in the drama. It was filmed in both the non-accessible staff areas and public galleries at Tate Britain. The use of Nollywood's style of 'soap opera' storytelling, with its cast of good and bad characters with whom the hero must deal, but filmed in Tate Britain as part of the research process, created an 'ironic' as well as documentary view of the art museum. The scenes of 'behind the scenes' or 'below stairs' at Tate Britain were of documentary as well as dramatic purpose serving to heighten the 'above stairs' effect of the grand façade and opulence of the galleries in which the fairy-tale romance based upon a chance meeting was enacted.

Case study 5

Jacqueline Ryan joined the Tate Encounters study in her first year as an undergraduate arts management student. She was a member of the pilot group who first visited Tate Britain with the project in September 2006 and continued as a co-researcher until April 2009. In addition to proposing her own documentary film, *Trading Cultures*, based upon her mother's experience of migration, Jacqueline also worked with Sarah Thomas on an ethnographic film based upon visits to the family home in Scunthorpe and a visit they made to Tate Britain.

Jacqueline Ryan's own proposal as a co-researcher was entitled, 'Is Britain a Cultural Melting Pot or a Cultural Vacuum?' and was as follows:

> In the Twenty First Century, Britain is home to every nationality in the world. Education and employment opportunities and developments in relationships in the EU and international have encouraged a global community. How do ethnic groups and individuals out of their cultural home, maintain their cultural identity?
>
> I look at my own perspective in relation to my mother migrating to this country from Malaysia, what challenges she met and how she feels connected to her own culture and if and how she feels a part of British identity. My mother will be the main focus of research, but it will be interesting to compare the thoughts and opinions of my siblings and myself and how we feel attached to that part of our family's cultural heritage.
>
> Also I plan to conduct short interviews with other candidates that may add to the value of this research:

(i) 'Grandma' (not my real grandma) – she has lived in this country for more than twenty years and yet cannot speak more than 'Hello hello'. [I will subtitle this interview]

(ii) Linda Chan – moved from Hong Kong to the UK when she was six years old, educated at state school in regular community. Linda now 38 years old, has a husband and two children and maintains very traditional conservative views and is struggling to pass that down on to her British-born children.

(iii) Jay – is 24-year-old student from China. She came here to study her A-levels and then went on to Central St Martins to study Fine Art. She is currently doing her Masters. Jay's work explores many personal and cultural aspects to do with her coming to this country and her relationship with British art and how she and her art work fit in to that.

(iv) TBC – Chinese contemporary artist exhibiting in Britain
The other element to this research project is the representation of British art within the Tate Britain and what my research subjects response to that is. In

relation to the topic of the Tate Britain collection in particular I will focus on my mother, Jay and the Chinese artist.

The research will be presented in a documentary format.

Jacqueline visited Britain's national art institutions in London during her youth, as an offshoot of her family life. The eldest of four siblings, she was born and brought up in an English town in North Lincolnshire. She was of mixed parentage with a Chinese Malay mother and a white English father. Her mother migrated to England during early adulthood, where she met and married Jacqueline's father before becoming involved in trading East Asian goods in the UK. Chinese Malay and British cultural networks thereby became generated in Jacqueline's family through family connections. The retail business that Jacqueline's parents eventually set up also connected Jacqueline's family to different nationalities through their customer base, which reflected a mix of people engaged in Chinese and other East Asian cultures. Furthermore, the advancement of the business involved Jacqueline's parents in sourcing a range of goods – foodstuffs, furniture and other household items – from various importers around the UK. Indeed, Jacqueline travelled to London during journeys on which she accompanied her parents to meet suppliers and wholesalers. As she got older, Jacqueline was able to spend increasing amounts of time independently of her parents during their London business trips. Jacqueline used such time to further her interest in art, visiting art galleries, museums and national institutions situated in the capital.

Taken together the two films, one directed and produced by Jacqueline and the other directed and edited by Sarah Thomas, contain extensive interviews with Jacqueline's mother in which she discusses the relationship between her own migrational journey and her settlement in Britain, establishing a family and a business. The films are structured around the narrative device of journeys and the participation of her parents and siblings in her Tate Encounter. The family visited Tate Britain on two occasions during the project. The first was a family visit to Tate Britain, which was filmed by Sarah Thomas. The second was to attend the screening of Jacqueline's film, *Trading Places*, during the Research-in-Process event. Jacqueline's choice to pursue the link between her own life as a student in London, participating in Tate Encounters and the migrational story of her mother, was, as she said an opportunity to be able to work on something with her mother and to be able to find out more about her while documenting something of her life and perspectives. The question of the Britishness of Tate Britain had been taken up by Jacqueline as an opportunity to investigate what constituted a multiculture.

This is the case with all of the co-researchers' material it is why, in the final analysis, it is regarded here as analysis, rather than to be analysed. Accepting the co-researchers' submissions as analysis from the perspective of audience, the research allowed for a larger shift away from the discrete (missing) subjects of the art museum. Instead it emphasized a move towards the art museum's processes of subjectification, now seen through the process of research.

The co-researcher's submissions to the Research-in-Process event are figural of both 'transcultural' experience and 'transmedial' approaches to documenting that experience. Such an approach to the material acknowledges that such submissions are part of, as well as demonstrations of, the much larger idea of the ways in which the new hybrid of the distributed museum operates. More concretely, the Tate Encounters co-researchers' submissions are part of the distributed museum by virtue of the methodology established by the research. The co-researchers did not supply evidence of subject presence to be subsequently analysed as such. Rather they presented an analysis from a position of audience/producer, or conventionally, but more problematically, evidenced what a visitor could produce given an extended period of time. As an illustration, this is one way of seeing a core, repeat visitor in longitudinal terms. In the current case, the co-researcher was a visitor with whom the museum remained unfamiliar. What sustained the co-researchers' encounter with the art museum was not 'membership' of an art club, nor 'participation' in an art culture but the expression of a questioning position towards, or more accurately a trajectory through the museum.

6

RECONCEPTUALIZING THE SUBJECT AFTER POST-COLONIALISM AND POST-STRUCTURALISM

Seeing the human subject as a figure drawn to move between different national and cultural settings remains critical for understanding the implications that contemporary global conditions have for museums. The centrality of a global context to a reconceptualization of the human subject was made evident in the last decades of the twentieth century through the conjuncture between post-structuralist thinking and post-colonial conditions. An intense dialogue with the post-structural thought of Derrida, Foucault and Deleuze could be seen in key works by post-colonial thinkers, such as Gayatri Spivak (1988) and Homi K. Bhabha (1990). Equally, post-colonial conditions can be seen to have influenced the thinking in post-structuralist texts, such as those composed by Derrida and Cixous, who were themselves born in the colonial setting of French-dominated Algeria. Indeed, in a piece discussing the ways in which Jews living in Algeria under French rule negotiated their relation to French, Maghreb and Jewish culture, Cixous wrote of 'a belonging constituted of exclusion and non-belonging' (Cixous 2004). Such comments emphasize the relation between concerns centred on experiences of non-belonging and questions articulated in the body of post-colonial thought. As such, the relation between post-colonial and post-structural critique provides clues to the ways in which notions of the human subject were reformulated. The particularity of the relation should be regarded as a 'sword that cuts both ways'.

Several post-structuralist tools were seen in operation among the positions advanced within post-colonial critiques. For instance, Derrida's problematization of the notion of 'origin' (Derrida 1976: 74) was seen as a useful means of derailing any attempts to situate the colonial subject in a mythologized (original or aboriginal) past. By abandoning 'origin', focus could be placed on the contemporaneous struggles against imperialist legacies and postcolonial social realities (Spivak 1988). Similarly, Derrida's rendition of the 'supplement' as a device that creates a void at the same time as generating a replacement[1] was seen as a useful means for thinking through the ideological function of nationhood in a post-colonial setting: 'The nation fills the void left in the uprooting of communities and kin, and turns that loss into the language of metaphor' (Bhabha 1990: 291). The unsettling of notions that had been central to the grounding of the foundational subject, such as nation and origin, were seen as key aims in the post-structuralist project – aims that coalesced with concerns elaborated in post-colonial critiques.

The work of Gayatri Spivak provides an incisive discussion of why the positioning of the foundational subject as a dominant paradigm of human subjectivity can be regarded as a central problem. For the purposes of the current argument, the foundational subject can be seen as a coherent, integrated, self-identifying figure. Such a figure is founded on a sense of self-presence that is guaranteed through indubitable self-knowledge, as articulated through the Cartesian cogito: 'I think therefore I am'.[2] Conceptions of human subjectivity that rely on such a rendition of a fixed and undivided self become problematic for Spivak. In her celebrated work, 'Can the Subaltern Speak?' (Spivak 1988), she elaborated the difficulty in terms of the reality of the economic conditions imposed on the human subject by international capitalism, which, rather than producing fixed and coherent subjects, generates subjects that are divided and dislocated. This is particularly true of the colonized subject during the successive phases of international capitalism dominated by Western European imperialism. For, in those phases, colonized subjects were included in systems of commerce as consumers and traffickers of goods while they were themselves trafficked as indentured or enslaved labourers. Successive phases of the expansion of international capitalism have made conditions less stark (through the abolition of the Atlantic Slave Trade in the nineteenth century, for example). However, the rendition of the subject as coherent and fixed remains untenable when one recognizes the conditions in which the human subject, even after colonization, is inserted in an internationalized system of capital, commodity and labour exchange.

Post-colonialism's dialogue with post-structuralism highlights the way in which the internationalized system divides the human subject in its political modality. Through a celebrated critique of Foucault and Deleuze, Spivak's work elucidated a necessary distinction in different ways of understanding representation. Representation as the aesthetic portrait of a people ('darstellen') tends towards a resolved and coherent image *of* the people – the public, the peasantry, the natives, the community – as well as images *for* the people – community leaders, patriots, heroes. A different kind of modality is at work when one speaks of representation by political proxy ('vertreten'), an expression of political will that tends towards heterogeny, reflecting the competing and mutable interests that articulate the realities of everyday economic and social life. Spivak's legacy means that we must set aside the political formulations made available by debates surrounding the so-called 'politics of representation', as representation itself is not clear-cut.

The views advanced within the field of cultural politics, extant in the latter years of the twentieth century in Western Europe and, particularly, North America, need to be abandoned. As Spivak pointed out, the conflation of 'representation as resolved image' with 'representation as different interests' generated a categorical error. By setting the two apart, one can recognize the division of the human subject: on one hand there is what one might term the 'politics of the proximate', dealing with the economic realities of working life (What to produce? What to consume? How and where to invest?). The politics of the proximate are situated in a heterogenous field of different interests, sometimes competing, sometimes enjoying moments of allegiance and solidarity. The politics of the aesthetic portrait, on the other hand, is a politics of remoteness. The represented 'image of the people' functions only as an abstraction. Different human subjects experience it through its mediation in political discourse as well as media networks: 'black and minority ethnic', 'Muslim communities', 'black and Asian artists' – all function as representational abstractions in those terms. Reifying the unified image of the people, whether generated through public policy or cultural politics, in place of the heterogeny of interests can only end in frustration. For, in such circumstances, the heterogenous demands have been subjugated and, therefore, can never be met.

The imperium becomes an important backdrop against which to understand the work of representational abstractions and the politics of remoteness. Empire becomes meaningful, of course, through the subjugation of the specificities of the proximate to the abstractions of the remote. The heterogenous give themselves up to the unified. The everyday competing interests of a given locality become subject to a resolved and remote image of imperial rule. The face of the monarch stamped on a coin, for instance, stands for sovereignty – the fixed image that mediates and resolves disputes of value, status and law. By unsettling the operations of the imperium, by refusing the subjugation of the politics of the proximate to the politics of remoteness, one allows for a field of competing interests to open up. The key modalities become negotiation rather than command, arbitration rather than order, temporary settlement rather than established resolution. Divided and differentialized interests, then, can be fully articulated rather than having to undergo the subjugations imposed by imperial rule.

The period of Western European imperialism, from Portuguese and Spanish expansionism in the fifteenth century to British and French imperial dominion in the nineteenth/early twentieth century, can be seen as key phases in the consolidation of the internationalized system of exchange. The history of the internationalized system must be grasped in terms of its drivers leading towards the division of the subject and the fragmentation of socioeconomic life. Equally, focus must be placed on the historic use of representational devices – the empire, the king, the republic, the self – to resolve the fragmentation created by the exchange system into an abstraction. The positioning of the United States as successor to the British Empire and the French Republic, following the ravaging of Europe in World War II, has been noted among scholars (Said 1978: 4). It would not, therefore, be controversial to cite the US as providing the dominant resolving abstraction of the late twentieth century – America – which is not a geographical territory so much as an idea.

The US-dominated period reached its apogee with the defeat of the Soviet Union in the Cold War. The subsequent demise of the Soviet Union alongside the reintegration of Russia, Poland, the Baltic states and a slew of European countries into the internationalized system can be remarked upon as the characterizing of a further phase of expansion of a system still dominated by the US imperium. The US, through its post-World War II reconstruction of Europe, laid the foundation-stone for the later establishment of the European Union (EU). However, the creation of a transnational space in the EU, declaring, as one of its principal aims, the free movement across its member-states of goods, services and people signalled the beginning of challenges to US pre-eminence in the internationalized system. China's integration into the internationalized system, culminating in policies that surrounded the tail-end of the British Empire with the ending of the lease of Hong Kong in 1997, becomes a productive benchmark to begin characterizing the latest phase of international capitalism. This phase can be termed the beginning of hyper-capitalism – a form of capitalism the global reach of which has been systematically intensified and accelerated through the mediation of digital and satellite technologies. What is interesting to note, however, is that, at this stage, hyper-capitalism is marked by a lack of a global imperium governing the newly expanded internationalized system of exchange.

If the human subject in the period of Western European imperialism could be seen as dislocated and divided by the demands to participate in international systems, to what extent can we say that the same applies to human subjects in this latest phase of hyper-capitalism? The clearest phenomenon to remark upon has been the effect of the latest expansion of the internationalized system on finance capital. As Lipovetsky has noted in his critique of hypermodernity:

> ... we are witnessing a formidable expansion in the size and number of financial and stock market activities, an acceleration in the speed of economic operations that now function in real time and a phenomenal explosion in the volume of capital circulating across the planet.
>
> *(Lipovetsky 2005: 32)*

The interconnectedness of finance capital with the production and circulation of commodities, brings the human subject into the picture as a consumer of commodities in the 'hypermarkets and shopping centres that are increasingly gigantic and offer a whole plethora of all kinds of products, brands, services ... ' (Lipovetsky 2005: 32). Museum shops, with their emphasis on merchandising, remain an explicit part of this. The museum collection itself also remains implicated through its insertion into systems of acquisition that facilitate the global circulation of artworks and museum artefacts. The museum visitor is assigned a place in the system through patterns of consumption within the museum. The visitor as consumer appears in various guises: as collector, as shopper, as café visitor and as online viewer looking at museum websites that display the highly-prized commodities that museums have managed to acquire. When museum visitors are staged as 'members of the public', a politics of remoteness displaces visitors' role as consumers, placing them instead at the centre of a 'resolved image of the public'. Museum authorities, cultural policy-makers or others claiming authoritative roles, as 'spokespersons' or 'community leaders', can thereby state what should or should not be 'in the interests of the public'. Set against this is a politics of the proximate where different people articulate their own interests and needs. In the current formulation of the national cultural institution, it is only in the role of individuated consumer that museum visitors come close to articulating their heterogenous demands. Cultural institutions need to look at ways of reformulating themselves with the main aim of addressing the heterogeny of viewers, if they want to get beyond or, even, build on the consumerist approach.

Accelerated consumption is a key aspect of the human subject embedded in the most recent phase of hyper-capitalism. Emphasis, though, also has to be placed on the effects on human subjects as producers of commodities through their labour. One such effect is the intensification of the demand for the mobility of labour, with workers needing to follow finance capital in extending global networks of investment and return. National migration, through increased urbanization in China and India, meets its corollary in international migration. The phenomenon of transnational migration ('crossing countries without borders') also becomes more pronounced through the establishment of transnational economic areas, such as the EU. This has a direct effect on the construction of the human subject, as Kevin Robins has written:

> It is clear that geographical transformations are now being brought about through the international restructuring of capitalist economies … At the same time there has been a consolidation of supra-national blocs (such as the European Community) and a new salience for sub-national territories (regions and localities) … As territories are transformed, so too are the spaces of identity.
>
> *(Robins 1999: 17)*

Such transformation of territories and spaces of identity through migrational patterns hold massive implications for museum practices, particularly in considering the location of national museums, like Tate Britain, situated in the international metropolitan centres, such as London, which experience the shifts in global population flow.

The oceanic scale of the distances originally breached by the international system of exchange in the fifteenth century has been exacerbated by the global speed at which those distances have been breached in the twenty-first century. Such speed and ease has been facilitated by advances in aviation alongside developments in cabled telecoms as well as satellite communications, secured through radio and space technologies. It has produced the phenomenon of global transitory migration or, more accurately, transmigration, whereby human subjects are able to move in a lifetime between several sites of settlement located in different national territories across the globe. Such mobility serves, of course, the purposes of the internationalized system, which demands the mobility of labour, in all forms, not least as managers of production, distribution and finance, as well as other highly skilled practices. Pools of mobile semi- and unskilled labourers must also be guaranteed to provide a resource of labour wherever it is needed at prices that employers are prepared to pay. Global transitory migration, then, becomes the corollary of global transitory capital, which follows international flows recognizing few borders in search of areas of investment and return.

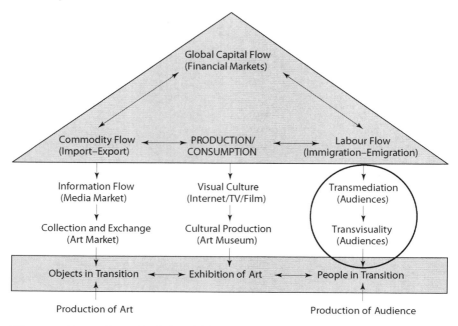

FIGURE 6.1 Transculture: Capital and labour flow. Tate Encounters research synthesis

The impact of transmigration as a way of thinking about contemporary subjectivity, even if its actualization remains inconstant, has to be addressed, in order to understand the contemporary metropolis and the role of any national cultural institution situated within it. One aspect to consider is the way in which a migrational pattern that involves several sites of settlement can invite different modes of engagement with the various national cultures encountered. Living in South America one year, followed by Western Europe the next and being propelled to West Asia the following year, does not necessarily produce an engagement with the different cultures encountered in a unified form. Can the human subject, in the process of transmigrating across several different national territories, engage in each national culture through the same modalities?

What role might a museum play in shaping the cultural landscape of a city that a transmigrating subject might inhabit for a time? The role of a cultural institution, like Tate Britain, in performing its role of displaying the national collection of British art, can be addressed in terms of the methods that a person living in Lagos then in London then in Los Angeles needs to use to negotiate their experiences.

The key differences between migration and transmigration centre on the fact that transmigration emphasizes the possibility of dynamic and, even, accelerated movement – the migration to one country precipitating the subsequent migration to another – such is transmigration. Persons undertaking transmigration also undergo transcultural experiences, as they pass through one cultural setting to another; they begin to recognize that cultural artefacts, habits, customs and behaviours continually shift from culture to culture, from place to place and from time to time. The recognition of such perpetual change leads to an acceptance of the mutability of all cultural paraphernalia: music, food, dress, even the way people hold themselves and move become culturally specific. An acceptance of the shifts from culture to culture becomes emblematic of transcultural experience.

Despite an awareness of shifts in migrational patterns as a result of successive radical transformations in global economic conditions, it remains difficult to conceptualize the human subject in terms of what it has so recently become. What are the main things to consider in respect of the transmigrating person undergoing so many different experiences of national cultures and their institutions? Prominent sociologist Anthony Giddens points toward the adjustments that take place as traditional social structures undergo changes as a result of the experience of globalization. He writes of the emergence of 'post-traditional society':

> [A] world where no one is 'outside' is one where pre-existing traditions cannot avoid contact not only with others but also with many alternative ways of life. By the same token, it is one where the 'other' cannot any longer be treated as inert. The point is not only that the other 'answers back', but that mutual interrogation is possible.
>
> *(Beck et al. 1994: 96–7)*

Recourse to post-colonial discussions of migrational experience would remind us that such mutual interrogation takes place between human subjects who are always already divided – with human beings implicated in disparate activities taking place across the globe – sugar grown in the Caribbean meets milk drawn from the local dairy meets coffee picked in Papua New Guinea, all because one orders a cappuccino rather than an Americano for early morning coffee. Images of metropolitan life can serve to smooth over the different locations from which our commodities are sourced. Equally the promise of a cosmopolitan existence can serve to embrace the different situations that transmigrational subjects will encounter as they move from one national culture to another in search of work or love or just a different way of life. Images and promises can never resolve the differentials, though. They can never breach the divide. In facing the realities of migrational experience, no image of resolution can hold together the fractiousness of different cultural encounters awaiting transmigrating subjects, as they journey across the globe.

On the journey of the transmigrating subject, each national location, with different notions of social interaction, different ideas of value, different approaches to meaningful exchange, provides a bewildering array of difference. The legacy of post-structuralist thinking invites a turning away from any resort to a resolving image or an over-arching embrace in mitigation of differentiating effects. Instead, the different conditions of the multiple environments in which the human subject now engages need to be opened up. The step forward from post-structuralist thinking moves the divided subject to engage with dynamic networks distributed across the globe. The notion of the distributed museum works on the understanding that a museum can be conceptualized as comprising a series of networks of interest and expertise going beyond any singular institutional setting. Working across multiple environments, the distributed museum links differentially located practices, centred on different subject-positions. An image of a street scene in Johannesburg gets commented on in Brisbane and sent on to Jakarta to produce a network of interest in which the museum can partake. In this model, the conventional museum paradigm gets turned on its head: it is not about finding ways for the world and its peoples to participate in the museum; it is about finding ways for the museum to participate in the lives of people of the world.

The distributed museum moves against the established model of the contributive museum – a model that defines the institution as a place to which tribute must be paid: charitable donations; sponsorship; bequests; even just paying a visit works as a contribution to the centripetal model of the contributive museum. At the centre of such a model lies the deposit of artworks held on reserve. By operating only on the contributive model, the museum misrecognizes an entirely different set of networks through which images circulate. Like a currency tied to the gold standard while all other economies have abandoned it, the contributive museum fails to see things any other way. The distributed museum, on the other hand, positions the institution as a space of circulation, a node in a network across which images consistently flow. Multiplicity and polyvocality, which acted as central tropes of post-colonialism and post-structuralism, can be seen at work in such a concept. Further

FIGURE 6.2 'In-transit'. Photo Tracey Jordan 2008. Tate Encounters

steps need to be taken, however, to understand how the space of multiplicity, as envisaged in post-colonialism and post-structuralism, is not the end of the road. Rather, it acts more like a port, setting out a vast array of flight-paths, rail-tracks, shipping lines and airwaves that in themselves link the different aspects of the fragmented subject to other aspects of other fragmented subjects distributed across the world.

The model of contributive museum makes little sense in an era in which the human subject is constructed as divided and networked. Relying on the payment of tribute to a recognized order, the contributive museum draws on a universalized system of knowledge in which every object in the world can be determined as a valuable artefact or otherwise. In turn, every object judged to be a recognizable artefact is assigned a place in a universalized system of order. In the light of such practices, conventional museological studies have to acknowledge the implication of the contributive museum in colonial history: the earliest public museums in England, for instance, such as the Musaeum Tradescantianum and, later, Oxford's Ashmolean Museum, were based on collections augmented by John Tradescant the Younger (MacGregor 1983) who brought materials back to London from his journey to the Colony of Virginia in the early 1600s.[3] Museum collections were connected to different periods of imperial expansion, which, in turn, were directly related to the development of international capitalism through the role of the imperium in securing the establishment of an internationalized system of exchange. The history of the US state of Virginia provides an engaging example: securing its status as a Royal Colony in 1624, Tradescant was able to transport objects from it that once belonged to indigenous peoples, establishing them, later, as relics for his collection. Museum artefacts and artworks act as highly prized commodities, flowing through the internationalized system, alongside other commodities, such as tobacco and timber. The system that established the conduits to facilitate the growth of Western European empires also supported the development of museum collections, such as the Ashmolean alongside the Louvre, the British Museum and the Tate.

Working on a model of centre and periphery, with tribute flowing from the (colonial) margin to the (imperial) metropolis, the contributive museum presupposes uni-directional flow. Tribute goes to the centre, while an established set of values is disseminated to the margins. The notion of acculturation is crucial to this model, where those migrating from the margins head towards the metropolis to acquire its culture and its values. Transculturality, with its emphasis on the mutability of cultural value, depending on time and location, works against the hierarchies presupposed in acculturation. In a transcultural model, movement from one cultural context to another unsettles hierarchies of cultural value, as it shows that such hierarchies are never fixed. Rather, hierarchies of cultural value remain conditional, ever dependent on time and place. For the transmigrating subject, the contributive museum's insistence on disseminating its hierarchical values becomes no more than a rhetorical stance. The transmigrating subject, unlike the migratory subject, is not fixed enough in one location to absorb the museum's rhetoric – to become acculturated. Instead, transmigrating subjects experience transculture. They operate through a modality of mutability, moving from place to place in such a way that there are no more margins, no more centres but just a distributed plane.

The distributed museum becomes a better model to work alongside the transmigrating subject. By working as a 'hub', the distributive museum provides a platform to support the circulation of knowledge and experience established between people globally. Postcolonial critiques discussed the ways in which the human subject became divided through the demands of migration:[4] movement across a cultural divide fractured the migrating subject, leaving migrational subjectivities inhabiting an irresolvable space (Bhabha 1994: 224). Transmigrating subjectivities take the fracture as a starting point. Continually coming up against different cultures, subject-positions continually undergo differentiation – experiencing the constant rearticulation of cultural difference. The opening up of lines of difference becomes the ground for the constitution of the transmigrating subject. By emphasizing the divided subject's partaking in networks circulating beyond the museum, the distributed museum becomes a resource to extend lines of difference.

Institutional spaces that assert a fixed view of cultural value, such as the contributive museum, become redundant to the needs of a subject-position constructed around continual differentiation. National art institutions, such as Tate Britain, cannot operate in terms of difference, where networks circulating beyond the museum render the cultural institution's assertion of value completely tangential or even insignificant. Preoccupation with contributive models underlines the narrow and restrictive way in which the rubric of image circulation gets applied in national art institutions. For, the contributive museum facilitates the circulation of particular forms of finance capital (donation, sponsorship, bequest); specified commodities (recognized artworks); and restrictive pools of labour (specialist workers, invested audiences). International finance capital appears in its most explicit form as sponsorship, with the multinational BP providing a high-profile example through its sponsorship of Tate Britain's programme of British displays. The counterpart to such sponsorship remains the donations that the museum elicits from its wealthy donors. The processes for acquisition or loan of art objects stimulate the circulation of highly-prized commodities held by different collectors or passing through the hands of dealers and auction houses situated in key locations across the globe. By drawing on, as well as feeding, an international pool of expertise in conservation, interpretation, archiving, audience-management and curating, the museum supports the circulation of labour. Concerns arise, though, in respect of the labour pool that makes up the museum's audience. Tate Britain draws on the active interests of stakeholder audiences – in the form of the social and cultural capital they invest with an expectation of high returns. It is in such terms that there is a need to assess the extent to which the museum mobilizes the different interests of its wider public.

The notion of the 'wider public' must be analysed as a 'resolving term', masking a heterogenous set of interests. What happens when one steps beyond the unified and resolved image of the museum's wider public to address the varied interests advanced by the vast range of individuals that lie behind it? By definition, the museum's understanding of the persons that might constitute the 'wider public' must remain remote. For, 'wider public' acts as a representational term, substituting the plurality of interests that lie behind it for a singular notion that can perform numerous institutional functions. The principle function is that of legitimation: it is on the public's behalf and in the public's name that the museum is able to retain its status as a national cultural institution.

In terms of national art institutions, the question of national heritage emerges: what are the consequences when it becomes possible for some people to recognize their patrimony in a national museum while for others such possibilities are impeded? In answering such a question, one can refer to the writing of art historian and museologist Donald Preziosi who, in his work *Brain of the Earth's Body: Art, Museums and Phantasms of Modernity*, wrote about a surprise discovery of an image of his recently deceased father during a visit to the US Holocaust Memorial Museum in Washington, DC (Preziosi 2003: 45). Preziosi explained how disturbed he had been by the unexpected sight of his father in a photograph in a museum that he had been visiting for the purposes of furthering his museological research. He confessed that his subsequent inclusion of the event in his writing was a way of working through the turbulence he had felt on first being confronted with the image. Preziosi's account demonstrates the wide range of ramifications that follow when a man's father literally becomes part of his patrimony – his national heritage. A corollary issue also emerges: what happens when a man or a woman's forebears do not and cannot form part of the established national heritage? What are the steps to take, when the construction of a cultural heritage is impeded?

Using the American setting of Washington's Holocaust Memorial Museum, as a starting point, a series of related questions emerge concerning the construction of cultural heritage among transmigrational peoples who choose the US or Angola or Britain or Brazil as a point of settlement. How do transmigrational peoples respond to the discourses of heritage that they encounter in the countries through which they move? Such questions shift focus of debate from the museum to the viewer as the primary site of cultural action. Contemporary conditions of transnational movement act as a starting point for a rethink of the principal considerations. Living in a transnational world, the viewer remains open to continuous migration from one country to another.

In order to negotiate the vast array of cultural encounters that they experience, persons going through transmigration have to produce and reproduce their subjectivity. Ways of seeing, the means of negotiating the various visual terrains in different national contexts, become a part of that exercise. The forms of visuality that accompany transmigration thereby increase in significance: transvisuality becomes critical to consider as a particular way of seeing – a form of seeing on the move. The term 'transvisuality' works as a means of theorizing the experience of 'seeing on the move'. Transvisuality stresses the shifts in the conditions of visuality that take place as the subject moves from one national context to another. Shifts in conditions of visuality reflect changes in discursive conditions that accompany moves between national contexts: languages, practices and objects change, as one moves across the globe. As such, transvisuality becomes the visual component of transculturality. It implies that changes in cultural settings entail the production of different conditions of viewing – the things that can be seen differ from one cultural context to another. Transvisuality, first and foremost, encompasses the changes in what can and cannot be seen; it signifies variations in what constitutes the field of the visible itself.

Gillian Rose outlined the intellectual terrain surrounding the notion of 'visuality' in which she emphasized the discursive aspects of what people are able, unable, provoked and compelled to see (Rose 2001: 6). According to this argument, different subject positions, how and where people are located in culture, do not just impinge on their outlook; they constitute the field of vision. A young black man's visual field is structured differently to that of an elder white woman. Different visual fields coincide to constitute a general field in which the same things are seen from all subject-positions. There are, however, things that fall out of the general field – things that can only be noticed or observed from a particular subject-position. In such terms, what people see remains visible because of their subject-position. That which remains unseen is not merely invisible; it is undervisualized or even unvisualized.

When phenomena are undervisualized because of certain subject-positions, such phenomena go unnoticed or even get disregarded. Such disregard takes place for a variety of reasons – different subject-positions bestow varying levels of awareness so that certain subjects cannot even know that a given phenomenon exists. In that sense, people see what they know. What they do not know, they fail to notice. Undervisualizing, as a concept, then, is, based on an understanding of a differential treatment of the things encountered visually. Not everything is given the same attention. Some things are allowed to slip out of the field of vision or are not even noticed at all. When objects are completely unvisualized, the subject-position determines that things remain completely unseen. This is not simply failing to notice; this is being unable to see something because it cannot be imagined as possible to be seen. Subject-position bestows the possibility of seeing: age, sexuality, gender, race, location – in short, situation makes a difference as to what can be imagined as possible to be seen.

Location is a key factor in shaping visuality. The things that are unvisualized, under-visualized and over-visualized shift according to location. The unnoticed and the over-exposed are just different points on a spectrum of visualization. The over-visualized or the over-exposed lie at one end of the spectrum, the under-visualized or the unnoticed remain at the other. Different cultural contexts change how things fall on that spectrum of visuality. For instance, particular national contexts render certain things visible while others do not. By entering a different national context, people become exposed to the sight of things that might have previously gone unnoticed. By beginning to notice what had previously been disregarded, shifts in the field of visuality take place. This shows that such a field is not fixed. It can be changed if conditions change. What was over-exposed in one context can suddenly be disregarded in another. National context provides a key set of conditions influencing how things are routinely visualized. When the national context changes, the field of visuality alters.

Those who transmigrate become more adept at recognizing the consequences that follow a change of national context. The shift in pace, the change in volumes of speech, the difference in uses of colour, all become more readily anticipated by those who get used to moving from one site of settlement to another. Consider, for instance, the changes in the social exchanges of looks: a national context will influence who can look at whom, in what way, at what degree of intensity and even for how long. In some national contexts, it becomes a breach of a social code to look at certain other persons; in others, it becomes a breach of the code not to look at all. Such conventions point towards the mutability of visual conditions in relation to national contexts. Those who transmigrate develop skills to negotiate such mutability, as they encounter it again and again. They anticipate the restructuring of the field of visuality. What in one country went unnoticed gets over-exposed in the next. Those who transmigrate expect to have to look at things differently. They accept that the field of visuality is mutable. Such acceptance is the ground of transvisuality. This is seeing on the move.

Migration produces changes in the human subject. Museum visitors who participate in migrational cultures do not merely change location, they shift subject-position. Transmigration – movement across several national territories – points towards a constant modulation of subject-position. The consequence of such modulation is a change in the structure of the visual field. By transmigrating, people are forced to confront the constant modulation of the structure of the visual field: a recognition that the visual field is mutable not in stasis; it can and must change. In taking a transvisual approach, a museum must work to recognize the mutability of the visual field. This is a massive challenge to any institution that sees its role as asserting value, working on the basis that a particular facet of the visual field – art objects and museum artefacts – can be fixed.

Transvisuality emerges because the dominant model becomes less about being fixed than being in flow. The intensification of flows of finance capital in hyper-capitalism find their corollary in the strengthening of currents of labour moving from rural to urban settings as well as from country to country. Hyper-capitalism creates such conditions – conditions that increasingly shape the contexts in which national cultural institutions operate. Museums benefit from the changed conditions by being able to draw on internationalized and, therefore, much more competitive labour markets. Particularly in respect of public interface functions – gallery attendants, visitor services, cloakroom attendants, security, shops, cafés and bars – museums are able to find staff to provide them with a cosmopolitan feel thereby contributing to their sense of being a heterotopia – a museum of the world. National cultural institutions, like Tate Britain, struggle to understand, however, that they are also museums in the world – situated among pools of migrating and transmigrating labour, flowing to places like London as a result of hyper-capitalist conditions. The forces that change the faces that make up the museum's staff also change the faces that populate its publics.

Alongside the increased flow of labour, hyper-capitalism incites the circulation of commodities. This has contradictory effects on national art institutions. On the one hand, the intensified flow of commodities increases the range of available goods and merchandise in the museum's retail outlets. On the other hand, the more highly-priced commodities placed at the heart of conventional museum's function – artworks – have to work against the intensified flows driven by hyper-capitalism. Their status as belonging to the elite stratum of luxury goods depends on a tacit guarantee that their supply will be restricted. The effect of hyper-capitalism's stimulation of the flow of finance capital, therefore, is not to cause an increased proliferation of artworks but to encourage increases in price. The contributive museum is assigned a role in this process: by taking objects out of circulation and holding them 'on reserve' in a collection, the museum provides a 'stop-lock', limiting circulation and, thereby, helping artworks and artefacts retain their value. The emphasis on this role of the museum is augmented by rules governing the museum's retention of art objects once they have entered the collection – restricting the ability to sell, gift, destroy or find any other means of disposal of art objects that they hold. In such terms, the museum keeps a 'reserve' function, holding back objects that might otherwise circulate.

Part of the museum's reserve function is to negotiate the relationship with other objects that circulate without reserve. This is of note in respect of merchandise, such as prints, greeting cards, t-shirts and ornaments that have a direct relationship to the paintings, sculptures and other artefacts held by the museum. The institution sets up a relationship between the artworks and artefacts it holds on reserve and other objects – proxies – the value of which depends on their relation to the reserve artworks. Good quality reproductions, true colours, accurate proportions – all begin to characterize the fidelity of the proxy to the reserve. The proxy also takes on an important role in keeping the reserve object in circulation. Such a role is critical, as it helps the museum escape a trap in which its elite functions drive it towards becoming increasingly tangential to the needs of hyper-capitalism. For, newly emerging elites established by hyper-capitalism need to gain access to the flow of commodities in the elite stratum of luxury goods. Conventional contributive museums, with their non-disposal regulations, stand in the way. Equally, ordinary people subject to increased urbanization and movement make use of images as part of their everyday lives. The reserve function of the museum renders it increasingly irrelevant without the work achieved by circulating its reproduced proxies.

The contributive museum needs to understand the critical work of its reproduced proxies and find ways of increasing their global distribution. The proxy, thereby, begins to partake of the politics of the proximate – engaged in the heterogenous needs and practices of people moving across the world. As images form a crucial part of the way in which experience is mediated, either in print media or digital media, people use images as part of the way in which they get what they need. By stimulating the circulation of reproductive proxies, the contributive museum moves more towards a distributed model. It allows the museum to play a part in the lives of the world's peoples rather than expecting the world's peoples to play a part in museum life.

Tate provides an example of the way in which the contributive museum has responded to hyper-capitalism's demands. The pressure to engage with the need to increase the flow of images, to provide sound and media content to populate media networks has been met with two mutually dependent responses: first, the museum has been complicit in platforming artists as signature figures, with a series of high profile artists' names being foregrounded, among them – Ai Wei-Wei, Grayson Perry, Chris Ofili became at Tate prominent examples; secondly, the museum develops an ever-increasing reliance on the Tate brand. The use of the Duveen Galleries Commissions at Tate Britain and the Unilever series of commissions in the Turbine Hall at Tate Modern exemplify the ways in which the two approaches work together with signature names – Martin Creed, Anish Kapoor, Olafur Eliasson – promoted as a means of maintaining Tate's presence within media networks. Again this representational strategy allows the figure of the artist to stand-in for the hosts of images that Tate does not allow to circulate. Reasons for restricting image circulation abound, such as matters regarding artists' copyright, conditions of donation and other intellectual property matters. However, the museum needs to find ways of moving closer to the mores of the distributed model with an acceptance that digital technology now provides the default mode of communication in London and other metropolises throughout the world.

The transmigrating subject presents the museum with a new model of subjectivity. The model moves away from established conceptions of the migrating subject's need for acculturation, wherein people who journey from the (colonial) margin to the (imperial) centre learn how to read cultural values disseminated by central institutions, such as Tate. Emergent conditions within hyper-capitalism lead to the abandonment of centre-periphery models. Instead, the move is towards a model of people crossing distributed planes. Such movement encompasses crossing cultures (transcultural) and nations (transnational) while developing practices and habits to cope with the demands of such constant movement (transmigrational). Among such habits are ways of seeing that allow people to anticipate the changes in the visual construction of different environments (transvisual).

The model of human subjectivity that emerges (trans-subjectivity) responds to the decline of the pre-eminence of dominant languages, cultures and nations that have defined the shape of the world since the inception of modernity. As Giddens has argued, such cultures have primarily been situated in the West:

> The first phase of globalization was plainly governed primarily by the expansion of the West and institutions that originated in the West. No other civilization made anything like as pervasive an impact on the world, or shaped it so much in its own image.
>
> *(Beck et al. 1994: 96)*

The end the US imperium has been signified above all by challenges to US hegemony in respect of the global economy. Ironically, the contribution that the US made to the globalization of the international system of exchange led both to the apogee of the US imperium (*c*.1990–2001) and its subsequent decline. The ambition to establish a global imperium to rule the international system of exchange no longer seems to be in the hands of the US. Indeed, the appearance is that the world will now operate more as a distributed plane with continental and regional distributions of power – countries in Asia, Africa, Europe, Australasia, North and South America will all have a role. It is in relation to such an outlook that the model of the migrating subject moving from margin to centre becomes redundant. Rather, the transmigrating subject crossing the distributed plane becomes the most efficacious concept to elaborate. Such a model equips the world for the shifts in cultural hegemony that follow the changes in economic hegemony. Museums need to be aware of such changes. The implication of cultural institutions in the West in broader Western colonial projects is clear. Being so mired in the formation of Western modernity and the subjectivities it inspired, museums need to connect with the trans(formation) of that modernity and the (trans)subjectivities that it now demands.

PART III
Hypermodernity and the art museum

7

NEW MEDIA PRACTICES IN THE MUSEUM

Why is a consideration of new media so central in considering the current operations and future of the museum and why is it so important to the argument about audiences in this account? Historically, museums have engaged with digital technologies and networked communication as Bearman (2010: 48) suggests, in a cautious and defensive manner and yet as things stand now there is a veritable tide of enthusiasm in the arts and cultural industries, including the museum for all things digital. Now digital technologies are looked to as the means to globally expand the reach of collections and the space of the museum in virtual form and in doing so develop new audiences. Gone is the suspicion that the virtual museum will make the analogue museum redundant along with the view that the 'aura' of the original will be undermined by its digital rendering. Part of the museum's current enthusiasm for the potential of digital technology and networked communications lies in recent developments that have seen technology become a ubiquitous feature of everyday life, especially in the potential for communication with audiences represented by the phenomena, 'social media'. Another obvious reason why museums have adjusted to computing is because over the past two decades, institutions of every kind have emphatically shifted from the management of knowledge, whose primary mode of organization and communication was paper-based, using analogue print, typewriters, fax machines, filing systems, landlines and face-to-face meetings, to the management of information, in which most internal and external operational functions related to programming and content generation are based upon digital data and networked computing. Museum workers, like most information workers, now live and work with computers. However, the museum's current embrace of computing does not change the overall conservatism displayed by museums towards the potential of computing and in general as cultural institutions they continue to follow, rather than lead innovations in the application of computing to both organizational management and public engagement.

One area of computing in which museums have had a considerable involvement over a longer period of time is the 'digitization' of collections and online archives. This is reflected in the considerable investment in and international co-ordination for what has now coalesced around the term 'digital heritage', led internationally by sub-committees of the International Council of Museums (ICOM). Through ICOM, a common international vision has emerged for digital heritage, in which networked computing provides the platform for joining up digitized collections and making them searchable. All of these applications of computing to the differing operations and functions of the museum are for the most part conventional and unsurprising and reinforce the view taken here that current enthusiasm masks a continued conservatism and hesitancy based upon a sense the museum has of new media's radical agency and power to unsettle and invade its deeper networks of intent. The radical potential of new media and the museum's management of the risk to historic and settled purposes is charted in what follows by looking in detail at Tate's uses and development of networked computing. The key to the argument advanced is that new media entails open collective practices, while digital heritage is a project of institutional closure, a distinction that will become apparent through a grasp of the idea of the museum as a distributed network in digital culture.

What is the specific work that the term 'new media' can do as opposed to 'digital media', 'online media', 'social media', or, more specifically, as technology has been applied to the museum, 'digital heritage'? What does 'new media' signal, or, contain that the other terms don't and why is it the preferred term in what follows? There is no single defining term that could encompass the social, economic, scientific, technical and cultural discoveries, applications and uses of computing on a global scale over the last quarter of a century. The world wide web and the internet form only one part of the spread of computing within and across human affairs in a tendency, noted by Baudrillard (1985: 128) for technology to produce, 'ever greater formal and operational abstraction of elements and functions and their homogenisation in a single virtual process of functionalisation'. This is necessarily abstract but its import is palpable. Applications of computing in medicine, banking, transport, manufacturing, distribution and communication become ever more central to the operation of production and reproduction.

Initially the term 'new media' delineated the application of computing to human communications, which historically have depended upon the material organization of separate analogue mediums. Over the latter half of the twentieth century, media became the collective noun for major public broadcast and print media, which had developed from the second half of the nineteenth century in the form of national daily newspapers, publishing, film, cinema, radio and television, etc. In these terms the BBC (British Broadcasting Corporation) was a key conduit for a public representation of British culture and its consumption within new forms of mobile privatization in domestic life in the immediate post-war period (Williams 1976). The technologies and cultural forms of these analogue media overlapped in terms of shared aspects of material technology, i.e. sound recording and the photo-mechanical process, as well as in terms of their cultural forms, such as journalism in print and broadcasting. In this sense, radio and television extended and reproduced the organization of public knowledge first developed by newspapers in the eighteenth century. The different technologies of analogue media and the prevailing organization of economic production gave rise to a media industry based upon separate ownership, product, plant, distribution and institutional organization. The introduction of digital technologies from the later 1980s brought with it increasing technical and cultural convergence across media industries in technology and ownership (Negroponte 1995). Image, sound, text, movement could all be produced and reproduced as a single binary code in electronic form. The creation, rendition, transmission and storage of what was previously thought of as valued knowledge became a generic mode of information in its translation into digital form. The advent of a single, universal digital code also gave rise to the project of 'digitizing' previous orthographic, photographic, sound and textual cultural archives.

On one definition, the term 'new media' encompasses the historical forms of commercial and public communication media, while the term 'digital heritage', often encouraged by government and funding as part of widening access, has come into use to delineate the cultural project of digitisation of archival museum collections. Other cultural and institutional delineations of the new media project engage in the same process of apportionment of digital technology to existing cultural practices and institutions, for example, digital photography, digital film, digital art and so forth, just as the previous industrial and institutional organization of media and its studies seek to delineate additional practices such as online media or social media, from previous broadcast forms. The recent term 'social media', used to define a collection of interactive, user-generated practices, perhaps illustrates the conceptual problem with most attempts so far to either encapsulate and separate off discrete cultural practices within the ecology of new media, or create digital taxonomies based upon technology. The term social media privileges the distributed, non-linear interactive characteristic of networked computing, which has been dubbed a 'many-to-many', as opposed to a 'one-to-many' form of communication. To define this aspect of networked communication as 'social' says something about the way in which previous analogue media, the one-to-many form of public and commercial broadcasting, understood itself and the ways in which the social now enters into the equation. Is it, by inference, the case that public broadcast and commercial media never have been social? Such a position opens up the question of what kind of sociality, or social relationships are being defined by networked user behaviours against established models of analogue media communication. Historically, for the museum, as for public broadcasting, the 'social' was cast in terms of an abstracted as well as representational public, which was addressed by the cultural authority and mediation of publicly funded cultural institutions. If the public is understood as the representational term for the people of a nation-state, then the social has been understood as the persistent structures of human relationships that make up collective ways of life or society. What has been called up in this account is that the representational systems by which the public is recognized and the social acknowledged have been put under pressure by the increasing globalized processes of the movement of capital and labour. The distributive forms of production and informational economies are bringing the human world to the point where the nation-state and its persistent structures of human relationship are revealed as localized, parochial and relative arrangements of larger networks of affiliation and interest, whose space is dissociative from place and the historic continuity of time.

The term 'social media' does indeed reintroduce the very idea of the social into media technology and its organization but not as an idea confined to the sum of networked interaction in and across a series of privately owned internet portals and applications, however politically dramatic some of the effects of mass user behaviours have been. New media has given rise to the need to rethink the social, not as something already given as a label attached to certain behaviours, but rather as something to be demonstrated in and across the networks of associations in which humans interact with machines and in those established institutional networks where the idea of the social has currency (Latour 2007: 3). One of the key reasons for this need to demonstrate the social is that what has previously been defined as the social in terms of structures and affiliations, cannot simply be converted and totalized as a number of internet users, because net behaviours are not necessarily governed nor restricted by an external supra-notion of the social. For the museum, as well as other state-funded cultural institutions, the term 'social media' raises not only what the social consists of and how it is demonstrated, but as a corollary it brings the very idea of 'the public' to the forefront of argument. What does 'the public' of public service and the public realm consist of, when it is clear that 'social media', the 'many-to-many' is short-circuiting the civic forms of both the social and public?

The term 'new media' is intended here to call into question the naturalization and normalness of applications of technology in order to temporarily suspend the business and busyness of the digitization of everything along existing institutional and organizational lines as if nothing has really changed. Instead of thinking about the 'digital' as a conventionalized add-on to existing forms, codes, conventions and practices of both media and institutions, new media draws attention to the larger dimension of a set of fundamental changes in human communication being made possible in the human-computer interface. Communication through graphical user interfaces, the desktop icons of personal computers, increasingly defines all human interactions with data, in the sense that software applications mediate the user's access to and manipulation of stored data. The 'raw' data, the zeros and ones of mathematical algorithms, require an intermediary platform (for all but computer scientists and programmers) in order for humans to interact with machines. In this important sense, a new and cultural dimension to media communication applies to human-computer interactions with networked digital data because interfaces necessarily code cultural purposes. It is in this recognition of the extension of coding meaning, now in a much wider set of mediated communications, which the term new media seeks to include. The term 'new media' can be thought of as a temporary place marker to hold open an exploration of a fluid moment of global economic and technological change and to resist a settlement based upon the continuity of existing forms of knowledge use. The term new media is a central acknowledgement that culture itself is now digital and that digital remediation is the new default of culture. This proposition is argued in more detail in what follows.

The central characteristic of new media is then the convergence and remediation of analogue media through digital technologies. However, while the technologies of microprocessing, digital code and computing are the necessary conditions of new media, they are not its exclusive defining feature. As a number of commentators have pointed out, it is not the technology in itself that is producing social and cultural change, rather it is the economic and institutional organization of technologies and the things humans do with them.[1] Essentially, this is a two-way street and to regard machines and their algorithms as providing an additional technical medium for achieving existing strategic aims and delivering outcomes in museums (at present those of archival documentation of collections and visitor engagement in marketing) is a reduction of more complex interactions between humans and machines. Technologies do things for and to us and our relationship with them is becoming ever more symbiotic and requires an understanding of the human-computer interface that recognizes new patterns of labour as well as intimacy (Turkle 1997: 180). What it is to be human, in particular the recognitions and embrace of multiple and relative subjectivities, now need to be understood as part of knowledge-formation processes and their institutional expressions, divisions and organization. Thus the stage is set not only for a reconsideration of what constitutes the social but also any fixed or ultimate notion of our humanness; both terms are being renegotiated in theory and in practice, which is a stark reminder to any limited project of digital heritage applied to the museum, that much more is at stake.

The immediate impact of such recognitions upon analogue museological practices is a challenge to existing models of knowledge (re)production in collection, conservation and interpretation. The reproduction of collections in digital code, which simulate textual, photographic and motion graphic constructions of analogue objects amounts to much more than an extension of analogue forms of traditional documentation (Cameron and Kenderdine 2010: 81). Digitization, as Cameron points out, does not produce self-evident data, but rather constitutes an entry, or log in a non-linear interpretative field. Support for this perspective derives not only from studies of the behaviours of the uses of digitized collections,[2] but also from post-structuralist theoretical perspectives that stress the essential arbitrariness of the linguistic sign. Not only is the production of knowledge now considered as relative rather than singular in its forms of truth, but the circulation and uses of knowledge are no longer confined within the institutionally legitimate boundaries of subject classification. Rather, as Lyotard first articulated, knowledge has become, not only a relative truth, but a tradeable commodity in contextually specific forms of consumption. Such understandings of both the behaviours of online users and post-modernist epistemological perspectives call into question the cultural authority upon which collection and interpretation practices in the museum are based.

The recognition of the polysemic nature of the human-object relationship, the multiplicity of interpretation and the changeability of context has been brought to the fore through the technocratic project of digitization, but equally applies retrospectively to analogue truths and their disciplinary regimes or in a further understanding of the term epistemic technologies. This, as Foucault so fully articulated, opened new ways to look at old technologies as well as to reverse the flow of historical truths through excavating the layers of knowledge construction and, in doing so being able to identify particular discourses or 'master narratives' by and through which knowledge orders had been assembled (Lyotard 1986: 18). Put another way if new media can be defined as a practice of remediated knowledge, then the analogue museum can by analogy be described as a mediating 'technology', whose historical form and the certainties it carried can, in the Foucauldian model, have an archaeology that can be excavated. The objects of collection and the penumbra of knowledge and scholarship attached to them can be understood as constructed and selective rather than transparent truths with universal reach as ably examined by Hooper-Greenhill (1992). This model of analysis of the historic development of the museum as a technology or disciplinary 'regime of truth' has produced scholarly perspectives on the museum's relationship to forms of power and exclusion, most notably in the post-colonial critique (Hardt and Negri 2001: 23). The understanding of new media as a profound remediation of the museum is a new alert to a new moment which is prior to, or at least in the process of becoming, a reordering of the historic museum with new economic and technological imperatives behind it.

In the world before mechanical reproduction, drawing, oil painting, etching, bronze casting and stone carving were the media of their day. This makes the contents of most international art museums, collections, media specific to a given mode of historical reproduction. From the perspective of new media, museums are archives of previous media whose content is not only as Marshall McLuhan would have it a previous medium, but can also, as Raymond Williams discussed with the development of television, be understood as an archive of the social relations which produced a particular medium (Lister et al. 2003: 78). In considering how these two perspectives derived from understandings of previous media applied to the new (digital) media it is possible to identify three defining conceptions, which can be thought of as layers, which make up the computer simulation of analogue representations. The first surface layer of an analogue medium resides in what is depicted and what is of general, cultural historical interest to the viewer, or as Barthes' notion of the 'studium' defines it, the spectators average interest in detail, manners and customs of a period (Barthes 1984: 51). The second layer consists of the cultural form, the cultural codes and conventions to which the object conforms, which in European art since the Renaissance has operated in relationship to the paradigm of representational theory (Lovejoy 2004: 15). The third layer is that of the object's materiality, consisting of the technical knowledge of its construction, its technicity. Manovich (2001: 11) describes new media in very similar terms when he defines four principle dimensions for understanding new media as: the digital medium itself – its material and logical organization; the human-computer interface – the operating system; the software systems that run on top of the operating system; the illusions – appearance based upon digital images used on software applications; and the forms – commonly used conventions for organizing a new media object as a whole.

Reframing the objects of the art museum as examples of historical media, from the vantage point of new media comes up against the subject taxonomy of the discipline of art history, and more significantly questions the category of art collection based in the exchange value of the art market. In the academy there are many currents within what has come to be understood as 'new' or 'radical' art history (Harris 2001: 9), which over the last four decades has developed perspectives on the work of art as part of the more general social processes of communication: in particular, materialist thinking about the work of art as social communication focused upon the material object as both a mediation in terms of encoding of conventions and reproduction, and, as a commodity in terms of its production, ownership, collection and exchange value (Berger 1972; Baxendall 1988). Such art historical scholarship and analysis has contributed to a broader understanding, if not a new set of museological benchmarks, for the interpretation of the work of art in education, the museum and media journalism. A knowledge and understanding of the historical conditions of the production of the work of art is now recognized as a significant means of increasing appreciation and making the meanings and values of the work accessible beyond expert knowledge. While the understandings of the new art history and the corpus of knowledge it has produced constitute a new norm in classrooms and lecture halls as well as providing a narrative thread for television art documentaries, it presents the art museum with an unresolved set of problems in interpretation and learning when faced with aesthetic modernism's refusal of interpretation.

The root of this problematic for all aspects of art museum practice rests upon the encounter with the work of art and the predominance of the aesthetic modernist trope. In aesthetic modernism curating, the individual, for that is the irreducible core of the construction of the modernist authentic self, approaches the work of art and stands before it, unencumbered in order that the work of art, that mute object as Preziosi (2011) terms it, can communicate, or 'speak' directly to the perceiving subject. In the act of encounter, the individual exercises aesthetic judgement. Art museum exhibition practice continues to wrestle with how exactly the mute object communicates and how the cultural position and knowledge of the subject engages the object in the degree to which it recognizes that the museum is itself an intermediary between the object and subject in its inescapable staging of the object for the viewer. At the risk of caricature, at one end of a spectrum of aesthetic modernism curatorial theory and practice lies the educated and informed autonomous individual with the resources to exercise aesthetic judgement in encountering the work of art. For this individual, any additional resource, even possibly a caption, is unnecessary and a distraction as would be the presence of other museum visitors upon the space between herself and the work. Such an encounter is imagined as essentially abstract and private. Thus for a modernist, the encounter with the work of art is an exercise in disinterestedness, both of the intentions of the artist in making the work of art, the work itself and its subsequent appreciation in what Kant theorized as the non-cognitive pleasure of the aesthetic and the need for art to be essentially separate from nature, science and labour in order to attain universality (Pietz 2009: 111). However, as Pietz goes on to point out, referring to the work of Derrida, the problem for such a view of the universal apprehension of sensate objects is the inevitable intrusion of the logos, which everywhere translates phenomenal apprehension into signs. In arguing for the arbitrariness of the sign and hence the constructedness of meaning, post-structuralism clearly softened the harder edges of modernist purism in the art museum, which, at the other end of the modernist spectrum of museum theory and practice, was expressed in the historical shift to the enabling museum. Here those without a knowledge and training in art, while remaining conceptualized as the foundational subject of the modernist individual, are thought not to be in possession of the resources to engage in aesthetic judgement and therefore require the intersession of the museum.

Prior to the emergence of new media and the definition of a new field of practice and study, academic discussion of late twentieth-century media had already led to a series of understandings of the expansion of the field of study of visual communication to include commercial television and advertising (Berger 1972) that, over the next two decades developed in the academy to various calls for the systematic study of visual cultures. Studies of the increasing influence of the visual in everyday life took place in the growing discipline of cultural and media studies as well as having an impact upon studies in anthropology, which had long used media as a means of observational recording, as well as in art history, which had been the historic discipline within European universities in which understandings of visual paradigms and codes were discussed. In focusing here on the art museum, understandings of art history, cultural and media studies and anthropology will need to intersect with as well as be rethought in studies of new media (Henning 2006: 71).

The greater predominance of the visual in the reproductive means of communication in late capitalist culture has, according to Mirzoeff (1999: 31), provoked a 'visual crisis of culture'. For Mirzoeff, this is a situation, 'caused by modernism and modern culture confronting the failure of its own strategy of visualising'. One of the consequences of this articulation over the past decade has been the emergence within the academy of a newly constituted approach to the study of culture, which has set itself the task of defining an 'expanded field of the visual'. There is a sense of critical urgency attached to this new delineation of the visual in culture, because, it is argued, visualization is a locus of globalized cultural change and it is here, precisely, that the larger and more general crisis of European/Western historical culture is met once more. The overall urgency given to this visual crisis of the cultural suggests that criticality cannot be limited to defining new objects of interest and subject framing within the due process of academic scholarship, nor the traditional sites of the collection and display of the visual, but is to be found in a much wider set of contexts, institutions and practices involved in the production, distribution and consumption of the visual.

To study visual culture was thus to bring the new topography of a globalizing world under some form of intellectual, educational and above all practical scrutiny and to reframe epistemologies that have previously only privileged a Eurocentric account of seeing and being seen. The legitimating project of Mirzoeff's 1999 book *An Introduction to Visual Culture* was to call for a reconfiguration of the scholarly study of art, media and communication built around new perspectives and theoretical perspectives of the postmodern. The introductory chapter, 'What is Visual Culture?', rehearses the problematic of the foundational subject/object distinction in visual representation established by the European Renaissance and questioned by modernist discourses that positioned visuality as a relationship between representations and reality. Mirzoeff insists that the new condition of visuality is that of an unstable set of relationships in which representations of the real are constitutive of the real. As he says in the panoramic opening paragraph, not only does modern life take place on screen as part of everyday life, it is everyday life for millions of people (Mirzoeff 1999: 1).

In the intervening decade since *Visual Culture* was published, the case for understanding culture through its media of communication and in the context of global spaces and flows is no less urgent. The tendencies noted by Baudrillard (1985: 129) of technological society's irreversible move towards miniaturization and functionalization of informational processes has become more pronounced in social and economic life and continues to be a focus of critical and political attention. Debord's (1977) 'society of the spectacle' (see Debord 1999) is no less compelling in the continuation of commodification, just as Lyotard's (1986) observations about the impact of the changed conditions in the production of knowledge still hold. The examples cited to support the significance of the visual in culture have changed; modern life still takes place on screen, but it is the screen of virtual space, rather than broadcast TV. Electronic surveillance has become an accepted fact of life but mobile technology and YouTube have given power to those previously surveyed. Social media was only dimly in the critical sights of the forms of convergence articulated at the millennial moment and is now the primary example of the complex interplay between multiple forms of mediation and everyday life. In short, Mirzoeff's original argument remains compelling and can be extended to take account of a further decade of change. Now the emphasis might be less upon having to argue for the centrality of the visual over the previous domination of print, but upon the digitization of all forms of analogue registration and their relationship to the human sensorium in a continuous intertextual process of remediation. What is becoming much clearer is that the representational model of mediation, which reached a scientific and technical 'perfection' with mechanical indexicality, is now inadequate to understand how the human-computer interface to network data establishes the real and the represented.

The other armature of Mirzoeff's argument, developed from Appadurai (2000) underlined the importance of the impact of the new patterns of global migration upon national cultures of identity and continues to be highly relevant to this account. One of the central social aspects of this globalized landscape in Britain can be found in the newer forms of transnational migration, making London, as the former capital of the British Empire, a global city, a transcultural centre, operating as an intense networked hub in which individuals experience a heightened sense of clashing, converging and co-existing cultures. The newer forms of the transnational in which migration is a more fluid and diasporic process brings with it the idea of the transcultural, which, as Appadurai points to has produced and reproduces the tension between 'sameness' and 'difference' at every level of life and consciousness and it is this tension that lies at the heart of the visual crisis of culture. For the art museum, however, the visual crisis of culture centres, as elsewhere, upon the unravelling of singular discourses of panoptic mastery (Bennett 1995) even as they are still promulgated and can be recognized in the profound disjuncture between the homogenized cultural register of curation and authorial voice and the heterogeneity of unregistered audiences.

What is of local importance here is how the expanded field of visual culture and the cultural crisis it invokes, now quickened by networked computing, acts back upon a specific national cultural guardian, Tate Britain and its National Collection of British Art. How, specifically, do transcultural experiences generate positions of spectatorship in the art museum and how does the museum acknowledge such positions? Within the curatorial practices of the art museum, the value of the expanded visual field has in many ways been framed within the post-colonial critique of the overriding tendency of museums towards Eurocentrism (Bhabha 2001: 193) and by a Foucauldian form of analysis of the disciplinary function and civilising mission of the public museum (Hooper-Greenhill 1992: 45; Bennett 1999: 89). Such critical positions, while slowly seeping into museological consciousness, have also, in the counter embrace of the spectator as consumer, been contained and eschewed in terms of an institutional stand-off between the museum and academy in which there is a claim that the post-colonial moment has passed. It follows from this that to suggest that the crisis of culture, centred upon the visual and generated by globalization, is still very much of the here and now for the art museum, requires the investigation of positions beyond the disciplinary and post-colonial critique of the museum, precisely because critical discourse is confined to the academy and market-driven commodification of the visual has been assimilated by the reflexive modernization of the art museum and corporatized in 'the image experience'. If this is true, then it begs the question of how new investigations of the status of the visual in the art museum can be framed, which do not start from or end with the academic critique.

A number of scholars have extended Benjamin's argument that the functions of both fine art and media were transformed in relationship to the technological advances of the second half of the nineteenth century to a consideration of the impact of digital technologies upon existing analogue modes of reproduction (Henning 2006: 71; Lovejoy 2004: 62; Bolter and Grusin 2000: 74; Robins 1996: 31). There is a broad consensus among these scholars that the complex interactions within and between digital technological and cultural systems now challenge established ways of thinking about art, reproduction, representation, knowledge and cultural authority. This is Mirzoeff's 'crisis of visuality' (1999: 3) and Lovejoy (2004: 33) goes as far as to say that digital technology has brought to an end the paradigm of visual representation that has been in place since the European Renaissance. Such recognitions make it clear that the challenge for museums of whatever kind is not only to recalibrate the relationship between analogue objects and their digital simulations, but to consider the larger shift taking place in cultural value systems that are recalibrating the relationship between the museum and everything that hitherto it was not.

Museums have engaged with and understood new media over the past two decades in ways that remain tangential to the knowledge orders of collection and exhibition practices of objects as well as learning and marketing practices of audiences. It would be surprising if this were not the case given the relative newness of digital media against the much longer history of national museums and analogue collections and it is only in this recent period focused upon the importance and composition of audiences that museums are turning to the potential of new media. There are two fundamental aspects to this intersection. Firstly, museums continue to preserve the uniqueness of their institutional and historic culture based upon collection, but now feel obliged to extend that in digital form as a matter of access and record. In their engagement with new media, museums are confronted by an expanded, global and transnational field of symbolic meaning which is reshaping national cultures and challenging traditional cultural authority. Secondly, the potential of new media to recode and distribute the cultural meaning of collections in the emerging practices of the art museum's online presence comes up against an organizational hierarchy that arranges curatorial and editorial practices within the logic and status of accumulation of the collection. The organizational structure of Tate, as has been argued, channels knowledge and practices of art and culture through selective and discrete networks which maintain a 'hard-walled' separation between the values of collection and those of embodied audiences, with exhibition and display acting as an interstitial zone of mediation. In contrast, knowledge in the 'global spaces of flow' (Castells 2010: 432) is increasingly dissolving boundaries, crossing territorial limits and repurposing uses. It has already been argued that the transnational field of potential meaning, predicated upon new patterns of global urban migration is leading to specific forms of transvisuality, which are understood as 'relative viewing positions' based in 'recognitions of difference' and aligned to 'remediated digital forms'. In this light, the discussion of new media and the museum can be seen as a contestation between maintaining institutional knowledge boundaries developed through an analogue world and the aspiration to reconfigure knowledge based upon user experience in a digital one.

The evidence of Tate Online, expressed in its editorial practices, points to a struggle to both embrace the possibilities of new media, while containing a series of perceived threats to traditional forms of cultural authority and provenance posed by the openness and reach of the internet. Tate Online contains competing definitions and conflicting purposes as the subsequent account will show. Tate developed its website and online presence from the 1990s, in a period in which the internet was still characterized as Web 1.0, built upon destination websites with textual read-only content, through to the development of Web 2.0 from roughly 2002 to the present, in which information sharing, interactivity, participation and user-generated content became possible through technical developments in computing speed, volume, scalability and software development. Social media and participatory net behaviour is still working its way through institutional understandings of the use of the web. It continues to represent the greatest challenge to institutions and organizations seeking to use the internet to communicate with their traditional constituencies as well as to reach out to groups and communities of users who have become visible through new cultures of participation as well as those who are conceptualized as beyond or outside of identified participation. The question can now be put of how have public sector institutions, such as Tate, responded to and organized the potential of new media?

Three defining institutional conceptualizations of how museums have responded to new media can be articulated which broadly follow the historical development of the web. Such defining conceptualizations can also be understood as distinct forms of the staging of the web by organizations and the staging of organizations on the web over a historic period in which the modes of production and exchange shifted from a vertical organization of capital and labour in capitalist nation-states, to the horizontal reorganization of distributed capital and labour (Harvey 2000: 142). What is outlined here in the example of the art museum might equally well apply to other publicly funded institutions in health, education and government. Organizations visibly display as well as conceal their organizational hierarchies in the transposition of knowledge to a virtual counterpart on web pages and in navigational tools. The conceptualizations examined here in relationship to museums are: i) the web understood as a marketing tool across a period in which public sector organizations were encouraged to recast themselves as corporations operating in relationship to market forces; ii) the potential of the web to produce a universal archive, cast as digital heritage and developed within a technocratic culture; and iii) the web understood in terms of social media as an interactive media, framing the virtual visitor as an expanded audience and to a lesser extent the user as a generator of valued content.

All three conceptualizations of the web articulated above apply to Tate Online. New media objects are defined as collectable works and hence fit within a genre of curatorial and collection practices, i.e. electronic art, digital art, or the curation of Intermedia at Tate.[3] Tate, along with most other national and international museums, locates new media within the zone of mediation (functions 4 and 5 in Figure 7.1).

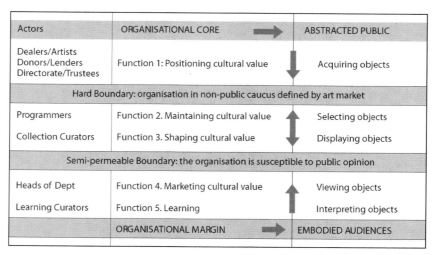

FIGURE 7.1 Diagram of Tate's organizational functions. Research synthesis, Tate Encounters 2009

New media as a mediation of the museum has, in the short history of a fast medium, primarily functioned as a replacement of print and broadcast publicity as a part of marketing. As might be expected in the early stages of the remediation of analogue content into digital form, the first iterations of Tate's online website followed other corporate and highly marketized branding models. The larger point of the argument is that the wider potential of digital technology as a radical new communication medium has, in the hands of the brand managers, been contained. New media's power to disrupt, supplant and even transform cultural knowledge practices are managed as a new set of risks to the analogue of material collection based as has been argued in the exchange values of the fine art markets. The emergent social and cultural forms of digital technology and online media, which are fundamentally altering the relationship between sender and receiver, author and reader, producer and consumer, are still largely perceived by the museum through the prism of pre-digital culture. However, museums in general and Tate's strategic approach in particular to new media, while fully acknowledging the success of Tate Online and the completion of the online collection, still confines the radical potential of new media to shift cultural authority within the boundaries of corporate communication on the one hand and a technocratic discourse, whose project is the rationalization of knowledge as information in digital form on the other. There is at the heart of this problematic a contradiction between the rhetoric of the creative potential of new media to enfranchise audiences as producers and the reality of the regulation of online content.

From the point of view of the homogenization of online collections in the European project of digital heritage, Tate Media's development through the period 2000–10 was in many respects a diversion from the digital heritage project. Tate's Online presence is better understood as a corporatist, rather than technocratic extension (McLuhan 1994) or remediation (Bolter and Grusin 2000: 5) of print and television because it was primarily a process of transferring cultural forms of analogue content to a digital platform. Historically, analogue publishing was based upon a one-to-many model of communication in which the means of production were technical and costly and concentrated in private ownership. Likewise, broadcasting followed the same model, but with the important difference that in Britain in particular a strong public broadcaster was established with the BBC in 1927 as the potential of radio was grasped by government. In contrast, the world wide web was constructed as a non-centralized system and digital technologies have made the means of production of broadcast quality media cheaply and readily available. More importantly for the discussion at hand, the internet is technically and culturally an interactive medium allowing for instantaneous response and self-directed navigation through non-linear hyperlinking.

An initial starting point for elaborating the corporatizing of the web can be gleaned from looking at Tate Online and its mode of public address. Tate relaunched its website in March 2000, to coincide with the opening of Tate Modern. The website was designed by Nykris Digital Design, with a brief to produce a 'clean, stylish and contemporary look which complements the new Tate corporate identity' (Zappaterra

2001: 22). Nikki Barton of Nykris elaborated on the brief as to 'disseminate the brand to a global audience' and that it needed 'to build international awareness, attract visitors and supporters and increase sales and attendance at exhibitions', in addition to making the collection available and fulfilling one of Tate's central tenets of access and education. The order of the aims is important in that, as with the organization, so in the strategy, 'access and education' are attendant upon marketing and serve to demonstrate the impact of the museum through expanded visitor awareness and virtual visits.

The brief for the 2000 website relaunch follows closely what Damien Whitmore, director of communications at Tate between 1992 and 2001, has outlined as the development of the Tate brand. Whitmore's account of his experience at Tate is a narrative of the transformation from the role of the informational services of the museum in a culture of public and civil service, to one of commercial and private enterprise led by the corporate needs of a museum aspiring to be a world leading brand and world centre for modern art. This is clearly exampled in the way in which Whitmore described the culture he found on his arrival at Tate in 1992. It was, he says, 'old fashioned', based upon paper memorandums and hierarchical formality. He sketched a Tate with little sense of the importance of audience and exclusively focused upon the needs of curators and their discussions with artists on who and what was considered important to acquire and exhibit. These traditional curatorial practices were to be expanded and reorganized through the vision and plan to create a new gallery of modern art in London. Whitmore describes the galvanizing effect of the decision to build Tate Modern at Bankside in which everything became about delivering the message that Tate would build Tate Modern. A decade on, the overriding logic of maintaining Tate as a world brand for modern art continues to dominate in the organizational networks of Tate through the creation of Phase Two of Tate Modern's extension. But what is of more immediate relevance is understanding how Tate's online architecture and navigational hierarchies were fashioned by the strategic interests of building expansion. As Whitmore put it, the website was an add-on to the building, rather than as it existed in the wider commercial sector, or as it was being discussed in wider academic circles, as a new medium of exploration and enquiry. In fact it was the conventional media of newspapers and television that were more significant to the strategic project of building Tate Modern and which shaped Tate's approach to its online presence. Whitmore describes the excitement of the controversy surrounding Carl Andre's 'Bricks', entitled 'Equivalent VIII' (1966) and purchased by the Tate Gallery in 1972, which were headlined on the front page of the *Daily Mirror* on the 16 February 1976 as 'What a Load of Rubbish', with the byline 'How Tate dropped 120 Bricks'. Familiar as this populist hostility to the modernist art project was in the British press of the period, it served as an example in Tate of the gulf between its ambitions and popular support at that time. If Tate Modern was to get built, the public's attitude towards it would have to change and Whitmore is clear that Tate became heavily invested in what he referred to as the 'spin politics' of the period.[4] The Turner Prize was strategically used to insert art into a rising celebrity media culture, which, he claims, worked to get the tabloids and government on side as illustrated by the £50 million grant it received from the Heritage Lottery Fund, Millennium Commission as well as *The Sun* tabloid newspaper's support for the opening of Tate Modern by sending three 'Page 3' models to be photographed in the building. Over this period, the older, civil service-styled Department of Information became the Communications Department, which introduced extended and specialist press consultancy. In Whitmore's experience, establishing the Tate brand became the primary driver and the website was seen as an adjunct to the needs of both corporate communication and income generation as Tate Online also became operationally important, with the introduction of online advertising acting as a box office, as well as publicizing an expanded events programme. Following Whitmore's move to the Victoria and Albert Museum in 2001, he was succeeded by Will Gompertz,[5] who, between 2002 and 2009, was to change the Department of Communications into Tate Media, before leaving to become the BBC's news arts editor. Gompertz had a background in successful innovative publishing, creating the early multimedia enterprise *Shots* and a combined arts magazine *Zoo*, which also developed a website. What had struck Gompertz in the emergent multimedia publishing environment was that it was possible to have new kinds of conversations about culture across different established fields and that publishing had become cheaper through technology.

Whitmore and Gompertz shared the view that the emphasis in their respective roles changed from establishing the brand to developing the brand after Tate Modern had opened. From a publisher's point of view, Gompertz grasped that Tate was potentially a content business because it had unlimited access to the collection, Turbine Hall commissions and exhibitions. What it did not have was the full means to exploit that content. Gompertz formulated his publishing interests in terms of Tate's public mission to increase public access, understanding, appreciation and enjoyment of art, as enshrined in the 1992 Museums and Galleries Act. His pitch to his fellow directors and to the Tate Trustees was that Tate Media should develop production facilities and become a broadcaster and publisher as the best way forward in developing its online presence. Gompertz stresses that Tate's phenomenal brand success had made it attractive and that Tate Media flourished because it had considerable sponsorship from the financial and business information company, Bloomberg. Such sponsorship allowed Gompertz to develop the video publishing arm, 'Tate Shots', which enabled him to employ an executive producer, and, through British Telecom (BT), which sponsored the website, hosting, technical and creative support. He also stressed the fact that the success of Tate Media had a lot to do with being at the boardroom table as a director because it was here that decisions on what to fund were made. His aim was to get the money for a production unit and people who could make high quality and entertaining content and to develop a website led by editorial expertise. In building the Tate Media department, Gompertz detailed his publishing and narrowcasting strategy and underlined four key aspects required to operate successfully; a deep understanding of multiple media platforms; an understanding of its content; an understanding of audiences; and finally editorial skills. As a publisher at heart, Gompertz was a professional who instinctively realised that media was a storytelling business and that Tate Online could be a microbusiness within the Tate brand.

The website Gompertz left in 2009, along with the end of the BT sponsorship, is very much the website as it remained until it was redesigned and relaunched in April 2012. This pre-2012 website, remained the Mykris design in its bare architecture, only with the addition of ten years of additional content and the innovations Gompertz led in editorial programming for audience sections, such as Tate Kids, Tate Shots and Tate Learning. Its navigational hierarchy continued to mirror the material and institutional organization, with a strongly retained corporate mode of address of the four constituent museums, nested within the overall Tate brand. Given the high costs and time required in major redesigns, websites in general tend to lag behind both technical and conceptual developments. The pre-2012 Tate website contained a large amount of archival material buried away in dusty navigational pathways, and pages with selective modes of search. A simple content analysis of the site map reinforced the view that the main purpose of the homepage was to maintain the Tate brand with categories such as Tate Channel, Tate Publishing, Tate Collection, Tate Kids and Young Tate; indeed the word Tate appeared more than 20 times as a prefix on the homepage. The organizational hierarchy could be read from right to left along both the horizontal navigation bars, one for the four museums, the other started with the collection and ended with the shop. The vertical navigation columns expressed the organizational structure of Tate. This was all conventional and, while institutional design styles differ, the V&A or MOMA for example, Tate's pre-2012 website conformed to established homepage navigation, mixing content areas with selective address to audience and the post-2012 redesign editorially reasserts aesthetic modernism's paradigm of the artist.

What distinguished Tate within the museum field in 2004, as John Stack, Head of Tate Online has noted[6] was its high number of visits and the range of content it made available. In presenting a new online strategy to the Tate Trustees in 2010, Stack gave a balanced, but candid view of the strengths and weaknesses of the existing Tate website. He appraised it as having deep content and some interesting interactive projects, but was 'relatively flat, monolithic and impervious', a view shared by the analysis above. In adopting the strategy the Trustees approved a complete overhaul of Tate's website in order that it could become an interactive 'platform for engaging with audiences'. Launched in April 2012, the redesign will, the strategy suggests, put audiences at the centre (Ringham 2011). It has moved from an organizational structure to a navigational interface that aids expectations, fosters discussion, debate and participation. The aim of the redesign is to move from a command transmission and broadcast model to one based upon shared experiences, multiple voices and cultural exchange and inclusivity. The strategy places much greater emphasis upon permeability and a differentiation of Tate voices and organizationally intends to repurpose and redistribute its current content in an interface that gives much greater predominance to a search function. In a compendium document, *Tate Social Media Communication Strategy 2010–12* (Ringham 2011), the social media dimension of the overall strategy for redesign was elaborated. The document lists the 'communities' that Tate will operate, including Google, Facebook, Twitter, Flickr and YouTube. The strategy acknowledges that the main aim of Tate's relationship to social media is grounded in marketing but widens that to an aim to engage in dialogue with its online communities as opposed to merely broadcasting, or product placement. The strategy aims to develop a small number of initiatives tied to the themes of the programme that invite deep engagement through user generated content as well as to create specific streams for specific targeted audiences, especially those defined as developmental audiences. The strategy recognizes a new resource demand for such initiatives to succeed.

How successful the relaunch of Tate's website will be in achieving the aims of the strategy will take some time to assess and certainly a number of its aims would support a shift away from existing central editorial control to a more open and distributed form of the many-to-many. In whatever way the relaunch develops, it will set the tone for Tate's 'fifth museum' for the second decade of the new millennium and should signal a move away from corporatism and towards the interactive museum. There is, however, a recognized tension within the strategy between new possibilities; those of open dialogue, and the function of the website in maintaining and refreshing the brand. This is evident in the balance both documents strive to achieve between the market goals expressed in the strategy for the new website to expand visitor numbers, develop and reward brand loyalty, and the use of social media as a form of product placement, while emphasizing a user-led approach. There is also a serious misrecognition about the relationship between the core institutional practices and those of web-users that threatens to limit the larger aspirations of the strategy, which resides in the reassertion of the Tate brand and what it consists in. John Stack expresses the core of Tate's brand value as 'the collection' and the foregrounding of art and artists, which on the face of it seems incontrovertibly what Tate is about as an art museum. However, as this book endeavours to show, the collection and acquisition of works of art, the production and reproduction of the artist and art, can be understood, not as static and given things/values in a pre-given social order, but also as networks in which humans and objects generate and secure agency in order to secure meaning and value in the creation of the social (Latour 2007). The meanings and values of museum collections of art objects reside not in the objects on their own, nor in the objects plus historical expertise, but in networks that constitute the collection. Such networks operate along active lines of communication in which meaning is maintained, challenged and developed through performing the network.

The point to labour here is that the collection is already social, not something to be made social by engagement with an audience recognized and constituted outside of the network. However, as Latour (2007) has pointed out, the social, which is understood here as the collection, is itself not given but has to be traced in the performance of a network of associations. Hence, if the collection is already social by virtue of its position in capital networks, then in order for Tate to achieve the dialogic and interactive encounter with its publics, the networks of collection and acquisition will also need to be made public. As has been argued elsewhere, at present the organization of Tate is such that the function of acquisition is hard-walled and not open because it overlaps with the networks of private collection and the art market. The success of the ambition of Tate's new website to be dialogic, open and communicative depends upon the degree to which Tate's professional community and the internal stakeholders within its differential knowledge and value networks grasp this central problematic, which new media brings to the fore.

In 2009, during the Tate Encounters public panel discussions in the strand 'Resolutely Analogue: Art Museums in Digital Culture', Tate Media had already successfully organized itself within a corporate model of online publishing. The growth in its operation reflected an overriding editorial strategy, such that the two other dimensions of new media's growth in relationship to museums (the digitisation of collection and the interaction with users) were less visible and smaller projects. While Tate, like most big international museums, was belatedly beginning to relate its relatively 'closed' corporate web enterprises to social media, social media offered museums a corporate answer. Successful sharing and search websites such as Flickr, YouTube, Facebook and Google were grasped by Tate Media as 'social' add-ons, a second tier of soft marketing for the organization in which members of such websites would be encouraged to create a focus of interest around Tate. Social networking sites offered Tate a means of claiming wider engagement through these networks, while using them, as Google does, as a means of gathering market information. The potential of social media for distributing Tate's digitized assets in one direction, while opening its web portal to different forms of authorship in the other is set against Tate's current practice of using social media as a selective interface for additional content management in line with corporate understandings of audience. This approach casts the virtual visitor as predominantly a consumer, whose 'production' consisted of an interface personalization of the Tate brand.

The practical and political reason why a technocractic solution to new media is being embraced by museums is also because it is the way in which funding for digitizing collections is being organized (Knell 2003) and, more abstractly in this argument, because it minimizes the risks to the values and practices of analogue collection by maintaining a curatorial separation between material objects and their virtual, informational simulacra. This, as suggested, has had the consequence of positioning new media organizationally in Marketing and Learning in the functional zone of mediation. The technocratic constitution of new media in the museum has so far framed the limits of the major projects of new media in the museum, whose ultimate drive is, in an echo of Baudrillard's (1985: 132) analysis of the irreversible direction of technological development, a drive to create a totalizing virtual museum through the digitization of collections in a single harmonized interface. The emergence of a cultural technocracy can be traced back as Knell (2003) demonstrates to certain political recognitions in the US and Europe during the 1990s of the need to develop a knowledge-based economy in the face of shifts in global production and exponential growth in the economies of India and China, among others.

Whilst this technocratic framing is facilitating the development of new digital resources and forms of access to collection and interpretation, it also comes into conflict with and contradicts historical sections within the formation of the internet.

In his analysis of the social shaping of the internet, Castells (2001: 37) notes four distinct tendencies, or communities of interest, which continue to establish goals and create values within the internet. In particular, he notes the importance of the 'virtual-communitarians and Hacker subcultures', intent on creating accessible bridges between technical and social goals, evidenced historically for example in the development of Open Source code and the connected belief that the internet represented an opportunity for new kinds of human freedom and association, unfettered by the hierarchies of existing institutions and their organization of power and authority. Interestingly enough Castells argues that museums have the potential to be cultural (re)connectors of people and place in a global virtual world in which time and space have vanished and cites Tate Modern as one such example. In looking at the uneven consequences of the Information Age, Castells provides an important part of the argument about what is at stake for museums as a guardian of the materially embodied public realm, which networked spaces are short circuiting, a recognition not lost on other scholars of museums in a digital age (Castells 2010: 430).

The unhappy term 'digital heritage' has become the place marker for all that is at stake in new media and museums within the technocratic framework, operating to locate and classify culturally consecrated information within the project of the single navigable database. The problem from the perspective of the analysis presented here is that digital heritage brackets out a consideration of visitor experience. It ignores the wider sense of convergence in digital form of all cultural content and, crucially, the digitization of broadcast and entertainment media. The acceptance of the technocratic solution to the framing of the relationship between new media and museums also means that the potential of the user to act back upon or reinscribe meaning is reduced to a function of consumption on the one hand, and limited interactions as a follower on the other hand; a means by which to demonstrate audience numbers for the purposes of auditing and public funding reporting. Outside of this narrow technocratic and commodified discourse, digitization is creating forms of media and cultural convergence within contemporary global cultures of both space and place on an unprecedented scale, which in turn is changing the established system of representation. As recognized by many scholars (Parry 2010), this convergence is creating new opportunities within academic study and to a lesser extent museum practice to reconceptualize understandings of collection, exhibition and audience and crucially challenges institutional lines of cultural authority.

In effect, what the term 'digital heritage' reproduces is a much older distinction between differently valued cultures. Ultimately it is a Eurocentric distinction between that which is culturally consecrated (by the museum) and everything else. Building such a distinction into the very architecture of developing the museum's relationship to digital culture ensures the reproduction of a conception of stratified audience, between those who know and attend and those who don't know and don't attend, which runs counter to the belief in the radical repositioning of cultural authority engendered by technology. In contrast, the convergence looked at here is that between the art museum and what to date has been referred to as the expanded field of visual culture, which it is argued is present for audiences but not as yet for the museum. It is present for the audience because the expanded field of sense perception, representation and communication, most simply recognized in the nexus of internet exchange, is the given of everyday life, but absent for the museum because its institutional practices remain defined by aesthetic modernism's object based, exclusive market logic, which sets it apart from the everyday. Thus, museum professionals still largely see their task as one of being the custodians of object collections, whose symbolic value is assured and beyond reproach, as well as proselytizers for the social and personal benefits of contact and communion with the museum. However, it is not enough to rest the argument on the problem of the museum grappling with the everyday in the terms first set out by Bourdieu (1979: 65). The argument for an expanded field of visual culture has already been overtaken by developments in new media in which the digital is now the default of culture and this changes the way in which we understand both the museum and everyday life.

Castells (2010: 433) poses the relationship in new terms. Firstly, he sets out a new contradiction between what he calls 'technological creativity and global cultural communication' and 'the fragmentation of societies and a lack of shared codes of communication between particular identities'. This, he says, is a fundamental rupture brought about by the networked society, which if left unchecked, could mean the end of society. He elaborates this problem in terms of three elements of global change: the replacement of common codes of communication by individualized hypertext messaging that alienates the individual from the lived experience of the group; the compression and transformation of time into atemporality; and the replacement of the space of particularised identities by global space of flows. This analysis of the impact of technological systems upon global production echoes what others have outlined as the features of the condition of post-modernity (Harvey 2000: 259). What Castells calls for in redressing the fragmentation in time and space of the previous real scenes of our lives in historically sequential time and place (a strong echo of Baudrillard 1985: 126), is a new form of common communication protocol that could act as cultural connectors of time and space. In reaching for both a mode of communication and a spatial location that might act as a cultural connector, Castells identifies the art museum as an institution and public space that could provide a reconstructive link. He cites Tate Modern as an example because 'of its openness and its mix of temporalities, in other words, its capacity to link the present, the past and the future within a multicultural initiative'. Castells sees Tate Modern, along with the Guggenheim in Bilbao and the San Jose Tech Museum in California, to which he has personal links, as illustrations of his argument that museums can connect up the global and local dimensions of identity, space and local society, through the communication of art, science and human experience (Castells 2010: 429). In its simplified form, Castells' view continues a long tradition of civic and reformist thinking in which the museum is once more being asked to fulfil a regulatory function of public representation in the face of social fragmentation (Bennett 1995: 2). Castells' view of the museum as a form of society also accords with more recent British cultural policy perspectives in which the museum was given a forward-looking role in the creation of social cohesion,[7] when he says: 'Museums should play the same role in the field of cultural innovation as hospitals are currently playing in medical research' (2010: 434). However, while Castells suggests a somewhat utopian role for the future of museums, this is not unqualified by his own recognition that museums operate within determined social contexts. Some museums operate only along the lines of the preservation of heritage and in Castells' view are doomed to be mausoleums, while less obviously articulated, other museums are aligned with global cosmopolitan culture, based upon elite networks operating within the 'space of flow' rather than with the 'multiple local identities based upon particular codes drawn from local experience' and hence enjoyed only by a few. For museums to be the required cultural connector, he envisages they would need to become in his own words 'not only repositories of heritage but spaces of cultural innovation and centres of experimentation' (Castells 2010: 433).

Castells' conclusion brings us centrally back to the closer discussion of how new media could be entailed in the museum in ways that would make them spaces of cultural innovation and centres of innovation as many other commentators have also recognized (Lankshear 2002: 1). In the recorded dialogues of Resolutely Analogue, the reframing of new media's relationship to the knowledge and cultural authority of the art museum was very much framed as an argument for dissolving the hard-walled boundaries between the museum and everything else and the development of a dialogic, rather than editorializing the relationship with the art museum's audiences. Such an aim need not necessarily lead to a loss of definition or purpose for the art museum. But there is a central problem in Castells' simplification of the universal role he accords to art as a means of overcoming the dissociation between the local and the global, the temporal and atemporality, which resides in his notion of art as follows:

> In this world art without having any institutionally assigned role, without trying to do anything special, but by the mere fact of being art, can become a communication protocol and a tool for social reconstruction.
>
> *(Castells 2010: 429)*

Art is indeed a particularized form of more general human communication, which encodes experiences of what it is to be human in often powerful ways. In this sense Castells' assertion that art is capable of restoring the unity of human experience beyond oppression, differences and conflicts, has a deep resonance with what many people will have experienced in some form or other. But what is left out of this essentialist view of art and its universal language is a description and understanding of how such experiences occur within any given culture for groups or individuals. As Williams (1965: 42) put it, for art to exist at all a message has to be actively communicated and actively received, below this threshold art simply cannot exist. Such an understanding is perhaps implicit in what Castells intends by art as a communication protocol as well as his view of art and the art museum reconstituting codes of communication. However, art is no less coded by its conditions of production and exchange than any other object of post-modern consumption and the art museum's marketing of contemporary modernist art to multiple local communities of identity has been a conspicuous failure over more than two decades. What is being argued here is, in important respects, a reverse of Castells' traditional privileging of art in a media saturated environment. The crisis is not one of the end of society brought about by global individualized hypertextual atemporalities, but one in which societies are experiencing the end of a historically dominant mode of representation of which the modernist art museum was at the centre of its cultural authority. In the argument made here, the museum needs what new networked media has to offer more than the net needs the museum, because the dynamic of networked cultures is reinventing the social, while the museum continues to obscure its relationship to the public.

8

THE DISTRIBUTED MUSEUM

Museums remain firmly established as singular, bounded institutions, considered foremost for what they are rather than what they do. In this familiar regard, museums are buildings situated nationally, regionally and locally, which house object collections both great and small. The buildings, objects, the professionals who collect, conserve and curate and the daily stream of visitors, make up the established institution of the museum. However, when considering what museums do, attention is drawn more to the processes and organizational arrangements by and through which the entire material and spatial collection and edifice of the museum is maintained, extended, represented and reproduced. In considering both what museums are and what they do a much more complex and diffused picture emerges in which they are constituted across different organizational and operational spheres, made up of countless components and operations. This view of the museum is consistent with and in part derived here from Latour's (2007: 131) view of the 'operations of networks', or – as Law's (1999: 4) description of the two aspects of organizational complexity that actor network theory attempted to grasp – 'relational materiality', or even as Callon (in Callon et al. 2001: 35) defined the situation of a 'hybrid forum'. The term designated here for understanding the networked, relational, hybrid and performative dimensions of the museum, is the distributed museum, which involves two very different and not to be confused understandings of networks, as Latour is at pains to point out:

> Network is a concept, not a thing out there. It is a tool to help describe something, not what is being described. The consequence is that you can provide an actor-network account of topics which have in no way the shape of a network – a symphony, a piece of legislation, a rock from the moon, an engraving. Conversely, you may well write about technical networks – television, emails, satellites, sales forces – without at any point providing an actor network account.

(Latour 2007: 131)

FIGURE 8.1 Research-in-Process event, Duveens Studio, Tate Britain, March 2009. Tate Encounters

The distributed museum involves both what Latour calls a technical network, that of the internet, and network as a concept which can be applied to an organization. In the case of the museum and the internet, both the technical and conceptual sense of network apply, however, the model of the distributed museum developed here cannot be reduced to the online or virtual museum, any more than the internet can be understood as only a technical network. The point of interest is that both the internet and the museum are entailed in representational systems of the social. To understand what is intended by the idea of the distributed museum and its relevance to thinking about audiences it will be necessary to consider how digital culture is impacting upon the analogue museum as well as more widely upon representational forms of communication.

What the internet is producing is not a radical replacement of society by a machinic network simulating reality, nor a breakdown in sociality, but a radical reconfiguration of how 'the social' is registered through the operations and functions of communication and knowledge. This is a reconfiguration of the technical and cultural organization of representation, which is occurring because of two major forces of the distribution of people and things. Firstly, global internet traffic involves complex, large-scale interactions between humans and electronic machines that take place in systems and networks that are themselves a joint product of humans and computing. It is the uses of the internet that are circumventing established forms of the control of communication. This is because the global digital network and its

connected databases is a distributed, rhizomatic, networked structure designed to
'avoid' a centralized system of 'command' and in this sense cannot be 'controlled' in
traditional analogue ways. In addition, the human-computer interface is a cybernetic
system, an extended 'feedback loop' that requires user interaction. It is the combination of these technical features and the intended and unintended uses to which
they have been put, which has produced the many-to-many mode of communication now operating as an alternative to and replacement of the one-to-many culture
of analogue print and broadcasting in which the analogue museum functioned: which
is to say that the art museum in particular is a part of the system of representation that
is now challenged. However, the crisis, or, radical reconfiguration of the established
representational system that new media is provoking cannot be understood only as a
matter of technology. The second force of distribution is the globalization of production and consumption, which has brought about a movement of people and
objects on a scale far greater and faster than all previous forms of capitalist expansion
and historic empires. The increased movement of people is breaking down bounded
notions of identity sustained by national borders, while the greater movement of
money and objects produces the paradoxical counter tendencies of cultural homogeneity
and heterogeneity, sameness and difference across space and place.

At its most abstract and encompassing level of description, the organization of
subjectivities, space, place, objects and communication amounts to a general definition of a system of representation, through which human collectivities are organized.
Such a definition is an extension and reworking of the analytic project to identify the
structures of human agency on the one hand and the structures of language on the
other. In the specific emphasis upon communication taken here, the effects of a
radical reconfiguration of representational systems are understood as focusing upon
the processes of recognition and, importantly, misrecognition of changes in codes and
conventions. Representational systems involve ways of seeing and ways of acting.
Visual representation is an encoding of space and place through the development of a
specific constructed optic, made up of schemas, tropes, diagrammatic and pictorial
recording equivalents and translations. All representational systems construct the subject and object and encode a mode through which they become visible. A society's
representational system is thus a complex nexus that produces subject positions and
the realities in which they operate. The representational system of democracy; the
representation system of Cartesian geometry underlying perspectival projections;
the photograph's representation of the latent image of reflected light; and the representation of the human biological subject as a biographical individual determined
by chronological time, all emerged and coalesced in and through the European
Enlightenment project of modernity. It is the bonding of all of these elements in an
historically evolved formation that is being loosened by the newest forces and which
in cultural terms is being deemed here as a crisis of representation. The production of
art and the art museum have, necessarily to be included in the organization of the
system of representation, which has been outlined above and therefore are part of
the processes of reconfiguration being alluded to. The Western world's developed
systems of representation are not about to disappear, but they are being

reconfigured and one of the most visible organizations of that change can be seen in the human–computer interface.

For museums, who have so far seen technology and its networks as supplementary to their main purposes, the question is not what additional technology is needed to optimize performance, but how these new communications networks are changing the museum's mediating relationship between people and cultural value. In the detail of the argument being developed here the challenge presented by human/computer networks is not to the existence of the museum per se, but rather to the ways in which the museum has been and is understood in the sociological and political projects of late modernity (Latour 2007: 247). The recognition that society is itself a system of communication (Castells 2010: 428) is an important reminder that communication is a necessary process in the production of the human subject and of the relations between subjectivities, which is to say that communication enters into and is constitutive of the complex nexus of unequal and differential relations between humans. Put this way, a system of communication understood 'as society' cannot be thought of only in terms of its formal logic, code, technical apparatus, institutions and mode of representation, but also has to be grasped as a system of relations between humans in which humanness itself is produced. The society/communication nexus, including economic networks, has historically produced unequal access to and distribution of cultural and material resources and thus manifests inequality along national and global lines. In the cultural arena, the terms of the struggle for communicable meaning and action turn upon competing and conflicting interests through which particular subjectivities are formed and reproduced.

The internet is one important and increasingly central network of the whole communication nexus through which competing attempts at – and often opposing definitions of – meaning are mounted. On the internet, the competition for meaning and hence the struggle for consensus, collectivity and equality, is waged at all levels, from technical encoding, ownership, commercial dominance, creative innovation, applications and user interaction. This is obviously true of large corporations and governments setting the terms of individual access and control to the internet and evident in cyber-wars waged by nation-states in pursuit of their perceived security interests. It is also clear that the internet and mobile technology is increasingly being used as an intelligence device by people against governments – as events in Egypt demonstrated in 2011 – as well as by rioters in London in the summer of 2011 to produce their own counter-intelligence in confronting as well as avoiding police. It is often less clear that network communication is also the site of contestation over the forms of communication. The conflict is expressed between the homogenizing tendencies of networked communication in work and consumption that is producing reductive, regimented and repetitive behaviours, and the uses of interactive media which establish collective, playful and open ways of communicating and sharing what is important about humanness. However, this description might suggest that the competition and struggle for meaning is waged only in terms of a private (hyperlinked) messaging system projecting discrete content across the spaces of the technical networks. It also needs to be recognized that competition is also waged in terms of the network's algorithms and simulated cultural codes, or what, in analogue terms, can be more widely understood as the system of representation. The struggle in and over the forms and terms of representation is important in understanding what is happening in the practices and spaces of the public realm and it is this which has significant impact upon the practices of the public art museum and contemporary art practice. Networked behaviour is, as most commentators have noted, changing life in the 'real' world. However, it is equally noted that life on screen or virtual reality, is not as good as real life, which beyond the explicit value judgement, is to say that real life remains continuous and embodied, but now in a relationship with a networked system made possible by computing (Turkle 1997: 70). The comparison between online and offline behaviour draws attention to the relationship between embodied and virtual spaces, which once more brings attention back to the public museum, recognized as an embodied space but now operating in a distributed and interactive system of messaging.

Interactivity, as it has been taken up by a range of new media practitioners operating outside of the corporate and technocratic spheres, offers the most promising line of enquiry in understanding the analogue museum in a digital culture because dialogic process, as has been noted by others, is new media's foundational stone (Manovich 2001: 55). Interestingly, Manovich goes on to dismiss interactivity as a myth of new media because, he says, the concept is too broad to be truly useful. But the opposite can be advanced precisely because interactivity combines the concept of a technical system with an important way of describing the process of general communication. It is the generality of the concept of interactivity that new media has brought back into the discussion of media and their meaning-making processes and in doing so foregrounds questions of audience and more crucially the public in new ways. The language of human-computer interfaces, based upon the technicity of cybernetic feedback loops, has entered the discussion of the cultural coding of communication in such a way that to say that reading a book, looking at a painting or listening to music is interactive gives renewed agency to the reader, viewer, listener. It is in relating the technical and cultural meanings of interactivity that new media can be grasped as a form of cultural as well as technical remediation of older cultural forms and analogue mediums (Bolter and Grusin 2000: 56).

The argument of remediation, made from the vantage point of digital culture, is that we can see in the historical tradition of Western visual technologies, a persistent although not chronological tendency to do two apparently contradictory things: to both erase the technical apparatus of the medium in order to maximize the effect of the transmission of equivalents of 'the real' (immediacy), while creating technical apparatuses that privilege the human control of mediated vision (hypermediacy). For Bolter and Grusin (2000), remediation is a kind of uneasy 'war' between these competing logics, which are present in both old (analogue) and new (digital) media. The aim of immediacy – whether it be the oil painting that optically persuades us we are looking through or beyond the surface into a credible three-dimensional world arranged to converge upon the eye of the spectator, or the special effects of a Hollywood film, or the vector graphics which render immersive imagined worlds on the computer screen – is to bring the image and optical reality closer together. With the fixing of the photographic image the path of immediacy followed the development of mechanical reproduction, first in photography, then film, in which, as Benjamin (1999: 73) says, the image could keep pace with speech. In the subsequent tradition of thinking, which flowed from Benjamin, about the social and cultural effects of continuous developments in technical mediation, we are also led back to the crisis of representational systems from a different direction. In the technological account of visual culture, the digital is considered to have not only remediated analogue media's extensions of the human powers of sense perception (McLuhan 1994), but introduced a transformation in visual culture, which is 'relocating vision to a plane severed from the human observer' (Crary 1992: 1). In contrast, the historical path of hypermediacy lies in the fascination with multiplicity and the many forms and devices through which the human sensorium can be engaged. In old media, hypermediacy was, for example, evident in the medieval cathedral, which combined illuminated stained glass windows, music and smell to produce heightened religious observance. Another example of an analogue form of hypermediacy can be seen in the baroque cabinet of curiosities, or 'Wunderkammer', with its intricate sets of drawers housing collections of eclectic objects. Museums are also hypermediated environments in which the visitor is presented with a multiplicity of objects, text and illustrated panels, screens and lighting effects that they 'navigate' in the structured spaces of galleries. In new media, hypermediacy has most closely followed the path of development of the human-computer interface in which the current 'windowed' style of the desktop interface on the computer screen allows for multiple applications to be present; importantly the human-computer interface is both technically and culturally interactive. Remediation is the double logic of immediacy and hypermediacy and the apparently contradictory interest, on the one hand, in removing all traces of mediation in order to experience immediacy (a digital example being immersive games in virtual environments) and, on the other hand, making mediation highly present in order for the user to experience the hypermediacy of multiple applications. Currently digital technology in its most present form of the internet is busily remediating the nexus of mechanical reproduction, with direct consequences for art and the art museum.

A full understanding of how the technical and cultural languages of new media intersect in the process of remediation has still not been worked out and will require further research and theoretical analysis to produce a synthesis of computer and cultural (re)coding. Nevertheless, the equal emphasis given here to the cultural within technology underlines the point in what follows, that it is not the technology but the uses to which it is put that matter and this emphasis has led many, for good reason, to insist that new media is neither new, nor a medium, but a revised set of tools. In independent practitioner terms, the emphasis upon new media as a tool is a useful counter to technocrats, who see technological systems as providing rational solutions to non-technological problems, and, to technophiles who see technology as providing an unobstructed, alternative world of creative freedom. However, to insist that new media is no more than the latest in a long line of technical means at human disposal is to miss the fact that tools are fashioned by humans for human purposes and hence culturally code the limits as well as possibilities of their use. Further, unlike all previous analogue media, the system of networked computers connects the producer and consumer in the same processes of mediation, hence the current meaning given to the terms 'prosumer' and 'user-generated content'. It is important to underline that this is not only a description of a technical code, but a recognition that precisely because of the unitary technical code of the digital, 'digital tools' are at the same time 'digital content', which is what places the producer and consumer in the same position in relationship to all that metadata has so far remediated.

Materialist cultural theory has long advanced the view that analogue objects are densely coded forms of social relations and value, which could be revealed or decoded as such by abstract analysis (Goldmann 1976). With new media, its culturally coded 'content', i.e. the simulation of the analogue form, is constituted on the surface, for example in the 'long tail' of the internet, and this is its radical import and challenge for cultural institutions, which were established as a result of the need to relay, mediate and interpret the analogue object's code. This aspect of the unitary code of the digital along with human-computer interactivity is one strand of the argument, which insists that digital culture is no longer an horizon, articulated as a possible future state of the mode and relations of representation, but now its cultural default. The parallel, related and equally important part of the same argument, is that the labour of culture, i.e. the mode of its relations, is no longer organized by the boundaries of the nation-state, because of the intersection of new economically driven patterns of migration, which lead to transcultural production and consumption. The enormous scale of intra- and transnational human movement to urban centres has produced a new axis between multiple localities defined by their cultural and historical singularity and contemporary spaces of cultural plurality. It is the combination of these two forces, the space of global flows in online networks and human migration to cities, which is producing both new recognitions of the limits of culture organized along national and analogue lines as well as new forms of creative extension. It is the force of these immensely complex networks of human activity, which is bringing to an end a system and paradigm of representation, which has dominated in Western European-based cultures since the Renaissance (Lovejoy 2004: 8). However, it remains the case that in received and popular ways of thinking about the process of communication in art and broadcast media, the model remains stubbornly that of a one-way transmission, from the artist through the work to the viewer. This now residual historical model of communication understands transmission to be creatively active and reception as conventionally passive, which misrecognizes the necessary (inter)active process of reception because of the exigencies of established institutional practices and the capital mode of exchange.

Many of the more abstract points surrounding this discussion of new media have been expressed concretely in accounts of practice given in the presentations and discussions of the project's discussion programme 'Resolutely Analogue: Museums in Digital Culture'. Such discussions reflected the use of new media in open as well as playful ways in applying its communicative and aesthetic possibilities of the medium in new public contexts and stand in marked contrast to the command model of new media practices in the art museum as represented by Tate Online, Tate's website managed within the department of Tate Media. The predominance of the corporate project of Tate Media in 2009, however, overshadowed the projects of both the digitized collection and Intermedia, both of whose curators, James Davis, online collections editor at the time and Kelli Dipple, curator of Intermedia Art, were in different ways pursuing new media's project of two-way interaction.[1] In the Resolutely Analogue sessions, Davis outlined his concerns in thinking about the differences between an encounter with a material work of art in a gallery and the virtual encounter with its reproduction. He pointed out that Tate currently held 67,000 works in its collection, which is growing all the time. Of that total, 35,000 works are by Turner of which, 30,000 are Turner's sketch book pages. At any one time the four Tate galleries can display only a fraction of the total collection, with the remainder in various stages of storage, transit, or conservation and a large proportion of works from the last century have copyright clearance issues, which means that they can only appear as a text entry in the online catalogue. Notwithstanding these organizational and legal difficulties, Davis saw the potential of the digitization of the collection to gain an understanding of the ontological difference between the analogue object and its digital image. He used John Everett Millais' painting 'Ophelia' (1851–2) in the Tate collection as an example of his preoccupations. Davis pointed out that when Millais' famous painting is on display at Tate Britain it can be approached in the gallery, hung at the standard height and viewed in its frame through protective glass. At any one time, the gallery will have varying numbers of people who will observe and who may, or may not, obscure or interrupt each other's view and flow of thought. Further, Davis reminded his audience that the visitor's thoughts at any particular point of viewing will be influenced by who they are, who they are with, why they are there, how they got there and what they are going to do afterwards. In short, Davis pointed to the sociological as well as phenomenological experience of the object in that the direct spatial apprehension of the object takes place in a continuous flow of time within everyday life. 'Ophelia' is also the best-selling postcard in Tate Britain's shop. More widely, the image is extensively reproduced in books, accompanied by scholarly or other textual information. It is a popular and abiding British image with strong associations with Shakespeare's *Hamlet*, from which Millais took his subject matter. Turning to the image online, Davis pointed out that in a Google search, Tate is the number one destination, with millions of results, for the death of Ophelia. He observed that clicking on the Tate website to access the image will open it in different operating systems as a small thumbnail, along with a display caption and a series of grey tabs for other connections. The appearance of Tate Online also varies depending upon the browser and screen used to access the site. The image online does not change its indexicality, it remains the image of Ophelia, but the delivery context does. In addition, to accessing the image online, Tate Online offers an art on demand print and framing service in conjunction with a commercial company, which will produce a print from a choice of sizes and deliver to your door. The point Davis was at pains to make is that, while both the painting and its digital counterpart are encountered in ways that are specific to its medium, nevertheless, in all its forms of reproduction, the image is a floating signifier in an endless chain of possible signified meanings. Davis' view of the essentially distributed nature of the indexical image fits with much that has been said regarding the transmedial nature of meaning and has the potential to inform the ways in which Tate organized its search function as well as providing a clue to digital knowledge taxonomies that involved dialogue with users understood as generators of meaning.

In a separate discussion in the same series of recordings, Kelli Dipple, curator of Intermedia at Tate, reinforced the essential dialogic nature of new media, emphasizing its open character in which process rather than product is valued by specific communities of users. For Dipple, the project of Intermedia at Tate was to explore these qualities of new media, as led by artists, and in this sense artists provided the location and legitimation of the project in the art museum. As was noted in the previous chapter, locating technology within the culture of art conforms to the conceptual model of subject annexation along the lines of 'technology and', in this instance, a delineation of technology and art practice. This is foremost a project of institutional legitimation and a means of giving new media provenance and value as a category within the terms in which art museums exhibit, collect and archive new media objects. It is also a categorization within which art historians have legitimated a modernist genre and avant-gardist notion of artists working with interactive machines (Rush 1999: 217). This has been the pattern at the Whitney Museum (Paul 2003: 7), and MoMA[2] with which Tate's Intermedia[3] project has links. Dipple's perspective is amply expressed in saying: 'We can shift in thinking of technology as a tool to technology as a medium and a sociopolitical context in which to make work.' This is an important extension of understanding the argument in relationship to the art museum in that the argument does not separate out a realm of artistic activity, thought of as separate from the realm of politics, and the practices of a new medium. In this respect, Dipple sees the art museum as providing a selective portal to and a platform for a different network of practices. The curation of Intermedia projects provides Tate with a means of retaining curatorial control in selecting projects considered to have provenance as new media artworks, while at the same time appearing to embrace the radical potential of the medium because of the separation of new media art from new media as the digital default.

In elaborating a view of new media as a political space of artistic activity, Dipple cited the influence of art practices that arose in the 1960s within certain forms of community art practice using analogue media such as radio and video. Dipple's view that the leading edge for a new generation of new media practitioners operating in relationship to contemporary art institutions resides in the possibilities for new forms of access, the value of process over product and dialogue, albeit still led by artists, represents a challenge to the central and continued dominance of the modernist aesthetic project as framed by object-based acquisition and collection practices. New media, thought of as a new medium for artists, offers, as Dipple said, a form of inclusiveness and engagement with specific communities and addresses the fundamental shift represented by a new means of communication whose central feature is dialogue.

New media, thought of as an art form, has been historized as part of a longer interest on the part of artists employing, working with and making machines a subject and part of their art of which computers are a relatively new addition (Gere 2008: 78). What inevitably falls out of such a view is a whole series of questions about how the art museum, specifically Tate, might conceptually regard the collection of work that is essentially part of a distributed network, but nevertheless has an aspiration to being an art form, as well as include the communities of use and interest in networked art practices as part of the museum's audience. It also introduces the question of why such new media networked practices continue to look to the agency of the art museum, rather than operate in and across networked communities. In addressing both of these questions, the argument will return to understandings of audience and that of the public realm. Both the project of Tate Intermedia and the online collection are open to larger questions of the relationship between the knowledge of the art museum and the knowledge of audiences in ways which neither the corporate, nor the technocratic project of media in the museum currently are. For the corporate project of the virtual museum, it is still the case that the brand must come first and that the openness of the medium has to be managed as a risk to the brand. In the case of the technocratic project of the digitization of collections, the problem remains one of the central defining relationship between curatorial knowledge of object collections and a technologically determined view of accessibility, not recognizing the transformation of the object in digital form.

The question of how the interactivity of the online user relates to existing notions of audience in terms of the public realm arose in a further session of *Resolutely Analogue*. Peter Ride, senior research fellow at Westminster University led a discussion with Marc Garrett (new media artist and founding member of Furtherfield), Matt Locke (commissioning editor for the UK Channel 4 online youth programming), Anna Colin (director of Gasworks, a London-based gallery and artist studios) and Honor Harger (artist, curator and director of Lighthouse, a Brighton-based arts organization). For Locke, innovation in online media arises from what he terms 'the commons', or the communities of users rather than from technologists, whom he saw as having to play catch-up with the inventive and collective practices of young people. This is the now familiar insistence that it is use rather than the technology itself that matters. Locke offered a taxonomy of social media, identifying new spaces created by users that have replaced the public realm. The public realm created through analogue broadcasting has, as Locke saw analogue media's own response to new media, been fractured by recent developments. Previously, for an individual or group to be able to enter and use the public realm at a mass scale required access to the means of broadcast and licence to speak. Now, in online media, access and permission are no longer such a problem and this is leading to a reformation of the public realm in terms of its enlarged scale and its user-centred identity. Locke makes these points as someone whose job it is to understand net behaviours in order to match potential television content to potential new young audiences. Locke's understanding carries with it a practical imperative to give a cultural shape to what would otherwise be about statistics of essentially anonymous

behaviour and his mapping of six spaces of interaction are useful as an initial reconceptualization of the broadcast public realm based upon marketized notions of a
national demographic. For Locke, secret spaces, group spaces, publishing spaces, performing spaces, participation spaces and watching spaces define the new relational
behaviours of new media and replace the conditions and conventions of a now
decommissioned public space. Such an account emphasizes the importance of the
agency of the user, in what Locke, citing Henry Jenkins, has criticized as the vague-
ness of the term 'viral media', wanting instead a fuller understanding of audiences'
vernacular role in retransmitting and spreading media in what he relates as the gift
economy (Jenkins 2006).

The question of changes in the mode of access and permission to speak in the
public realm which are being ushered in by a new technological means was given a
different historical perspective by Honor Harger, who emphasized continuity rather
than rupture: 'Technology isn't relevant in itself, let alone its oldness or newness, but
what you do with it. Let's concentrate on bringing in a new kind of practice rather
than think about bringing in new technologies.' Again, this is a plea from a practitioner perspective not, as she put it, to mistake the tools for the purpose. Harger gave
an example of an artist-led project, 'Polar Radio: Antarctica FM radio station', which
for her, demonstrated that an 'old' analogue technology could be based upon network thinking rather than network technology and produce both a new type of
thinking and user-generated content. Harger, like Dipple, referenced the historic uses
of radio as a protest as well as community movement in demanding that the airwaves be
considered as public space rather than controlled and licensed. People's radio and free
radio could be considered as precursors to Wi-Fi access to the internet and Harger cited
the work of Tetsuo Kogawa on the potential of translocal media and the conception of
polymorphous space in the low-tech development of radio as both transmitter and
receiver, enabling a heterogeneous form of non-hierarchic communication.

What is important for the larger argument being made here is the recognition that
the concern for participatory cultural and technical forms of communication arose
historically in cultural contexts beyond and outside of the institutions of public
broadcast and consecrated culture, and most definitely outside of Tate and other
national art museums. The import of and continuity with such historical community
models of creative exchange using analogue media is not lost upon contemporary
practitioners who see very clearly the potential for artists and curators to work in
non-institutional spaces defined within the spaces of global flows made possible by
online communication. The creation of new open channels and organizations for the
creative use of new media can be seen in the London-based organization Furtherfield, a new media artist's collective, which sees the importance of controlling the
organizational context in order to create a platform for critical expression. Furtherfield was founded by artists Ruth Catlow and Marc Garrett in 1997 and their vision is
succinctly summed up on their website: 'We believe that through creative and critical
engagement with practices in art and technology people are inspired and enabled to
become active co-creators of their cultures and societies.'[4] This puts Furtherfield in
the context of other independent organizations, such as Eyebeam, MUTE, Rhizome,

among others, who see new media as a means of repositioning socially responsible art practice, of recasting the practices of art in terms of co-creation and of embedding such practice within new media ecologies and networked communities. In these ways there is a remapping of the public realm in online culture as the much older idea of the creative commons, through which a contemporary democratic politics of culture and society can be registered and expressed. However, there is a significant gap between this and the art museum's commitment to the modernist art project, with its embrace of art and politics and notions of democracy and public participation entailed by new media.

How are such participating publics to be made visible, or, now in the language of interactivity, to generate content in the space of the museum? How is the museum to be made public? (Weibel and Latour 2007). In asking these questions, the museum's position within the communication nexus in which 'the social' needs to be traced leads back to the question of how the art museum understands its audiences. In the online space of networks there is great scope, as Furtherfield has shown, to constitute individual and group affiliation, association, residency, as well as the more obvious follower and subscriber, at the centre of the practices of online organization. But how, in the terms of interactivity so far discussed, can what Garrett calls 'co-creation' take place in the space of the art museum and in relationship to analogue collections? Interactivity has been identified with new media's potential for the user to 'act-back' upon the resources embedded online and the emphasis in the *Resolutely Analogue* discussions moved beyond reductive notions of user interactivity based upon monitoring net traffic and gaining 'user profiles', while users sit patiently at their screens clicking through pre-set pathways. The interactivity expressed by the term co-creation stresses the reciprocity, contingency and interdependence of interactivity (Blackmann 1998: 136) and not simply the technical feature of the human-computer interface, nor the navigational hierarchies of hyperlinking. For Blackmann and others, interactivity is conceived as engagement and as encounter in which the user re-appropriates and repurposes the resources previously held within the hierarchical spaces and discourses of analogue institutions (Blackmann 1998: 132).

In summarizing the discussion of interactivity as a liberating concept of new media, as it relates to the embodiment of audience in the art museum, there are some notable caveats. In the art museum and in contemporary art culture, interactivity has been most successfully promulgated in terms of a distinct practice of art and artists, rather than a practice of audiences, even though it has been recognized that such practices put audiences in a new relationship to what is being created, authored or said. It is also the case that many of the practices of new media art, net art, digital art or computer art (and here it is clear that the defining historical title for the canon has yet to be settled) have revived a politics of art and an art of politics. This is precisely because of new media's imbrication in the most powerful forms of communication and exchange through which power itself is exercised. However, the canonization of a selection of new media art practices in the late modernist project of the art museum has to be seen as a reduction and containment of the potential of new media to set the museum on a more open and non-hierarchical course; one in which the museum's users are at the centre and whose experience forms the basis of knowledge exchange. But how might such interactivity be achieved in the visitor experience of the spaces and objects of the museum and why is this important?

New media has been present in museums and galleries for more than two decades. The National Gallery in London opened its Micro Gallery as far back as 1991, offering a screen-based interactive and personalized tour of the collection and displays. The application was designed by Cognitive Applications, a British company specializing in multimedia designs in the cultural sector, who have subsequently gone on to work with many world leading museums. The Micro Gallery can be seen to have ushered in the very corporatized and technocratic paradigm which has been shown to be so limiting. Its conceptual and business model has been adopted by major museums since and has set the terms in which museums seek partnership and sponsorship for technological applications and services. Two major limits of this approach need articulating again. Firstly, technology in the museum is conceived as an aid to the visitor's experience of object displays rather than as an object and display on equal terms with analogue objects. Screens, audio-guides, smartphone applications are framed as a secondary source of information and interpretation that operate discretely to augment the visitor experience of objects. The installation of computer terminals, touchscreens as well as handheld devices in gallery spaces are presented and used to transmit curatorial 'content', which is regarded as generated from a separate domain of knowledge. In this, the technological carrier of that content is deemed neutral with respect to the message received and user experience and the technology is considered therefore not to compete with but rather complement the experience the viewer has with objects and spaces. This is clearly a case of the reverse of 'it's not the technology, but what you do with it', since clearly it is the technology that has led and still leads development. The privileging of the technology, rather than the (new) medium, leads to a second limiting feature of mainstream development, which is that the business model of working with technology partners confines the discussion of new media's augmentation to the latest technology applications. The limit here is that commercial applications, whether through the software or hardware come with culturally coded uses, in this case as one-way informational devices. The whole discussion of new media's essentially dialogic, user-generated and many-to-many characteristics are ignored in an application that limits the use of technology to repurposing exhibition texts in audio-visual form. From the point of view of the weight of argument being presented here, such applications and the model of their production are designed to reproduce the same relations of cultural authority and to maintain the public in the same position of supplicant that was the greatest achievement of the historical analogue modernist museum. The cultural authority of the museum, first expounded in the nineteenth century and modified throughout the twentieth, works within a model of civic society and the public realm, which, as has been repeatedly been pointed out, has changed.

The current interactivity available to users in the many-to-many forms of 'social media' in online media constitutes one of the important cultural and technical networks by which the invisible non-technical networks of the distributed museum could be traced and made visible. The concept of remediation with its double logic of immediacy and hypermediacy also assists in bringing together understandings of the practices of 'user-generated content' in online communities and the uses of new media to augment visitor experience, whether as dedicated guides or in the permitted use of visitors' own mobile media in the analogue space of the museum. Remediation is a useful overarching concept for thinking about what is happening when digital recording devices are used in encountering the art museum as much as it is for understanding the digitization of collections. In the case of the online collection, the image is multiplied and hence hypermediated in different contexts and environments. Hypermediation is also present in the deployment of mobile guides which augment an encounter with museum objects by the addition of textual, visual and audio information. The use of cameras and videos in museums is also a form of hypermediation, standing between the object and the perceiving viewer through the optics of the camera, the resolution of the screen and duration of recording. The import of such understandings about the hypermediated nature of the uses of new media online, as well as in the space of the museum, can be added to the considerable knowledge that viewing, or spectatorship is already a highly conceptualized and cultural process of interaction and mediation (Hall 1999: 25). Returning to the research at Tate Britain, the student co-researchers in Tate Encounters used a range of online and digital recording media over an extended period in the galleries and in pondering how such production related to these multiple cultural and technical processes of mediation the research analysis developed the concept of transmediation as a means of bringing its work on contemporary diverse spectatorship as a transcultural experience (as described in Chapters 4–6), together with the discussion here of new media and the museum.

The concept of transmediation has been developed in North American high school education from Siegal's definition of 'taking understandings from one system and moving them into another sign system' (Siegal 1995: 455). There are a number of published accounts of its application, which also emphasize the polysemic aspects of the approach, which rather than privileging a 'correct' reading of a given media text based upon the acquisition of expert knowledge, opens the way out for the learner to create new structures of meanings drawing upon their implicit knowledge of other media lexicons in the expanded field of visual culture and, by implication, from their extended life worlds and from their language.

> When we talk about teachers and students engaging in transmedial experiences, we are referring to their abilities to engage in multiple ways of mediating knowing between sign systems. Such critical engagement does not involve only passive reading and writing; rather, it involves an active textual analysis through a multiplicity of perspectives and critical methods.
>
> *(Semali 2002: 5)*

Transmediation, as the use of one media to transcribe another, is a literal description of what is involved in mediating knowledge between sign systems. To leave the matter here, however, would be to ignore the cultural context and subject position involved in the process. Transmediation is certainly based upon technical recoding, but it also operates for the spectator at the cultural level through subject positioning and that, as has been said, rests upon the globalizing processes of transculturality within the expanded field.

The processes of transmediation, a means of recoding messages from one formal value system to another, are entailed implicitly in the practices of everyday life across a range of activities wherever receiving and authoring media is involved. Transmediation is entailed in the art museum as both part of the staging of objects and in the viewing strategies of visitors. Modernist art curation is conflicted about its mediating role, with one school of thought in denial of the very processes of mediation, insisting that the art object must 'speak for itself' and that the spectator must approach the work of art unencumbered and experience it directly, while the other school of thought of constructivist pedagogy believes in providing additional information and activity to prompt or promote the viewer's engagement. Modernist curation stops well before the recognition that transmediation is happening in people's heads, because it does not acknowledge that remediation is now a dominant trope, a digital default, and hence structures vision. The result of this is that modernist curatorial practice has yet to reach the conclusion that transmediation is a possible practice through which their own knowledge could be mediated between sign systems and well as providing a means for a transactional relationship with audiences.

If the two identified senses of a contemporary visual crisis in culture, the first stemming from post-colonialism and embodied in the transnational subject, and the second arising through the processes of remediation and particularly the logic of hypermediacy, are brought to bear upon the student co-researchers' recordings in Tate Britain a new insight is possible. In terms of what is happening for the viewer in the art museum, a new intersection can be identified between the mediation involved in the position of the transcultural subject and the remediation of the visual field in the technical networks. From this new intersection, thinking about the art museum visitor standing in front of a painting, it is no longer possible to imagine that the viewer can sustain a relationship to the painting without the effects of remediation and the transcultural being present. The stance of informed scholarship and the position of the confirmed aesthete will only work to hold such effects in abeyance for so long. Come what may, the subject is confronted by a new and contradictory sense of distraction and hyper-attention. No longer is it possible to enter the scene depicted in an unmediated way because every reproduced image and every different person stands metaphorically between the subject and object.

Remediation and the transcultural are the new historical default positions of contemporary visuality. Such an intersection is a location within the distributed museum. Such an understanding begins to make sense of the relationship between historical objects made in technical and social conditions both different from, yet continuous with the present and the contemporary spectator. Every spectator arrives in front of the culturally consecrated object with a different history, sense of time and position within networks and yet every spectator is differentially subject to the homogenizing processes of mediation. This new recognition presents a challenge to the traditional cultural authority of the museum as well as to all institutions of media literacy, since it places the spectator in the same position with respect to the cultural processes of remediation as museum professionals. The recognition of this new position of the viewer also highlights the limits of much of the thinking about interactivity through the use of technology in the museum. If the field of enquiry is contained around the ways in which the art museum evolves in relation to new technology it could be argued that the Tate Encounters experience demonstrates three concurrent positions articulated by Peter Ride.[5] Firstly, that new media is narrowly understood by the museum as technology, which is then seen to play a supportive role in externally facing marketing and internally augmenting visitor experience; here the museum accommodates and absorbs technology to existing core and strategic purposes. Secondly, technology is understood by the museum as a new publishing media that can be used to engage a wider debate and interest in the museum and its role in collecting and curating contemporary art. Thirdly, technology is understood by the museum as a new cultural medium of communication, which changes the ways in which audiences view works of art and confronts the knowledge practices of the museum with a need to rethink the question of cultural value.

The main thrust of the argument is not that museums and the art museum in particular are ignoring their audiences, far from it. Tate Britain, as the research example used here has demonstrated, has come to engage with its audiences far more fully over the past two decades. It has done this, on the one hand, in response to a more general commodification of culture, by creating the museum consumer and presenting art as a spectacle and, on the other hand, through a structured response to government policy, which focused upon culture as a means of social inclusion. The stage of the argument reached here is that art museums and maybe museums in general have yet to find ways, conceptually and practically to connect with the knowledge of their embodied audiences and distribute their accumulated knowledge in ways which are meaningful to museum professionals. One strand of the problem remains the professional adherence to a taxonomy of communication which continues to distinguish art as a special category of objects above others and categorically separates objects from humans, a problem that has been identified as the separation of use value and exchange value and hence the separation of capital and labour. A further problem is the continued over-reliance upon a social taxonomy, based upon class, race and ethnicity as the means to understand audience and attendance at the museum. A third problem, extensively discussed throughout this account, is the continued organizational practice of an essentially non-transactional model of communication in the use value of the museum itself, in which the knowledge of the viewer is considered private and individual, while expert knowledge is considered public. All of these factors amount to a profound misrecognition of the position of audience and of the potential of new media to bring the viewer closer to the museum and the museum closer to the public and, in doing so, to make the networks of the distributed museum visible to all concerned.

9

MUSEUMS OF THE FUTURE

The troubling of settled notions in the art museum's relationship to culture and society, which has been argued so far, can be summarized in three key understandings. Firstly, the utility of transmediation, as the emergent form and lexical index of cultural communication in the many-to-many environment of online media, is leading to the demise of singular forms of cultural authority previously mediated by traditional institutions. Secondly, the established and normative notion of spectatorship entailed in aesthetic modernism, based upon the idea of a singular and exceptional transaction between two foundational subjects in the encounter with the work of art, is unsustainable in the face of new subjectivities engendered by transcultural conditions and its new trope of the transvisual. Thirdly, a combination of the transmedial and transcultural, and the global economic and technological conditions in which they are entailed, is unsettling the system of representation which has hitherto stabilized the relationship between subject and object. A consequence of this confluence of related factors is that rethinking audience becomes the urgent task since the spectator has been put in a new relationship to traditional objects of cultural value.

In thinking about art museums of the future it will be necessary to rethink audiences simultaneously as individuals, consumers and collectivities, as well as in the more particular senses of being users and even 'prosumers'. Understanding what audiences are doing in the museum, as has been argued, is an urgent and primary task for thinking about the museum of the future because the established formation of the public realm and its modes of representation are rapidly changing in the face of global economic and technological change. The task of understanding the recent growth in museum attendance in major international cities, the character and composition of visitors, their motives, interests and experiences in museums is connected to how the museum of the future will continue to produce cultural value, a question that has historically turned upon notions of the public realm and civic society. This is a time of uncertain transitions in which the established institutional apparatuses of the representation and communication of cultural value are all still in place, but are now cut across by the new situation of a convergent, interactive, global network. Cultural value, as posited by the historic public and cultural realm, rested upon the authority of academics, keepers, curators, critics and broadcasters, acting as sole arbiters of what and how universal, national and common meanings were constituted and maintained. Historically expert cultural authority emerges from and resonates with the cultural values of a predominantly privately educated elite minority, while passing by and largely ignored by a state educated popular majority (Bourdieu 1979: 25). The current constitution of cultural authority written into national collections in Britain as in other European societies still has at its core an assemblage of cultural tastes, judgements, consuming practices, patterns of patronage and ownership and education of the historically defining social elite. However, educated elites are not monolithic and their individual and group composition and fractions is constantly replenished and varies with changes in the distribution of education, wealth and patterns of consumption. Twentieth-century museums were part of the changing networks of knowledge acquisition in terms of the objects they acquired and through their modes of exhibition, display and interpretation. It is possible in outline to schematize how these historical changes in museum practices have moved from the connoisseurial museum through to the current state of the post-modern corporate and business orientated organization with audiences now positioned as consumers.

In quantitative terms, the argument for why questions of audience need to be put at the centre of thinking about the future of museums might seem redundant given

Organisational development of the Art Museum: historical, consecutive and concurrent practices			
Connoisseurial	Modernist	Post-modernist	Transcultural
TATE BRITAIN	TATE MODERN	MUSEUM OF THE PRESENT	MUSEUM OF THE FUTURE
The Art Academy	Art Museum	Museum of the Spectacle	Social Art Museum
Historical Hang	Thematic Hang	Contingent Hang	Remediated Hang
Authority of the Expert	Authority of the Curator	Authority of the Educator/Media Editor	Authority of the Viewer
Aesthetic trope: Beauty and Taste (historical canon)	Aesthetic trope: Art and Modernism (formalist/abstract)	Aesthetic trope: Post-modernist (thematic)	Aesthetic trope: Transmedial
Audience: Cultured	Audience: Educated/educatable	Audience: Consumers	Audience: Curators

FIGURE 9.1 Diagram schematizing curatorial models at Tate. Research synthesis, Tate Encounters 2010

the buoyancy of numbers and the continued popularity of Britain's major museums. On the face of it, since the 1990s, museum audiences are a success story and there is no reason to suppose that current audiences will desert the museum in the near future. For as long as the museums are full, why should audiences be troubling? Museums gather demographic data in broad terms in order to know who is and is not turning up. The 2010 Annual Accounts to the Board of Trustees, reported a total of 7,125,000 visitors to its four galleries, of which 1,150,000 visitors went to Tate Britain. Tate reported a figure of 257,000 (3.6 per cent) visitors from an ethnic background and 344,000 (4.8 per cent) from NS-SEC 5–8, which comprises people in occupations classified as lower supervisory, technical, semi-routine, routine and unemployed. These attendance figures are unrepresentative of the population as a whole. For those who work in and regularly visit Tate Britain, this demographic picture is not surprising and bears out what one Tate Encounters research participant from London South Bank University described:

> When I went to Tate Britain I did feel uncomfortable because it was a museum in an upper class environment and I have to try not to be myself too much especially reacting to a painting I like or hate e.g. not to talk too loud or laugh.[1]

The cultural policy drive of the British New Labour Government (1997–2010) to make museums more accessible and inclusive to a social majority provided the rationale and funding for the Tate Encounters research used in this book[2] and it led initially to framing the question of who the absent social segments were and why they did or did not use museums. London South Bank University (LSBU) recorded a total of 25,441 students enrolled in 2009/10, the latest figures available, of which 58 per cent were female and 50 per cent were full-time. Apart from being local to Tate Britain, the university was selected as the key institutional collaborator on the Tate Encounters research project, not only for its research specialism in sociological studies of race, but also for the demographic profile of its students, of which the 42 per cent recorded as 'white' were in a minority, and because as a 'new university' it would have a greater number of students from lower socioeconomic backgrounds, (NS-SEC 5–8). From a research point of view, the profile of Tate Britain's audience and that of LSBU's students were diametrically reverse.[3]

In answering the essay question 'What is the Britain in Tate Britain?' in 2007, a sample cohort of 260 first-year undergraduate LSBU students wrote about their views and feelings of visiting Tate Britain and living in Britain. A number of strong common narratives emerged, some, as might be expected, consistent and enmeshed with other contemporary media narratives of Britain. A somewhat surprising theme, from a group with an average age of 22 years, was of Britain as a nation in decline. The narrative of decline was predicated upon the idea of Britain as a once strong nation, associated with the period of its imperial rule, strongly echoing what Paul Gilroy has termed 'post-colonial melancholia' (Gilroy 2005: 42). The historical sense of the economic and military decline of Britain, in the student accounts, was coupled with a sense of loss of national and cultural identity. National identity was associated with a monocultural tradition whose figurehead is the monarchy, which has been replaced by a multicultural society brought about by immigration, as one essay put it, Britain is, 'a multi-ethnic island awash in a sea of intolerance'. However, immigration and cultural diversity were seen overwhelmingly as progressive features of modern Britain, a positive aspect of social change and an inevitable outcome of globalization and, while there was a recognition of social tensions associated with migration, especially focused upon religion, this was more than offset by the greater benefit of increased tolerance and the mingling of cultures.

A further strong narrative thread in the student accounts was the sense of a divided Britain, although this was tempered by a recognition of the media's role in constructing such oppositions. Nevertheless, a number of 'fault lines' in British society were consistently referenced between an older more settled Britain and a newer and uncertain one. The divide between rich and poor, rural and urban, polite and rude and between classes were all present. Such narratives were under-scored by a sense of unbridled consumption replacing tradition and constraint with the effect of a 'cheapening' or hollowing out of traditional British values of tolerance, fair play and moral rectitude. Rising knife crime, binge drinking and high rates of teenage pregnancy were contrasted to an image of a more settled mainland Europe in which traditional values persist. Britain, it was often asserted, was caught between the unbridled power and culture of the USA and its European neighbours. But such pessimism as this suggests was more than countered by an optimistic belief that Britain remained a strong liberal democracy and had a role to play in the world.

What interpretative substance if any should be accorded to such narratives in rela-tionship to the cultural logic of modernist cultural authority? Overall the accounts of Britain and the subject positions expressed through the narratives bear out what Harvey (1992: 260) first noticed as some of the effects of time-space compression. From the early 1980s, Harvey, Jameson and Baudrillard articulated, through different formulations, the outline of newer subjectivities encountered in the condition of post-modernity. This newer subjectness was, they argued, produced by an emergent set of practical and institutional technologies responsible for the increasing globalized flows of capital and labour. The new narrative of the post-modern subject was that of a radical decentring of identity, characterized by a constant state of uncertainty. This seems to fit with the subject positions described by the student cohort, only without the pessimism of Baudrillard, or the critical rejection of post-modernism, entailed in Harvey and Jameson's Marxism. The personal resources of the student participants, in so far as it can be said to belong to a group, are those of social mobility and adaptability and an embracing of the value of difference and living with uncertainty.

The function of established forms of cultural capital, such as those associated with the appreciation of art through visiting public art museums and galleries, are in this more relative and impermanent world now contingent with and often subordinate to the forms of subjectness established by the networked practices in everyday life. In

Britain, the question of recent changes in generational modes of subjectivity, recognized as more fluid and plural, come up against continued narratives and reconstitutions of nation and identity as officially represented and recognized. The bifurcation of Tate in London at the millennial moment is a case in point.

Tate Britain came into existence at an historical moment of an organizational separation, conceived, not along an axis of geography, as with Tate Liverpool and Tate St Ives, but in terms of a conceptual division between historical time and historical space, between two powerful imaginaries, modernity and nation. Tate was founded in 1897 as the National Gallery of British Art and from its inception the complexities of the classification of British art and artists was written into its collection practices (Morris 2003: 170). Moreover, the foundation of Tate as the National Gallery for British Art made it a site of contestation over what could and could not be collected from the outset (Fyfe 1996: 221), and it is this that continues to provide the organization with its central binary drive and logic. In the branding exercise conducted by Wolff Olins, which eventuated in the public face of Tate Britain and Tate Modern, the British imaginary and the question of Britishness re-emerged, but now in a post-colonial and post-modern world. A world in which nation and the modern are now uncertain terms, cut adrift by the distance from Empire and the decline of manufacturing capitalism, reduced to floating signifiers in a hypermediated textual universe.

The Tate Gallery at Millbank opened as Tate Britain on 27 March 2000, with building works still in progress to provide a new entrance at lower ground level along its western elevation but with new displays in place. The new Manton entrance and reception hall would create a contemporary urban space in marked contrast to the original neo-classical entrance into the Rotunda and axial Duveen galleries on the riverside. The new Manton entrance at Tate Britain was a development that mirrored the new entrance into the Turbine Hall at Tate Modern, both of which were described as making the entrances feel less intimidating and more publicly accessible. The planning strategy for the relaunch of Tate Britain and the opening of Tate Modern adopted a graduated approach involving the launch of a series of new presentations of the collection at Tate Britain starting in 1999. According to Morris (2003: 171) it was the conceptual shift represented by the rehanging of the collection, one that set about disrupting the historical and chronological hang, which embodied a new vision of British art. What was that vision based upon and how did its embodiment pose a new relationship between museum and visitors, objects and viewers? From the perspective of new media and the distributed museum, the move to a thematic curatorial conception contains something of a non-linear approach in which objects can be grouped and juxtaposed outside of their historic and canonical sequencing. But by what new logic should objects be placed together and based upon what cultural authority? As director of Tate Britain, Stephen Deuchar presided over the relaunch of the gallery with its thematic approach to the hang of the collection in 2000. The cultural logic of the approach was a hybrid of modernist fine art formalism and modernist social contextualization, based on the cultural authority of the curator. In this moment, the potential for the development of many more hybrids in which objects and ideas could be connected was limited by an organizational network, invisible to the public, connecting continued acquisition to curatorial expertise. The logic of the modernist museum as a singular cultural authority was reinforced, rather than relaxed, by thematic hanging and carried out at the expense of opening up the collection of objects to many more contingent networks extending beyond those of the organization and its controls. What did the singular cultural authority of the modernist museum mean for its contingent audiences in a period when audience was also seen to be necessarily constitutive of Britishness?

Unlike the industrial economy that had built Bankside Power Station in the earlier part of the twentieth century, the economic and political climate of late capitalism in which the project of Tate Modern was conceived, was defined by global neo-liberalism. Over this period in Britain, manufacturing continued to decline as an overall percentage of GDP, while the financial markets continued to be deregulated, delivering spectacular profits and a healthy return to the Treasury, while a burgeoning public sector was kept going by a mixture of privatization and public borrowing. The US banking crisis, signalled by the collapse of Lehmann Brothers in 2008, which triggered the European banking crisis and brought around the threat of global recession, was a sobering reminder of the risks and excesses of unfettered market freedom and in Britain brought the New Labour project to a close. Beyond national perspectives and local political fallout much deeper patterns of global economic change had been noted over the previous three decades (Harvey 2000), bringing about new alignments and configurations of nation, capital, labour and production. Of the many changes, realignments within international corporate capitalism, the change from production-led to consumption-led economic development had a decisive impact upon the cultural sector.

For Tate Modern, as with other museums, the new dynamic of consumer-led demand came as a surprise in the spectacular visitor rate achieved in its opening years, which was subsequently sustained. Growth in visitor rates can be attributable to the more general commodification of culture and heritage in Britain, which Tate grasped and pursued vigorously in adopting global market branding techniques, maximizing the potential of the private patronage networks that significantly contributed to the building of Tate Modern, putting in place greater and more prominent consumer opportunities for shopping and eating together, with thematic programming approaches, and an extended range of related media activities. There is some ground for arguing that commissioning, programming and marketing now follow a more deregulated and distributed mode of (re)production in which art museums co-opt smaller cultural producers, exploit niche marketing, outsource curating, import strategy and above all increase output, all of which are characteristic of post-Fordism with its predominant mode of just-in-time delivery.

This evident shift from production-led to consumer-led approaches to museum programming is reflected in a corresponding shift from object-led to visitor-led art museum professional practices, noted for the museum sector generally by Hooper-Greenhill (2000). Conceiving of the art museum visitor as consumer is antithetical to the tradition which regards museums as continuing, albeit problematically, the

Enlightenment values of critique, freedom and progress (Lord 2006: 11). The argument that post-modern consumer ambience in the affluent world brings with it, on the one hand, a world of interesting and pleasurable lifestyles, choices and cultural aesthetic distractions, while on the other, it abolishes tradition and detaches the individual from a representation of reality, has continuing purchase in theorizing forms of deliberate agency of the art museum visitor.

Although embodied attendance at Tate Britain continues to reflect long-term historical social and cultural patterns, Tate can now point to a large and increasing number of virtual visitors – 18.86 million recorded unique hits in 2010/11[4] – as both an optimistic sign that the social and cultural demographic might be changing in favour of a more heterogeneous range of interests in art, as well as demonstrating the scale of the potential of the web as a new means of engaging and sustaining a dialogue with a global audience. The post-modern notion of the heterogeneous audience as a collection of consumers masks certain structural absences, however. Most obviously, it conceals the absence of those who do not, as the sociological argument and cultural policy-makers have it, have the 'cultural capital' to exchange in the art museum and for whom the art museum remains wholly discontinuous with their everyday life. The current British museum demographic continues to show that in percentage terms migrant and diasporic groups (black and minority ethnic) do not attend museums in proportion to their numbers in the population as a whole, nor, as has been equally demonstrated, do less educated and lower socioeconomic income groups.[5] Such structural exclusions do not accord with the historic notion of the public museum as a demonstration of the collective wealth of the people, nor do they fit with the rhetoric that consumption has levelled social difference.

But the problem of the creative agency of audiences, as it emerges through this argument, is not merely one of the physical absence of numerous and classified bodies. The missing audiences of cultural diversity policy (whoever they are constituted to be), are considered to be absent because there are barriers to access, some of which are rooted in factors related to: their continuous everyday worlds; their remote perceptions of museums; the organization of their time; their supposed lack of developed 'codes' with which to see meaning; the absence of work in collection and exhibition that reflects or celebrates their life worlds and identities; and in their negative reactions to the architectural organization of space with which they are not familiar (Hewison and Holden 2004: 8). Learning and education departments of museums, and indeed museum research projects, identify such barriers and set about constructing strategies and practices through which absent people can be made welcome and develop a sense of conviviality, meaning and purpose. Such strategies have so far been limited in converting targeted groups into recurrent visitors and in one important sense the approach of targeting missing demographic sections misses the crucial issue that all visitors are in one important historical sense invisible in the face of the museum, which is organized to legitimate the singular creativity of the production of art and its private collection and ownership.

This is because for the audience to be visible in the art museum would entail an active form of participation in the production of their own subjectivity and identity both individually and as representative people, which modernist aesthetics believes happens only privately. Of course the mode of producing aesthetic subjectivity in the encounter with a work of art does largely go on in people's heads, but the limit imposed by the museum has to date accepted the unequal distribution of cultural capital. In adopting constructivist and dialogic strategies, as the means to creative engagement with works of art, the question urgently arises about how the knowledge produced in the encounter becomes known and more widely shared. In order to make multiple subjectivities visible in the public domain, the art museum needs to find ways of demonstrating that what is (coded) in people's heads as the experience of the museum has a direct and meaningful relationship to the forms and organization of exhibition. Making the art museum public, or social, would require the organization of the museum to embrace a new form of general communication about the value and uses of collection in which new media and the distributed museum now represents an opportunity to grasp this central misrecognition entailed in the privatization of aesthetic experience.

How does the argument for a public aesthetic relate to the ways in which museums currently understand the challenges of the future? In July 2009, the London School of Economics (LSE) hosted an event to mark the 60th anniversary of the publishing company Thames & Hudson to which they invited Neil MacGregor, director of the British Museum, and Nicholas Serota, director of Tate to discuss 'The Museum of the 21st Century'.[6] The event was chaired by BBC broadcaster John Wilson who introduced the event as bringing two of the world's most pre-eminent and powerful museum directors together and to 'spark off each other' producing an 'alchemy of new ideas'. By any standard, the event did little to live up to Wilson's aspiration, which is not to detract from the considerable achievement of both men in successfully leading major developments in their respective museums over the past 25 years, the clearly crowning achievements of their working lives. What is of interest here is how what was said by both Serota and MacGregor plays into and with current conceptions of object collections, audiences and networks. In response to an opening question on personal motives, MacGregor highlighted the pleasure and privilege of being able to be alone with some of the greatest and unchanging objects in the world, while Serota highlighted his pleasure in working with artists. Although Macgregor also cited his equal pleasure in witnessing the great volume of different kinds of people who engage with great works, both men nevertheless placed their own immediate subjectivity and identity in their relationship to the individual possession of objects and proximity to their makers, one as a keeper, the other as curator. This opening gambit, by consummate patricians, thus restated the essential, historical modernist purposes of museums by addressing the private experience of the individual in a world that they recognized had changed dramatically over their working lives. MacGregor noted that when Serota was appointed director of Tate in 1987, contemporary art in Britain was publicly rejected. Serota agreed and added that coverage of contemporary art in the press had been transformed and that the success of Tate had changed political debate in which a significant case for the art of the present had been made in non-instrumentalized terms.

London in the 1980s had not yet experienced super-migration, MacGregor said, but now the world lives in London and Britain, which, more than in France or the USA, has embraced multiculturalism allowing difference to co-exist. London, MacGregor told the audience, is an extraordinarily exciting diasporic city in which the old distinction between 'home' and 'abroad' no longer makes sense. He saw the British Museum's Imperial collections as a unique world resource representing a conspectus of the world that cannot be found in any other city. The British Museum now holds these world collections in trusteeship for the whole world and its expertise is available to the world in a new way. The British Museum and Tate now have world stature and serve a world purpose. This new role for world museums and their collaborators was, as MacGregor put it, a context 'where the world can look at the world' based upon 'shared human culture, inheritance, history and identity', a 'world of diasporas and not simply national identities'. In the context of the discussion, MacGregor was making the case for the continued pre-eminence of the British Museum's collections and its scholarship and expertise but now on a world stage in which it is a major attraction for visitors to London as well as marking a pre-eminent standard for museology in the world. MacGregor may well be accurate in his esti-mation of the stature of the British Museum, but this glosses over the central issue of the cultural interpretation objects and differential access to its narratives for diasporic peoples. Indeed, there is a case for interpreting MacGregor's view of the position of the British Museum on a global stage as being continuous with the premium position of Britishness occupied by the British Empire, from whence a great deal of its historic collection came. Serota also wanted to make a case for Tate on a world stage, but in different terms. Tate too needed what he termed 'a defensible position in the world', which, he said, had meant Tate some years ago rethinking its understanding of international contemporary and modern art beyond the comfort of the European/ USA axis to include South America, Southeast Asia and the Middle East. Serota agreed that museums in Britain foster civic cohesion and make great objects equally available to all. Museums are free to visit and free from political interference. Tate, Serota emphasized, was run by curators in collaboration with artists who do things by conviction not by public opinion, he went on to say that Tate is able to assemble great objects in a great museum because it is has powerful networks of individuals who can support its projects and who are not swayed by local politics. MacGregor emphasized the depoliticized role of the British Museum, which enabled it to look at the world from other positions. Such comments, far from being depoliticized, suggest, on the contrary, that on the new world stage, museum collections and their ambassadors play a more prominent role in cultural diplomacy than they have in the past.

The majority of the discussion focused upon the traditional role of the museum in acquiring, conserving and exhibiting objects of collection, now on a global scale for global consumption. The educational role of the museum was used to underscore the value of collection practices and this was the perspective extended to the new means of communication in which technology was seen as a tool for learning from collec-tions. In the brief discussion of new media, it became clear that both directors primarily saw new media technology as offering the museum a means of broadcasting expert views, which should not be confused or blurred with the use of new media for audiences to comment and exchange views among themselves. Both insisted that the new channels of broadcast as they saw them would maintain the cultural authority of the museum and that online media presented an opportunity to stage the museum to a world audience. The internet will, as MacGregor put it, give museums a better understanding of what audiences are looking for and establish more direct lines of communication between people, curators and objects.

While both men saw the potential of the new medium within the now conventional terms of extending the authority of their collections and organization, there was a dawning recognition that communication through a many-to-many medium meant that the audience have something to say. Again, the conventional response has been that tracking and quantifying net behaviours is a form of advanced market intelligence and clearly the algorithms can differentiate and group a wide range of choices and selections, as witnessed in iTunes and Google personalized applications. But what was not recognized, and indeed eclipsed by the very stress on the importance of the internet to museums, was any sense of how the qualitative dimension of interaction can or indeed should be registered by the museum. This, as has been repeatedly pointed out, is because the boundary between the audience and object collections is hard walled and requires, in Latour's term, a constant process of purification less the significance of the object, guaranteed by the associations that keep it in view, are contaminated by the new associations made possible by the internet whose provenance is unknown and untested (Latour 1993: 10). The provenance of the knowledge of the subject network is the new 'other' to the established object network of the museum.

Two British museums, the British Museum now exhibiting the world to the world, and the Tate exhibiting British historical and 'international' modern and contemporary art to Britain and the world. There remains much that the naming of nation reveals about the relationship national and international organizations have to time and historical circumstances and how these bear upon its sense of continued operation and future direction. Names are a clue to less obvious narratives, just as they are transparent in conferring evident purposes. In considering here questions of the future of the art museum and its relationship to digital culture, the naming of Tate Modern and Tate Britain and the differences between them have usefully illuminated the problematic of larger contemporary changes in a system of representational cultural value. The naming of Tate Modern and Tate Britain connoted differences between national identity and temporality in which, paradoxically, the art collection was understood, on the one hand, as both historic and modern, and on the other, as both British and international. This binary classification based upon territory, (Britain and its dominiums), and temporality (past and present), continues to frame and give meaning to a collection of objects in terms of an historical narrative of identity and progress in which modernity remains the central thread. But, as has been forcibly argued to this point, both nation and linear time are unevenly experienced depending upon place and space, and now recognized, as well as lived, as more fluid categories. Such relativities, as has been argued, have impacted upon the representational system in which the online space of flows challenges the hold analogue institutions, such as the museum and broadcast media, have had over definitions of and practices within the public realm. The same techno-global forces that are reshaping subjectivities and challenging analogue institutions have also undermined modernism's confident construction of temporality and geography.

How have such issues and debates been addressed in the practices of the art museum and particularly in the practices of Tate over the recent period? What evidence is there that Tate has engaged with such ideas? It was evident in the LSE discussion that both Serota and MacGregor acknowledged the greater force of a consuming public and the importance for the museum of understanding their interests. Yet at the same time, there was an insistence upon maintaining forms of cultural authority derived from the Enlightenment and modernism's view of history, or at best an extension of European modernism to a world modernism. However, the distinction between the historic and modern has been flattened and compressed in and through the experience of post-modernity, such that the meaning of objects is no longer secured by an historical order, since historical time and multiple temporalities can no longer follow a singular overarching chronology. What does this mean for the logic of analogue-object relations? How does the singular discourse of object selection operate in a world of hybrid networks? In March 2009, the Tate Encounters research project staged a month-long Research-in-Process event at Tate Britain, marking the end of a two-year fieldwork period and intended to engage a community of interest in its research questions. Some of the recordings made over that period, in particular the Resolutely Analogue discussions, have formed the basis for much of the discussion here.[7] At the same time as the Research-in-Process events were taking place, Tate Britain invited Nicolas Bourriaud, to curate the Gulbenkian sponsored Tate Triennial, which he did in an exhibition entitled *Altermodern*.[8] Bourriard's altermodernism was intended as a provocation to post-modernism, to fill what he saw as the intellectual void it had created and to announce its demise. In the same vein as scholars seeking to make sense of culture through the continuation of modernization in its globalized form, Bourriaud focused on an alternative to global economic standardization and its homogenizing cultural effects, pointing instead to multiple temporalities and what he terms, 'post-colonial heterochrony'. Altermodernity thus embraces plurality and difference as the way out of the post-modern malaise as well as modernism's singularity and essentialist view of culture and the separate elements of a multiculture. In curatorial terms Bourriard saw a plurality of voices co-existing in what he calls a hybrid arrangement. In terms of contemporary art practice he argued that artistic styles and formats must be viewed from the standpoint of diaspora and migration (Bourriaud 2009: 1). At Tate Britain in 2009, Bourriaud's *Altermodern* exhibition and the Tate Encounter's Research-in-Process events ran concurrently and there is more than a passing connection in the ideas both dealt with, even though their paths never formally crossed. Both events were a response to the impact of global migration and economic standardization upon the contemporary cultural practice of the museum.

Lipovetsky also announces the end of the post-modern era:

> The 'post' of postmodern still directed people's attentions to a past that was
> assumed to be dead; it suggested that something had disappeared without
> specifying what was becoming of us as a result, as if it were a question of pre-
> serving a newly conquered freedom in the wake of the dissolution of social,
> political and ideological frameworks. That era has now ended. Hypercapitalism,
> hyperclass, hyperpower, hyperterrorism, hyperindividualism, hypermarket,
> hypertext – is there anything which isn't 'hyper'?
>
> *(Lipovetsky 2005: 30)*

The import of the idea of the hypermodern here is not a simple embrace, as if
recognizing what it notices about the present is the same thing as agreeing with the
terms of the argument offered. As a description of the present, in the account it gives
of contingency and temporality, it has real resonance and accords with other recognitions already noted about the relationship between new subject positions and new
functional systems. Lipovetsky posits the idea of 'paradoxical individualism' as a
product and characteristic of hypermodernity, which combines both autonomy and
dependence in ever increasing processes of personalization. Lipovetsky is grappling
with the same paradoxical situation revealed by Latour's analysis that a science of the
social cannot conflate the existence of the social with the political project of society
and that the alternative reveals 'the sheer difficulty of assembling collectivities made
of so many members once nature and society have been simultaneously put aside'
(Latour 2007: 259). The present is, for both arguments, a moment of great uncertainty for the political project of humanity in how to imagine and transform individuals
and collectivities, however assembled, into a new common unity.

The discussion of the museum and its audiences, or more abstractly the museum
and its publics, whether framed through the possibilities of technologies or not, now
turns upon how are the great numbers of people who visit museums, whether
embodied or online, to be understood both as individuals and as collectivities; how in
fact can we detect the social in the museum's networks? Taking the first part of the
question it is now clear that it is necessary to go beyond the idea of the museum
visitor as consumer to ask what is entailed in the process of consumption, what is the
product, how is it consumed and how does it constitute an exchange? As the Tate
Encounters ethnography[9] has shown, the consumption of the past or the present in
the art museum involves reflexive subjectivity, which is to say that the viewer is
involved in a relational process in which biography, memory and identity are no
longer given but to be discovered. The museum and its objects are thus entailed in
the consumption of individualized identity and this takes place in the current configuration of museums privately. This private consumption of tradition bound the
individual to a world of continuity and value in a world where the past was understood through modernism to be intrinsically linked by a continuous thread to the
present. In contrast, the world of hypermodernity is built upon the consumption of
tradition in the same terms as the consumption of everything else and it is this that

the museum can no longer guarantee because it no longer holds the authority over the relationship between tradition and the individual consumer. No longer can the museum legislate for how to respond or receive the value of an object or image, nor can it know how the visitor makes sense of the process. This is why the enabling modernist museum moved to see the space of the museum as the space of encounter and engagement between the individual, the object and object maker.

The modernist museum was conceived as the black box, or white cube (O'Doherty 2000: 16) in which it need do nothing other than present an event. What is left out of this account, and what the museum is missing is the means of dialogue in the engagement such that private consumption can be reconnected to a notion of public, a conduit that tradition once provided. In the hypermodern, post-traditional society tradition cannot be revived, other than as heritage, but subjectivities can be made visible and shared, and this is a necessary step in assembling new collectivities. The networks of the distributed museum, the cultural archives of the connected databases together with the work undertaken by the consumer in fashioning subjectivities provides the framework, or network, within which the process of identity formation can form a new commons and a replacement for representational systems that no longer connect with the hypermodern subject. From the perspective of the argument being made here, there still remains a need to see how a confrontation with the paradoxes of the hypermodern has been intellectually arrived at and tracing the outline of the way the argument has been constructed will be helpful.

What does it mean to be modern? This question was asked by Bruno Latour nearly two decades ago in a calculated and sustained response to the intellectual uncertainty represented by the theoretical project of post-modernism (Latour 1993: 10). Nearly 20 years on, it might be equally useful to ask what is the practical purchase of the idea of the hypermodern in relationship to the future of the art museum. Scholars of science and technology studies and proponents of Actor-Network Theory, have long been aware of Latour's argument that 'We have never been modern', a phrase that provided the title of the book in which he expounded the idea. For the purposes of the argument here, Latour alights upon a formative moment of the intellectual formation of modernity in the competing work of Robert Boyle and Thomas Hobbes in the middle of the seventeenth century. With due acknowledgement to the work of Shapin and Schaffer (1985) in the social history of science, Latour identifies in Boyle's and Hobbes' work a fundamental epistemological division in the production of knowledge. Latour argued that the division between the domains of science and politics was central to the formation of the Enlightenment project, the consolidation of European bourgeois society and the emergence and shape of modernism.

> They have cut the Gordian knot with a well-honed sword. The shaft is broken: on the left they have put knowledge of things; on the right, power and human politics. ... [I and my colleagues are] attempting to retie the knot by crisscrossing, as often as we have to, the divide that separates exact knowledge and the exercise of power.
>
> *(Latour 1993: 3)*

According to Latour, secular rationalism was organized upon the division between science and politics, such that science dealt with and explained the objects of nature, while politics organized human affairs in the field of society and culture. Latour shows how this division contained a double paradox in regarding nature and society as both transcendent and constructed. In the first paradox, nature is conceived as a non-human construct and therefore transcendent and surpasses humans infinitely, while society is conceived as the free construction of humans and therefore immanent to action. In the second paradox, the reverse is stated, that nature is artificially constructed in the laboratory and is hence immanent, while society is not constructed by humans and hence transcendent. The constitutional guarantees of the modern are, as Latour expresses them, 'that even though we construct nature, nature is as if we did not construct it' and 'even though we do not construct society, society is as if we did construct it' (Latour 1993: 32). Thus the foundations of the epistemic project of modernity, its forms of knowledge, are based upon an ontological distinction between nature and society, which must be kept distinct in order that the affairs of science and politics can proceed and be distinguished from the superstition and irrationality that was the ancient and feudal. What the project of science and technology studies sets out to show and Actor-Network Theory facilitates is that the world never did conform to the project of modernism and its ontological divide. The collapse of the Soviet Union, the pandemic of AIDS, world famine and the crisis of the planetary ecosystem, first noted by the post-modernists as signs of the end of modernity, are reinterpreted by Latour as demonstrating the existence and proliferation of hybrids of nature and culture. Hybrids are new types of entities or beings, which mix nature and culture in what Latour calls networks of things both human and non-human, which modernity attempts to 'purify' by means of its primary ontological division. Latour engages anthropology to show that combinations of nature and culture, his hybrids, were embraced by the cosmology of 'pre-modern' knowledge, but distinguished and 'purified' (his term) by secular rationalism. Latour's rediscovery of hybrids in the modern world allowed him to claim that 'we were never modern'. In Latourian terms, the art museum is still in the process of the purification of objects, however, when looked at as the distributed museum through its networks of practices it is better thought of as a 'tainted' hybrid.

This condensed account of Latour's analysis of the modern might seem something of a counterintuitive detour in establishing the utility of the hypermodern, since if modernity is revealed as a flawed epistemic project, whose end was signalled by post-modernity, what need can there be to cling to the historicizing force of modernity in idea of the hypermodern? In *Modernity and its Futures*, the final volume of four sociological textbooks written for an Open University course entitled, 'Understanding Modern Societies: An Introduction', the editors explain that the course and the reading material,

> ... adopt a dual focus aiming on the one hand to explore the central, substantive features of social reproduction and transformation in the modern epoch and, on the other, strives to highlight the nature of the theories and

categories that social scientists draw upon in order to make sense of those processes.

(Hall et al. 1992: 10)

Conceptually, the position of the Open University course of the 1990s distinguished the concept of modernism from the conditions of modernity or, modernity's institutional nexus. Latour might possibly balk at this distinction, seeing in it another example of sociology's complicity with modernity's separation of a social science from the networks in which it fashions its account. However, he would also acknowledge that Hall and his colleagues, were engaged in the same scholarly enterprise in responding to the twin experiences of globalizing changes in the conditions of the world's economic, technological and political arrangements, together with a corresponding sense of major uncertainty in European academia surrounding the intellectual project of modernity. A distinction between conceptions of the conditions of modernity and the conditions of modernity's conception can be extended to a consideration of post-modernity and post-modernism (Webster 1995: 190). Scholars such as Harvey (1992) and Jameson (1991) saw a different 'cultural logic' working its way across the globe as the capitalist economic system increased accumulation through flexible production and distributed modes of production, which they identified as a postmodern set of conditions. In contrast, Baudrillard (1985: 127) and Lyotard (1986: 4) among others, concluded that the post-modern conditions identified were of such magnitude that they had also produced a fundamental rupture in the modernist epistemological project and hence demarcated a break with its intellectual modus operandi and the certainties and guarantees it produced. Modernity was a form of scientific rationalism, which configured history in terms of a progression away from the irrationalism and tyranny of the past and a resolution of the contradictions of the present by the future. This was true for both liberalism, which saw capitalism as capable of reform and control, as well as for Marxism, which saw capitalism as a fatally flawed stage of human progress towards communism. The confident paths to the future outlined by these opposing accounts of historical progress in the terms of scientific rationalism, have most recently been finally vitiated in the simultaneous triumph and crisis of neo-liberalism and the ecological crisis of the planet. How then is the contemporary post-industrial Western world to think of its history and proceed in the future? As noted, Hall and his Open University collaborators, rejected an either/or choice between the modern and postmodern, finding instead new complexities in the late modern period which reflect arguments on both sides. Alternatively Beck (in Beck et al. 1994: 25), Bauman (2007: 2), Giddens (in Beck et al. 1994: 57) and Lipovetsky (2005: 30), while taking seriously the account of the post-modern critique, have argued for a new theorization of contemporary social and political life along a number of parallel and critically engaged lines including, reflexive modernization (Beck), post-traditional society (Giddens), liquid modernity (Bauman) and hypermodernity (Lipovetsky). Each argument has a bearing upon the museum and its relationship to cultural value and starts from the post-modern recognition of the triumph of consumerism and the paradox of ever greater processes of individualization alongside an ever greater process of homogenizing functionalization. One of the roles of the museum, which is in a sense continuous with many points in its history, is to understand the cultural import of a world that is creating humans who are both more individualistic in terms of the multiplicity of time, subjectivity and activities, while at the same time equally aware of being more connected than ever.

Within these debates can be found the new terms of an argument for framing the discussion of the museum and the public realm. It is no longer productive to think of the museum in isolation, either as a kind of monolithic relic from the nineteenth century, nor simply as a modern corporation. Instead, it has been suggested that the art museum is a distributed organization, which operates across a number of partially connected networks, the most notable being the global art market and its mobilizing capital accumulation, and the other the remediated channels of global media communication. To think of the art museum along these lines opens up new perspectives on the thorny questions of the production of cultural value, founded upon curatorial knowledge and judgement. Equally, it is no longer productive to think of the art museum's audience as a representation of society, in which policy-makers and educators are driven to find ever more ingenious and novel ways to identify and entice the socially 'missing' audiences, while failing to articulate or explore the silent accord between the culture or its core audience and that of its professionals. The continued framing of 'social' experience in the terms of race and class by journalists and professionals remains troubling, but is also hollowed out by a global dynamic of human movement and exchange, which demands a new language and understanding of what constitutes the bonds and divisions between and within collectivities. How the art museum understands the current terms of debate and whether it takes up the challenge of putting audience at the centre of its networks and thinking is the subject of the final section of this book.

10

POST-CRITICAL MUSEOLOGY

Reassembling theory, practice and policy

The problem of theory and practice

The Tate Encounters research project arose as a product of a separation between policy, research and practice, in which research is seen to be able to bridge the space between policy and practice at points where implementation of policy runs into difficulties on the ground. The writing of this book and its forms of analysis were based upon an understanding of a double separation between theory and practice and the museum and the academy, constituting a kind of epistemic fault line. While the institutions of government, museums and universities involved in policy and practice have a common public remit to the production and dissemination of knowledge in pursuit of their stated aims, the separation of their institutional functions replicates a separation between certain kinds of theory and certain kinds of practice, in which knowledge and understanding is disaggregated for operational purposes. The constitution of a double theory/practice divide in the museum and academy as well as between them is manifest at two points. Firstly, within the academy there is a division between theoretically informed reflection in research and contingent operational knowledge in teaching, and in the museum between the know-how of operational practices and the know-why of strategic knowledge. Secondly, there is a theory/practice division between the academy and the museum, in which the museum is posited as the concrete operational sphere considered as the object of abstract reflection by the academy.

This double separation constitutes a yawning gap between the academic production of certain kinds of cultural theory and the concrete practices of the museum, in which there is little reflexive overlap. Put another way, even though certain academics, their students, and museum professionals act upon the possibility of a common (meta) theoretical discourse, constituting common objects, ideas and language, which speaks across the gap, theory and practice are, for all practical purposes, organized as different discourses, belonging to different institutional arrangements, involving the production of different functionalized objects and forms of knowledge. A 'non-critical', conventional understanding of the relationship between the practices of the museum and academy would understand the museum and its operational sphere as a legitimate object of study, research and analysis by the academy in its role of specialized knowledge producer. The knowledge produced about the museum in this conventional relationship is subsequently mobilized within the museum and within a nexus of government funding for teaching and research and the more general dissemination of knowledge though media. In this conventional model, the academy produces commissioned, applied and speculative knowledge about museums because the division of theory and practice, as well as being an epistemic division, is also a practical division of labour and interest. The museum, on the other hand, recognizes and understands itself as an organization of contingent practices, to be studied by the academy and its discipline methods, because it is not dedicated to the production of an abstract knowledge of itself and its operational sphere.

Speculative knowledge production within the academy is directed at revealing the problematic nature of given concrete arrangements in which theory is offered as a prescription for progressive transformations in the concrete, real world. The main reason for the museum not easily responding to the offering of museology's critical theory is because the critical project, operating as one side of the double separation, can only overcome the separation of theory and practice, by the production of more theory. There are a number of consequences for the museum of the annexation of critical knowledge to the realm of theory (re)production, an important one being an anti-theory response. Museum managers can often see no practical or immediate relevance of theoretical critique and seek instead to constitute a professional body of knowledge about the museum through external consultation led by marketing and others.

The current state of play of museum/academy relationships is likely to involve a combination of the following responses to the production of different registers of theory. Firstly, there are those in the academy whose interests lie in maintaining the academic project of criticism, often for institutional purposes of research funding and status, who see museum practices as problematic, but who believe that a meta-discourse is possible and necessary to any transformation of the museum. Secondly, there are those in the academy and museum who subscribe to a view that theory is itself unproblematic and can be mobilized in the production of practical knowledge to improve the museum. Thirdly, there are those in the museum who subscribe to an anti-theory view who see the museum as a separate professional sphere of operation based upon its own reflexive knowledge. Finally, there are a smaller number of academics and museum professionals, mostly likely identified with the educational mission of the museum and university who, like the authors here, have experienced collaborative and embedded research in which audiences, museum professionals and academic researchers co-produce knowledge, but are left unsure of what the status of such knowledge is and for whom.

Throughout the organizational study of the Tate Encounters research, it became clear to what extent a relationship of doubt and scepticism had emerged between the academy's own theoretical ruminations on the museum and its perceived lack of connection with the 'real work' of the museum and the everyday practices, practicalities and realities in which decisions are made. It is perhaps most notable at this particular conjuncture of theory and practice that the conditions of non-engagement between the academy and the museum have been and continue to be most defined, ensuring that the common sense, sedimented language of the museum and the theoretical language of the academy rarely meet outside of an educational context, if fleetingly there. How to get beyond, the theory/practice impasse was a key research objective of Tate Encounters.

The limits of museum studies

The establishment of a body of critical knowledge of the museum and its relationship to society owes its institutional origins in Britain more generally to the period of expansion of higher education from the 1960s onwards, which led by various routes to both the legitimation of new areas of study as well as to the functional system and economy of present-day university education. The expansion in the scale and scope of universities in Britain brought with it new kinds of purposes that are recognized today in the intention to educate a majority rather than a minority at tertiary level and to connect universities more closely with industry and everyday life. The expansion of higher education in Britain brought with it greater social differentiation in the student body and among academics, together with a greater focus upon the perceived problems of contemporary society. The discipline of sociology expanded considerably in and through the polytechnics of the 1970s, which later became the first institutions of higher education to be incorporated into a unified university system.

The established universities of the period also witnessed the emergence of studies of popular and common culture, which developed from traditional subjects, such as English, from which British cultural studies, media studies and post-colonial studies were legitimated, often not without internal resistance from traditionalists in the humanities disciplines. What these developments sought to frame for serious study and inclusion was a politics of contemporary culture and to a lesser extent to mobilize such studies, both in teaching and scholarly activity, within cultural and social practices, in effect to make knowledge useful, or in the more abstract sense, emancipatory (Johnson 2006: 75). In critical theory's focus upon culture and its relationship to economic and political power, the museum came into view as a site of universal values and narrative histories. The museum was by turns presented as a technology of panoptic mastery and the disciplinary gaze, a state institution of civilizing ritual and civic reform and a structure for the exercise of social distinction (Duncan 1995: 18). The museum was located by the project of critical theory as a site of contested power in the public realm. What evidence might exist or analysis offered of how museums responded and adjusted to critical theory's analytical perspectives remains to be understood, but what is evident is the incorporation of critical theory in academic studies of museums.

If critical knowledge has confined itself to the production of theory, with all the dangers that theoreticism entails, by institutional processes of knowledge reproduction carried out by its academic practitioners, museum practitioners are equally locked into a reproduction of professional operational practices without end and with few mechanisms for either 'criticality' or 'reflexivity'. Both the expanded British university system and the professionalized British museum sector have been transformed through the greater functionalization and speeding up of knowledge systems and economic exchange rendered by hypermodernity. For practice in the art museum, separated from its own theoretical project, the primary effects have been the maintenance of the organizational separation between the systems of objects and the system of humans, such that the knowledge of and about audiences remains misrecognized, while the system of objects remains concealed by the annexation of acquisition networks. In Latourian terms, the modernist art museum has to expunge all hybrid networks in order to maintain its own logic and trajectory, but without seeing the nature of its own hybridity. As a consequence, modernist art museum professionals are locked into operational forms of knowledge, or what might be thought of as specific zones of expert informational exchange. The threat of hybrids (other networks of people, ideas and objects) is constantly managed through the assessment of risk to the central logic of the modernist project.

Traditional museology can be seen as sitting alongside conventional art history, providing the tools to put into practice the insights offered by art historical knowledge (artist, genre, form, school, nation, historical period). Critical museology emerged out of a critique of established museological practice and conventional art history, questioning the view that there can be a robust universal standard by which the value of objects can be ascertained and meaning assigned. Critical museology advanced by means of a series of theoretical analyses and standpoints. The research recognized this as problematic, since criticality emerged more from a distanced elaboration of theory rather than from an embedded working through of museum practices. The approach advocated by a Post-critical Museology, which emerged from the methods of the Tate Encounters research, did take on existing theoretical critiques, but in doing so it tested them against what Thrift calls a 'radical empiricism' and 'a poetics of the release of energy' in experimenting with how the experience of encountering Tate registered (Thrift 2008: 12). The research recognized the exhaustion of the insights provided by the critique of the museum, while recognizing that new museology (Macdonald 2011), contains many elements of analysis, which parallel the arguments made here. However, the proposed practice of Post-critical Museology, is a provocation even to progressive academic museology, since it wants to insist that research relating to the problems of contemporary practices in museums, whether conceptualized analytically or met operationally, takes place in and with museums and their extended collaborators in a reflexive methodological mode. This leads to a working method that involves processes of translation between different registers of knowledge and dialogic iteration in which theory and practice are equally questionable.

Methodology

The methodology developed by Tate Encounters had three practical dimensions; it was organized and conducted collaboratively and fully embedded in the site of research; it developed a transdisciplinary approach; and it adopted a reflexive method to the gathering of data and its analysis. Embedding research in Tate Britain meant that the practical organization of collaboration forced an interaction between the practices producing the critical conceptual framework, reflected in the research questions and the everyday, practical and contingent world of Tate's practices. The accumulative effects of this reflexive process, over a two-year period – such as a recognition of the constructed nature of the research object; the relative position of facts and values; the recognition of the relative position of theory and what it framed – were all in accord with some of the tenets of the philosophy of pragmatism and its critique of foundational theories of knowledge (Rorty 2011: 370). A third and connected element in the methodological triangulation was the value placed upon reflexivity (Alvesson and Sköldberg 2009: 222).

Reflexivity has become a benchmark in recent sociological research as a mechanism for recognizing that the agency of the researcher is an active ingredient in shaping meaning in the design, execution and interpretation of data. Reflexivity offered the research a means of acknowledging that what was being examined and the method of examination needed to be understood as both object and subject and cause and effect. Reflexivity also offered the research a method by which its findings could be verified over the duration of the research in terms of the acknowledgement of the reflex of 'acting back' upon hypothesis and data. Put another way, reflexivity was a tactical companion to the pragmatic perspective on theory and practice, which allowed the agency of the researcher to be acknowledged as a constituent of knowledge formation. Reflexive research lies within a constructivist tradition within sociological research and privileges: i) the primacy of interpretation and the position of the interpreters and their understandings; ii) an awareness of the political character of research; iii) the problem that research carries no representational authority; and iv) insists upon a clarity of the logic of collecting and processing empirical data (Alvesson and Sköldberg 2009: 11).

As much as the research pursued its original questions and created data from which to provide answers, the design of the research was developmental and dialogic, by which it is meant that the research methods were open to change in the process of establishing relationships with and between Tate and the co-researchers. This is where the central value of reflexive methodology can be understood. It would have been perfectly possible to have conducted a research programme at a distance from Tate Britain, in the standard default position of external research, which sought access from the institution to the objects relevant to research. Such an approach would not have been collaborative nor interdisciplinary, nor would it easily have been able to engage 'action orientated' social science methods. The fact that half of the research team of six were employed by Tate evidences the embedded nature of the research approach, and which located the project as a part of the learning and public programme of Tate Britain.

Advancing a reflexive position through embedded practice necessitated the progressive abandonment of critical positions that could only be theoretically sustained. In their place, a closely situated problematic was framed, focused on difficulties exposed through experimental practices within the museum. The perspectives that developed from this process, emerged as much from museum practice as they did from theoretical argument. The embedded and collaborative method of Tate Encounters brought theory and practice reflexively together in and through the specificity of the encounters in the museum. The analysis of the Tate Encounters research brought a particular historic critique of the art museum, which had identified the absences and exclusions of particular histories and the occlusion of the role of audience in making meaning through a series of separations between curatorial and intellectual knowledge practices, to a new practice threshold.

Collaboration, transdisciplinarity and reflexivity in the embedded context of carrying out the research at Tate Britain, produced a close collaboration between investigators, Tate professionals and student participants, which resulted in a particular research ethic that emphasized the importance of achieving an equality of voice for all those involved in the research enterprise. Put more abstractly, the reflexive and collaborative methodology of Tate Encounters underpinned the aim of a research democracy, which in turn directed the practical forms, types and uses of data and analysis. In expanded and formal detail, the production of knowledge based upon research democracy becomes synonymous with what is being proposed here as the practice of the post-critical.

Of necessity the post-critical locates itself in the everyday and in spaces 'outside', 'between' and 'beyond' those of the foundational boundaries of knowledge disciplines. This is because, as Lyotard, has argued, the legitimation of knowledge, which historically required a consensus that in turn relied upon the grand narratives of progress and emancipation, have for some time now been thrown into doubt. For Lyotard, as with this research 'consensus is an horizon never to be reached' and its remaining function is as 'a component of the system, which manipulates it in order to maintain and improve its performance' (Lyotard 1986: 61). Discipline knowledge has been co-opted within the informational system Lyotard describes as the institutional management of risk, which in the case of the disciplinary production of knowledge about the museum, limits the agency of that knowledge. The limit comes about when highly specialist knowledge is treated through the informational mode in order to maximize its market potential and in doing so removes the specificity and concreteness of its location and hence, in social and cultural theory, removes its politics (e.g. external commissioned consultancy research).

In contrast to the disciplinary project, the post-critical seeks to formulate, confront and solve problems of the everyday through a dialogic method embedded in practice worlds. The basis of the position advanced resides in arguing that in the case of museology, the agency of disciplinary knowledge positions, based upon a critique of established, embedded and implicit knowledge practices of the museum, circulate in closed, self-serving networks, rather than practically confronting their objects. The problem of post-criticality is a complex one, involving a reflexivity towards the work of theory and practice. The post-critical calls for new understandings of what being critical entails and what criticality produces and this can be approached by turning theory's illumination back upon the means by which theory generates knowledge. Equally the post-critical requires a reflexivity towards the subjectivities, associations, performances, mediations and collectivities that constitute the production of ideas, things and relations in the everyday. The problem of how to enmesh and hold together the processes of theory generation and the processes of subjectification in embedded life worlds is inimical to advancing post-critical practice. The post-critical arises from an entanglement of theory in the pragmatics of performance and in this case the post-critical was an outcome of the embedded location of the research at Tate Britain and the methods it developed as a consequence. As such the position of post-criticality was arrived at through a process of action and reaction over time. In what follows, an account of the 'journey' of the method of the Tate Encounters research is given as a way of showing how both research democracy and the position of post-criticality were arrived at.

The Tate Encounters research started from an acknowledged interdisciplinary model, which formally sought the joint expertise of art history, anthropology and sociology. The final research team brought together the additional inflections of studies of new media, the practices of curatorship and visual culture studies. The starting point of interdisciplinarity was based upon the recognized specialism of each individual member of a research team of six people, which were aligned with three research strands, policy, visuality and media production, which led to a body of data comprising ethnographic film-making, an organizational study, student surveys and participant recordings. During the process of mapping disciplinary concepts and concerns in relationship to the initial research questions of what are the barriers to access to Tate Britain and what constitutes the Britishness of its collection, a set of objects came into view that were not within the disciplinary framing with which the project began.

The new objects in sight, such as the identification of selective networks and the operations of the transcultural and transmedial, were peripheral objects of the disciplines in play, but moreover, the analytical means of their identification were not within the view of the disciplines involved. The emerging analysis of Tate Encounters was moving not only between the parameters of the disciplinary mix, but taking in other perspectives, which were themselves questioning their own disciplinary base, such as science and technology studies, Actor-Network Theory and non-representational theory. This reframing of the original objects of study through the generation of new objects of study led to a recognition that the method that had evolved in practice was not interdisciplinary but transdisciplinary and it was the transdisciplinary that offered the possibility of a synthesis of the new complexity, which the research came to define as the distributed museum. Transdisciplinarity as a description of the method adopted by the research paralleled other objects and ideas, which stood outside and between the existing mix of disciplinary framing of studies of the art museum, which were first assembled in the formation of Tate Encounters. The prefix of 'trans' to disciplinarity parallels its appendage in the research analysis to culture, visuality and media in the terms transcultural, transvisual and transmedial, as a means of signalling precisely the movement of people and things in which agency was being identified across multiple locations and practices.

In line with the democratic ethic of the research, the relationship between the researcher and the researched was not performed as one of observer and the observed in which the authority to define a situation in research terms lay exclusively with the researcher, but instead understood as the co-extensive generation of knowledge. This was formalized after the evaluation of a three-month pilot project at the beginning of the Tate Encounters fieldwork, in which participants who wished to continue with the research submitted a proposal to undertake their own project, which the research team would facilitate. While the model for this was implicitly educational in terms of facilitation, in terms of ethnographic research it was a practical method through which Tate Encounters could resolve the problem of the unequal relationship between researcher and those volunteering to be subjects of the research. The 12 student participants who volunteered to continue for a further year by means of a nominated project, were given the status of co-researchers. This was intended to signal the ambition to achieve an equality of voice and authority in relationship to the ethnographic process of documentation in the research outputs and more complexly in the analysis and findings. Co-researchers enabled more grounded accounts of individual encounters with the museum to be constructed, in contrast to the ways in which certain 'missing' audiences had been constructed by policy categories.

The perspectives offered by the co-researchers in their projects and presentations, what have been termed here as transcultural perspectives and transmedial productions, looked at Tate Britain obliquely, or rather they looked directly at what they saw as an oblique object. For the co-researchers, the status and purposes of the relationship between Tate Britain and the research remained unclear, while their perspective remained detached, sceptical and questioning. They viewed Tate Britain as positioned outsiders, not looking for membership, but curious and interested nevertheless of how Tate Britain configured itself in relationship to contemporary culture and Britishness. Moreover, in answering the research question put to them about Britishness and cultural identity, they politely refused racial, ethnized or national categorization and instead demonstrated a relationship to identity based upon the co-ordinates of time and space. This paralogic and highly relativistic approach to identity is what allowed the research analysis to name the process of transculturality.

Fundamental to building such co-research with its grounded and embedded accounts was a commitment to establishing a sustained longitudinal enquiry and analysis, which could not only test the working assumptions of the research framing and the practices of the art museum and its audiences, but ensure that a sufficient timescale was realised in which to generate a significant depth of practice-based and participant qualitative data which would go beyond a snapshot of most commissioned audience research. The establishment of a strong empirical basis for the research and the embedded organisation of the fieldwork at Tate Britain meant that an 'uneasy' passage of dialogue opened between Tate's professional need for short-term operational knowledge and the slower process of generating an analysis from the research data, which could be useful in the practices of the museum. Over the two-year fieldwork period, Tate Encounters often had to resist operational questions seeking instrumentalized answers to the problem of absent audiences and the reason given for this was that the time frame of qualitative research is much slower than that of operational knowledge, which seeks immediate answers. The sustained empirical base of the Tate Encounters research was more than locally pragmatic, since it was the practical means by which theory and practice could be connected. The empirical method of the research went hand-in-hand with a pragmatist perspective, which emphasized the localized and practical utility of knowledge.

It has already been suggested that the co-researchers' submissions to the Research-in-Process event are figural of the emergent condition and practices of the transcultural and transmedial, which is to say that such submissions are part, as well as demonstrations of the new hybrid of the distributed museum. More concretely, the co-researchers' submissions can be seen as aspiring to be part of the distributed museum as expressed through the methodology established by the research. The co-researchers did not supply evidence of subject presence to be subsequently analysed as such, but instead presented an analysis from a position of audience/producer, or conventionally, but more problematically, evidenced what a visitor could produce given an extended period of time. As an illustration this is one way of seeing a core, repeat visitor in longitudinal terms, only in this case the co-researcher was a visitor the museum was unfamiliar with. What sustained the co-researcher encounter with the art museum was not 'membership' of an art club, nor 'participation' in an art culture, but the expression of a questioning position towards, or more accurately a trajectory through the museum.

What is important in drawing together the argument for the position of post-criticality from the basis of the Tate Encounters research is to what extent the model of co-research, which has been presented as a form of collaborative 'problem solving', between experts and non-experts constituted across as well as outside knowledge disciplines, can be extended to the conditions of the museum's relationship with visitors. Notwithstanding the obvious differences of scale in resource investment, the question arises, does the apparent 'disinterest' of the position of the transcultural and the ubiquity of the transmedial fit the contemporary conditions of spectatorship? This is of course a conceptual modelling of audience, but is no different in kind from other existing models of audience engagement, as can be seen in Tate's current adoption of a motivational segmentation of its visitors, which it developed and adapted with Morris, Hargreaves and McIntyre over the past ten years. At the practical level, the differences between the co-researchers and Tate Britain's audience might be seen to turn upon the motivations of students in full-time higher education, as against the many other positions of age and circumstance of Tate's visitors and non-visitors. At the conceptual level, the profound shift in the organization and distribution of knowledge brought about by the informational economy has changed the ways in which people meet and interact with what is considered important and necessary to know and engage with.

The informational economy continues to have an intense impact upon young people and students just as it does upon most forms of employment. While there are many real and practical 'digital divides', in terms of access to and understandings of computer mediated data, it has to be accepted that digital media has become the 'digital default' of local and global communication and culture. In the specific case of the student participants in the Tate Encounters research, while their participation in higher education marks them out as part of the 42 per cent of 18–24-year-olds currently studying in British higher education institutions, it does not mark them out as part of any elite privileged statistical demographic group for whom the culture of the museum and university experience is a class and family norm. The co-researchers maintained part-time jobs in order to fund themselves through their courses, had various and diverse migrational family experience and were for the most part, what is euphemistically termed 'non-traditional' entrants to higher education. Indeed, in the initial formulation of the research they were constituted in the terms of demographic groups who Tate Britain wished to 'target' as museum non-attendees, a definition that fell apart through the refusal of participants to accept such racial and social classification terms. What is being insisted upon here is that, while specific material and cultural differences abound between and within both Tate Britain's visitors and the student population from whom the co-researchers were drawn, the communication systems in which cultural value is registered and through which individuals participate are converging and interactive and hence it is possible to speak of a commonality organized along a radically horizontal plane of access. The possible objection that the modelling of a form of sustained encounter with the museum presented in the research is in some way limited to a privileged sample, is countered not only by the demographic profiling of the group, which places them outside of established art museum culture, but by the larger argument of the degree to which they were part of a much larger group configured within the same axis and necessary participation in the informational networks.

The transcultural is a lived and reflexive form of cultural relativism, whose affects cannot but help test values across different 'life worlds' as mobile subjects navigate multiple passages through the everyday. The transcultural is similar to what, de Certeau calls 'the science of the ordinary', which consists of being 'a foreigner at home':

> And since one does not 'leave' this language, since one cannot find another place from which to interpret it, since there are therefore no separate groups of false interpretation and true interpretation, but only illusory interpretations, since in short there is no 'way out', the fact remains that we are foreigners on the inside [because] there is no outside.
>
> *(de Certeau 1988: 13)*

De Certeau is here referring to the domain of the use of language in which the forms, modes and pragmatic rules are dependent upon 'forms of life'. In this there is a parallel with Lyotard's attempt to construct a possible and useful epistemology in the face of the crisis of the legitimacy of science, brought about through the commodi-fication of knowledge. Where de Certeau draws attention to language's relationship to 'forms of life', Lyotard draws attention to its relationship to the social bond when he says 'that the observable social bond is composed of language "moves"'. De Certeau and Lyotard make common recourse to Wittgenstein's sociolinguistic approach to the study of language as a 'game' in which the rules of language do not carry with them their own legitimation, but are the object of a contract between the players. The players do not necessarily invent the rules, but without a rule there can be no game and that an utterance that does not satisfy a rule does not belong to the game they define (Lyotard 1986: 10). De Certeau parallels Wittgenstein's thesis when he insists that language is 'an ensemble of practices in which one is implicated' (de Certeau 1988: 13). It needs to be recognized here that the example of Lyotard and de Certeau's specific emphasis upon the relationship between the modes, forms and uses of language in the transaction of meanings and values is an historical response to the intellectual crisis of modernism and a specific response to structuralism's final goal of revealing the external and abiding structures governing human forms of symbolic meaning. The continued importance of the provisional and contingent nature of language to the analysis here is not focused upon language per se, but upon the position of the knowing subject relative to the means of knowing, or the status of performative action relative to the practice of performance. The latter emphasis upon performativity, escapes the limit of the language games in favour of a wider assemblage in time and space of action and event, but both trains of thought mark out the intellectual movement away from macro models of power and knowledge fixed in structures, towards the micro focus upon how knowing is constituted in subjectivity. This brings the argument back to what can be said of the knowingness of the art museum visitor.

Transvisuality

> We need a critical literature that in addition to analysing how museums con-struct meaning and project an ideal viewer in the abstract, will also give us a theory of the viewer that emphasizes individual responses to both complex interior impulses and conflicting external messages.
>
> *(Rice 2003: 92)*

In the Tate Encounters analysis, the transcultural is both a mode and a condition. It is both a way of seeing/speaking based upon crossing life worlds as well as constituting a life world in itself. The experience of migration is the paradigmatic form of the transcultural, although crossing other sub-cultural life worlds given by social mobility also produces the transcultural. In the context of spectatorship, transculturality pro-duces what was earlier referred to as 'seeing on the move', and in combination with the transmedial produces transvisuality, which is a way of signalling the specificity of a dynamic and relative position of seeing and subject position. Hypermodern transna-tional migration is creating a new life world, which is experienced both here and not here, or indeed in multiple localities, a form of belonging and not belonging, which are simultaneously connected through the global space of flows (Castells cited in Webster 1995: 200). These new conditions of the life world of transnational migration are bringing about new subjectivities whose defining features are the transcultural and transmedial.

The paradigm of transculturality taken as a mode (of language), rather than as a condition (of a life world), becomes applicable to all museum visitors in the context of the distributed museum because of two important new recognitions. Firstly, users experience transculturality through the differing registers of network cultures, which require a crossing of informational codes. Secondly, the space of the museum can no longer be taken as a universal public space, in its historically civic sense, but now appears as a specific spectacular space in multiple localities. In both of these senses transculturality, and its special case of transvisuality becomes for the art museum a new general mode of viewing and spectatorship, replacing the historically given vertical alignment of seeing within specific aesthetic tropes, cultural locations, objects and places, in the example under scrutiny here, aesthetic modernism.

While the transvisual (as a special product of the transcultural) is a new default way of seeing, it does not by itself encompass a second condition of the distributed museum, which is that the viewer is also a producer. The Tate Encounters analysis introduced the concept of transmediation as the companion to the transcultural precisely to deal with the remediating effects of new media in the distributed museum. The transmedial operates as a further crossing of cultural codes, only in this case media or language coding in which the producer/viewer repurposes messages from one media register in another. In the Tate Encounters analysis, the productions of the co-researchers mostly met both of the conditions of the transmedial and transcultural in exhibiting both a relative view of the museum's organization of space, objects and purposes as well as viewing objects within differing media modalities. While it is possible to consider museum visitors as having a new default viewing position set by the transcultural and transmedial in the form of transvisuality, the aggregate of all visitors is not equal to the historic representational public and this sets up the problem of having to consider them one by one if the paths of subjectivities towards collectivities are to be established. This is one more reason why the model of the co-researcher in the museum prefigures the producer in the distributed museum.

How the co-research model might be scaled-up in order that the museum professionals, now constituted as an audience in the distributed museum, can gain a knowledge of the new producers presents a logistical and economic problem, rather than a conceptual one. Of course one of the ways in which the museum is considering the networked audience as prosumers is, as discussed previously, through limited forms of consumer attraction in social networking sites. The gap between the possibilities of audience as producers and the reality of current museum practices of audience as consumers returns the discussion to current understandings of how meaning is coded in and by global capital and its forms of production and consumption. But what is now unambiguous, is that in future the discussion of the art museum's audience can no longer meaningfully be conducted in terms of a relationship between given cultural authority and cultural deficit. The museum of the future – the distributed museum – will have to refashion the space of the public and that will require a profound shift in understanding the recoding and transcoding processes of its visitors.

At present, national at institutions such as Tate Britain do not operate as distributed museums but rather act on a contributive basis. Functioning through the historical legacy of a colonialist logic, the contributive museum works on a model of centre and periphery, with tribute flowing from the (colonial) margin to the (imperial) metropolis. The contributive museum presupposes uni-directional flow. Tribute goes to the centre, while an established set of values is disseminated to the margins. The notion of acculturation is crucial to this model, where those migrating from the margins head towards the metropolis to acquire its culture and its values. Those deemed to be coming from the margins, whether as artists or theorists, those characterized as BME or any other category of difference were marked by the contributive museum as outside the body of opinion that shaped cultural value. Rather they were regarded principally in one of two ways, either they were politically excessive and therefore requiring the neutralization offered by policy initiatives, or they were socially excluded and in cultural deficit in which case they were in need of accommodation and acculturation. The distributive museum refuses the cultural positionings of the contributive model and instead relies on transculturality. Transculturality, with its emphasis on the mutability of cultural value, depending on time and location, works against the hierarchies presupposed in acculturation. For the transmigrating subject, the contributive museum's insistence on disseminating its hierarchical values becomes no more than a rhetorical stance.

The distributed museum becomes a better model to work alongside the transmigrating subject. Transmigrating subjectivities take the fracture as a starting point. Continually coming up against different cultures, subject-positions continually undergo differentiation – experiencing the constant rearticulation of cultural difference. The opening up of lines of difference becomes the ground for the constitution of the transmigrating subject. By emphasizing the divided subject's partaking in networks circulating beyond the museum, the distributed museum becomes a resource to extend lines of difference.

Theory and practice at Tate

Within the account and analysis of the Tate Encounters organizational study, three strong messages emerged. The first is that the consideration of and address to audience was peripheral in the production of the exhibition and this gave a first clue as to the distribution of differential notions of audience carrying various degrees of significance along the networks of practice. Secondly, that cultural diversity, which was a code for both 'a missing audience', the politically sensitive 'imaginary multicultural audience' and in the case of The Lure of the East: British Orientalist Painters, 'a Muslim audience', was engaged in terms of the management of risk to other networks of interest and practice of Tate, which led in this sense to cultural diversity being used as a code for 'the other' within identifications of difference. Thirdly, and arising from the first two, *The Lure of the East: British Orientalist Painters* study began to build a picture of organizational practices in which Tate was one institution, but many networks in a more distributed organization. The study showed that, while sharing a strong corporate structure, ethos and brand, different practices within Tate are not necessarily internally connected to each other, nor do they necessarily cohere in common over-arching purposes.

If the model of Tate as a series of connected/disconnected, internal/external networks shown by the organizational study has any purchase, then it suggests that the agency of its departments or operational groups is differential in impact and reach. The connections and disconnections between people, ideas and works are produced by mediators in the networks, such that their agency and meanings can change, bifurcate, multiply. Thus for example in the Learning Department, the agency of audience, modelled through a constructivist pedagogy of engagement with works of art, is not the same audience as imagined or understood in the curatorial networks of expertise, nor the income-generation audience whose purchasing power is calculated in the retail shop, nor the nation-state audience who the directors address in seeking strategic funding. The limits upon the agency of all these audiences is organized by the separation of the network of people from the network of objects, in which the latter largely operates beyond Tate, but in which Tate is an important agent in establishing the exchange value of objects.

In a further example, it is possible to see that Tate Media is more than one thing. It is responsible for managing the network interface (an intermediary in the Actor-Network Theory sense), which transports meanings about the spaces and objects of the museum, without obviously changing their terms to the users of the website. But it is also a network hub (a mediator in the opposite Actor-Network Theory sense), which translates and changes meaning operating between other organizational nodes and their networks within Tate and between Tate and all the other networks of the internet. This places Tate Media in both a strategically advantageous as well as representationally onerous position. This was evident in the uneasy balance between maintaining the brand and opening the network; between retaining cultural authority and relinquishing control of authorship, expressed in the Online Strategy. The modelling of Tate's organization in terms of embodied and virtual networks, and the intersections, connections and disconnections they contain is a means of understanding how existing values and practices are maintained as well as potentially predicting obstacles in the path of the creation of new networks of value. Actor-Network Theory, which informed the Tate Encounters organizational study and analysis of *The Lure of the East: British Orientalist Painters* exhibition, brought the new hybrid of 'the distributed museum' into view, now no longer thought of as a relationship of the museum to society, in which the public realm stood as the intermediary, but as a mediating assemblage in a network of networks in which the social has to be traced. The social is no longer configured as something standing outside of the museum (and it should be added the research), as a given set of structures, but as something unpredictable to be identified in the agency of things that act or perform through heterogeneous associations.

Such an analysis arose from, as well as being applied to, the data. The qualitative datasets repeatedly showed how meaning in the space of the museum was derived from sources outside of the museum and that meaning 'events' in the museum flowed out through other associations. In this sense, it becomes hard to sustain an idea of Tate as one thing, as a unified organization, or singular entity. Tate, as its professionals would most likely confirm through experience and in commonsense terms, is many things to many people. In the research context, the tracing of what those things are and how they are tied to subjects and collectivities becomes the object of the exercise. One of the most significant traces to arise from the analysis of the relationship between subjects, visuality and exhibitionary practices, can be found in the connection between Tate practices and those of distributed media, as producers and consumers, curators and visitors adjust to new media and global migrational networks. Such networks represent the largest forces at work in the reconfiguration of cultural value and authority and, as has been argued, entail the museum and Tate in particular in a reconfiguration of representational systems.

The period of modernization of the museum, marked out in the research and this book as being from the early 1990s to the present, was encapsulated by new building projects, refurbishments and above all by the branded museum, of which Tate was a spectacular early example with the launch of Tate Modern. The corporate museum emerged as part of changing patterns of consumption and commodification with the effect that the museum visitor could be understood as cultural consumer (Prior 2002: 52). In what can now be discerned as a cultural movement in Britain over the past two decades, expressed by policies, practice and academic study, museums became policy vehicles for progressive social change. A progressive alliance between the cultural politics of the British New Labour government, academics and specific sections of museum professionals was forged to transform the museum's social function. This was to be achieved through a combination of targeting groups not present in the core of museum visitors, providing greater contextualization of objects in order to draw out their relevance, to consider museums as a site of entertainment as well as scholarship and to acknowledge the visitor as a more active agent in the making of meaning, registering what Anderson (2004: 1) describes as the museum's paradigmatic shift from 'collection-driven institutions' to 'visitor-centred organizations' (Macdonald 2011: 2).

It remains something of a puzzle that the reflexive modernization project of the art museum took place under the conditions of post-modernity and in the intellectual context of post-modernism. What kind of modernity was being installed in the museum and how did it square up to understandings of the post-modern subject? The characterization of the present as hypermodern is the latest in a number of attempts to identify changes between peoples and societies, subjects and systems and to understand the forces that are currently shaping individual and collective life. Like other scholars of the period surrounding the political events in which the Berlin Wall came down, Giddens (in Beck et al. 1994: 57) discusses a number of intellectual endings surrounding modernity and argues that what was emerging in the millennial moment was a post-traditional society, brought about by a reordering and extension of forces within modernity. The import of the post-traditional lay in the dynamic relationship between, on the one hand, the extension of 'modern institutions universalized via globalizing processes' and, on the other, the 'radicalizing of processes of intentional change', which were forcing an evacuation and problematization of tradition. Giddens thus provides a way of accounting for the continuation of modernizing forces at work in the museum.

In the same discussion in which Giddens posits the post-traditional, Beck puts forward the idea of reflexive modernization in which, he argues, that the more societies are modernized the more agents (subjects) acquire the ability to reflect on the social conditions of their existence and to change them through the new modes of information work and general consumption. Reflexive modernization involves greater processes of individualization in which 'agency is freed from structure'. In a critical riposte to Giddens and Beck, Lash points out that the new globalizing post-Fordist forces, which bring reflexive modernization into being, create winners and losers. Both locally and globally, changes in the movement of capital and labour create greater polarization between those in the informational economy and those in the downgraded service economies (Beck et al. 1994: 127). While the debate between Giddens, Beck and Lash is now historical, it remains relevant to the discussion of the museum on two counts. Firstly, because it forms a basis for considering the differential nature of the idea of 'agency freed from structures', in relationship to both forms of institutional relationship and to consumption. Secondly, and more urgently, because it entails the question of how social regulation is to be understood in the new spaces of global networks. In Lash's argument, the older regulated normative structures have been replaced by networks of information and communication structures, which have outstripped the historical forms of representational regulation.

For Lash, the need for a new explanation of social action in no way removes the question of a politics based upon the recognition of inequalities and the burden of his thinking is precisely to seek new ways of addressing how humans can better live together in shared and common collectivities. This is also the case with Latour's project of separating a 'science of living together', from sociology's historical entanglement with the project of social regulation. Latour makes this clear when he says: 'To state that domination breaks down bodies and souls is one thing, whereas concluding that hierarchies, dissymmetry, inertia, powers and cruelties are made of social stuff is a different argument altogether' (Latour 2007: 52). The manifest recognition in both Lash and Latour of continued inequalities, but the need to think differently about the mechanisms which produce them, has a new and direct impact upon cultural policy and public support for the arts and for the ways in which museums think about audiences.

The demographic of Tate's visitors, based upon audits using national statistical classifications, continue to show that its core audience differs markedly from the demographic composition of Britain's metropolitan centres and to the population as a whole. But what does it mean to measure an audience in this way using a demographic, which numerically encodes a society according to markers of race, ethnicity, education and income? What would Tate and all the other museums look like if, in some hypothetical world, they managed to produce a proportional demographic audience, 'perfectly reflecting society' based upon classifications of race and class? On the evidence of the analysis presented here, in which the museum is not a single entity but a distributed network, it is unlikely that 'in a perfect world', Tate would be recognizable. The example is intentionally absurd, but it underlines the point that museums are recognizable precisely because of all the things they assemble – including their visitors.

The reflexive modernization of the modernist art museum can be seen in similar terms to the argument outlined by Beck and Giddens, as recognized by Prior (2003: 52) when he suggests that museums have adapted by being 'self-reflective agents of social and cultural change themselves'. As a product of the reflexive modernizers of museums, audiences have been reconfigured as consumers and this has been widely recognized in a range of studies in which museums were seen to 'serve different purposes for different people' and 'their ability to give various publics a variety of experiences across a broad museological landscape' (McClellan 2003: 40). This characterization of the project of reflexive modernization makes powerful sense of the organizational changes, which led Tate into its highly successful corporate branding and correspondingly the reflexive consumer is evident in Tate Modern's spaces of circulation and exchange, although less so as yet at Tate Britain. But what is not at all clear is how the reflexivity of the expert and that of the consumer are related in and through the museum.

Lipovetsky's characterization of the hypermodern as the extension of greater processes of individualization is also couched in terms of a post-traditional society in which he argues that nothing can be taken for granted any more and therefore only the urgent questions of protection, security, the defence of social benefits, humanitarian aid and the safeguarding of the planet matter. Lipovetsky argues that 'through its operation of technocratic normalisation and the loosening of social bonds, the hypermodern age simultaneously manufactures order and disorder, subjective independence and dependence, moderation and excess' (Lipovetsky 2005: 50). People are made more responsible for themselves, on the one hand, but are more free from rules and regulations on the other. One of the major consequences of the rupture of tradition has been a reordering of social time such that time is also wrenched from its linear sequence, fragmented and structured by presentness in which consumption not production is the new regulator. The consequences of this are again paradoxical in that in hypermodern societies, people are subjected to the constraints of rapid time one the one hand, but able to make greater subjective choices and reflect upon themselves on the other.

With hypermodernity, reflexivity is given a time dimension, which Lipovetsky introduces as chrono-reflexivity. For the art museum and its visitors, these emergent forms of self-awareness and action involve the absence of tradition and the speeding-up, as well as atemporality of time, which position identity in the proliferating inflation of memory in the marketing and consumption of people's relationship to time.

The formidable expansion in the number of objects and signs that are deemed worthy to belong to the memory of our heritage, the proliferation of museums of every kind, the obsessions with commemorations, the mass democratization of cultural tourism, the threat of degradation or paralysis hanging over heritage sites because of the overwhelming floods of tourists – this whole new insistence on everything old is accompanied by an unbridled expansion, a saturation, a boundless broadening of the frontiers of our heritage and our memory: and in these we can recognised a modernization taken to its logical conclusion.

(Lipovetsky 2005: 134)

Lipovetsky's description of the hypermodern places considerable emphasis upon the mediation of cultural capitalism, which in turn raises what has been referred to here and by others as provoking a continuing crisis of representational systems. Lash points out that as well as the informational economy, outlined as noted by Lyotard (1986: 5), with its accumulation of conceptual symbols replacing capital in the mode of production, there is also, as articulated by Baudrillard (1985: 130) a semiotic side of the informational economy made up of signs, images, sounds and narratives. Whereas the circulation of information creates the conditions for conceptual reflexivity, the sign economy creates the conditions for a 'mimetic' or, aesthetic reflexivity founded upon modernism in the arts.

On the one hand as the commoditized, intellectual property of the cultural industries they belong to the characteristically post-industrial assemblage of power. On the other, they open up virtual and real spaces for the popularization of aesthetic critique of that same power/knowledge complex.

(Baudrillard 1985: 135)

Reflexive modernization distinguishes between a cognitive dimension of reflexivity operating in the expert domain of the informational economy and an aesthetic dimension grounded in the principle of 'expressive individualism' operating in contemporary arts and consumer capitalism. The import of this conceptualization for the modernization of the art museum means that its historic representational function within the public realm now operates within the conceptual and aesthetic economies of information. What is of crucial importance here, and is something of a hypermodern paradox, is that Tate, along with other modernist art museums has and continues to be the guardian of the core discourse of aesthetic modernism, based upon expressive individualism in which the veneration of the artist and fetishization of the art object are paramount. Hypermodernity offers an explanation of a world of consumption which at first caught up with the expressive and representational practices of aesthetic modernism, then widely disseminated aesthetic modernism through many forms of cultural consumption, and finally has outstripped aesthetic modernism by hypermodernity's double logic of the speeding up of the informational modes and in nostalgia, through which modernism is memorialized as heritage.

The emptying out of aesthetic modernism does not, however, make aesthetic reflexivity redundant, precisely because aesthetic modernism has been stripped of its logic in the representational system. Aesthetic reflexivity has been operating upon the mode of extended media production and consumption, of which music and fashion are the prime examples. With the emergence of new media, aesthetic reflexivity now has an extended mode of expression and circulation in photography and video, as witnessed in social sharing websites.

> The challenge that museums face in a time of transition is obscured on the one hand by theoretical rhetoric that interprets museums from a distance and ignores their concrete vulnerabilities, and on the other, by too close a focus on the immediate exigencies of circumstance, which then discourages speculative contemplation.
>
> *(Hein 2000: ix)*

How is the central account given in this book of the entanglement between the art museum, research, audiences and the representational systems connecting them to be concluded? In essence the argument marks out a shift from, an understanding of the [individual – museum-society] relationship in terms of fixed subjects, objects and relationships, to one in which art and media producers, the art museum and its consumers, are thought of an assemblage, currently struggling to see itself as a new collective formation in the production of aesthetic reflexivity. In this emergent model, the visitor is no longer to be considered as a representative individual, who shuttles backwards and forwards between society and the museum, which is also no longer thought of as a single entity comprised of its institutional organization, architectures and objects, no longer located by another sets of institutions and organizational structures where the social resides. In the hybrid, which is the distributed museum, with its assemblage of people, ideas, objects and things, the social and the aesthetic has to be traced through the agency of 'actors' who perform in networks.

The conception of the museum as a distributed network offers new ways of thinking about the agency of all the elements operating in and across the organizational and communication networks and allows for a radical reconfiguration of the older analogue museum conception in which unnamed museum professionals worked away behind the scenes for a representative audience and anonymous visitors configured in a public space. In the distributed museum, all those configured in and by the network are audience, including and centrally all those who are positioned as producers of the museum experience. Just as museum professionals become the audience, conversely, those who were previously conceived as the audience of the museum become producers of the distributed museum. But can the distributed museum be manifested as a visible reality, against the weight of practices, which continue to confine the agency of the visitor to an affect of the production of objects by professionals? Can the existing networks along which agency travels be made visible and can the separation between the organizational networks of acquisition/collection/curation and exhibition/interpretation/spectatorship be connected? The vexed question in this new equation of audience-as-producers in the distributed museum is what happens to the notion of the public realm. How is a public to be configured in the networks?

From the point of view of the Tate Encounters research, the aesthetic and conceptual dimensions of reflexivity were arrived at in terms of the articulation of the transcultural and transmedial as culturally reflexive practices, whose conditions were those of the impact of global migration and information. It is the centrality of the interactive and remediating dimensions of the human-computer interface, which now makes reflexivity a greater possibility, if not a limited requirement of its operational modes. Remediation, or transmediation, has become a necessary act within the cultural digital default, just as transculturality is a new condition of subjectivity and belonging in place and space. The binary distinction between the conceptual and mimetic, leading to the separation of the aesthetic response, also appears redundant in the new informational economies and the transcultural and transmedial are intended as active and performative terms within the practices of everyday life. Transmediation certainly operates in relationship to existing representational tropes and systems, but its end is not so much representational as it is processual.

Hypermodernity is one expression of the cultural impact of such changes, as was Harvey's time/space compression in the period identified with post-modernity (Harvey 1992: 211). Thrift goes beyond the identification of a general crisis of representation in developing a set of general principles and their applicability to what he terms 'non-representional theory' in an attempt to move beyond constructionism and relativism. Thrift's account is a positive contribution to what he calls 'a geography of what happens' and is intended 'as the beginning of an outline of the art of producing a permanent supplement to the ordinary, a sacrament to the everyday, a hymn to the superfluous' (Thrift 2008: 2). In its ambition, but not its method, Thrift's work accords with that of de Certeau (1988) in theorizing the practices of everyday life and with Latour (2007) in wanting to reassemble the social. Thrift's belief is that the aim of epistemology should be to capture movement and what he terms the onflows of everyday life and to get in touch with a full set of registers of thought by stressing affect and sensation. Thrift's theoretical model is designed to capture the 'spillage of things' and the 'sense-catching forms of things' as telling us more about the current state of the world than existing representational models (Thrift 2008: 9).

Thrift shares with Latour the idea that humanness cannot be separated off from the assemblages and hybrids of science and nature created by human relationship to objects and space. He stresses the technicity of assemblages and the materiality of practices. In this last respect, Thrift's approach is anti-biographical and pre-individual, emphasizing that the world is made up of all kinds of things brought in to a relation with involuntary process of encounter. While Thrift ultimately refuses to grant an invariant reflexive consciousness the centre stage of humanness, he stops short of the position of the 'post-human'. He retains a minimal humanism because humans live with and accept that they have a conscious will and even though that may in a full account be illusory, illusions are also 'real' and human's self-possession of consciousness is a basis for joint action (Thrift 2008: 13). The Tate Encounters research did not set out with Thriftian precepts in designing the research methodology, nor did it use them in the first iterations of analysis. However, in reaching for a conceptual and transdisciplinary synthesis, in order to make sense of the experience of the research in Tate, non-representational theory offers strong parallels with Actor-Network Theory in rejecting representational models of 'society', 'individuals' and 'action' and seeks alternative explanations in affects, performativity and assemblages of humans and things. In doing this it abandons the old certainties of labour, class and community, but seeks to rework the agency of group formation and point to new ecologies of belonging. Finally, Thrift's view of how to go about a geography of how things happen, strikes a chord with the Tate Encounters methodology, when he argues that research should retain a radical empiricism, which values the immediacy as well as interpretation of experience and an embrace of experimental method capable of capturing the trace, what he deems 'a kind of poetics of the release of energy which might be thought to resemble a play' (Thrift 2008: 12).

What might a geography of what is happening in the art museum and at Tate look like? To start with the forces of global technology, capital and labour impact upon the pre-eminent system of representation in manifold ways in the distributed museum, which can be seen in three related practices. The crisis of representation is sharply focused in the fields of aesthetics, exhibitionary practices and cultural policy. In the field of aesthetics, the crisis is acutely focused upon objectness and materiality, which the informational mode challenges. As Henning has pointed out, the work of art gained a new kind of singularity in the museum age predicated upon the Romantic notion of aesthetic experience in which there is a direct passage of communication between the material work of art and the human soul:

> The fact that this kind of experience was to be had in even the most systematic and pedagogic arrangements is not in spite of the museum but because of it. That is, the very act of turning something into a museum object makes it available for aesthetic contemplation. The museum animates objects as the source of knowledge, and simultaneously as aesthetic, auratic things.
>
> *(Henning 2006:18)*

But what is the aesthetic of the informational mode, which has no singular objecthood? The digital removes objecthood and replaces it by the screen or projection upon which digital code remediates inscriptions of objects, people, spaces and ideas. More than that the human-computer interface removes singularity and replaces it with multiplicity, it replaces the depth of an object with the surface of the screen and replaces narration with interaction. The very immateriality of the informational mode makes the identification of a digital aesthetic a vexed question. Within aesthetic modernism, the problem is resolved by recourse to the status of the artist and the role of curator, as the discussion of Tate Intermedia demonstrated. However, the solution of legitimating the digital aesthetic through the provenance of the modernist artist using the informational mode can only be a temporary one because authorship in the informational mode is replaced by collaboration in the network. As Lankshear points out in relationship to museums and digital heritage, the informational mode brings about changes in the world of objects because of changes in the relative significance of and balance among different modes of knowing associated with digitization (Lankshear 2002: 3). Hawkey has also pointed out that digital technology is predisposed to unite the functions of scholarship and education, such that the user becomes a privileged participant in the knowledge construction of objects (Hawkey 2001: 24). Such views fit with the Tate Encounters research and its argument that the embrace of new media as a medium of the practice of audience is one way out of the aesthetic impasse of the object. But in order for that step to be taken aesthetic modernism has to permit new media to enter the space of the object.

The crisis of representation is expressed in aesthetic modernism's exhibitionary practices at a number of levels all of which are connected to its need to ensure that the hybrids that abound in the distributed museum are, to use Latour's phrase, 'purified'. The modernizing of the art museum and its attendant forms of reflexive modernization are based upon the museum being able to produce the singularity of objects within a mode of attentiveness such that the object continues to produce the experience for the subject, rather than the subject producing a meaning for the object. Exhibitionary practices are intended to animate objects simultaneously as a source of knowledge and as auratic objects, which produces the tension for the art museum between the object's presence and its interpretation (Henning 2006: 71). The distributed museum threatens to dispel the fetishization of the object and reveal the various meanings/values the object performs in the networks, such as the objects exchange value, commodity value and value as spectacle.

The distributed museum not only suggests a reversal of the polarity of object and subject in a proliferation of meanings, but also constantly promotes connections between disparate objects through hypertexual, or hypersigned practices in hyper-consumption, which finally dissolve the dualism. The impact of such hybrids is most obviously seen in virtual spaces of flows of the informational network with which, as has been seen with Tate Media, the museum has no quarrel since they can be kept separate from objects in embodied space. New media currently enters the embodied space of the object through bodily augmentation in the form of audio/visual devices, understood not as extensions of the (aura of the) object, but as extensions of human memory and interpretation. This recognition of the separation of technological aug-mentation from the object of sensation raises the converse equation of what augmented objects would look like in the spaces objects inhabit. Screens have accompanied objects in many museums as a means of providing visitors with additional and con-textual knowledge. More and more screens are appearing in museums and Tate has established practices of placing display screens in entrance and exit spaces related to particular artists' works. Tate also has a number of discretely placed computer term-inals through which visitors can access contextual material, but what, as yet, cannot be entertained is the interactive informational mode occupying the same space of the object, a possibility which could produce a merging of object and subject, or as Macdonald puts it, 'scope for readings beyond those anticipated – question as to what extent visitors are sufficiently provoked to experiment with forming and voicing their own views' (Macdonald 2011: 21).

In the analysis here, visitors are embodied while audiences are abstracted and both make up the collective agency of the public. The crisis of representation is unsettling understandings of the relationship between visitors and audiences, such that whilst the art museum can count its visitors, sort them demographically and segment their motivational interests, it no longer knows what significance to accord this information in relationship to its exhibitionary practices. This is because the system of representation by which publicly funded art museums could rationalize the relationship between the object and viewer through aesthetic modernism no longer corresponds to the embodied visitor as consumer or the online visitor as user. This separation between representative values of audience and consuming values of visitors challenges the ethos and values of the public museum, which has so far assumed that its core demographic audience has the tacit and informal training that matches the aesthetic mode of experience, while non-attending, marginal or new audiences need to be enabled to understand or appreciate the transformative experience that objects can produce. However, as Henning has pointed out in her discussion of Benjamin's articulation of the aura of the work of art, the emphasis the modernizing museum places upon experience has the effect of displacing the emphasis on artefacts, such that in some forms of aestheticizing display the object functions as a prop or stimuli for transformative experiences (Henning 2006: 113). This is the current paradox of aesthetic modernism in that the more the art museum attempts to make the object directly sensate, the more layers it has to put between the object and the subject in maintaining the network that produces the subject of aesthetic modernism, which is precisely the network that excludes all other non-conforming hybrids. In contrast, new media is bringing about a convergence of previously separate media and their cultural forms such that only by the most deliberate energies can they be kept separate and it is this energy that the Tate Encounters research demonstrates, which, it is argued, the art museum could harness as a means of reassembling the social and moving on from the crisis of representation. Without such a process, the project of aesthetic modernism will be reproduced as a pastiche of itself or, more accurately, as heritage in the recycling of historical period.

What is of direct interest here, in bringing the arguments to a conclusion, is how the account of a twinned epistemic/disciplinary and practical/operational problematic bears upon the position of the account itself, in effect the project of the production of this book. This is a reflexive point in which the critical and analytical narrative of the argument needs to be subjected to a scrutiny of its own methods, conditions, interests and networks as a means of understanding its own limits. The optic through which a reflexive knowledge of the research project and its methods of analysis can be established has two lenses, firstly in an extension and updating of the position of post disciplinarity, which Lyotard proposed as a consequence of the new conditions of the production of knowledge (Lyotard 1986: 60). Secondly, the danger of reproducing the project only as theory is answered by pragmatism, which adopts a view that the production of knowledge is always historical, constructed and conditional and always met in embedded circumstances (Alvesson and Sköldberg 2009: 33).

The dangers inherent in what is being attempted here in making a call for a position of post-criticality are evident and recognized. Is it possible to critique the critical project in terms, which are themselves critical and theoretical? Is there some unseen flaw such that the claim to be offering a different order of knowledge through collaborative and democratic research models is really a continuation of the politics of critical theory, smuggled into the museum under false pretences? If that were the case then surely it would be an act of bad faith both to academic peers, whose intellectual space the authors share, and to colleagues at Tate in accepting its genuine offer to collaborate. Might there be a sleight of the critical hand not apparent to the authors in the labour of rendering the account and now in the completion of the architecture of its argument, too late to reverse. The book is certainly not written in the language of the everyday, nor is it a language of professional practice, and it retains the conventions and style of academic writing. The book is offered as the outcome of a collaboration in which the generosity of Tate to make itself open to question is acknowledged. The defence offered is that the book attempts at many points a form of translation, both across different discipline concerns and into the concerns of practitioners. In this it tries to establish a form of dialogue across the fault line that has been identified. This book is not a project of the post-critical, but the post-critical can be glimpsed in more than outline in the course of the collaborative research upon which the book is based. Here there is a need to offer a more analytic justification for the position, which involves describing the perspectives offered by post-disciplinarity and pragmatism.

In his discussion of knowledge in computerized societies, Lyotard argued that the status of knowledge had been altered. In summary, Lyotard laid out a set of changes in the technological systems of communication in which knowledge had ceased to be an end in itself and its use value had been replaced by its exchange value. Lyotard argued that knowledge had become a commodity by virtue of being operationalized in new channels of communication dealing in quantities of information.

> It is not hard to visualise learning circulating along the same lines as money, instead of for its 'educational' value or political (administrative, diplomatic, military) importance; the pertinent distinction would no longer be between knowledge and ignorance, but rather, as is the case with money, between 'payment knowledge' and 'investment knowledge' – in other words, between units of knowledge exchanged in a daily maintenance framework (the reconstitution of the work force, 'survival') versus funds of knowledge dedicated to optimising the performance of a project.
>
> *(Lyotard 1986: 6)*

An important aspect of Lyotard's argument is that as a consequence of the same conditions of postmodernity that had altered the status of knowledge, knowledge about society and the nature of the social bond required a different epistemological model. Again, in brief, Lyotard argued that events in the world no longer support grand narrative explanations of historical social progress in terms of a unitary goal of social improvement, nor in critical explanations of the dualism of opposing social forces, which would be reconciled by social transformation. Lyotard rejected the idea that critical theory could achieve unity by the force of rational argument alone because communication is itself not free from disturbance and contradiction. He concluded that the goal of dialogue between competing explanations is not consensus, but 'paralogy', what he calls a 'fruitful dissensus', which undermines prevailing discourses and poses not a representational system of correspondence between subject and object, but knowing and proximate constructions (Lyotard 1986: 61; Alvesson and Sköldberg 2009: 191). The new conditions of knowledge production and exchange have led many to suggest that knowledge reproduced through single disciplines and even in their combination and overlap in multidisciplinary and interdisciplinary modes of research can no longer encompass multilayer realities and the complexity of their networks (Thompson Klein et al. 2001).

The implications of the post-disciplinary have been taken up in a number of applied fields of research and, not surprisingly given the subject of argument and the complexity of human interactions, quite forcibly in education and social work in which dialogic and collaborative approaches are encouraged and tried out both in teaching and research (Roberts 2003: 133; Sharland 2011: 6). The central and highly abstract over-arching argument of Tate Encounters is that, while cultural institutions hold on to cultural dualism in order to manage their missions and practices, changes in the world and Britain have outstripped the capacity of this binary logic to explain what is currently happening. While the classificatory systems and practical institutional technologies of people and things are all still in place, their explanatory power is near exhaustion. Tate Encounters is not alone in reaching for a model of cultural practice that centrally recognizes the transformations taking place in the processes through which cultural value is currently being lived.

What is incontrovertible on the basis of the evidence of the co-researchers and the participants of the Research-in-Process events presented in the analysis is the museum needs to rethink who does and does not come through the doors of the museum and why, but no longer on the basis of representational thinking, which simultaneously reproduces the isolation of aesthetic modernism and a deficit modelling of culture. Moving beyond representational models will involve findings ways of understanding how the museum experience, now understood as the sum of agents in a network, establishes proximal relations to the life of each and every person and how the currency of such relations are enmeshed in the practices of everyday life. One way in which this might be attempted is simply for the museum 'to get out more often' in order to enter other networks, as well as giving permission for other networks to operate in the museum. Turning the museum 'inside out', would create a more porous museum and enable it to embrace and map new groupings and collectivities, those which are busily reshaping the public commons. The same could be said by and large for academia, which, while teeming with the everyday life of its student body, still abrogates research to a separate realm of experts.

The art museum's profound lack of acknowledgement and engagement with the realm of the everyday provides a clue to the knowledge needed to turn Latour's rebuke of critical sociology for conflating politics and science into what he terms a new science of living together (Latour 2007: 259). This book has laid out the ground for a Post-critical Museology to develop in bringing together and attempting to synthesise a number of normally separate discussions. Those discussions travel across the three main sections of the book whose themes covered discussions of cultural policy and museum practices, post-colonial perspectives and spectatorship and new media and the museum. The important strands concern the production of knowledge, representational systems and what counts as the social and the account drew the finer threads together around the Latourian ideas of tracing associations and following the agency of people, ideas and things. In the discussion of method, the account laid out how Lyotard's insights into the changed conditions of the production of knowledge relate to more recent discussions of how cultural value is established in post-traditional and hypermodern societies and what position the art museum and academy occupy within this. The central ideas of the book are the importance of the transcultural and transmedial as providing a framework for understanding new ways of seeing, or more inclusively new ways of being. The elaboration of the transcultural and transmedial could be programmatic and lead to a host of further collaborative and transdisciplinary research, projects and practice. The position of post-critical museology is an optimistic one and the hope is that it will form the basis of a new network of associations and interact with other hybrids in the distributed museums of the present.

NOTES

Introduction

1 Mindful of Lyotard's hypothesis. 'that the status of knowledge is altered' and that 'scientific knowledge is a kind of discourse' (Lyotard 1986: 3), the book attempts to be reflexive about the limits of erecting a meta-theoretical narrative or general theory of the different objects to which it attends.

2 Raymond Williams used the term 'vague and baggy monster' in his discussion of the future of cultural studies, as a reminder of the larger social and political project of cultural studies, against discipline specialization that arose within its academization and institutionalization (Williams 1989).

3 Stuart Hall (2006) discusses 'ambivalent mainstreaming' as a 'tricky' position of apparent inclusion of black British art as represented in cultural policy perspectives associated with New Labour (1997–2010).

4 Under the Museums and Galleries Act of 1992, the Tate Gallery's status as part of the Civil Service was terminated and it was reconstituted as an independent organization with incorporated status.

5 The research was funded as a major project within the AHRC Migrations, Diasporas and Identities national programme directed by Professor Kim Knott.

6 A podcast giving an overview of the formation and development of the research is available on the AHRC Diasporas, Migrations and Identities website, www.diasporas.ac. uk/Podcasts/Tate%20Encounters%201%20of%202.mp3, accessed 24 January 2012.

7 The findings were summarized in a project report, *Tate Encounters: Britishness and Visual Cultures* (2011) available as a PDF on the research papers of Tate Online, www2.tate.org. uk/tate-encounters/edition-6/pdf/Papers-AHRC-Final_Report-Selected_Sections.pdf, accessed 7 June 2012.

8 The external research participants were: Peter Ride, Senior Research Fellow at Westminster University; Dr Malcolm Quinn, University of the Arts; Dr Sophie Orlando, Sorbonne; and Dr Raimi Gbadamosi, artist and writer.

9 'Tate Encounters' is used throughout the book to refer to the *Tate Encounters: Britishness and Visual Cultures* AHRC-funded research project (2007–10).

10 The book draws heavily upon the ideas of Actor-Network Theory (ANT) as exposed in Latour (2007).

11 The idea of the 'expanded field of visual culture' was a central aspect of redefinition of the new art history, also connected with studies of the visual within cultural studies (Mirzoeff 1999).

12 The book is indebted to the fine account of qualitative research methodology given by Alvesson and Sköldberg (2009) in their book *Reflexive Methodology: New Vistas for Qualitative Research*.

13 Grub Street existed on the margins of eighteenth-century London's journalist and literacy scene and has been subsequently used as a pejorative term for impoverished hack writers.

14 This is a similar point to that first made by Raymond Williams in his lecture on 'The Future of Cultural Studies', in which he argued that the original impulse of cultural studies lay in a broad popular cultural movement, which he saw as becoming de-politized through its academic institutionalization (Williams 1989).

1 The post-traditional art museum in the public realm

1 'Education Practice at Tate Since 1970', a series of nine recorded interviews conducted by Victoria Walsh 23–7 February 2009 as part of the Tate Encounters public engagement programme, Research-in-Process. All interviews available at http://process.tateencounters.org/?cat=3 (accessed 30 January 2012). For full programme information see www.tate.org.uk/britain/eventseducation/talks/17860.htm. For a summary review of all the interviews see http://process.tateencounters.org/?page_id=799.

2 Interview accessible at http://process.tateencounters.org/?p=287, accessed 30 January 2012.

3 See the account on the Tate website www2.tate.org.uk/archivejourneys/historyhtml/people_public.htm, accessed 30 January 2012.

4 www2.tate.org.uk/archivejourneys/historyhtml/people_public.htm, accessed 30 January 2012.

5 Interview with Tim Marlow accessible at http://process.tateencounters.org/?p=210.

6 Interview with Sylvia Lahav accessible at http://process.tateencounters.org/?p=232.

7 Interview with Andrew Brighton accessible at http://process.tateencounters.org/?p=259.

8 Nicholas Serota's speech to open the 2008 Association of Art Historians conference on the theme 'Location: Museum, Academy, Studio', 2 April 2008.

9 Interview with Simon Wilson accessible at http://process.tateencounters.org/?p=171.

10 Indeed, Wilson carried out 'tests' across the curatorial division to assess the range and register of language used by curators mapping their texts next to different newspaper styles, both broadsheet and tabloid, to demonstrate the levels of communication revealed. The optimum style that communicated difficult technical knowledge and concepts with ease was represented by *The Economist*.

11 Michael Compton discussed the creation of the education department in his interview accessible at http://process.tateencounters.org/?p=170.

12 See Wolf Olins website www.wolffolins.com/work/tate.

2 The politics of representation and the emergence of audience

1 BBC news footage of Tony Blair 'Tribute to Diana', 11 August 2009, www.youtube.com/watch?v=x5Q_h_ZDGBk& feature=related.

2 See Selwood (2002:7). Quote from *Arts and Sport: A Report to the Social Exclusion Unit*, London: DCMS, 2. The Social Exclusion Unit defined social exclusion as 'a shorthand term for what can happen when people or areas suffer from a combination of linked problems such as unemployment, poor skills, low incomes, poor housing, high crime environments, bad health, poverty and family breakdown' (Sandell 2003).

3 Chris Smith, 'Government and the Arts', Lecture at the RSA in London, 22 July 1999 (text reproduced in Wallinger and Warnock 2000: 14–15).

4 See William Packer, 'A Black Mark for the Tate', *Financial Times*, 13 January 1996, 14; Richard Dorment, 'Slaves to the Stereotype', *Daily Telegraph*, 10 January 1996, 14; Tania Guha, *Art Exhibitions*, 10–17 January 1996; Richard Cork, 'Old Black and White Truths in Colour', *Times*, 2 January 1996, 11.

5 Interview with Leon Wainwright 2011, *Tate Encounters*, accessible at www2.tate.org.uk/tate-encounters/edition-6/dewdney_dibosa_walsh_interview_dr_leon_wainwright.shtm

6 Nicholas Serota, transcript of speech, 'The Art of the Unexpected', Commission for Racial Equality, December 2006.

7 Gordon Brown, *The Governance of Britain*, HMSO, July 2007, 54.

8 See Hew Locke's website entry for 'King Creole' at www.hewlocke.net/kingcreole.html, accessed 30 January 2012.

9 Quote taken from the panel discussion 'Ambiguous Mainstreaming: The Artist's Perspective', Research in Process, recording available at http://process.tateencounters.org/?p=776, accessed 30 January 2012.

10 See Fallon's PowerPoint presentation 'A New Frame for Art' (2007), www.slideshare.net/Mattspringate/apg-awards-tate-collections, accessed 30 January 2012.

11 See Morris Heargreaves Macintyre company website and Tate project pages, www.lateralthinkers.com/tate.html, accessed 30 January 2012.

12 For more information about the Target Group Index see the Arts Council of England audience research at www.artscouncil.org.uk/what-we-do/research-and-data/arts-audiences/target-group-index-tgi, accessed 5 May 2012.

13 Raimi Gbadamosi interviewed by Paul Goodwin (2011), *Tate Encounters, Edition 6,* recording available at www2.tate.org.uk/tate-encounters/edition-6/paul_Goodwin_interview_raimi_gbadamosi.shtm, accessed 9 May 2012.

14 Mike Phillips in interview with Victoria Walsh (2008), *Tate Encounters*, Edition 2, available at www2.tate.org.uk/tate-encounters/edition-2/walsh-phillips.shtm, accessed 9 May 2012.

15 Faisal Abdu'allah interviewed by Mark Miller (2011), *Tate Encounters*, Edition 6, recording available at www2.tate.org.uk/tate-encounters/edition-6/mark_miller_interview_faisal_abduallah.shtm, accessed 9 May 2012.

16 See the exhibition website at www.tate.org.uk/britain/exhibitions/eastwest/default.shtm, accessed 30 January 2012.

17 Will Gompertz participated with Damien Whitmore, his predecessor in the panel discussion 'New Media and Museums: Channels for the Future', available at http://process.tateencounters.org/?p=446, accessed 9 May 2012.

3 Tracing the practices of audience and the claims of expertise

1 See The Lure of the East microsite at www.tate.org.uk/britain/exhibitions/britishorientalistpainting/default.shtm, accessed 23 March 2012.

2 Orientalism Revisited: Art and the Politics of Representation, www.tate.org.uk/britain/eventseducation/symposia/14267.htm, accessed 23 March 2012.

3 See conference programme at www.tate.org.uk/britain/eventseducation/symposia/14267.htm, accessed 23 March 2012.

4 See event publicity as part of Late at Tate programme at www.tate.org.uk/britain/eventseducation/lateattatebritain/lateattatejuly.htm, accessed 23 March 2012.

5 See exhibition information pages online www.tate.org.uk/britain/exhibitions/nahnoutogethernow/default.shtm, accessed 23 March 2012.

6 'Contemporary Art in the Middle East' took place in January 2009. For conference programme and themes see www.tate.org.uk/about/projects/contemporary-art-middle-east, accessed 9 May 2012.

7 Interview with Anna Cutler accessible at http://process.tateencounters.org/?p=253, accessed 23 March 2012.

8 Interview with Helen Charman accessible at http://process.tateencounters.org/?p=281, accessed 23 March 2012.

4 Canon-formation and the politics of representation

1 Organizational Study Papers M.
2 For closer discussion of the epistemological register of rumour see Butt (2005).
3 Sandy Nairne, speaking at 'The Changing Status of Difference: Cultural Policy 1970–present', Tate Encounters: Research in Process, Duveen Studios, Tate Britain, 19 March 2009.
4 Ibid.
5 Organizational Study Papers O: 9.
6 In particular, Hooper-Greenhill's work within the Research Centre for Museums and Galleries (RCMG) in the Department of Museum Studies at the University of Leicester, England, is acknowledged as having contributed to policy as well as practice. Her work on the Learning Impact Research Project (2002), which led to the development of the Inspiring Learning for All framework (ILFA), has been widely cited in respect of its formulation of 'GLOs' (Generic Learning Outcomes) for museums and galleries in England (Coles in Bellamy and Oppenheim 2009: 95).
7 Organizational Study Papers A: 3.
8 ibid.
9 Said did, in fact, make reference to Delacroix in his seminal work, *Orientalism*. However, the discussion can be said in Said's own terms to have been 'scant': '[I]n the nineteenth century, in the works of Delacroix and literally dozens of other French and British painters, the Oriental genre tableau carried representation into visual expression and a life of its own (which this book unfortunately must scant)' (Said 1978: 118).
10 Organizational Study Papers A: 3.
11 ibid: 5.
12 Thin Black Line(s), curated by Lubaina Himid with Paul Goodwin, Tate Britain, BP British Art Displays, 22 August 2011–18 March 2012.
13 'Thin Black Line(s) in discussion: Paul Goodwin with Lubaina Himid and Claudette Johnson', Late at Tate, Tate Britain, 2 December 2011.
14 Into the Open, selected by Pogus Caesar and Lubaina Himid (Mappin Art Gallery, Sheffield, 1984); The Image Employed, curated by Keith Piper and Marlene Smith (Cornerhouse Gallery, Manchester, 1987); The Essential Black Art, curated by Rasheed Araeen (Chisenhale Gallery, London, 1989); and The Other Story, curated by Araeen (Hayward Gallery, 1989).
15 Dislocations selected by Veronica Ryan (Kettles Yard Gallery, Cambridge, England, 1987).
16 'Mona Hatoum', press release, Tate Britain, 6 December 1999.
17 Marlene Smith, email to David Dibosa.
18 *State of the Art*, (dir. Geoff Dunlop and John Wyver), Illuminations Films. Broadcast on Channel 4 Television, 1987.
19 See illustrations for Mercer and Julien (1992).
20 '[Kobena] Mercer also suggested that inIVA's "unpopularity" was due in part to a perception of its "bureaucratic insitutionalisation of cultural theory"' (Hylton 2007: 115).
21 Platform 1 ('Democracy Unrealized') took place in the Akademie der Künste in Vienna and the Haus der Kulturen der Welt in Berlin. Platform 2 ('Experiments with Truth: Transitional Justice and The Process of Truth and Reconciliation') was organized in the India Habitat Centre in New Delhi. Platform 3 ('Créolité and Creolization') was a workshop on the West-Indian island of Saint Lucia. Platform 4 ('Under Siege: Four African Cities – Freetown, Johannesburg, Kinshasa, Lagos') took place in the Nigerian megalopolis of Lagos. http://casestudiesforeducationalturn.blog.hu/2011/05/24/doc umenta_xi_platforms, accessed 11 January 2012.

5 Tate Encounters: Britishness and visual cultures, the transcultural audience

1 www2.tate.org.uk/tate-encounters/editions.shtm, accessed 14 May 2012.
2 http://process.tateencounters.org/?tag=co_researchers, accessed 14 May 2012.

3 The full programme of the Research-in-Process event is given at http://process.tateen counters.org.
4 http://process.tateencounters.org/?tag=co_researchers, accessed 14 May 2012.
5 The Art of the Sikh Kingdoms, Susan Stronge (curator), V&A Museum, London, 25 March–25 July 1999.
6 http://process.tateencounters.org/?page_id=540, accessed 11 July 2011.
7 Adekunle Detokunbo-Bello, *Nollywood: Losing the Plot,* South London Gallery, London, 26 November 2010.
8 See films such as *Sarraouinia* (dir. Med Hondo, Franco-Mauritania, 1986). For discussion of Hondo, see also Ukadike (1999).

6 Reconceptualizing the subject after post-colonialism and post-structuralism

1 'But the supplement supplements. It adds only to replace. It intervenes or insinuates itself in-the-place-of; if it fills, it is as if one fills a void' (Derrida 1976: 145).
2 It has been argued that emphasis should move away from a preoccupation with the renowned formulation 'cogito, ergo sum' – I think therefore I am – as Descartes does not provide such a formulation himself in his most significant elaborations of self-conceptualization in his work *Second Meditation*. The more prescient rendition is cited thus: 'this proposition, I am, I exist, is necessarily true whenever it is put forward by me or conceived in my mind' (Descartes, *Second Meditation*, vol 2: 17, Standard Edition, Adam, C. and Tannery, P., as cited in Broughton, J. (2002) *Descartes's Method of Doubt*, Princeton University Press, Princeton and Oxford, 107).
3 Note the use of 'Powhatan's Mantle' in educational work at the Ashmolean Museum, www.ashmolean.org/education/takeone/?s=powhatan, accessed 14 May 2012.
4 '[M]igrant culture … dramatizes the activity of culture's untranslatability; and in so doing, it moves … towards an encounter with ambivalent process of splitting and hybridity that marks the identification with culture's difference' (Bhabha 1994: 224).

7 New media practices in the museum

1 Honor Harger and Marc Garrett made this point forcibly in the audio recorded session, Resolutely Analogue as part of the Tate Encounters: Britishness and Cultures, Research-in-Process events at Tate Britain in March 2009.
2 James Davis, who worked for Tate as the online collections editor was keenly aware of the mismatch between an analogue conception of collection and the behaviours he observed of online users, http://tateencounters.org.
3 Now archived, the Intermedia Art programme ran 2008–10. The Intermedia Art pages also contain the archive of Tate's netart projects from 2000 onwards, www2.tate.org.uk/intermediaart/about, accessed 24 January 2012.
4 The references made to Damian Whitmore come from an audio recording of his participation in Resolutely Analogue: Museums in a Digital Culture. Accessible at http://tateencounters.org.
5 The references made to the views of Will Gompertz are taken from the same audio recording session that Damian Whitmore participated in.
6 The references made to the views of John Stack are taken from an audio recording of his participation in Resolutely Analogue: Museums in a Digital Culture. Accessible at http://tateencounters.org.
7 See for example DCMS (2005).

8 The distributed museum

1 James Davis and Kelli Dipple took part in the Resolutely Analogue: Museums in a Digital Age discussions held at Tate Britain in March 2009 and available as audio recordings at http://tateencounters.org, accessed 24 January 2012.

2 MoMA supports a range of multimedia art related projects, hosted on its website, www.moma.org/explore/multimedia, accessed 24 January 2012.

3 The Intermedia Art programme ran 2008–10. The Intermedia Art pages also contain the archive of Tate's netart projects from 2000 onwards, www2.tate.org.uk/intermediaart/about, accessed 24 January 2012.

4 www.furtherfield.org/content/about, accessed 24 January 2012.

5 Peter Ride was a co-chair of the Resolutely Analogue discussions and wrote a summary of the week's discussion, published in *Tate Encounters* as 'Shiny and New: Reflections on "Resolutely Analogue? Art Museums in Digital Culture"', www2.tate.org.uk/tate-encounters/edition-5/Peter-Ride-Shiny-and-New.pdf, accessed 3 May 2012.

9 Museums of the future

1 A not untypical extract from unpublished research data of 260 essays written by first-year undergraduate humanities students for an assessed assignment entitled 'What is the Britain in Tate Britain?'.

2 Tate Encounters received a three year grant of £639,442, calculated at full economic cost, from the British Arts and Humanities Research Council under a national research programme entitled Diasporas, Migration and Identities.

3 Source: LSBU annual student survey, key statistics, 2009.

4 Source: Morris Hargreaves McIntyre unpublished Tate commissioned visitor survey report May 2011.

5 DCMS Annual Report (2006) Efficiency Review, www.culture.gov.uk/images/publications/DCMS_AR_06pt2b.pdf, accessed 17 May 2012.

6 The event was audio recorded and is accessible at http://richmedia.lse.ac.uk/publicLecturesAndEvents/20090707_1830_theMuseumOfThe21stCentury.mp4, accessed 8 January 2012.

7 The Research-in-Process event took place in the Duveen Studio over four weeks in March 2009 and was a publicly advertised event. More than 72 speakers participated in the event and the sessions were audio recorded and are available at http://tateencounters.org, accessed 8 January 2012.

8 The exhibition Altermodern was the 2009 Tate Triennial, which took place between 3 February and 26 April at Tate Britain.

9 Source: Published research data of co-researchers' media productions at http://tatencounters.org, accessed 8 January 2012.

BIBLIOGRAPHY

Adam, G. (2011) 'The Lure of the East', *The Art Newspaper*, issue 2020.

Adorno, T. (1991) *The Culture Industry*, London: Routledge.

Allen, F. (2008) 'Situating Gallery Education', *Tate Encounters*, Edition 2, www2.tate.org.uk/tate-encounters/edition-2/tateencounters2_felicity_allen.pdf, accessed 9 May 2012.

——(2009) 'Border Crossing', *Tate Papers*, www.tate.org.uk/download/file/fid/7281, accessed 9 May 2012.

Alvesson, M. and Sköldberg, K. (2009) *Reflexive Methodology: New Vistas for Qualitative Research*, 2nd edn, London: Sage.

Anderson, G. (ed.) (2004) *Reinventing the Museum: Historical and Contemporary Perspectives on the Paradigm Shift*, Walnut Creek, CA: AltaMira Press.

Appadurai, A (1990) 'Disjuncture and Difference in the Global Cultural Economy', *Theory, Culture & Society*, 7: 295.

——(2000) 'Grassroots Globalization and the Research Imagination', *Public Culture*, 12(1): 1–19, reprinted in A. Appadurai (ed.) (2001) *Globalization*, Durham, NC: Duke University Press, 1–21.

——(2003) *The Social Life of Things: Commodities in Cultural Perspective*, Cambridge: Cambridge University Press.

——(2010) 'How Histories make Geographies', *Transcultural Studies*, 1: 4–13.

Araeen, R. (1984) *The Art Britain Really Ignores*, London: Kala Press.

——(1991) 'The Other Immigrant: The Experiences and Achievements of Afro Asian Artists in the Metropolis', *Third Text*, 5(15): 17–28.

Araeen, R. and Chambers, E. (1988/9) 'Black Art: A Discussion', *Third Text*, 2(5): 51–62.

Araeen, R., Kingston, A. and Payne, A. (1987) *From Modernism to Postmodernism: Rasheed Araeen, a Retrospective: 1959–1987* (exhibition catalogue), Birmingham: Ikon Gallery.

Armitage, J. (2000) *Paul Virilio: From Modernism to Hypermodernism and Beyond*, London: Sage.

Armitage, J. and Roberts, J. (2006) 'From Organization to Hypermodern Organization: On the Accelerated Appearance and Disappearance of Enron', *Journal of Organisation Change Management*, 19(5): 558 –77.

Arts Council of England (ACE) (2007) *Taking Part: The National Survey of Culture, Leisure and Sport*, London: ACE.

Ashcroft, B., Griffiths, G., and Tiffin, A. (2000) *Post-Colonial Studies: The Key Concepts*, London: Routledge.

Barker, E. (1999) *Contemporary Cultures of Display*, New Haven and London: Yale University Press.

Barr, J. (2005) 'Dumbing Down Intellectual Culture: Frank Furedi, Lifelong Learning and Museums', *Museum and Society*, 3(2): 98–114.

Barringer, T.J. and Flynn, T. (1998) *Colonialism and the Object: Empire, Material Culture and the Museum*, London: Routledge.

Barthes, R. (1984) *Camera Lucida*, London: Flamingo.

Baudrillard, J. (1985) 'The Ecstasy of Communication' in H. Foster (ed.) *Postmodern Culture*, London: Pluto, 126–34.

——(2005) *The System of Objects*, London: Verso.

Bauman, Z. (1997) *Postmodernity and Its Discontents*, Oxford: Blackwell.

——(2007) *Liquid Times: Living in an Age of Uncertainty*, Cambridge: Polity Press.

Baxandall, M. (1988) *Painting and Experience in Fifteenth Century Italy: A Primer in the Social History of Pictoral Style*, Oxford: Oxford University Press.

Bearman, D. (2010) 'Standards for Networked Cultural Heritage', in R. Parry (ed.) *Museums in a Digital Age*, London: Routledge, 48–63.

Beck, U., Giddens, A. and Lash, S. (1994) *Reflexive Modernzation: Politics, Tradition and Aesthetics in the Modern Social Order*, Cambridge: Polity Press.

Beech, D. (2008) 'Include Me Out!', *Art Monthly*, April: 1–4.

Belfiore, E. (2002) 'Art as a Means of Alleviating Social Exclusion: Does it Really Work? A Critique of Instrumental Cultural Policies and Social Impact Studies in the UK', *International Journal of Cultural Policy*, 8(1): 91–106.

Bellamy, K. and Oppenheim, C. (2009) *Learning to Live: Museums, Young People and Education*, London: Institute for Public Policy Research and National Museum Directors' Conference, www.ippr.org/images/media/files/publication/2011/05/learning_to_live_ 1693.pdf, accessed 11 May 2012.

Benjamin, W. (1999) 'The Work of Art in the Age of Mechanical Reproduction', in J. Evans and S. Hall (eds) *Visual Culture: The Reader*, London: Sage, 72–79.

Bennett, T. (1995) *The Birth of the Museum: History, Theory, Politics*, London: Routledge.

——(1999) 'Useful Culture', in D. Boswell and J. Evans (eds) *Representing the Nation: A Reader, Histories, Heritage and Museums*, London: Routledge, 380–93.

——(2005) 'Civic Laboratories, Museums, Cultural Objecthood and the Governance of the Social', *Cultural Studies*, 19(5): 521–47.

——(2007) *Critical Trajectories: Culture, Society, Intellectuals*, Oxford: Blackwell.

Bentkowska-Kafel, A., Cashen, T. and Gardiner, H. (2009) *Digital Visual Culture: Theory and Practice*, Bristol: Intellect.

Berger, J. (1972) *Ways of Seeing*, London: BBC.

Bhabha, H.K. (1990) *Nation and Narration*, London: Routledge.

——(1994) *The Location of Culture*, London: Routledge.

——(2001) 'The Postcolonial and the Postmodern: The Question of Agency', in S. During (ed.) *The Cultural Studies Reader*, London: Routledge, 189–208.

Bishop, C. (2006) *Participation*, Cambridge, MA: MIT Press.

Blackman, L.M. (1998) 'Culture, Technology and Subjectivity: An "Ethical" Analysis', in J. Wood (ed.) *The Virtual Embodied: Presence, Practice, Technology*, London: Routledge, 132–47.

Bolter, J.D. and Grusin, R. (2000) *Remediation: Understanding New Media*, Cambridge, MA: MIT Press.

Boswell, D. and Evans, J. (eds) (1991) *Representing the Nation: A Reader, Histories, Heritage and Museums*, London: Routlege.

Bourdieu, P. (1977) *Reproduction: In Education, Society and Culture*, London: Sage.

——(1979, reprinted 2007) *Distinction: A Social Critique of the Judgement of Taste*, Paris: Editions de Minuit, London: Routledge.

Bourriaud, N. (1998) *Relational Aesthetics*, London: Routledge.

——(2009) 'Altermodern Manifesto', www.artsandecology.org.uk/magazine/features/ nicholas-bourriaud–altermodern-manifesto, accessed 17 May 2012.

Bradley, C. (1998) *Mrs Thatcher's Cultural Policies: 1979–1990: A Comparative Study of the Globalized Cultural System*, New York: Columbia University Press.

Bragg, S. (2007) *Consulting Young People: A Review of the Literature, a Report for Creative Partnerships*, London: Open University and Arts Council England.

Bridgwood, A., Fenn, C., Dust, K., Hutton, L., Skelton, A. and Skinner, M. (2003) *Focus on Cultural Diversity: The Arts in England: Attendance, Participation and Attitudes*, London: Office for National Statistics, Research Report 34.

Broughton, J. (2002) *Descartes's Method of Doubt*, Princeton: Princeton University Press.

Burger, P. (1992) 'On the Problem of the Autonomy of Art in Bourgeois Society' in F. Frascina and J. Harris (eds) *Art in Modern Culture: An Anthology of Critical Texts*, London: Phaidon Press (originally published in German in 1972).

Butt, G. (2005) *Between You and Me: Queer Disclosures in the New York Art World, 1948–1963*, Durham, NC: Duke University Press.

Button, V. and Searle, A. (1998) *The Turner Prize*, London: Tate Publishing.

Callon, M., Lascoumes, P., Burchell, G. and Barthe, Y. (2001) *Acting in An Uncertain World: An Essay on Technical Democracy*, Cambridge, MA: MIT Press.

Cameron, F. and Kenderdine, S. (2010) *Theorizing Digital Cultural Heritage: A Critical Discourse*, Cambridge, MA: MIT Press.

Carbonell, B.M. (ed.) (2004), *Museum Studies: An Anthology of Contexts*, Oxford: Blackwell.

Castells, M. (2001) *The Internet Galaxy*, Oxford: Oxford University Press.

——(2010) 'Museums in the Information Era: Cultural Connectors of Time and Space' in R. Parry (ed.) *Museums in a Digital Age*, London: Routledge, 427–34.

Chambers, E. (1988/9) 'Destruction of the NF', *Third Text*, 2(5): 45–50.

Charman, H. (2005) 'Uncovering Professionalism in the Art Museum: An Exploration of the Key Characteristics of the Working Lives of Education Curators at Tate Modern', *Tate Papers*, Spring 2005, www.tate.org.uk/download/file/fid/7342, accessed 9 May 2012.

Charmaz, K. (2006) *Constructing Grounded Theory: A Practical Guide*, London: Sage.

Chong, D. (2002) *Arts Management*, London: Routledge.

Cixous, H., (2004) *Portrait of Jacques Derrida as a Young Jewish Saint*, trans. B.B. Brahic, New York: Columbia University Press.

Clifford, J. (1993) 'On Collecting Art and Culture', in S. During (ed.) *The Cultural Studies Reader*, London: Routledge, 57–76.

Cooke, J. (2005) 'Heterotopia: Art, Ephemera, Libraries and Alternative Space', *Art Documentation*, 25(2): 34–9.

Crary, J. (1992) *Techniques of the Observer: On Vision and Modernity in the Nineteenth Century*, Cambridge, MA: MIT Press.

——(1999) *Suspension of Perception: Attention, Spectacle and Modern Culture*, Cambridge, MA: MIT Press.

Crimp, D. (1983) 'On the Museum's Ruins', in H. Foster (ed.) *The Anti-Aesthetic*, Port Townsend: Bay Press, 43–56.

Crooke, E (2007) *Museums and Community: Ideas, Issues and Challenges*, London: Routledge.

Cuno, J.B., McGregor, N., de Montebello, P., Lowry, G.D. and Wood, J.N. (eds) (2003) *Whose Muse? Art Museums and the Public Trust*, Princeton: Princeton University Press.

Dabydeen, D. (1985) *Hogarth's Blacks: Images of Blacks in Eighteenth-Century English Art*, Kingston-upon-Thames: Dangeroo Press.

Dean, C., Donnellan, C. and Pratt, A.C. (2010) 'Tate Modern: Pushing the Limits of Regeneration', *City, Culture and Society*, 1(2): 79–87.

Debord, G. (1999) *The Society of the Spectacle*, New York: Routledge.

de Certeau, M. (1988) *The Practice of Everyday Life*, Berkeley: University of California Press.

Deleuze, G. and Guattari, F. (1980) *A Thousand Plateaus: Capitalism and Schizophrenia*, trans. B. Massumi, Minneapolis: University of Minneapolis Press.

Dempsey, A. (2002) *Art in the Modern Era: A Guide to Styles, Schools and Movements, 1860 to the Present*, New York: Harry N. Abrams.

Department for Communities and Local Government (DCLG), (2007) *The Bicentenary of the Abolition of the Slave Trade Act 1807–2007*, London: DCLG.

Department of Culture, Media and Sport (DCMS), (2005) *Understanding the Future: Museums and 21st Century Life: The Value of Museums*, London: DCMS.

——(2007) *Culture on Demand: Ways to Engage a Broader Audience*, London: DCMS.

Department of National Heritage (1993) *National Museums and Galleries: Quality of Service to the Public*, London: National Audit Office.

Derrida, J. (1976) *Of Grammatology*, Baltimore: Johns Hopkins University Press.

——(1987) *The Truth of Painting*, Chicago: University of Chicago Press.

Desai, P. and Thomas, A. (1998) *Cultural Diversity: Attitudes of Ethnic Minority Populations Towards Museums and Galleries*, London: Museums and Galleries Commission.

De Saussure, F. (1986) *Course in General Linguistics*, Illinois: Open Court.

Dewdney, A. (2008) 'Making Audiences Visible: Gallery Education, Research and Recent Political Histories', *Tate Encounters*, Edition 2, www2.tate.org.uk/tate-encounters/edition-2/ TateEncounters2_Andrew_Dewdney.pdf, accessed 9 May 2012.

——(2011) 'Transmediation: Tracing the Social Aesthetic', *Philosophy of Photography*, 2(1): 97–114.

Dewdney, A. and Ride, P. (2006) *The New Media Handbook*, London: Routledge.

Dewdney, A., Dibosa, D. and Walsh, V. (2010) 'Cultural Inequality, Multicultural Nationalism and Global Diversity', *Tate Encounters*, Edition 6, www2.tate.org.uk/tate-encounters/edi tion-6/pdf/Papers-Cultural_Inequality-Multicultural-Nationalism-and-Global-Diversity. pdf, accessed 20 May 2012.

Donnellan, C. (2011) *Establishing Tate Modern: Vision and Patronage*, thesis submitted, London School of Economics.

Doy, G. (2000) *Black Visual Culture: Modernity and Postmodernity*, London: I.B. Tauris.

Duncan, C. (1995) *Civilizing Rituals: Inside Public Art Museums*, London: Routledge.

Duro, P. (ed.)(1996) *The Rhetoric of the Frame: Essays on the Boundaries of the Artwork*, Cambridge: Cambridge University Press.

Dyer, R. (1997) *White*, London: Routlege.

Dyer, S. (2007a) 'Can't Non-white People Ever Just Make Art?', *Spiked Culture*, www. spiked-online.com/index.php/site/article/3396, accessed 30 Jaunary 2012.

——(2007b) 'Boxed In', *Spiked Culture*, www.manifestoclub.com/aa-diversity-ace, accessed 30 January 2012.

Enwezor, O. (1999) 'Between Worlds: Postmodernism and African Artists in the Western Metropolis', in O. Oguibe and O. Enwezor (eds) *Reading the Contemporary: African Art from Theory to the Marketplace*, Cambridge, MA: MIT Press, 245–75.

——(2002) 'The Black Box', in H. Ander and N. Rottner (eds) *Documenta 11: Platform 5* (exhibition catalogue), Ostfildern-Ruitt: Hatje Cantz Publishers, 42–55.

Esmel-Pamies, C. (2010) 'Into the Politics of Museum Audience Research', *Tate Encounters*, Edition 5, www2.tate.org.uk/tate-encounters/edition-5/Cinta-Esmel-Pamies-Into-the-Politics-of-Museum-Research.pdf, accessed 14 May 2012.

Fanon, F. (1994) *Wretched of the Earth*, New York: Grove Press.

Featherstone, M. (1990) *Global Culture: Nationalism and Modernity*, London: Sage.

Fisher, J. (ed.) (2000) *Reverberations: Tactics of Resistance, Forms of Agency in Trans/cultural Practices*, Maastricht: Jan van Eyck Editions.

Foucault, M. (1970, 2007) *The Order of Things*, London: Routledge.

——(1977) *Discipline and Punishment: The Birth of the Prison*, trans. Alan Sheridan, New York: Vintage Books.

——(1984) 'The Masked Philosopher', in L.D. Kritzman (ed.) *Michel Foucault: Politics, Philosophy, Culture, Interviews and Other Writings 1977–1984*, London: Routledge.

——(2002) *The Archaeology of Knowledge*, trans. A.M. Sheridan Smith, London: Routledge.

Furedi, F. (2004) *Where Have All the Intellectuals Gone?*, London: Continuum.

Fyfe, G (1996) 'A Trojan Horse at the Tate: Theorizing the Museum as Agency and Structure', in S. Macdonald and G. Fyfe (eds) *Theorizing Museums*, Oxford: Blackwell, 203–28.

Gere, C. (2008) *Digital Culture*, London: Reaktion Books.

Giddens, A. (1990) *The Consequences of Modernity*, London: Polity.

Gilroy, P. (1987) *There Ain't No Black in the Union Jack: The Cultural Politics of Race and Nation*, London: Hutchinson.

——(1991) 'It Ain't Where You're From, It's Where You're At ... The Dialectics of Diasporic Identification', *Third Text*, 5(13): 3–16.

——(1993) *Black Atlantic: Modernity and Double Consciousness*, Cambridge, MA: Harvard University Press.

——(1996) *Picturing Blackness in British Art 1700s–1990s*, London: Tate Gallery.

——(2000) *Between Camps: Race, Identity and Nationalism at the End of the Colour Line*, London: Penguin.

——(2004) *After Empire: Melancholia or Convivial Culture?*, London: Routledge.

——(2005) 'Melancholia or Conviviality: The Politics of Belonging in Britain', *Soundings*, 29(1): 35–46.

——(2006) 'Multiculture in Times of War', lecture delivered 10 May at London School of Economics, reproduced as 'Post-colonial Melancholia', *Critical Quarterly*, 48(4): 27–45.

——(2008) *Post Colonial Melancholia*, New York: Columbia University Press.

Giroux, H. (1983) *Theory and Resistance in Education: A Pedagogy for the Opposition*, South Hadley, MA: Bergin & Garvey.

Golding, V. (2009) *Learning at the Museum Frontiers: Identity, Race and Power*, London: Ashgate.

Goldman, L. (1976) *Cultural Creation*, trans. B. Grahl, St Louis: Telos Press.

Gordon, D. (ed.) (2001) *Postmodernism and the Enlightenment: New Perspectives in Eighteenth-Century French Intellectual History*, London: Routledge.

Gray, C. (2000) *The Politics of the Arts in Britain*, London: Palgrave.

Greenberg, C. (1965) 'Modernist Painting', in F. Franscina and Harrison, C. (eds) (1982) *Modern Art and Modernism: A Critical Anthology*, London: The Open University, 5–10.

Greenberg, R., Ferguson, B. and Nairne, S. (eds) (1996) *Thinking About Exhibitions*, London: Routledge.

Grenfell, M. and Hardy, C. (2007) *Art Rules: Pierre Bourdieu and the Visual Arts*, New York: Berg Publishers.

Gretton, T. (1986) 'New Lamps for Old', in A.L. Rees and F. Barzello (eds) *The New Art History*, London: Camden Press, 63–74.

Hall, S., (1994) 'Cultural Identity and Diaspora', in P. Williams and L. Chrisman (eds) *Colonial Discourse and Postcolonial Theory*, New York: Columbia University Press, 392–403.

——(1999) *Representation: Cultural Representation and Signifying Practices*, London: Open University/Sage.

——(2006) *Black British Art: The Revolt of the Artists*, Tate Channel, channel.tate.org.uk/media/27535869001, accessed 17 May 2012.

Hall, S. and Back, L. (2009) 'At Home and Not At Home: Stuart Hall in Conversation with Les Back', *Cultural Studies*, 23(4): 658–88.

Hall, S., Held, D., and McGrew, T. (1992) *Modernity and its Futures*, London: Polity.

Hardt, M. and Negri, A. (2001) *Empire*, Cambridge, MA: Harvard University Press.

Harris, J. (2001) *The New Art History: A Critical Introduction*, London: Routledge.

Harvey, D. (1992) 'The Condition of Postmodernity', in S. Hall, D. Held and T. Mcgrew (eds) *Modernity and its Futures*, London: Polity Press.

——(2000) *The Condition of Postmodernity: An Enquiry into the Origins of Cultural Change*, Oxford: Blackwell.

Hawkey, R. (2001) 'Innovation, Inspiration, Interpretation: Museums, Science and Learning', *Ways of Knowing Journal*, 1(1): 23–31.

——(2004) *Learning with Digital Technologies in Museums, Science Centres and Galleries*, London: Futura.

Hayles, N.K. (1999) *How We Became Posthuman: Virtual Bodies in Cybernetics, Literature, and Informatics*, Chicago: University of Chicago Press.

Haxthausen, C. (2003) *Two Art Histories: The Museum and the University*, New Haven: Yale University Press.

Hein, G. (1995) 'The Constructivist Museum' *Journal of Education in Museums*, 16: 21–3.
——(1998) *Learning in the Museum*, London: Routledge.
Hein, H.S. (2000) *The Museum in Transition: A Philosophical Perspective*, Washington, DC: Smithsonian Institute Press.
Henning, M. (2006) *Museums, Media and Cultural Theory*, Maidenhead: Open University Press.
Herman, D. (2004) 'Toward a Transmedial Narratology', in M.-L. Ryan (ed.) *Narrative Across Media: The Languages of Storytelling*, Lincoln: University of Nebraska Press, 47–75.
Hewison, R. and Holden, J. (2004) *The Right to Art: Making Aspirations Reality*, DEMOS Report, www.demos.co.uk/files/TheRighttoArt.pdf, accessed 17 May 2012.
Himid, L. (1985) 'Introduction', in *The Thin Black Line* (exhibition catalogue), London: Institute of Contemporary Arts.
Holden, J. (2004) *Capturing Cultural Value: How Culture Has Become a Tool of Government Policy*, DEMOS Report, www.demos.co.uk/publications/culturalvalue, accessed 30 January 2012.
——(2008) *Democratic Culture: Opening Up the Arts to Everyone*, DEMOS Report, www.demos.co.uk/publications/democraticculture, accessed 30 January 2012.
Hooper-Greenhill, E. (1989) 'The Museum in the Disciplinary Society', in S. Pearce (ed.) *Museum Studies in Material Culture*, London: Leicester University Press, 61–72.
——(1992) *Museums and the Shaping of Knowledge*, London: Routledge.
——(ed.) (1994a) *Museum, Media, Message*, 2nd edn, London: Routledge.
——(ed.) (1994b) *The Educational Role of the Museum*, London: Routledge.
——(2000) *Museums and the Interpretation of Visual Culture*, London: Routledge.
——(2007) *Museums and Education: Purpose, Pedagogy, Performance*, London: Routlege.
Hylton, R. (2007) *The Nature of the Beast: Cultural Diversity and the Visual Arts Sector: A Study of Policies, Initiatives and Attitudes 1976–2006*, Bath: ICIA.
ICOM, (1997) 'Museums and Cultural Diversity: Policy Statement', http://icom.museum/diversity.html, accessed 30 January 2012.
Jameson, F. (1991) *Postmodernism: Or, the Cultural Logic of Late Capitalism*, Durham, NC: Duke University Press.
Janes, R. (2009) *Museums in a Troubled World*, London: Routledge.
Jantjes, G. and Serota, N. (1986) 'Introduction' in *From Two Worlds* (exhibition catalogue), London: Whitechapel Art Gallery, 5–8.
Jenkins, H. (2006) *Convergence Culture*, New York: New York University Press.
Johnson, R. (2006) '"Really Useful Knowledge": Radical Education and Working Class Culture 1790–1848', in J. Clarke, C. Critcher and R. Johnson (eds) *Working-Class Culture: Studies in History and Theory*, London: Routledge, 75–102.
Kirby, A. (2009) *Digimodernism: How New Technologies Dismantle the Postmodern and Reconfigure Our Culture*, London: Continuum.
Knell, S. (2003) 'The Shape of Things to Come: Museums in the Technological Landscape', *Museum and Society*, 1(3): 113–21.
Knell, S., Macleod, S. and Watson, S. (eds) (2007) *Museum Revolutions: How Museums Change and Are Changed*, London: Routledge.
Lahav, S (2012) *Interpretation in the Art Museum: Authority and Access*, unpublished thesis, University of London.
Lankshear, C. (2002) *The Challenge of Digital Epistemologies*, draft paper for the American Educational Research Association, New Orleans, www.geocities.com/c.lankshear/challenge.html, accessed 21 March 2005.
Latour, B. (1993) *We Have Never Been Modern*, Cambridge, MA: Harvard University Press.
——(2005) *Making Things Public: Atmospheres of Democracy*, Cambridge, MA: MIT Press.
——(2007) *Reassembling the Social: An Introduction to Actor-Network-Theory*, Oxford: Oxford University Press.
Law, J. (1999) 'After ANT: Complexity, Naming and Topology', in J. Law and J. Hassard (eds) *Actor Network Theory and After*, Oxford: Blackwell.

Law, J. and Hassard, J. (2004) *Actor Network Theory and After*, Oxford: Blackwell, 1–14.

Law, J. and Urry, J. (2003) 'Enacting the Social', Department of Sociology, Lancaster University, www.lancs.ac.uk/fass/sociology/papers/law-urry-enacting-the-social.pdf, accessed 30 January 2012.

Lindauer, M.A. (2003) 'Inside, Out, and Back Again: The Relationship of New Museology and Curriculum Studies to Museum Education', paper presented at Current Research in Museum Studies, a forum featuring the Year 2004 Smithsonian Fellows in Museum Practice, 4 December 2003, http://museumstudies.si.edu/lidauer.pdf,accessed 30 January 2012.

Lipovetsky, G. (2005) *Hypermodern Times*, London: Polity.

Lippmann, W. (2009) *The Phantom Public*, 9th edn, New Brunswick: Transaction Publishing.

Lister, M., Dovey, J., Giddings, S., Grant, I. and Kelly, K. (2003) *New Media: A Critical Introduction*, London: Routledge.

Lord, B. (2005) 'Representing Enlightenment Space', in S. MacLeod (ed.) *Reshaping Museum Space: Architecture, Design, Exhibitions*, London: Routledge, 146–57.

——(2006) 'Foucault's Museum: Difference, Representation, and Genealogy', www2.le.ac.uk/departments/museumstudies/museumsociety/documents/volumes/1lord.pdf, accessed 17 May 2012, originally published in *Museum and Society*, 4(1): 11–14.

Lord, C. (1993) '(An)Other Panic: The Mainstream Learns to Bash' in J.M. Basquiat, C. Lord and C. Gaines (eds) *The Theater of Refusal: Black Art and Mainstream Criticism*, University of Californa: Fine Arts Gallery.

Lovejoy, M. (2004) *Digital Currents: Art in the Electronic Age*, London: Routledge.

Lyotard, J.F. (1986) *The Postmodern Condition: A Report on Knowledge*, Manchester: Manchester University Press.

Macdonald, S. (2003) 'Museums, National, Postnational and Transcultural Identities', *Museum and Society*, 1(1):1–16.

——(ed.) (2011) *A Companion to Museum Studies*, Oxford: Wiley-Blackwell.

Macdonald, S. and Basu, P. (2007) *Exhibition Experiments*, Oxford: Blackwell.

Macdonald, S. and Fyfe, G. (eds) (1996) *Theorising Museums: Representing Identity and Diversity in a Changing World*, Oxford: Blackwell.

MacGregor, A. (ed.) (1983) *Tradescant's Rareties: Essays on the Foundation of the Ashmoleon Museum*, Oxford: Oxford University Press.

Macpherson, W. (1999) *The Stephen Lawrence Inquiry*, London: Sationery Office, www.archive.official-documents.co.uk/document/cm42/4262/4262.htm, accessed 30 January 2012.

Mannen, H. (2009) *How to Study Art Worlds: On the Societal Functioning of Aesethetic Values*, Amsterdam: Amsterdam University Press.

Manovich, L. (2001) *The Language of New Media*, Cambridge, MA: MIT Press.

Marstine, J. (2006) *New Museum Theory and Practice*, Oxford: Blackwell.

Mason, R. (2006) 'Cultural Theory and Museum Studies', in S. Macdonald (ed.) *A Companion to Museum Studies*, Oxford: Blackwell, 17–32.

Mattarasso, F. (1997) *Use or Ornament? The Social Impact of Participation in the Arts*, London: Comedia.

McClellan, A. (2003) 'A Brief History of the Art Museum Public', in A. McClellan (ed.) *Art and its Publics: Museum Studies at the Millennium*, London: Blackwell, 1–50.

——(2007) 'Museum Studies Now', *Art History*, 30(4): 566–70.

McDonald, G.F. (1992) 'Change and Challenge: Museums in the Information Society', in I. Karp, C.M. Kreamer and S.D. Lavine (eds) *Museums and Communities: The Politics of Public Culture*, Washington, DC: Smithsonian Institute Press.

McGuigan, J. (1996) *Culture and the Public Sphere*, London: Routledge.

——(2004) *Rethinking Cultural Policy*, London: Open University.

McLuhan, M. (1994) *Understanding Media: The Extensions of Man*, Cambridge, MA: MIT Press.

Meijer, R. and Scott, M. (2009) 'Tools to Understand: An Evaluation of the Interpretation Material used in Tate Modern's *Rothko* Exhibition', *Tate Papers*, www.tate.org.uk/download/file/fid/4467, accessed 5 May 2012.

Mercer, K. and Julien, I. (1992) 'True Confessions: A Discourse on Images in Black Sexuality', *Critical Decade: Black British Photography in the 80s*, 2(3): 40–1, 49.

Message, K. (2006) *New Museums and the Making of Culture*, New York: Berg.

Miller, T. and Yudice, G. (2002) *Cultural Policy*, London: Sage.

Mirza, M. (ed.) (2006) *Culture Vultures: Is UK Arts Policy Damaging the Arts?*, London: Policy Exchange.

Mirzoeff, N. (1999) *An Introduction to Visual Culture*, London: Routledge.

Morris, A. (2003) 'Redrawing the Boundaries: Questioning the Geographies of Britishness at Tate Britian', *Museum and Society*, 1(3): 170–82.

Morris, S. (2001) *Museums & New Media Art*, research report for The Rockefeller Foundation, www.cs.vu.nl/~eliens/archive/refs/Museums_and_New_Media_Art.pdf, accessed 18 May 2012.

Morsch, C. (2011) 'Alliances for Unlearning: On Gallery Education and Institutions of Critique', *Afterall*, Spring: 4–13.

Mouffe, C. (ed.) (2009) *Deconstruction and Pragmatism*, London: Routledge.

Muholland, N. (2003) *The Cultural Devolution: Art in Britain in the Late Twentieth Century*, Aldershot: Ashgate.

Muir, R. (2007) *The New Identity Politics*, London: IPPR, www.ippr.org/images/media/-files/publication/2011/05/New%20identity%20politics_1562.pdf, accessed 19 May 2012.

Myrone, M. (2000) *Representing Britain 1500–2000*, London: Tate Gallery.

National Museums Directors' Conference (NMDC) (2004) *Museums and Galleries: Creative Engagement and Valuing Museums: Impact and Innovation*, London: NMDC.

Negroponte, N. (1995) *Being Digital*, New York: Vintage.

Nowotny, H. (2003) 'Dilemma of Expertise: Democratising Expertise and Socially Robust Knowledge', *Science and Public Policy*, 30(3): 151–6.

O'Doherty, B. (2000) *Inside the White Cube: The Ideology of the Gallery Space*, Berkeley: University of California Press.

Okri, B. (1988) 'Leaping Out of Shakespeare's Terror: Five Meditations on Othello', in K. Owusu (ed.) *Storms of the Heart: An Anthology of Black Arts and Culture*, London: Camden Press, 9–18.

O'Loughlin, B. (2006) 'The Operationalization of the Concept "Cultural Diversity" in British Television Policy and Governance', *CRESC Working Papers*, Milton Keynes: Open University/CRESC.

O'Neil, P. and Wilson, M. (2010) *Curating the Educational Turn*, London: Open Editions.

Parry, R. (2007) *Recoding the Museum*, London: Routledge.

——(ed.) (2010) *Museums in a Digital Age*, London: Routledge.

Paul, C. (2003) *Digital Art*, London: Thames & Hudson.

Phillipi, D. (1988) 'Impatience of Signs' in *From Modernism to Postmodernism: Rasheed Araeen: A Retrospective 1959–1987* (exhibition catalogue), Birmingham: Ikon Gallery.

Phillips, M. (2007) 'Migration, Modernity and English Writing: Reflections on Migrant Identity and Canon Formation', Tate Encounters working papers, www2.tate.org.uk/tate-encounters/edition-1/Eng-Lit-and-Canon-Formation.pdf, accessed 5 May 2012.

Pietz, W. (2009) 'Fetish', in D. Preziosi (ed.) *The Art of Art History: A Critical Anthology*, Oxford: Oxford University Press, 109–14.

Pine, J and Gilmore, H (1998) *The Experience Economy: Work is Theater & Every Business a Stage*, Boston, MA: Harvard Business School Press.

Pollock, G. and Zemans, J. (eds) (2007) *Museums After Modernism: Strategies of Engagement*, Oxford: Blackwell.

Powell, W, and DiMaggio, P (1991) *The New Institutionism in Organizational Analysis*, Chicago: University of Chicago Press.

Power, M. (1997) *The Audit Society: Rituals of Verification*, Oxford: Oxford University Press.

Preziosi, D. (1989) *Rethinking Art History: Meditations on a Coy Science*, New Haven: Yale University Press.

Preziosi, D. (1996) 'Brain of the Earth's Body: Museums and the Framing of Modernity' in D. Preziosi (ed.) (2009) *The Art of Art History: A Critical Anthology*, Oxford: Oxford University Press.

——(2003) *Brain of the Earth's Body: Art, Museums and the Phantasms of Modernity*, Minneapolis: University of Minnesota Press.

——(2004) *Grasping the World: The Idea of the Museum*, Aldershot: Ashgate.

——(2011) 'Art History and Museology: Rendering the Visible Legible', in S. Macdonald (ed.) *A Companion to Museum Studies*, Oxford: Blackwell, 50–63.

Preziosi, D. and Farago, C.J. (2004) *Grasping the World: The Idea of the Museum*, Aldershot: Ashgate.

Preziosi, D. and Lamoureux, J. (2006) *In the Aftermath of Art: Ethics, Aesthetics, Politics*, London: Routledge.

Prior, N. (2002) *Museums & Modernity: Art Galleries and the Making of Modern Culture*, Oxford: Berg.

——(2003) 'Having One's Tate and Eating It: Transformations of the Museum in a Hypermodern Era', in A. McClellan (ed.) *Art and its Publics: Museum Studies at the Millennium*, London: Blackwell, 51–76.

Rancière, J. (2006) *The Politics of Aesthetics: The Distribution of the Sensible*. London: Continuum.

——(2007) *The Emancipated Spectator*, London: Verso.

Rectanus, M. (2011) 'Globalization: Incorporating the Museum' in S. Macdonald (ed.) *A Companion to Museum Studies*, Oxford: Blackwell, 381–97.

Rice, D. (2003) 'Museums: Theory, Practice, and Illusion', in A. McClellan (ed.) *Art and its Publics: Studies at the Millennium*, Malden: Blackwell, 77–95.

Ringham. J. (2011) *Tate Social Media Communication Strategy 2011–12*, www.tate.org.uk/research/publications/tate-papers/tate-social-media-communication-strategy-2011-12, accessed 16 May 2012.

Roberts, C. (2003) 'Applied Linguistics Applied', in S. Sarangi and T. van Leeuwen (eds) *Applied Linguistics and Communities of Practice*, London: Continuum and British Association for Applied Linguistics, 132–49.

Roberts, P. (1998) 'Rereading Lyotard: Knowledge, Commodification and Higher Education', *Electronic Journal of Sociology* 3(3).

Robins, K. (1996) 'Will Image Move Us Still?' in M. Lister (ed.) *The Photographic Image in Digital Culture*, London: Routledge, 29–50.

——(1999) 'Tradition and Translation: National Culture in a Global Context', in D. Boswell and J. Evans (eds) *Representing the Nation: A Reader, Histories, Heritage and Museums*, London: Routlege, 15–32.

Rogoff, I. (2000) *Terra Infirma: Geography's Visual Culture*, London: Routledge.

——(2006) 'What is a Theorist?', www.kein.org/node/62, accessed 8 April 2012.

Rogoff, I. and Sherman, D. (ed.) (1994) *Museum Culture: Histories, Discourses, Spectacles*, London: Routledge.

Rorty, R. (2011) 'Solidarity or Objectivity?', in R.B. Talisee and S.F. Aikin (eds) *The Pragmatism Reader: From Peirce Through the Present*, Princeton: Princeton University Press, 367–80.

Rose, G. (2001) *Visual Methodologies: An Introduction to the Interpretation of Visual Materials*, London: Sage.

Ross, J. (1988) 'The Timeless Voice for the New Language: Reflections on Imperatives', in K. Owusu (ed.) *Storms of the Heart: An Anthology of Black Arts and Culture*, London: Camden Press, 231–7.

Rush, M. (1999) *New Media in Late 20th Century Art*, London: Thames & Hudson.

Rushdie, S. (1988) *The Satanic Verses*, London: Viking.

Ryan, M. (2004) *Narrative Across Media: The Languages of Storytelling*, Nebraska: University of Nebraska Press.

Ryan, V. (1985) 'Artist's Statement', in *The Thin Black Line* (exhibition catalogue), London: Institute of Contemporary Arts.

Said, E. (1978) *Orientalism: Western Conceptions of the Orient*, London: Routledge.

Sandell, R. (ed.) (2002) *Museums, Society, Inequality*, London: Routledge.

——(2003) 'Social Inclusion: The Museum and the Dynamics of Sectoral Change', *Museum and Society*, 1(1): 45–62.

——(ed.) (2007) *Museums, Prejudice and the Reframing of Difference*, London: Routledge.

Sandell, R. and Janes, R. (eds) (2007) *Museum Management and Marketing*, Oxford: Routledge.

Scarman, L. (1982) *The Scarman Report*, London: Penguin.

Selwood, S. (1992) *Investigating Audiences: Audience Surveys in the Visual Arts*, London: Art & Society.

——(2002) 'Measuring Culture', *Spiked Culture*, 30 December, www.spiked-online.com/articles/00000006DBAF.htm, accessed 30 January 2012.

Semali, L.M. (2002) *Transmediation in the Classroom: A Semiotics-Based Media Literacy*, New York: Counterpoints.

Serota, N. (1996) *Experience or Interpretation: The Dilemma of Museums of Modern Art*, London: Thames & Hudson.

——(2006) 'Art of the Unexpected', transcript of speech given at the Commission for Racial Equality, www.juliushonnor.com/attheturningofthetide/anthology_23.html, accessed 30 January 2012.

Shapin, S. and Schaffer, S. (1985) *Leviathian and the Air Pump: Hobbes, Boyle and the Experimental Life*, Princeton: Princeton University Press.

Sharland, E. (2011) 'All Together Now? Building Disciplinary and Inter-Disciplinary Research Capacity in Social Work and Social Care', *British Journal of Social Work*, 42(2): 208–26.

Shaw, I. (2008) 'Situating Method: Accountability and Organizational Positionings', *Tate Encounters*, Edition 4, www2.tate.org.uk/tate-encounters/edition-4/isabel-shaw.pdf, accessed 19 May 2012.

Shukra, K., Back, L., Keith, M., Khan, A. and Solomos, J. (2004) 'Race, Social Cohesion and the Changing Politics of Citizenship', *London Review of Education*, 2(3): 187–95.

Siegal, M. (1995) 'More Than Words: The Generative Power of Transmediation for Learning', *Canadian Journal of Education*, 20: 455–75.

Slater, D. (1999) 'The Marketing of Mass Photography', in J. Evans and S. Hall (eds) *Visual Culture: The Reader*, London: Sage, 289–306.

Smith, D. (2005) 'Artist Hits at Tate "Cowards" Over Ban', *The Observer*, 25 September, www.guardian.co.uk/uk/2005/sep/25/arts.religion, accessed 9 May 2012.

Smith, M. and Holly, M. (2008) *What is Research – in the Visual Arts?*, Massachussetts: Clark Institute.

Solanke, A. (1986) 'Juggling Worlds', in *From Two Worlds* (exhibition catalogue), London: Whitechapel Art Gallery, 9–10.

Somerville, M. and Rapport, D. (2000) *Transdisciplinarity: Re-creating Integrated Knowledge*, Oxford: EOLSS Publishers.

Spalding, F (1998) *The Tate: A History*, London: Tate Publishing.

Spivak, G.C. (1987) *In Other Worlds*, London: Routledge.

——(1988) 'Can the Subaltern Speak?', in C. Nelson and L. Grossberg (eds) *Marxism and the Interpretation of Culture*, Chicago: University of Illinois Press, 271–313.

——(2003) *Death of a Discipline*, New York: Columbia University Press.

Sylvester, D. (2000) 'Mayhem at Millbank', *London Review of Books*, 22(10): 19–20.

Tate Gallery (1968–70) *The Tate Gallery 1968–70, Biennial Report*, London: Tate Gallery.

——(1976–8) *The Tate Gallery 1976–78, Biennial Report*, London: Tate Gallery.

——(1984–6) *The Tate Gallery: Illustrated Biennial Report 1984–86*, London: Tate Gallery.

——(1996–8) *Tate Report, Tate Gallery Biennial Report 1996–98, London: Tate Gallery*, London: Tate Gallery.

——(1988–90) *Tate Report: Tate Gallery Biennial Report 1988–90*, London: Tate Gallery.

——(1990, 2nd edn 1991) *Tate Gallery: An Illustrated Companion*, edited by S. Wilson, London: Tate Publishing.

Tate Gallery (1998–2000) *Tate Report: Tate Gallery Biennial Report 1998–2000*, London: Tate Gallery.

——(2004–6) *Tate Report 2004–6*, http://webarchive.nationalarchives.gov.uk/20061027114622/tate.org.uk/about/tatereport/2006, accessed 5 May 2012.

Taylor, B. (1999) *Art for the Nation: Exhibitions for the London Public 1747–2001*, Manchester: Manchester University Press.

Thompson Klein, J., Grossenbacher-Mansuy, W., Häberli, R., Bill, A., Scholz, R.W. and Welti, M. (eds) (2001) *Transdisciplinarity: Joint Problem Solving Among Science, Technology and Society: An Effective Way for Managing Complexity*, Berlin: Birkhäuser.

Thrift, N. (2008) *Non Representational Theory*, London: Routledge.

Trodd, C. (2003) 'The Discipline of Pleasure: Or, How Art History Looks at the Art Museum', *Museum and Society*, 1(1): 17–29.

Tromans, N (2008) *The Lure of the East: British Orientalist Painting*, New Haven: Yale University Press.

Turkle, S. (1997) *Life on the Screen: Identity in the Age of the Internet*, London: Phoenix.

Ukadike, N.F. (1999) 'New Developments in Black African Cinema', in O. Oguibe and O. Enwezor (eds) *Reading the Contemporary: African Art from Theory to the Marketplace*, Cambridge, MA: MIT Press, 166–213.

Vergo,P. (ed.) (1989) *The New Museology*, London: Reaktion.

Virilio, P. (1998) *Pure War*, Paris: Semiotext(e).

——(2000) *From Modernism to Hypermodernism and Beyond*, London: Sage.

Wainwright, L. (2009) 'On Being Unique: World Art and its British Institutions', *Visual Culture in Britain*, 10(1): 87–101.

——(2010) 'Art (School) Education and Art History' in R. Appignanesi (ed.) *Beyond Cultural Diversity: The Case for Creativity*, London: Third Text, 93–103.

Wallinger, M. and Warnock, M. (2000) *Art for All? Their Policies and Our Culture*, London: Peer.

Warf, B. (2008) *Time-space Compression: Historical Geographies*, London: Routledge.

Webster, F. (1995) *Theories of the Information Society*, London: Routledge.

Weibel, P. and Latour, B. (2007) 'Experimenting with Representation: *Iconoclash* and *Making Things Public*', in S. Macdonald and P. Basu (eds) *Exhibition Experiments*, Oxford: Blackwell, 94–108.

Williams, R. (1958) *Culture and Society*, London: Chatto & Windus.

——(1965) *The Long Revolution*, London: Penguin.

——(1976) *Television: Technology and Cultural Form*, London: Fontana.

——(1989) *The Politics of Modernism: Against the New Conformists*, London and New York: Verso.

Wilson, S. (1990) *Tate Gallery: An Illustrated Companion*, London: Tate Publishing.

Wood, J. (1998) *The Virtual Embodied: Presence, Practice, Technology*, London: Routledge.

Zappaterra, Y. (2001) *Digital Lab: Print & Electronic Design: Editorial*, London: Rotovision.

INDEX